FAMILY STRESS
COPING & RESILIENCE

CHALLENGES AND EXPERIENCES OF MODERN FAMILIES

GREGORY J. HARRIS · KRISTEN GREENE · FIORELLA L. CARLOS CHAVEZ

Kendall Hunt
publishing company

Cover image © Shutterstock, Inc.

Kendall Hunt
publishing company

www.kendallhunt.com
Send all inquiries to:
4050 Westmark Drive
Dubuque, IA 52004-1840

Copyright © 2019 by Kendall Hunt Publishing Company

ISBN 978-1-5249-3195-7

Published in the United States of America

Contents

PART V: Caregiving Stressors, End of Life Challenges, and Resilient Families

Acknowledgments

We express our thanks and professional gratitude to the support we received from the Kendall Hunt Publishing family for their patience and guidance as this project came to life. We wish to thank and acknowledge the guidance we received from Bev Kraus, our Project Coordinator and Whitney Wolf, our Acquisition Editor. We acknowledge the many students and colleagues who inspired this project. Their support as contributors or as sources of inspiration will never be forgotten.

We are forever grateful to the authors who contributed to this project. Their research and commitment to elucidating the problems families experience with life stressors are to be commended. Finally, we would like to thank our families for their continued support and dedication to the high ideals needed to advance scholarship in the field of family stress.

—Gregory J. Harris, Kristen Greene, & Fiorella L. Carlos Chavez

Introduction

Gregory J. Harris, Kristen Greene, and Fiorella Luisa Carlos Chavez

The first edition of *Family Stress, Coping, & Resilience: Challenges and Experiences of Modern Families* presents salient research and scholarly readings as an anthology of family stressors and demands impacting families across a myriad of life dimensions. Like conflict, stress seems to be an inevitable consequence of the human experience and family stressors are no different. All stress is not bad or damaging. However, as families encounter new and emerging family stressors it may become difficult for families to bounce back or emerge from the encounters. Likewise, as chronic stressors dominant the American family landscape, families are constantly flooded with its negative impacts without having the necessary tools to respond in a positive and healthy manner. In such cases, the deleterious impact of acute, episodic, and chronic stressors can wreak havoc on individuals and families as they try to manage daily and competing demands. Every system tries to reach a sense of balance or equilibrium in responding to such stressors. However, as stressors arise in the individual or family system, it causes the system to react in a variety of ways that may produce dysfunction, promote coping or a state of resilience. There are many ways to define stress depending on the discipline, context of the problem or issue.

For the purposes of this textbook, we define family stress as a "disturbance in the steady state of the family system" (Boss, Bryant, & Mancini, 2017, p. 4). We feel this definition is broad and encourages an understanding of multi-complexities of the family, its members, and the various encounters each member experiences and brings to the family context. Further, this perspective on family stress as shared by Boss and colleagues (2017) considers the internal and external components of many life stressors. Coping is defined as Patterson (1988) discussed and as detailed in Weber (2011) as "the transformation process of managing distress by each individual in the family" (p. 31). While coping implies the hope of adapting to adversities associated with stress in the family system, we define "resilience" as the ability to have flexibility and the wherewithal to bounce-back with a more positive orientation or at a higher level of adaptation (Boss, 2017). The experiences and challenges of families under stress can only be best understood within the context in which the problems or family issues arise, the historical manner in which problems have been appraised and dealt with in the past, the resources available to the family to deal with the stressors, and whether or not families adapt or maladapt to these impacts and emerge better off or fall into an immobilized state (Boss, 2017).

Goal of the Book

A major goal of *Family Stress, Coping, & Resilience: Challenges and Challenges and Experiences of Modern Families* textbook is to present current and salient research on the experiences and challenges of modern families dealing with a variety of family stressors across various domains and contextual areas of daily life. A portion of the *Family Stress, Coping, & Resilience: Challenges and Experiences of Modern Families* textbook will be devoted to critical physical, mental, and economic issues impacting families such as poverty, posttraumatic stress disorder, family violence, aggression, families with special needs children, caregiving, and host of other topics related to parenting, immigration, and end of life issues. The *Family Stress, Coping, & Resilience: Challenges and Challenges and Experiences of Modern Families* textbook is intended for scholars, graduate students, advanced undergraduates, policy makers, and practitioners in the fields of family science, human development, sociology, psychology, social work, health, and medicine. It has a multidisciplinary focus as it cuts across various disciplines academic interests and examines various scholarly approaches of dealing with the multifaceted nature of family stressors of modern families.

Overview of the Book

The *Family Stress, Coping, & Resilience: Challenges and Experiences of Modern Families* textbook includes five broad overarching parts, and several chapters within each part for a total of fourteen chapters: *Family Stress Concepts, Theories, and Models; Family Stressors, Parenting, and Mental Health; Family Stressors, Substance Abuse, Family Violence, & Trauma; Family Stressors among Vulnerable and Transitional Populations; and Caregiving Stressors, End of Life Challenges, and Resilient Families.*

Part I: Family Stress Concepts, Theories, and Models

The part on *Family Stress Concepts, Theories, and Models* focuses on the various conceptual models of stress and its application to modern families. A focus on integrating family resiliency into family stress theory is also explored. Pauline Boss, Chalandra Bryant, and Jay Mancini reflect on their work on family theories stress and the life course. Part I ends with the seminal work of Joan Patterson on integrating family resiliency and family stress theory to create a better understanding of the role of resiliency within the stress process theory.

PART II: Family Stressors, Parenting, and Mental Health

The part on *Family Stressors, Parenting, and Mental Health* addresses research on family stress within the context of the family unit and the mental and physical health consequences associated with child-rearing, special needs children, and general family functioning. Thus, authors Ming Cui and Peipei Hong explore issues of parenting and associated stress within the parenting context in families. Carmen Caicedo explores research relative to family stress associated with caring for special needs children and it impact on family health, general family functioning, and care burden. Part II ends with the work of Angie Schock-Girodano and Stephen Gavazzi on aspects of mental illness and mental health as concepts that must be understood in the context of family stress.

PART III: Family Stressors, Substance Abuse, Family Violence, & Trauma

The part on *Family Stressors Substance Abuse, Family Violence and Trauma* makes up several chapters focused on the complex impact of family stress and substance abuse in families, family violence, aggression, and trauma across the life course. Judith Fischer, Kevin Lyness, and Rachel Engler focus on families coping and the impact of alcohol and substance abuse in the family. This chapter is followed by the work of Madelyn Labella and Ann Masten with their research on the impact of the family on the development of aggression and violence. Part III end with Daniel Conner and colleagues providing an update on posttraumatic stress disorder in children and adolescence.

PART IV: Family Stressors among Vulnerable and Transitional Populations

The part on *Family Stressors among Vulnerable and Transitional Populations* addresses chapters focused issues of poverty, attention bias and anxiety, and family stress, immigration and cultural related stressors. Eric Finegood and colleagues focus on family poverty and the issues associated with attention bias and anxiety and how they interact in the context of daily hassles. The following chapter by Fiorella Carlos Chavez and Joseph Grzywacz explore issues of stress of immigrant families. Part IV ends with Kim and colleagues addressing the cultural influences on stressors, parental socialization, and mental health of immigrant children.

PART V: Caregiving Stressors, End of Life Challenges, and Resilient Families

The part on *Caregiving Stressors, End of Life Challenges, and Resilient Families addresses* chapters focused on caregiving of older adults, facts regarding stressful life events, disease risk, death and dying, and how families respond. The first chapter in Part V by Harris provides an expanded review of the challenges and experiences of informal caregivers with a focus on family stress, demands, caregiver resources, appraisal of stressors, and their overall impact on the concept of well-being which is a more positive orientation to caregiving. This chapter is followed by the work of Kim and colleagues on the relations between multiple informal caregivers and subjective physical and mental health status in older adults and racial differences. The final chapter in Part V by Cohen and colleagues introduce key facts about stressful life events and their risk of disease.

References

Boss, P, Bryant, C., & Mancini, J. (2017). *Family stress management: A contextual approach, 3rd edition.* London: Sage.

Patterson, J. M. (1988). Families experiencing stress: I. The family adjustment and response model, II Applying the FAAR model to health-related issues for intervention and research. *Family Systems Medicine, 6, 2,* 202–237.

Weber, J. G. (2011). *Individual and family stress and crisis.* London, Sage.

PART *I*

Family Stress Concepts, Theories, and Models

CHAPTER 1

The Contextual Model of Family Stress

In April of 2008, Jenifer, mother of two children (12 and 9 years old), lost her home (a six-bedroom house nestled on an acre of land) in Georgia because she couldn't afford the monthly mortgage payments after medical bills and a divorce. Her salary as a day care center director simply was not enough. She and her children moved to a two-bedroom apartment. Now, even her children worry about money. While grocery shopping, her 9-year-old son, noticing the price of milk, told her that they shouldn't buy it. He gets up after she goes to bed and checks all the doors to make sure that they are locked. Then he goes to her room and tells her that everything is safe so it's okay to sleep. He must have noticed that she no longer sleeps well. This child now worries not only about money but also about his mother. (Armour, 2008)

During the Great Recession of 2007 to 2009, stories about foreclosures, bankruptcies, job loss, and homelessness dominated the news media across the United States. For families, this crisis took its toll. Although the exact figures vary, most sources indicate that millions of people lost homes to foreclosure during this economic downturn (Bernard, 2014; CoreLogic, 2012; Schoen, 2010). According to a professor of economics at Princeton University and a professor of finance at the University of Chicago, between 2007 and 2009, about 8 million jobs were lost, and over 4 million homes were foreclosed (Mian & Sufi, 2014).

There are countless stories like this of family stress where the external and internal contexts of family life merge to increase family stress and also sometimes cause a crisis. In Chapter 1, we defined family stress as a change or disturbance in the steady state of the family system and illustrated family stress with a bridge metaphor. In the preceding story, the structure of the family's support was not a bridge but a house—the family home—which fell away. The family became disorganized, with a child now taking care of his parent. With all highly distressed families, a framework like the Contextual Model of Family Stress (hereafter referred to as the CMFS) helps practitioners and researchers to more fully understand how to assess and intervene with troubled families.

Here, in Chapter 2, we define and discuss all the constructs upon which the CMFS is built. Consider this chapter a glossary for a theoretical map. As you read, you may want to refer back to this chapter because definitions will not be presented again in such detail.

Family stress terms are notorious for their inconsistency. Our aim is to clarify definitions so that family therapists, educators, social workers, nurses, family psychologists, and researchers can all understand each other in their mutual goal of helping couples, families, and communities to manage stress. First, let us explain why a contextual model is essential for helping families in stress.

Why a Contextual Model?

All families, worldwide, experience stress, but not all are in trouble. Other factors in addition to the stressful event influence family vulnerability or breakdown. The end result of the stress process, whether the family and its members manage to avoid or survive crisis, is influenced by their internal and external contexts. The *internal context*, over which the family may have some control, is composed of structural, psychological, and philosophical dimensions, as well as the family's chosen beliefs and values and way of life. The *external context* consists of dimensions over which the family has little or no control—culture, history, economy, development, and heredity (including race, class, gender, age, sexual orientation, and physical constitution). This includes unemployment, terrorism, war, military deployment, financial recessions, illness, aging, natural catastrophe, and when and how one dies. Unique stories of coping and managing are less often in the newspapers and on the evening news than are catastrophic stories of disaster and loss. Family and community narratives about strength are only recently being documented to help us recognize and understand the processes of resilience and overcoming adversity.

On *20/20,* Barbara Walters once told the story of an African baby who was accidentally dropped into a fire by her 13-year-old mother (who was having a seizure). The baby girl, named Lydia, was taken to a hospital and given up by her parents. She miraculously survived, and today she lives a comfortable upper-middle-class life in the United States. After 38 years, married and a mother of three, she returned to the interior of Africa to visit her birth mother who could not believe the beautiful woman her nearly dead baby daughter had become. Such stories of resilience may help to balance the many stories of victimization that the media broadcast (Neufeld, 2001).

A family's external context influences how families and the individuals in them perceive what they experience. Those contextual factors play a role in determining whether families give the stressor a positive or negative valence. In the case of Lydia and her mother, their definition of the event and their interpretation ebbs and flows. Lydia's mother had been sold into marriage and poverty when she was 12 years old, so she had little power to influence her situation; Lydia, however, did. She had grown up in safety and comfort.

She obtained an education and resources to search for her birth mother. Paradoxically, the daughter who almost died in the fire and who had to have her legs amputated, had more mastery and control over her life than did her healthy but impoverished and oppressed mother. Knowing the great variations that exist in the family, we gain a broader repertoire for working with distressed individuals and families. For this reason, we contextualize this model of family stress. Whether in the time of Tolstoy or today, families are both alike and different, and the differences yield for us the most knowledge about how to strengthen families. We now move on to the CMFS and its definitions.

To define and describe terms that comprise the CMFS, we begin with the outside of the model in Figure 1.1 and move toward the middle. That is, we move from external context to internal context to the recursive ABC-X process of family stress management.

The Family's External Context

Individuals and families do not live in isolation. They are part of a larger context or environment, which is critical to understanding their ability (or inability) to manage stress and recover from

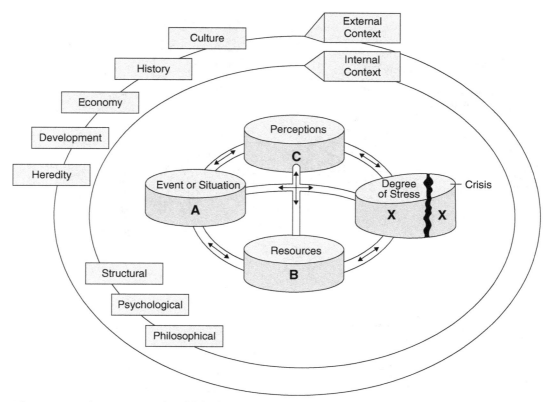

Figure 1.1 *The Contextual Model of Family Stress*
Source: Adapted from Boss (2002).

crises. Of the two different contexts in which family stress can be shaped—the external context over which the family has little or no control and the internal context over which they do have control—we discuss the external context first. The external context is composed of five dimensions that influence family stress management: culture, history, economy, development, and heredity (see Figure 1.2). The external context is the environment or ecosystem in which the family is embedded. It can, for example, include global politics, macroeconomics, and catastrophes caused by nature, war, political terrorism, or ethnic annihilation. It can also include societal pressures from discrimination and poverty.

Because the five dimensions are imposed on families from outside their system, the external context is a macro pressure over which the family has little or no control. It also includes the limits of time and place, in which a troubled family, through no volition of its own, finds itself.

Cultural Context

Culture refers to the beliefs and behaviors of a group of like-minded people who share unique characteristics such as race, religion, nationality, or ethnicity (e.g., Native Americans, African Americans, Asian Americans, Latin Americans, Pacific Islanders, etc.). (To differentiate from community, we note that while culture refers to customs, arts, religions, foods, and sports of a particular group of people, community often refers to where people live or meet—e.g., military base, religious convent, West Side neighborhood, parish church, etc. Of course, community has psychological elements. For more information on communities, see Chapter 8.)

Although the family's private beliefs and values are, for most of us, under our control and therefore part of the internal context, the larger society's *cultural context* may still provide the canons and mores by which families live. Culture defines the rules for problem solving and coping with

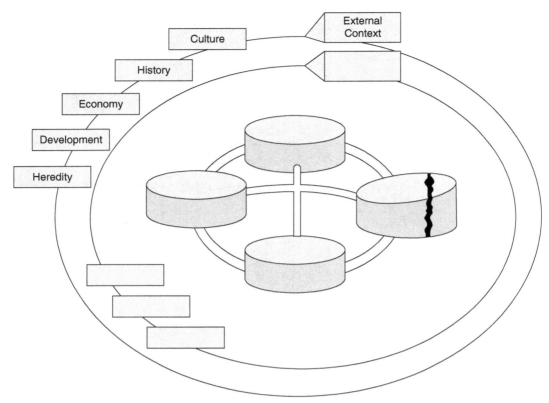

Figure 1.2 *The Contextual Model of Family Stress: External Context*
Source: Boss(2002).

prejudice and stigma and defines how to do this with accepted and legal methods for managing stress. The larger culture, then, provides the meta rules by which families at the micro level find their way to coping and managing.

Sometimes, however, a family belongs to a subculture *or* community whose rules conflict with those of the prevailing culture. In such subcultures, problems are often solved by group leaders or elders. When, for example, the Hmong tradition was for older men to marry 13-year-old girls, there was incongruity between our larger society's laws and Hmong cultural values, mores, and rules; the two competing models could not coexist. Cultural prescriptions and proscriptions conflict until rules and values shift to fit the law of the land. Hitting one's wife is another example. It may be accepted in one culture but not legal in the larger society. Also, on college campuses, perhaps another subculture, there had been a similar mismatch between cultural behavior and the law when it was found that about 25% of students felt it was okay to slap around a partner "if they needed it" (Grant, 2015). Such attitudes are clearly at odds with the laws of larger society. But imagine if you are part of a subculture where a number of people endorse hitting or abuse. What do you do? Accept it? Head to the authorities? Which authorities?

Historical Context

The *historical context* of family stress is the time in history during which an event or situation occurs to the family or a family member (Elder, 1974/1999; Elder & Giele, 2009). A past event may influence the family's meanings and ways in which members manage stress and crises today. When we try to understand family stress, we have to know what historical events have been influential (Bengtson & Allen, 1993; Bowen, Martin, & Mancini, 2013). For example, if the stressful event was loss of a job, it would mean one thing if the loss happened at a time of job scarcity and it would mean another at a time when jobs were plentiful. Other important historical events that influence meaning and perceptions about family stressors include human-caused events of prejudice (slavery, the Holocaust, uprooting and forced education of Native American children in government boarding schools to eradicate their Indian identity, the fight for civil rights, continued ethnic cleansing worldwide [from Cambodia in the 1970s to Syria today]). There are natural disasters (floods, droughts, earthquakes, tsunamis, and fires) and human-made disasters (war, terrorism, murder, torture, and abuse). At identifiable times in history, these traumatic events leave their mark on the cohort that manages to live through them and, often, on subsequent generations.

When we ascertain the historical context of a particular family in stress, we then know more about whether the event occurred in an environment of choices versus one of powerlessness, captivity, or discrimination or in an environment of vast resources, privilege, and empowerment versus limited resources. The environment gives us clues to understanding the problem and shaping more effective interventions, but the historical time of the stress also provides clues. Both the environment and time reflect context. Like a pebble tossed into the water, contextual time markers leave their traces through a ripple effect, from the external contextual level to the family level. For example, a military couple may have a marriage problem, but to deal with it, they must acknowledge their separate experiences: namely, the soldier's experience in battle and the spouse's experience at home. Furthermore, the historical period in which the war takes place may also make a difference in perception; for example, what couples took from the Vietnam and Gulf Wars versus World War II is very different. Subsequent generations may still reflect some of the previous generation's coping behaviors. We think of many films that illustrate ancestral trauma: *Schindler's List, Ten Years a Slave, Roots, Amistad, The Diary of Anne Frank,* and *The Hurt Locker.*

Economic Context

The community or society's economy forms the family's *economic context* at a macro level and influences how the family reacts to a stressful event. For example, during a strong economic period, being laid off from a job is not as stressful to a family as it is when the economy is weak, with high unemployment and scarcity of jobs. When the chance of getting another job is slim, losing one's job becomes a crisis. During the Great Recession in the United States, unemployment was high, family incomes plummeted, and middle-class families everywhere, and especially in Detroit, faced foreclosures and lost their homes. Yet, some couples and families remain strong despite loss of employment. For example, Elder (1974/1999) and other family scientists Conger and Rueter (Conger, Reuter, & Elder, 1999) and Kwon, Rueter, Lee, Koh, and Ok (2003) studied couple resilience to economic pressure and found that high marital support was a protective factor against loss of income. Family researchers Dew and Yorgason (2010) found this strength as well in retirement age couples.

Overall, however, the management of stress within a family is not only complicated by the fluctuating state of the larger economy but also by unexpected changes in family income. Boss, a family therapist, has worked with a family in which the stress of the husband's job loss was erased by an unexpected inheritance, but then marital and family stress increased because the husband began spending most of his time gambling and became addicted. More money is not always a solution for reducing stress.

Developmental Context

Here, development refers to the human maturation process controlled by biology. For the most part, it is not under the family's control. Children grow up and leave—or return home; grandparents become primary caregivers for grandchildren when parents are unable to function in that role. Elders become frail and die; one's parents grow older and may need help.

While the *developmental context* includes the individual's and family's place in the life cycle when a stressful event occurs (Aldous, 1978; Carter & McGoldrick, 1999; Papalia, Olds, & Feldman, 2001), we propose a less linear and less normative-based model (Boss, 1980a). Marriage and divorce, for example, can occur at any age, not just during young adulthood; families can be new even if the people in them are old. Today, pregnancies occur within a wider range of the developmental context as technology now makes it possible for women well into their 40s to have children. Nevertheless, the different levels of family stress caused by the same event (in this case, pregnancy) cannot be explained by theories of development without looking at developmental nuances that can occur. That is, a 16-year-old girl could be deeply distressed to find out she is pregnant, while a 40-year-old woman, more mature psychologically as well as more financially stable, could be elated to finally be pregnant. Such contextual differences in development often explain why people have different perceptions and coping strategies for the same event.

Other developmental milestones can create and exacerbate family stress. Having elderly parents, for example, may be more stressful today because technology has made it possible for them to live longer, thus increasing the number of people with dementia and other frailties needing full-time care. Unfortunately, family and societal policies have not adapted adequately to this new longevity of our elders. Most of us expect our parents to take care of us when we are young, but fewer of us are prepared to care for our parents when they are old and frail. To complicate matters, caregiving families may not have adequate resources to care for their elderly parent in their own homes if they so choose. Moreover, the cost of having a frail parent in a long-term care facility is incredibly expensive.

When elderly parents are chronically ill and frail, the burden of caretaking falls predominantly on adult daughters or daughters-in-law (National Alliance for Caregiving & AARP Public Policy Institute, 2015). The increased stress this presents for individuals in the middle generation, who may concurrently be launching adolescents, supporting adult children, or even preparing for retirement, places them in a generational squeeze. With pressure from both above and below, they have been called the "sandwich generation." Midlife families, and especially midlife women, are now considered high risk for not only stress but also mortality, because of simultaneous stress stemming from the needs of frail elderly parents, children, housework, employment demands, plus their own retirement plans (Navaie-Waliser, Spriggs, & Feldman, 2002; Yee & Schulz, 2000).

Hereditary Context

The family's *heritable* and *genetic context* affects the health and physical strength of the family members. Because of genes and strong constitution, some people, and even some families, are simply physically healthier than others. Such people and families have more stamina and resilience when under pressure. They not only have more energy to deal with an event but also have the strength to persevere when the stressful situation is of long duration. A strong constitution makes it easier to cope when pressure continues over an extended period of time such as with unemployment or a chronic illness.

Perhaps the most prolific body of research about heredity and stress was produced by social psychologist and epidemiologist Ernest Harburg, spanning the late 1970s to 2003. To determine the effects of heredity on stress as indicated by blood pressure and cortisol levels, he developed a "family set" research method, in which he used a primary family member, plus his or her sibling or first cousin as the "set." He also used a randomly selected unrelated individual for comparison (Harburg,

Erfurt, Schull, Schork, & Colman, 1977). In a classic series of studies, Harburg and colleagues found that for both Black and White participants, environmental variables, such as neighborhood, contributed more to variations in blood pressure than did their genetic differences (Chakraborty, Schull, Harburg, Schork, & Roeper, 1977).

Much more research is needed to determine the effects of heredity and genetics on individual and family stress. Family scientists have already joined scientists from other disciplines to conduct research (D'Onofrio & Lahey, 2010; Salvatore & Dick, 2015), showing that environment strongly influences the survival of the human body, perhaps despite genetic makeup. The important point is this: We can change our view of a stressor even if we cannot change our heredity. It is on this premise that we place the hereditary makeup of family members in the *external* context of the CMFS.

Historically and still today, people tend to describe those who have lived long enough to reach an old age as "coming from good stock." They saw a strong constitution, such as, in the late comedian George Burns, who lived to be 100 years old despite smoking cigars daily. On the other hand, people worry about youthful deaths such as that of Steve Jobs, the creator and chief executive officer of Apple, who died at age 56 in 2011 from cancer. While anecdotally, many of us rely on having a strong constitution and genetic makeup, much more research needs to address if or how heredity helps distressed individuals and families.

Summary

The external context of the CMFS consists of culture, history, the economy, development, and heredity, each of which constrains the management of stress because each is outside of the family's control. For this reason, we encourage family professionals, policymakers, and researchers to work for change in this larger arena (Ungar, 2012). The family is expected to be the keystone of society, but policymakers do little to strengthen the family for that larger societal role. In 2001, family psychologist Nadine Kaslow documented global trends and problems in families, most of which are influenced by the external context: shifting sociopolitical borders; changing male-female relationships; increasing domestic violence; increasing divorce rates; longing for greater spirituality; growing addictions; proliferating wars, starvation, and persecution; escalating crime and violence; more missing family members; growing numbers of homeless and throwaway children; increasing waves of immigration; rising incidence of uprooting; and increasing multicultural diversity (Kaslow, 2001). Sadly, the list remains much the same today. The external context needs to become more family friendly—family safe, actually. Asking families to be resilient is not enough.

While families are active reactors to the macro events of the external context, they are active shapers within the internal context. There, families have more volition, control, and mastery to not only react but also to shape their processes of coping and resilience. We now explain the internal context.

The Family's Internal Context
(Structural, Psychological, and Philosophical)

The *internal context* of the family is composed of three micro dimensions that are classified as structural, psychological, and philosophical. Change in the family's internal context is more readily possible because the family has relatively more control over it.[1] It comprises the family's values and belief systems and broadens the multicultural application of the contextual stress model. Note that in Figure 1.3 these dimensions comprise the inward ring around the core that is the family stress process.

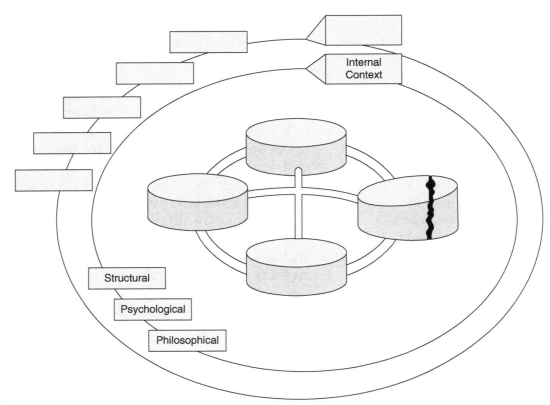

Figure 1.3 *The Contextual Model of Family Stress: Internal Context*
Source: Boss (2002).

Unlike the external context, which is composed of elements over which the family has little or no control, the *internal context* is composed of elements that the family, at least its adult members, *can* change and control (Figure 1.3).

Maintaining some control allows some choice about how and whether to shift gears and change; thus, even highly stressed families can change to survive, even thrive.

First, the *structural context* refers to the form and function of the family's structure: its boundaries, membership, role assignments, and rules regarding who is within and who is outside these boundaries. When the boundary of a family remains unclear (boundary ambiguity) (Boss, 2002), there is unclear support in the structural context and thus more stress in the system. More is said about boundary ambiguity in Chapter 5.

Second, the *psychological context* refers to the perception, appraisal, definition, or assessment of a stressful event by the family as a whole, as well as by its individual members. Here, we prefer the term *perception* because it embodies both cognitive (thinking) and affective (feeling) processes. How the family and its members perceive an event, mentally and emotionally, determines their ability to mobilize defense mechanisms and problem-solving strengths.

Third, the *philosophical context* of the family refers to its values and beliefs at a micro level. This is under the family's control. A particular family, for example, can live by rules that are different from those of the larger culture to which it belongs. Many immigrant and minority families in American culture still experience this incongruence. For example, when the larger culture provides government support for the institutional care of elderly parents but not for care within the family home, the external and internal contexts are brought into conflict and even more stress is created. Another example is the military subculture that sometimes imposes rules on family dependents that are inconsistent with those of the larger culture with secrecy about the whereabouts of a spouse or parent who is on a dangerous military mission. This leads to additional stress for families already worried about deployment. Such cultural incongruence may be even greater for military families living on installations in foreign countries. They must intermittently know and follow the rules of American mainstream culture, the military subculture, and the foreign culture in which they reside. It takes a strong family to synthesize such complexity into its private philosophy.

Population mobility also creates pockets of philosophical diversity and complexity. In almost any American city or town, there is a range of family beliefs that often directly oppose each other. For example, some families may believe that illness can be overcome by modern science and technology, other families put their trust in homeopathic remedies, and still others look to the healing powers of religion and prayer. As another example, some families believe that fighting back actively is the appropriate response to a stressor event while others believe in passive acceptance of whatever happens to them. Thus, even within the same cultural context, families may differ in their private philosophies.

Although such family beliefs and values are influenced by the external context, we note that a family's internal synthesis of beliefs and values (which become the family's own philosophy of being) directly influences the family's perception of a stressor event and how to deal with it. Consequently, we focus heavily in this book on the internal context—not because it is more important than the external context but because it is malleable. While both external and internal contexts are critical in determining which families remain strong, the internal context provides a more feasible window for change. It contains a possible set of leverage points that can be activated by family members themselves. It is for this reason that the internal context is of interest to family therapists and counselors who work with distressed and traumatized couples and families.

As we work with and study stressed families, we must ascertain their internal context before we can understand how the family sees the problem and whether change is possible. To further complicate matters, the family's internal context often shifts over time, with individual family members often disagreeing in their perceptions of the situation. Thus we need to ask family members, "What does this situation mean to you now?" (Boss, 2006).

Some families try to change their external context, but many remain powerless in the face of international politics and the devastation of war or plague. Although such families may try to eradicate such external stressors, they are rarely successful, at least in the short term. Often, the only option left is to change their perception of what is happening to them, which brings us back to the internal shift that they can control.

This ends our definitions of the CMFS's external and internal contexts. Keeping in mind that the following constructs are context-laden, we now move deeper into the model to define the ABC-X dimensions. We discuss them one at a time, beginning with the A factor, then B, C, and finally, X.

The ABC-X of Family Stress: A Frame for Definitions

When Reuben Hill (1958) formulated his ABC-X model, he provided a heuristic model for the scientific inquiry of family stress. He presented this model to a group of social workers in 1957, thus linking the work of family sociologists to that of practitioners. His framework for family stress theory focused on the following independent or intervening variables, which remain the foundation of family stress theory today:

   A—the provoking event or stressor
   B—the family's resources or strengths at the time of the event
   C—the meaning attached to the event by the family (individually and collectively)
   X—the outcome (coping or crisis)

Boss (1987, 1988, 1991, 2002) built upon Hill's heuristic ABC-X model but adapted it to be less linear, more contextual, and more focused on meaning and perception. With these major changes and additions, the CMFS was born. While other family stress models were developed, for example, the Double ABC-X model (Lavee, McCubbin, & Patterson, 1985), we find the parsimony and usefulness of the CMFS to be especially easy for practitioners and researchers to apply. Hill's work remains the heuristic core (Figure 1.4), but now the C factor is emphasized, which is what makes the theory a useful guide for intervention. From a clinical perspective, the family's perception of an event is often the most powerful—or only—window for change. Perception, however, is difficult to measure, which may explain why the C factor was the least investigated in earlier decades. Since 1973, the focus for Boss has been on the C factor, for which we encourage continued study.

Because developing family stress theory is an interdisciplinary endeavor, you will see that we have merged constructs and definitions from family science, child development, social work, and nursing literatures, among others, because all have contributed directly or indirectly to understanding the processes of family stress management and resilience. In addition, using a general systems perspective, we include both individual and group indicators. Moving now to the inside of the model, we define the components of its ABC-X core.

The A Factor: Stressor Event (Stressful Event)

A *stressor event* is an occurrence that is of significant magnitude to provoke change in the family system. A stressor event is not synonymous with stress. It is an event that marks a possible starting point for the process of change and subsequent stress in the family system. It disturbs the family's status quo.

The stressor event also has the potential to increase the family's level of stress, although it does not necessarily do so every time. Stressors may be positive, normative, or toxic. The degree of stress depends not only on the actual magnitude of the event but also on the family's perception of that event. Families often view the same event differently (e.g., one family is ecstatic over a move to a new country, whereas another is panic stricken or angry) or may perceive an event differently over time (e.g., the first time a family moved it was exciting, and small children were not disturbed, but after the 12th move in 15 years, the mother feels defeated, and high-school-aged children are angry).

The Danger of Circular Reasoning

Because a stressful event is only a stimulus, it cannot be synonymous with the outcome of that stimulus. This means that a stressor event is not the same as the degree of stress the family experiences

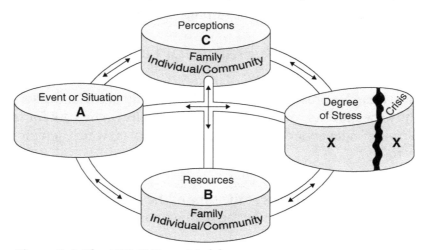

Figure 1.4 *The ABC-X Stress Model*
Source: Adapted from Boss (2002) and Hill (1958).

(see Figure 1.4). Were they the same, this would be a tautology (circular reasoning). A *tautology* is an untestable hypothesis because obviously "stress equals stress" or "change equals change." The correlation would be 100%. A researcher would be wasting his or her time trying to test such hypotheses. It would not provide an explanation or help us to understand nuance or complexity or move our thinking to action.

To avoid the danger of tautologies, we propose that the *type* of stressor event influences the *degree* of stress experienced. Thus, in the model in Figure 1.4, "type of event" equals "degree of stress" (rather than stress equals stress). This is a very important point. Not only does it avoid circular reasoning, but it also aids in parsimony and conceptual clarity. You will see how this equation becomes even more complex (but still testable) when we add "the family's perception of that event." Were we to add "community perception of the event," as recommended by family psychiatry researchers Reiss and Oliveri (1991) and Reiss (1981) and more recently by Mancini and Bowen (2009, 2013), there would be no danger for tautology.

Classification of Family Stressor Events

Stressor events are varied and multiple. Because it is essential to be able to identify them, the basic types are classified and defined in Table 1.1 for quick reference and better understanding. Here's the point: It is more useful to classify stressor events or situations by their characteristics and intensity than by the name of a particular event or disease.

Table 1.1 *Classifications of Stressor Events and Situations*

Source	
Internal: Events that begin with someone inside the family, such as addiction, suicide, violence, or running for an election	**External:** Events that begin with someone or something outside the family, such as floods, terrorism, or loss of job
Type	
Normative, Developmental, Predictable: Events that are expected during the life course, such as birth, puberty, adolescence, marriage, aging, menopause, retirement, and death	**Catastrophic, Situational, Unexpected:** Unforeseen events or situations, such as a young child dies
Ambiguous: Events or situations that remain unclear, such as facts about the status of a family member remain unclear or are unavailable	**Clear:** Facts are available, such as the family knows what is happening and how it will turn out
Volitional: Events or situations that are wanted and sought out, such as freely chosen job changes, college entrance, or a wanted pregnancy	**Nonvolitional:** Events or situations not freely chosen, such as being laid off, fired, divorced, or being given up for adoption
Duration	
Chronic: A situation of long duration, such as diabetes, chemical addiction, or discrimination and prejudice	**Acute:** Event that lasts a short time but is stressful, such as a broken leg
Density	
Cumulative: Events or situations that pile up, one after the other, so there is no time to cope before the next stressor occurs, such as families worn down by multiple unresolved stressors	**Isolated:** One event that occurs by itself or alone with no other stressor; it is easily pinpointed

Source: Adapted from Boss (2002).

When an individual is faced with a stressor event, either as a professional who works with stressed families or as a family member, it is important to identify the type of event before assessing or responding to the situation because the type will influence the entire process: the family's perception of the event, the degree of stress experienced by the family, and the managing strategies used or not used. In fact, the type of event may be highly correlated with the family's ability or inability to manage stress or recover from crisis. Certainly, the type called "ambiguous stressor events" has been identified as a major predictor of family stress that is difficult to resolve (Boss, 1999, 2006).

The types of stressor events in Table 1.1 provide a template for assessing the characteristics of stressor events, some of which will be problematic and others that are normative. Rather than focusing on a specific disease or event, Table 1.1 expands our thinking to include the nuances of what is stressful and why.

As you can see, we categorize stressors by source, type, duration, and density. To assess, we ask, Did the stressor originate inside the family or from the external context? Was it expected, clear, and volitional or the opposite? Is the stressor now chronic, becoming a situation and not just an event? Was it made more dense by piling on other stressors? While some of the subcategories in the table are more positive than others, all have the potential to disturb the family's status quo. We now discuss each subcategory.

Normal, Developmental, and Predictable Stressor Events

While normative stressors are usually expected events (e.g., children grow up), the normal and expected development of a child to adolescence, for example, tends to increase family stress, especially if the parents do not acknowledge the maturation and change. Retirement can cause a crisis in an older, traditional couple when the husband and wife continue to interact as if the husband still has a full-time job. To avoid conflict and dissatisfaction in the family, he may have to take on a new role, such as sharing the household duties with his wife, and she may have to adjust her activities to adapt to his increased presence at home. With many normative developmental events, a family must change at every transition point. Who is in the family and how? We define normative stressor events in terms of family boundary changes across the family life cycle; with each event, the family either loses or gains a member, and this means that its boundary is disturbed. When the physical presence of family members increases or diminishes, there is a ripple effect that causes stress at various degrees of the entire family system.

Catastrophic, Situational, and Unexpected Stressor Events

Catastrophic types of stressor events (Table 1.1) initially interested family stress theorists such as Reuben Hill more than 4 decades ago. They are unexpected (nonnormative) events, the result of some unique situation that could not be predicted and is not likely to be repeated. As a result, such events are usually highly stressful.

Negative examples of unpredictable and unique events include disasters and catastrophes such as the March 11, 2011 Fukushima triple disaster in northeastern Japan (earthquake, tsunami, and subsequent nuclear disaster); the Newtown, Connecticut school shooting of 20 grade school children; the disappearance of the Malaysian airliner and its 239 passengers; the BP oil spill; the AIDS epidemic of the 1980s; and other major earthquakes, volcanic eruptions, tornadoes, fires, and floods.

Unexpected events that are not catastrophic may also be stressful for families. Examples include finding lost relatives or receiving unexpected job offers or promotions. Such events are positive, but they create a disturbance in the family's routine and thus have a potential for increasing the family's level of stress.

Ambiguous Stressor Events

Ambiguity is created when facts can't be obtained about an event or situation. The whereabouts or fate of a kidnapped boy—even a lost pet—remains unclear for a long time, or an illness takes away the mind or memory of a family member. For example, a grandfather with advanced Alzheimer's disease is no longer the person he was and is now unrecognizable. The ambiguity lies in his being here but not here. An ambiguous stressor may be an event that is predicted but no one knows if and when it will really occur (e.g., tornado, hurricane, earthquake, Alzheimer's disease). In any case, with ambiguous stressors, facts are unclear or nonexistent. Families are pushed to the limit of what they can withstand. Many find resilience in surprising ways. When Microsoft scientist and Turing Award Winner Jim Gray was lost at sea in 2007, with no trace of his boat anywhere, his family and his colleagues searched the sea for a long time but found nothing to clear up the ambiguity (Boss, 2008). Eventually, his wife found new meaning through writing poetry, which allowed her to move forward with a new kind of life (Boss & Carnes, 2012). The pain of such stress is the ambiguity of losing a person who has disappeared. Categorizing such painful stressors as "ambiguous" and naming the culprit as "the not-knowing" is more effective than attributing blame to those who are, through no fault of their own, at the mercy of the ambiguity.

Clear Stressor Events

When clear facts are available about an event—what is happening, when, for how long, and to whom—a family is in a better position. There is no question about what is happening to them, the prognosis, and what will help to reduce their stress. If the event, such as a hurricane, cannot be changed, the family is at least clear about the duration of the storm, its logical progression, and what they must do to protect themselves.

Volitional Stressor Events

Volitional events are those that a family controls and implements. Making a move willingly or planning a pregnancy are examples of volitional stressor events. Thus, these events are classified by the degree of choice and control of the family members and the system as a whole. Other examples of volitional stressor events are a desired marriage, a wanted divorce, or a deadline that a family has chosen to meet. Some families actually enjoy challenge and thus choose vacations that include some stress; for example, white-water rafting, climbing mountains, running marathons, bicycling hilly terrain, or simply taking a road trip with small children.

Typically, in our culture, volitional stressor events are associated with lower degrees of family stress because the events are purposefully selected. The family remains in control of its destiny. Stories about some immigrant families, such as those of former U.S. Secretary of State Madeleine Albright (part of the Clinton Administration, 1997-2001) and the family of President John F. Kennedy, reflect a constant search for challenge and high-stress situations. The problem, however, is that not all members of a family may enjoy a high degree of stress all the time. Not everyone may be an adventurer or enjoy competition. There may be a shy person in a family devoted to public service. When we work with families, we have to be sure that all family members want an event to occur before it can validly be classified as volitional for the entire family.

Nonvolitional Stressor Events

Nonvolitional events are events that are thrust on a family. They originate in the outside context and are not a result of action by anyone inside the family. The key point is that the family has no control over the occurrence. Examples of nonvolitional family stressor events are family breadwinners being laid off from their jobs or a family member being robbed. Disastrous events that are called "acts of God," such as volcanic eruptions or earthquakes, are also categorized as nonvolitional. Even human-made disasters such as the nuclear bombings in Hiroshima and Nagasaki in 1945 can, at least from the Japanese people's perspective, be classified as nonvolitional; there was no knowledge of the nature of the bombs before they were dropped.

Stressor Situations

A chronic stressor is defined as a stressful situation (rather than an event) because it is characterized by (1) a long duration; (2) the probability of occurrence with other events, especially normal developmental transitions; and (3) the potential for high ambiguity in its origin (etiology), progression, and conclusion. The situation is difficult to change—that is, the stressor persists. Such chronic stressors may be an illness (e.g., alcoholism or Alzheimer's disease), an economic situation (e.g., poverty), or a social condition (e.g., discrimination against race, gender, and sexual orientation). Other examples of chronic stressors are living in constant danger (e.g., terrorism, persecution, or high murder rate in neighborhood). Other chronic situations may not be dangerous but are nevertheless a constant irritation (e.g., noisy atmosphere for people living near an airport or in some college dormitories). The key point is that a chronic stressor is a long-term situation rather than a one-time event and thus, more problematic.

Chronic stressors have special characteristics that affect the degree of stress experienced in a family. The following questions define the characteristics:

1. Is there ambiguity rather than predictability in the event or situation—that is, is there uncertainty regarding facts about the onset, development, and resolution of the situation? The chronic stressor of Parkinson's disease, for example, has more predictability (due to a known medication) than does the chronic stressor of autism (about which less is known).

2. What is the context in which the chronic stressor event develops—that is, is the stressful event a result of the larger context (e.g., inflation, living near an active volcano, or the closing of a factory) or the result of an individual action (e.g., a lifetime of smoking that caused a persistent illness)?

3. What is the visibility or nonvisibility of the situation? Some chronic stressors, such as diabetes or heart disease, are not physically noticeable, whereas others, such as loss of a limb or being blind are more apparent to outsiders and family members.

Each of these characteristics may affect the family's perception of the event, which will determine the degree of stress experienced collectively and individually. Therefore, we must obtain answers to the aforementioned questions when we work with chronically stressed families.

Even more than with short-term events, the subtle characteristics of chronic stressor situations call for special consideration in research methodology, clinical diagnosis, and assessment of family stress. Instruments must have the capacity to measure perceptual variables that are influenced by the duration and ambiguity of long-term stressor situations. Tests and measuring instruments must be sensitive to the possibility that the family members are denying what is happening to them. For example, the family may deny the existence of a persisting illness in one of its members.

Such denial occurs with many chronic illnesses, such as alcoholism, drag addiction, Alzheimer's disease, and end-stage renal disease.

Another characteristic unique to a chronic stressor situation influences research and therapeutic assessment: The family's perception of the situation may change during the family life cycle, According to Lynn Wikler (1981, 1986), a social work researcher, the painful reality of a chronic stressor such as severe intellectual disability is again inflated at each juncture of the life span when a developmental step would normally occur in the affected person. For example, when a child reaches the "age of high school graduation and cannot graduate and attend college or obtain employment as other children do, the family is newly reminded of the constraints on the child's situation. If the family maintains normal expectations, their chronic stress may be increased to a higher level at each developmental point. Disability as a chronic stressor event is an added complication when combined with the normal stressor events of developmental family life transitions that occur naturally during the life span. Another example is when a caregiver and the family may not be able to deal with both the stressor situation (e.g., a chronically ill family member) and normal stressor events (e.g., the death of an aged parent and an adolescent leaving home) happening during the same period. Managing all of these changes may become overwhelming. Therefore, it can be predicted that a family will be highly stressed whenever a normal developmental transition occurs simultaneously with a chronic family stressor situation, even though the family managed the illness reasonably well before the transition point and will do so afterward.

Acute Stressor Events

Acute stressor events are those that happen suddenly and last only a short time. Their duration is usually predictable. Examples are a child breaking a leg and wearing a cast for 6 weeks or a family member undergoing emergency surgery and staying home from work for a few weeks to recuperate. The major distinction between a chronic and acute stressor event is that the latter happens suddenly and then is over. The duration of the acute stressor event is short and reasonably predictable. Note, however, that aftereffects are not predictable and also can be long lasting. An example is the acute stressor of heart surgery followed by the ongoing chronic heart disease itself.

Cumulative Stressor Events

The accumulation of stressor events is a phenomenon in which several stressor events or situations occur at the same time or in quick sequence, thus compounding the degree of pressure on the family. The phenomenon is also called cumulative disadvantages or adversity (Gerard & Buehler, 2004; Lucier-Greer, Arnold, Mancini, Ford, & Bryant, 2015). The idea of accumulation is the basis of the frequently used stress scale, Schedule of Recent Events, developed by psychiatrists Holmes and Rahe (1967), which quantifies self-reported stressors piling up or accumulating for individuals (Rahe, Veach, Tolies, & Murakami, 2000) and the Family Inventory of Life Events and Changes Scale developed by family social scientists McCubbin, Patterson, and Wilson (1981), which quantifies stress pileup as reported by a family member. The concept of stressor pileup is important because it is the accumulation of several stressor events rather than the nature of one isolated event that determines a family's level of stress, its subsequent vulnerability to crisis, or its ability to recover from a particular crisis. An event rarely happens to a family in total isolation; normal developmental changes are always taking place as family members are born, mature, grow older, and die. The pileup of stressor events and situations is highly influential in assessing a family's level of stress.

Isolated Stressor Events

Isolated stressor events are single events that occur at a time when nothing else is disturbing the family status quo. This single event can then be pinpointed as the event that is causing one's stress, Life is good, but one day, you mistakenly park in the wrong place. Your car is towed, you are very upset, you hitch a ride to the tow pound, pay a considerable fee, and have your car back. The stressor event is over, although there may still be a credit card bill to pay off. Or, you break an ankle, you go to the hospital, they treat you and put your ankle in a cast, you experience more stress for 6 weeks or so as you limp around, they take the cast off, and you can walk again as normal. Such isolated stressor events are more easily (though not happily) dealt with in a linear fashion. Although we may be deeply stressed or in pain, it is clear what happened and what we need to do to fix the problem.

With this brief discussion of each classification of stressors shown in Table 1.1, we reiterate the core point: Classifying stressor events and situations by source, type, duration, and density will reveal the nuances of why some events are more immobilizing than others. Classifying stressors in this manner is more revealing than classifying them by disaster or disease. Nevertheless, there are some cautions.

Cautions About Defining a Stressor Event

Keep in mind what we said earlier: What is defined as a stressor event is highly influenced by the family's external context—the time in their lives and the place in which they live. Community and cultural contexts influence what the family defines as a "stressor event." Marriage, pregnancy, an adolescent leaving home, the loss of a job, women working outside the home, failing an exam, or even winning the lottery are all viewed differently. We cannot automatically assess such events as stressful without first asking the family, and its members, how they define the event. There are times when military deployment is a stress reducer rather than a stressor event. The same can be said for death, if a family member has been in great pain or in a coma for a long time.

Although neutral, a stressor event has the potential to be either positive or negative—or a mixture of both. Winning a large amount of money has as much potential to cause stress in a family as losing money. However, when a stressor is transformative and leads to growth, it is an example of making lemonade out of lemons.

Stressor events do not always increase stress to a crisis point. They can occur, and the status quo of the family can be disturbed, but the family's stress level can be managed if the system finds a new equilibrium.

On the other hand, when a stressful event such as sudden loss of income occurs, a family can refuse to acknowledge the event or to change their behavior (habits of spending freely). They act as if nothing happened, using credit cards and going deeper into debt. Here, the denial of the event (loss of income) prevents change and thereby increases the probability of crisis in the family.

A family cannot begin to manage stress or solve problems until they recognize that they have a problem. Families cannot deal with a stressor event until, as a group, they recognize that the event has occurred. If only one family member sees the problem, these are few systemic options: the rest of the family has to change their perceptions of the event; the dissenting person has to change his or her perception; or ultimately that dissenter is isolated, shunned, and has to leave.

Throughout the time a particular family is experiencing a stressor event, their resources for coping and managing are hopefully gathered, assessed, and set in motion. Resources can influence how a family responds to stress.

The B Factor: Resources (Individual, Family, and Community)

We now move to resources, the B factor in the CMFS. Family resources are the individual, familial, and community strengths and assets available to the family at the time of stress or crisis. Examples include financial stability, good health, intelligence, education, employable job skills, proximity of support, spirit of cooperation in the family, relationship skills, network and social supports, and resilience—both individual and collective. Family resources then are the economic, psychological, and physical assets from which the family can draw upon in response to stressor events or situations.

A question remains about whether resilience is a resource or an outcome in the CMFS. In this book, we present resilience as a process so it occurs in multiple places—but not at the same time. That would be tautology. For the most part, we see resilience as an outcome of the family stress management process (see Chapter 7).

The C Factor: Perception

The C factor is defined as the family's collective perception of a stressor event or situation. It is how they think about or view what they are experiencing. Hill originally called the C factor the "definition of the event," but that term was too narrow (Boss, 1988, 2002). Boss preferred the term "perception" because it included more than the family's definition of the stressor; it included—and elevated—the value of a family's subjective interpretation and meaning of a stressful event. If families are expected to act on their own behalf, to change or to transform, then honoring the sense *they* make of their experiences is the first step.

With perception (and thus meaning) now the central construct, a major theoretical shift took place; the focus in the CMFS was now on the social construction of meaning. This continues today, as symbolic interactionism remains relevant. While Boss built her early work on the symbolic interactionism of pioneer sociologist George Herbert Mead (1956), family sociologist Sheldon Stryker (1968), and especially sociologist Erving Goffman, (1959, 1974) (see Boss, in press for review), today, we also build on the social construction theory pioneered by Peter Berger and Thomas Luckmann (1966), David Reiss (1981), and psychologist Kenneth Gergen (1994, 1999, 2001), a major figure in the development of social constructionist theory and its applications to practices of social change. Like Boss (2006), Gergen agrees that loss is "a rupture in meaning" and "a relational disorder and not individual pathology" (2006, back cover). Meaning must be restored if a family and its individual members are to remain strong after loss. Today, we continue our emphasis on perception because it embodies both the cognitive (thinking) and affective (feeling) processes of family stress management.

The Primacy of Perceptions

In work with distressed families, it became apparent that unless we could identify, understand, and measure their perceptions, we would not have a valid view of what was happening to families or how to intervene (Boss, 1992). During Boss's initial studies with families of men declared missing in action in Vietnam and later with families in which there was Alzheimer's disease, she paid as much attention to qualitative narratives from family members as to quantitative data from questionnaires. The latter were often easier to analyze and much more acceptable as research data when she began in the 1970s, but it was the stories told by family members that informed her of the power of their perceptions of the situation. Hill (1949/1971) originally called this the family's "definition of the event," medical sociologist Aaron Antonovsky (1979) called it "appraisal," and Patterson and Garwick (1994) called it "levels of meaning." The latter reflects the growing consensus among family stress researchers that perception and meaning are central to understanding sometimes puzzling processes observed in distressed families.

For example, a student wrote:

> I work in a shelter for battered women and I am continually amazed and saddened by different women and children's perceptions of what is going on in their lives. Some women view the battering as just another event in their lives and take it in stride; others are unable to function from the hurt and shame. The meaning each woman attaches to her abusive situation is always different. It is often hard for me to understand their perception because mine varies drastically. Some women see abuse as normal stress, while others see it as a crisis. Most continue to function (going to work or school) while living in the shelter, while others are traumatized and barely able to take care of themselves. Some have to be referred to hospital or medical staff. My perception of their situation often differs from theirs. Even after I find out what their perceptions are, my values and standards block my ability to fully see where they are coming from. I am very sensitive to their situations and offer them several resources to become more self-sufficient and improve their lives, but I am still unable to totally view battering the way they do. My question is this: Is this a bad thing? Must I constantly remind myself that I am perceiving it differently and try to perceive it in the way they do in order to help them? Or do I just need to know their perceptions in order to fully understand the premise they are coming from?

This student began to answer her own question by framing her last question. Where she is "coming from" is influenced by her community and cultural context. We need to know the premise or meaning that all family members have about the family's situation. How do they define it? What meaning does it have for them and their community? We would never agree that being battered was normal, but if this is what a woman believes, it helps us to know this as we work with her. If she believes it is normal to be hit by her partner, she needs information and group experiences to show her that other options exist. In such cases, we work cognitively and psychodynamically to change perceptions so that everyone in that group or family becomes intolerant of abuse and more able to express feelings verbally.

How a family perceives an event or situation and the meaning it embodies is critical in determining the degree of stress they experience (i.e., crisis or coping). For example, the death of a parent is described as a loss, but it might *mean* the end of someone's world—a repossessed home; no car; no money for education, food, or clothes; even homelessness. In another family, the death of a parent is also sad but may simply mean the end of a long and good life.

In sum, you see that we support the primacy of perceptions, but we must also add that perceptions are not *all* that matter (Boss, 1992). Sometimes, the family's perception can be distorted, so other views are needed—the teacher's, the nurse's, the doctor's, or the social worker's view. Multiple views are needed to validate assessments. This is true for research as well as for professionals who work with families who are in disagreement or denial.

Collective Versus Individual Perceptions

And that brings us to collective perceptions. This means that everyone in the family agrees with how the stressor event or situation is perceived. As in any system, the whole is greater than the sum of its parts; the family's collective perception can overpower the meaning that any individual family member might give to the same event. When even one family member begins to see things differently, change is on the way for the entire family system. To determine the degree of incongruence among individual members' perceptions, we recommend using both individual and collective assessment of the C factor. In effect, we are assessing the degree of family agreement in perceptions of the event versus their degree of disagreement.

The X Factor: Family Crisis

Family stress sometimes results in crisis (Figure 1.4). A family crisis is (1) a disturbance in the equilibrium that is so overwhelming; (2) a pressure that is so severe; or (3) a change that is so acute that the family system is blocked, immobilized, and incapacitated. At least for a time, the family does not function. Family boundaries are no longer maintained, customary roles and tasks are no longer performed, and family members can no longer function at optimal levels, physically or psychologically.

The following case from Boss's own family illustrates this point. She shares her family's story of crisis;

> In the summer of 1955, the summer before the Salk polio vaccine was discovered, polio was rampant, and many of the young were stricken. Eddie, my younger brother, was a strong 13-year-old and the predicted star of the freshman football team. Disaster struck, however. He played football one Friday and died the next. The young football squad carried his coffin at the funeral, and the whole school and community were in shock. Our family was immobilized. Friends and people from the community came to our home with food. My parents could not function or work, so friends and neighbors had to chauffer them, help plan the funeral, and fill in for them at work. I was at the university but could not study. None of us could perform our usual tasks. Each of us withdrew into our own private grief. Our family rule of "we take care of ourselves" had to give way as friends and neighbors took over to help. Our family system was in crisis. We were immobilized by Eddie's unexpected and terrible death from polio.

When a family is in crisis, using the bridge metaphor means that the structure has collapsed. At least for a time, the family cannot function. Specific indicators of such family crisis are (1) the inability of parents to take care of themselves, their children, their work, or their business; (2) the inability of family members to make decisions or to solve problems (e.g., about the funeral, money, or work); (3) the inability of family members to perform daily tasks and roles so that outsiders are temporarily needed to do this; and (4) the care for each other as family members or spouses may retreat to private coping. In the case of Eddie's sudden death, the family was stunned and in deep grief, so it was others who drew them out to see the public support—the school community, the church congregation, the football team, relatives, and friends of all ages. As family members could no longer take care of each other, they were fortunate to have the support of the community to keep them going during this terrible time. When a beloved family member dies suddenly and all too young, the strongest of families can fall into momentary crisis and immobilization.

We want to emphasize that the terms *stress* and *crisis* cannot be used interchangeably. Whereas family stress is a state of disturbed equilibrium, family crisis is a point of acute disequilibrium. Therefore, family stress is a continuous variable (degrees of stress), whereas family crisis is a categorical variable (a family is either in crisis or it is not; see Figures 1.4 and 1.5). In crisis, the family system is immobilized and stops functioning. Like a bridge that collapses, a family crisis is determined by the point at which the family structure can no longer perform its intended functions. In a family, however, in addition to the pressures that outweigh the family supports, their perception and appraisal of what is happening can influence the point at which the break occurs or is avoided.

The Roller Coaster Model of Family Crisis

The roller coaster model of family adjustment after crisis developed by Hill in 1949 and adapted by others (Boss, 1987; Hansen & Hill, 1964) illustrates familial adjustment to crisis. According to the model, crisis is the period of disorganization and immobilization in which previous interactions and behaviors for managing and solving problems become inadequate, frozen, inoperable, or blocked. The system hits bottom. Depending on the amount of time needed to shift gears or change, the family reaches a turning point, begins to move again, reorganizes, and enters what Hill (1949/1971) called the period of recovery. The family reaches a new level of reorganization that is higher, lower, or equal to the one experienced before the onset of the stressor event (see Figure 1.5). Today we call this growth an indicator of resilience or post-traumatic growth (see Chapter 7). This means that a family does not have to be destroyed by crisis or immobilization.

Linking the ABC-X Model to the Roller Coaster Model of Family Crisis

While there is a difference between Hill's ABC-X model of family stress and his roller coaster model of family crisis, the two are linked. The roller coaster model (as adapted, Boss, 1988, 2002) illustrates the breaking point after increasingly wild gyrations of resisting until, finally, the family structure breaks under the pressure. Like an overloaded bridge, it is no longer functional. The family falls into crisis (as indicated by immobilization). Ideally, the family eventually reaches a turning point, which means they decide to start moving forward again, and they may function at a level lower than, equal to, or higher than before the crisis occurred (see Figure 1.5). We believe, however, that the roller coaster model represents only one portion of the broken X factor in Figure 1.4. There we show crisis as a state separate from high stress (note the broken line). Crisis is something other than simply the highest point of the stress continuum. That is, crisis is not a continuous variable: It is a categorical variable. You are either immobilized or you are not. Although hopefully temporary, crisis as indicated by immobilization is an outcome.

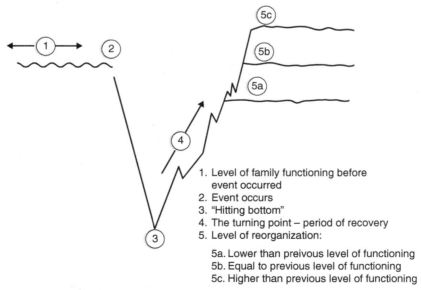

1. Level of family functioning before event occurred
2. Event occurs
3. "Hitting bottom"
4. The turning point – period of recovery
5. Level of reorganization:

    5a. Lower than preivous level of functioning
    5b. Equal to previous level of functioning
    5c. Higher than previous level of functioning

Figure 1.5 *The Turning Point in Family Crisis*
Source: Adapted from Boss (2002), Hill (1949/1971), and Koos (1946).

In contrast to the model of family stress shown in Figure 1.4, the roller coaster model in Figure 1.5 helps us to understand family recovery because it shows the disorganization and reorganization process in families. They are immobilized, hit bottom, and, hopefully, turn the corner to begin the process of recovery. Importantly, families often grow stronger after surviving crisis so that their levels of functioning can become even higher than before the *crisis*. Outcomes can range from low stress, meaning the family is managing, to high stress or crisis, meaning the family is still struggling.

The Turning Point: Family Recovery After Crisis

Crisis is painful and may debilitate the family, but the length of the debilitation may vary from hours to years. Given minor and some major crises, a family may often hit bottom, turn the corner, begin the recovery process, and repair itself (see Figure 1.5). This ability to recover marks the major difference between a mechanical system (the bridge) and an organic system (the family). A family system has the potential to grow and learn from a crisis, whereas a bridge does not. Therefore, for human systems, crisis may be simply a turning point, not an end point. This is a hopeful note for families in crisis.

When the ratio between the family system's support and the pressure on it shifts so that the pressure decreases and the support becomes stronger, recovery is occurring. Turning points result from (1) a change in the stressor event, (2) a change in the availability of resources for coping, or (3) a change in the family's perception of both factors. In the case of incurable illness or when the pressure of the event cannot be lessened, we can ease the stress level with the second and third factors. If, however, the family's resources cannot be increased, then we can intervene with only the third factor, changing the family's perception of what is happening to them.

Some families reach a turning point after the crisis by redefining the events that have been stressing them, or they redefine their existing strengths, resources, and supports. Even if nothing else changes, families may have changed their perception of what was happening to them or what resources and supports were available to them for coping. Clinicians call this process *reframing*. Such a change in perception can alter the ratio of family pressure to family support and thereby precipitate a turning point, which is the beginning of recovery for a family in crisis. This is important in crises in which the event, in this case, a loss, for Boss's family, cannot be changed. The family could not change the loss of Eddie, so they changed their perception and worked tirelessly to help others.

> After Eddie's death, our family took a long time to even begin recovering. While we began to work again, to eat, and even occasionally find a reason to smile, I never felt I recovered as such; rather I learned to live with the sadness. Perhaps that is what recovery means for some. Routines returned. Help from the outside was needed less and less. My parents met with others who had lost children. Perhaps what helped the most is that a year later, all of us in the family went door to door to collect donations for the March of Dimes, which at that time was funding research on preventing polio. We found a meaning in our sorrow and thus were no longer in crisis. After hitting bottom, we were on the way to becoming a new family system, one without Eddie, except in memory. The stress from that awful event of loss will always be with us, but we are no longer immobilized. Indeed, crisis does not have to permanently destroy a family. It can make them stronger.

Family Strain

Before we end this section on crisis as outcome, we need to clarify that not all families fall into crisis. Some are just highly stressed but managing; others are driven to the brink but holding on and still functioning. We call it *strain*.

Family strain can be likened to a bridge shaking but not collapsing. The structure is still functional—at least minimally—but it is bent out of shape, creaks, and shakes under pressure. Strain results from a mismatch at the point where pressures occur and the supports are grounded. In a family system, that means supports (resources and strengths) may exist, but they are not where they are most needed. For example, poor families who have seen trouble before and know how to survive may be more resilient than more privileged families who have not faced trouble before. Psychologically strong families are those who avoid the mismatch between the location of its strengths and pressures. Those families may still continue to function, albeit shakily, if there are some outside supports that come to help.

The danger of strain for a family is that if their structure begins to change at some time (which is quite likely because children grow up and parents grow older), the existing mismatch limits the family's degree of tolerance to adapt to stress. A strained family is brittle (the opposite of resilient). Thus, in an already strained family, the chance for total collapse (crisis) is high when an additional event occurs and even more pressure is added. The family becomes highly vulnerable.

Therefore, it may be more critical to avoid the mismatch of strain than to avoid the occurrence of stressor events. After all, a life without stress would be unusual. We need to know how much pressure we can handle and if we can handle more pressure at certain times than others. The family that is not strained can more easily manage and cope with everyday stressor events because resources can simply be directed to match pressures when and where they occur. In addition, although the mismatch that defines family strain does not always depend on the accumulation of stressor events, it is more likely to occur when events pile up persistently and exert increasing pressure at different points of the family structure, thus aggravating the dangerous mismatch.

For professionals working with families, the identification of vulnerable families may be easier if they search for this mismatch between stressors and strengths, pressures and supports, and rigidity and resilience to determine which families are fragile and which are strong. Some families can handle a lot of pressure, whereas others cannot. Strain, with its brittleness, more than stress or crisis, may be a distinguishing variable in identifying vulnerable families.

In the next chapter, we discuss a universal stressor—a death in the family. The responses, however, to the stress of losing a loved one to death vary across cultures and ethnicity. Focusing on this common family stressor through a multicultural lens, the following chapter shows us the urgent need for more inclusion of diversity in the study and practice of family stress.

Summary

Neither individuals nor families exist in a vacuum. They are a part of a larger context. Sometimes they have very little control over the context in which they find themselves embedded. Families generally have relatively more control over their internal context, compared to their external context. Thus, for example, although they cannot change their heredity (external), they can change their perceptions and appraisals (internal). Doing so can impact the outcome of a stressor event. Sometimes family stressors lead to crises, and crises can immobilize and incapacitate a family system.

CHAPTER 2

Integrating Family Resilience and Family Stress Theory

Joän M. Patterson University of Minnesota

The construct, family resilience, has been defined and applied very differently by those who are primarily clinical practitioners and those who are primarily researchers in the family Geld. In this-article, the family resilience perspective is integrated with conceptual definitions from family stress theory using the Family Adjustment and Adaptation Response (FAAR) Model in an effort to clarify distinctions between family resiliency as capacity and family resilience as a process. The family resilience process is discussed in terms of (a) the meaning of significant risk exposure (vs. the normal challenges of family life) and (b) the importance of making conceptual and operational distinctions between family system outcomes and family protective processes. Recommendations for future family resilience research are discussed.

The perspective that families, like individuals, can be considered resilient as they deal with the challenges in their lives has received increased attention from family scholars in the past decade. The popularity of this concept reflects the general trends in (a) family science, with more emphasis on family strengths (Stinnett & DeFrain, 1985) and resources (Karpel, 1986), rather than family deficits and pathology; and (b) psychology, with a greater emphasis on positive mental health and good functioning (Seligman & Csikszentmihalyi, 2000). However, with the proliferation of research on resilience and applications in practice, confusion has resulted in defining resilience and in deciding who is resilient, particularly when a family is the unit of analysis.

School of Public Health, 1300 South 2nd Street, Suite 300, University of Minnesota, Minneapolis, MN 55454 (patterson_j@epi.umn.edu).

Key Words: family adaptation, family protective processes, family resilience, family risk processes, family stress.

Joan M. Patterson, *Journal of Marriage and Family*, vol. 64, issue 2, © John Wiley and Sons.

There are multiple sources contributing to this confusion but three issues stand out. First, practitioners and researchers have used the concept of resilience differently. Generally, practitioners use the term to characterize an approach that focuses on family strengths versus deficits; most researchers, on the other hand, have been more interested in outcomes to explain unexpected competent functioning among families (and individuals) who have been exposed to significant risk(s). A second source of confusion follows from the first and relates to the lack of differentiation between (a) resilience as an outcome, (b) the characteristics or protective factors that contribute to families being resilient, (c) the nature and extent of risk exposure, and (d) the process of resilience. The third source of confusion is one that often plagues the family field with regard to other constructs and relates to the unit of analysis. How is a resilient family different from a resilient individual? Wolin and Wolin (1993), for example, wrote about resilient individuals in the context of having survived a toxic, dysfunctional family of origin. In their work, the primary unit of analysis is the individual and their attention to the family system is primarily as a significant source of risk. Is their work about *family* resilience?

In this article, I address the above issues and try to clarify the concept of family resilience. The theoretical foundation for the ideas presented is family stress and coping theory, particularly the stress models that emphasize *adaptation processes* in families exposed to major adversities. An effort is made to integrate the body of work of developmental psychologists who have been studying the origins of psychopathology in children. Empirical support for the perspective on family resilience developed in this article is drawn from studies of family adaptation when a child member has a chronic illness or disability, although the relevance of these ideas to families faced with other kinds of significant stress should be apparent.

What Is Family Resilience?

The concept of resilience emerged primarily from studies of children who functioned competently despite exposure to adversity when psychopathology was expected (see, i.e., Garmezy, 1991; Masten, 1994; Rutter 1987; Werner & Smith, 1992). Concurrently, researchers in disciplines other than psychology were noting similar competent functioning following risk exposure. Antonovsky (1987), a medical sociologist, introduced the concept of *salutogenesis* to describe the high functioning of many survivors of the Holocaust. Cassel (1976), an epidemiologist, introduced the idea of *host resistance* to describe the factor(s) that protected the host (person) from becoming ill. The field of family science was following a similar paradigm shift. McCubbin and his colleagues (McCubbin, Boss, Wilson, & Lester, 1980; McCubbin & Patterson, 1982), in explaining variability in military families' responses to the crises of war, observed that many families moved from crises to successful adaptation. The disciplines of public health, medical sociology, psychology, and family science converged at a similar place asking a similar question: "What accounts for why some stay healthy and do well in the face of risk and adversity and others do not?" The phenomenon of doing well in the face of adversity is now called *resilience.*

In these studies, the evidence for resilience was usually based on competent functioning in some domain (such as good social relationships or work success) after exposure to significant risk (such as being reared by a mentally ill parent or having a husband or father disappear in the Vietnam War). The risk was labeled significant because normatively, most persons exposed to it showed symptomatic or dysfunctional behavior. As these unexpected relationships between risk exposure and successful functioning were observed, attention was increasingly drawn to identification of the factors that moderated the relationship, which have been labeled protective factors. Integrating the work of many resilience researchers, Masten and Coatsworth (1998) clarified three conditions necessary for considering resilience in individuals. These three conditions can be adapted to family as the unit of analysis: First, a *family-level outcome* must be conceptualized so it is possible to assess the degree to which a family is competent in accomplishing the outcome. Second, there must be some *risk* associated with the expectation that a family will not be successful. Third, there is a need to understand what *protective mechanisms* prevent poor expected outcome(s). Any application of this perspective requires clear conceptual definitions of family outcomes, significant family risk, and protective mechanisms. Family stress theory has much to offer in formulating these definitions.

Family Stress and Coping Theory

Just as understanding of child resilience emerged from studies of stress and coping in children, family resilience can be examined from the perspective of family stress and coping theory (Boss, 2001; Hill, 1958; McCubbin, McCubbin & Thompson, 1995; McCubbin & Patterson, 1983; Patterson, 1988). In this article, the Family Adjustment and Adaptation Response (FAAR) Model (Patterson, 1988) will be used to emphasize the linkages between family stress theory and the family resilience perspective. In the FAAR Model, four central constructs are emphasized: families engage in active processes to balance *family demands* with *family capabilities* as these interact with *family meanings* to arrive at a level of *family adjustment* or *adaptation* (Patterson, 1988; 1993; see Figure 2.1). Family demands are comprised of (a) normative and nonnormative stressors (discrete events of change); (b) ongoing family strains (unresolved, insidious tensions); and (c) daily hassles (minor disruptions of daily life). Family capabilities include (a) tangible and psychosocial resources (what the family has) and (b) coping behaviors (what the family does). There are some obvious parallels between risk factors (resilience language) and demands, as well as between protective factors and capabilities. Both demands and capabilities can emerge from three different levels of the ecosystem: (a) individual family members, (b) a family unit, and (c) from various community contexts. The diagnosis of a child's disabling condition would be an example of an individual level demand; marital conflict about how to manage the child's condition would be a family level demand; and community stigma about disability would be a community level demand. Parent education, family cohesiveness, and good health and education services are examples of capabilities at each of the three levels, which could be used to help manage the aforementioned demands. Developmental psychologists also have emphasized that the resilience process involves transactions between multiple systems in the ecological context and that both risk and protective factors can emerge within individuals, families, and/or community contexts (Luthar, Cicchetti, & Becker, 2000). Among family stress theorists, Boss (2001) has emphasized the contexts of family stress and the need to take account of community and cultural contexts in which a family resides to understand why and how families are stressed, as well as to understand how families respond to stress.

Family meaning, an important construct in the FAAR Model, is less apparent in individual resilience perspectives but may add understanding to how the resilience process unfolds. Three levels of family meanings have been described in the FAAR Model: (a) families' definitions of their demands (primary appraisal) and capabilities (secondary appraisal); (b) their identity as a family (how they see themselves internally as a unit); and (c) their world view (how they see their family in relationship to systems outside of their family; Patterson, 1993; Patterson & Garwick, 1994). These meanings shape the nature and extent of risk, as well as the protective capacity of a family. The process of adapting to major, nonnormative stressors, such as the diagnosis of a child's chronic health condition, often involves changing prior beliefs and values as a way to make sense of the unexplainable and as a way to adapt (Patterson, 1993).

There are two types of family outcomes in the FAAR Model. On a daily basis, families engage in relatively stable patterns of interacting as they try to balance the demands they face with their existing capabilities to achieve a level of family adjustment. However, there are times when family demands significantly exceed their capabilities. When this imbalance persists, families experience *crisis,* which is a period of significant disequilibrium and disorganization in a family. A crisis is very

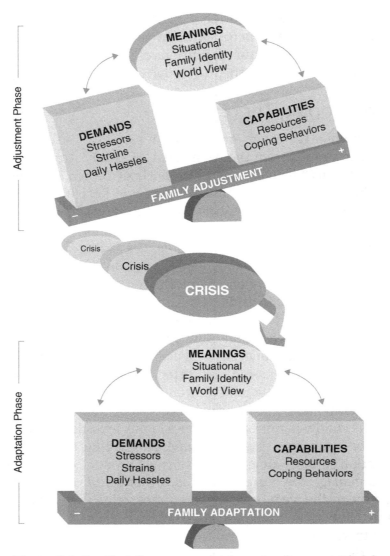

Figure 2.1 *Family Adjustment and Adaptation Response Model*
Note: From "Families Experiencing Stress: The Family Adjustment and Adaptation Response Model," by J. M. Patterson, 1988, *Family Systems Medicine, 6*(2), pp. 202–237. Copyright 1988 by Families, Systems & Health, Inc. Adapted with permission.

often a turning point for a family, leading to major change in their structure, interaction patterns, or both. A crisis can lead to a discontinuity in the family's trajectory of functioning either in the direction of improved functioning or poorer functioning. When the discontinuity is in the direction of improved functioning, this would be similar to the developmental discontinuities noted by Rutter (1987), Cowan, Cowan, and Schulz (1996) and others as an indicator of resilience. The processes by which families restore balance (reducing demands, increasing capabilities, and/or changing meanings) are called regenerative power in stress theory if the outcome is good (family bonadaptation). Of course, families can also engage in processes leading to poor adaptation, which is called *vulnerability* in stress theory (McCubbin & Patterson, 1983). Family resilience is similar to family regenerative power when good outcomes follow significant risk situations confronting a family. In the next sections, definitions of the key constructs underlying a family resilience perspective will be clarified by integrating conceptual definitions from family stress theory. A major source of confusion about family resilience is the two different ways this term is used for practice versus research. Generally, for practitioners, family resilience implies the capacity of a family to successfully manage challenging life circumstances—now or in the future (Walsh, 1998). Consistent with this view, McCubbin and McCubbin (1988) define family resilience as "characteristics, dimensions, and properties of families which help families to be resistant to disruption in the face of change and adaptive in the face of crisis situations" (p. 247). Used in this way, family resilience appears to be another name for family strengths. It is not always clear if or how this family capacity is distinct from family protective factors. For practitioners, there is less emphasis on the nature of significant risk exposure or on family-level outcomes that are conceptually distinct from family strengths or protective capacity. From a research perspective, however, significant risk, protective factors, and outcomes each must be distinctly defined—conceptually and operationally—to decide if a family has engaged in a process of resilience.

Most researchers view resilience as a process where there are interactions between risks and protective factors relative to a specified outcome. The processes by which protective factors moderate or mediate the risk and lead to good outcomes continue to be debated (Luthar et al., 2000). For example, protective factors can have direct effects on the outcome (e.g., the factor has a similar effect under conditions of high risk or low risk), or interactive effects (Zimmerman & Arunkumar, 1994). In the latter case, protective factors may only affect the outcome under conditions of high (vs. low) risk—true interactive effect—or the protective factor may be developed or strengthened following risk exposure and contribute to higher than normal competence in the outcome—an inoculation effect. These variations in functioning following risk exposure are similar to Hill's (1958) roller coaster model of family stress when he proposed that stressed families return to a level of functioning at, below, or above their precrisis level.

Psychologists wanting to differentiate between resilience as a trait versus a process have recommended that the term resiliency be used to refer to an individual trait (much like ego-resiliency) and that *resilience* be used to describe the process of successfully overcoming adversity (Luthar et al., 2000; Masten, 1994). If the family field were to adopt a similar convention, *family resiliency* could be used to describe the capacity of a family system to successfully manage their life circumstances and *family resilience* could be used to describe the processes by which families are able to adapt and function competently following exposure to significant adversity or crises. The latter raises additional questions. First, what does it mean for a family system to adapt and function competently, and second, what is significant risk?

Family as the Unit of Analysis

Family System Outcomes

To be considered family resilience (in contrast to individual resilience), the outcome of interest should be at the family system level, where a minimum of two family members are involved; that is, it should represent the product of family relationship(s). Examining this issue from the perspective of family stress theory, family adaptation is the outcome in the FAAR Model most relevant to resilience because it emerges following a crisis, which is a period of serious disruptiveness, implying significant risk exposure. Family adaptation has been defined as a process of restoring balance between capabilities and demands at two levels of transaction: (a) between family members and the family unit, and (b) between a family unit and the community. When the family is successful in this process, bonadaptation is observed in the family's (a) continued ability to promote the development of individual family members and (b) willingness to maintain their family unit so it can accomplish its life cycle tasks (Patterson, 1988). This definition acknowledges two issues relevant to resilience. First, the family serves as a bridge between the individual and other community contexts and is often central to the transactional processes evident when resilience occurs. Second, it points to at least two important functions families fulfill, both for their members and for society: (a) nurturance and socialization and (b) family formation and membership. These are two of the four functions Ooms (1996) has emphasized to policy makers as important in strengthening the capacity of families in contemporary society. The other two functions she identified were (a) economic support and (b) protection of vulnerable members. She advocated that public policies be examined relative to their impact on families' abilities to satisfactorily fulfill these functions. In Table 2.1, some ways each of these functions serves the needs of individual family members and the needs of society are elaborated.

One possible way to conceptualize meaningful family-level outcomes for assessing family resilience is the degree to which a family is competent in fulfilling one or more of these four functions. Although this structural-functional approach for defining family competence may no longer seem relevant to post-modern families, it may offer one way to maintain a distinction between family protective mechanisms and family competence as an outcome. Family functions are not the same as family functioning. The term *family functioning* is commonly used to describe relational

Table 2.1. *Core Functions of the Family for Individual Members and for Society*

| Family Function | Ways Each Function Provides Benefits To | | Examples of Positive (+) and Negative (−) Family Level Outcomes |
	Individual Family Members	Society	
Membership and family formation	■ Provides a sense of belonging ■ Provides personal and social identity ■ Provides meaning and direction for life	■ Controls reproductive function ■ Assures continuation of the species	+ Commitment to and maintenance of family unit + Addition of children is planned and desired − Divorce
Economic support	■ Provides for basic needs of food, shelter, and clothing and other resources to enhance human development	■ Contributes to healthy development of members who contribute to society (and who need fewer public resources)	+ Adequate food and clothing + Safe housing − Child neglect − Homelessness
Nurturance, education, and socialization	■ Provides for the physical, psychological, social and spiritual development of children and adults ■ Instills social values and norms	■ Prepares and socializes children for productive adult roles ■ Supports adults in being productive members of society ■ Controls antisocial behavior and protects society from harm	+ Family love and mutual support + Martial commitment and satisfaction + Securely attached children − Domestic violence − Child abuse
Protection of vulnerable members	■ Provides protective care and support for young, ill, disabled or otherwise vulnerable members	■ Minimizes public responsibility for care of vulnerable, dependent individuals	+ Family care for child with special needs − Elder abuse − Institutional placement of member with disability

processes within a family (Walsh, 1998). In other words, family functioning is the way in which a family fulfills its functions. These family relational processes are important in considering family protective mechanisms. To reduce confusion, I use *family relational processes* in lieu of family functioning to distinguish family functions as indicators of family-level outcomes.

Would a family have to be competent in all four of these functions to be labeled resilient? Psychologists have debated this issue and have agreed that a child does not have to be competent in all domains to be considered resilient (Luthar et al., 2000). Deciding which family function(s) are the most relevant indicator of family competence will vary depending on the population being studied and the research question(s) being addressed. For studies of resilience in families with a child who has a chronic health condition, the ability of the family to meet a vulnerable member's needs with internal and external resources is a relevant function (in contrast to the irrelevance of this function for a family who did not have a vulnerable member). However, competence in this one function may be insufficient in deciding if a family is resilient, given that the presence of a chronic health condition often creates risks that other family needs may be ignored or postponed (Reiss, Steinglass, & Howe, 1993). Clinicians have reported that when families live with chronic illness there is a tendency for some families to give a disproportionate amount of their resources of time, energy, and money to the illness needs at the expense of meeting the needs of other family members. When this skew toward the illness is prolonged, normal family developmental needs may be unattended, which would threaten successful accomplishment of the nurturance and socialization function of the family (Reiss et al., 1993; Steinglass, 1998). It would, therefore, be important to assess a family's competence relative to both of these functions in deciding about their resilience.

It is also possible that a family may show competence in one function but not others. For example, a teenager giving birth to an unwanted child is an example of lack of competence in the family formation and membership function. Challenges faced by unmarried teen mothers are well documented (Corcoran, 1998), and competence in meeting the nurturance, socialization, and economic functions may be difficult for them to achieve. However, over time, some young single parent families recover from this significant risk and move on to become competent in meeting the nurturance, socialization, and economic functions thereby becoming resilient.

If we accept that resilience is a process and not a trait, it follows that families would not necessarily be resilient for all time under all circumstances. Developmental psychologists, too, have pointed out that children are not necessarily resilient across all developmental stages (Luthar et al., 2000). Families may be resilient in responding to one form of significant stress but as new circumstances emerge, their ability to remain resilient could diminish.

Even though the label of family resilience does not require competence in meeting all family functions, these examples illustrate how closely interrelated success in meeting these functions can be. Moreover, when a generally successful family shows decline in meeting one of the functions, it is quite likely that they have encountered circumstances that would be labeled significant risk.

It is important to note that although these functions of the family are viewed as ubiquitous across racially and culturally diverse families, the way these functions are accomplished will reflect incredible diversity. This diversity will be apparent in the capacity or resiliency of the family—in the protective relationship patterns they develop to manage life's challenges.

Family Risk Exposure and Mechanisms

Significant Risk

One major issue related to risk exposure that seems to be viewed differently in research and practice is how significant the risk must be before a good outcome can be considered evidence of resilience. Masten and Coatsworth (1998) articulate the view of resilience researchers and define significant risk as emerging from: (a) high-risk status by virtue of continuous, chronic exposure to adverse so-cial conditions, such as poverty; (b) exposure to a traumatic event or severe adversity, such as war; or (c) a combination of high-risk status and traumatic exposure. From this perspective, every fam-ily would not have sufficient risk exposure to show evidence of resilience. Theoretically, everyone could be competent but only those exposed to significant risk who functioned competently would be viewed as showing resilience.

However, the perspective of practitioners about resilience seems to suggest that any family who functions competently would be an example of resilience (McCubbin et al., 1995; Walsh, 1998). Per-haps what is implied by this view is that life in general is sufficiently challenging to create risk ex-posure. All families at some time or another are faced with challenges to their usual way of relating and accomplishing life tasks. Hence, the notion of significant risk as a precondition for resilience may be less relevant to practitioners.

It is important to note that the significant risk perspective emerged from researchers who, as it happens, were studying populations at significant risk. The life-as-risk perspective was articulated primarily by practitioners (and some applied researchers) whose interest was the encouragement of approaches to prevention and intervention that focus on individual and family strengths rather than deficits. The two perspectives are related. Practitioners use the evidence produced by the sig-nificant risk researchers as the basis for their approach. Furthermore, resiliency-based practitioners hold the belief that most families can recover from stress and adversity and be successful. In this sense, the resiliency perspective is a philosophy and belief system oriented towards uncovering individual and family assets and strengths (Walsh, 1998).

The significant risk perspective relies on population-based observations of the negative out-comes experienced by the majority of families exposed to any given risk. This objective judgment of significant risk is based on normative data documenting poor outcomes. In family stress theory, a distinction is made between objective judgments about the severity of sources of stress and sub-jective judgments (i.e., the primary appraisal of the person or family experiencing the source of stress; Lazarus & Folkman, 1984). Subjective judgments are a critical component of the coping response, which influence behavior and hence, adaptation. In the FAAR Model, the first level of family meanings emphasizes the meaning a family gives to their situation and includes appraisal of the difficulty of the sources of stress and appraisal of the family's capabilities to manage the stress (Patterson & Garwick, 1994). It might be argued that the process of defining the situation is a criti-cal component in understanding resilience processes because these appraisals are a critical link in what Rutter (1987) calls the *chain of risks* or *chain of protective mechanisms*.

Family level meanings are distinct from individual meanings. Family meanings are the interpre-tations and views that have been collectively constructed by family members as they interact with each other; as they share time, space, and life experience, and as they talk about these experiences. Reiss (1981) emphasized that these family constructions of reality emerge from the family's shared process and that they are more than simple agreement among members. These implicitly shared explanatory systems play a crucial role in organizing and maintaining group process. Shared mean-ings reduce ambiguity and uncertainty about complex stimuli and make coordination of response among family members possible. Wamboldt and Wolin (1989) called shared family meanings *family reality* to differentiate them from what one family member might report about his or her family's meanings, which they called a *family myth*. A family myth is based on internalizations of family ex-perience and is how a person represents the family in his or her mind. Family reality is observed as the practicing family according to Reiss (1989).

The important point in the present discussion is that a family's shared meanings about the de-mands they are experiencing can render them more or less vulnerable in how they respond. These family appraisals and responses to discrete demands cumulatively create a pattern. A family's history and experience with successfully managing normative demands (which may not fit the significant risk criteria) can build their protective capacity or resiliency, increasing the likelihood of showing resilience if and when they were exposed to a traumatic event that would be defined as a significant risk. Conversely, difficulty in managing normative demands could cumulatively lead to a downward trajectory in fulfilling family functions, the inability to build a repertoire of protective family relational processes and perhaps high-risk status. From this systemic, process-oriented perspective, the punctuation point for defining significant risk exposure (of the sort where recovery from it would be called resilience) is less clear, particularly with regard to high-risk status as a necessary condition to be viewed as resilient.

Rutter (1987) articulated the view of many resilience researchers that risk should be examined in terms of mechanisms, rather than factors per se, emphasizing that there are processes by which exposure to a static risk factor interacts with a person in the context of his or her life. This perspective is similar to Boss' (2001) view that family stress expression and response must be examined within the social and cultural contexts of a family's life. For example, parenting a child with asthma is different for a poor family than for a middle-class family. A poor family is more likely to live in a social context with fewer social supports, have difficulties accessing health and education services, have less parental understanding of ways to minimize asthmatic attacks, have less control over the physical environment that exacerbates reactivity in the child's airways, and experience more challenges in meeting basic economic needs of the family (Mansour, Lanphear, & DeWitt, 2000). In such a context, the needs of the child with asthma may be minimized because other basic needs are viewed as more pressing. Inattention to the child's asthma needs may contribute to more medical emergencies, fewer preventative measures, school absences, and often, increased morbidity and earlier mortality.

Risks often cascade, with one risk leading to another, in a downward spiral (Rutter, 1987). McCubbin and Patterson (1983) used the phrase "pile-up of family demands" to describe such an accumulation of sources of stress. This cascading of risks often is related to having inadequate resources for meeting family needs. When a need is unmet, it can generate more problems, hence increasing the risks. When there are too few resources available relative to needs of family members, a demand-capability imbalance emerges, moving a family into crisis.

Normative versus Nonnormative Demands

Usually normative family demands (expectable family life cycle changes, such as getting married or having a child) would not be considered a significant risk for families. However, in some instances and contexts, they could pose significant risk. For example, if the timing of a normative change departs from societal expectations it may be harder to manage, such as a teenager having a baby. Or the meaning of a normative event, influenced by social and cultural factors, could increase the risk. Also, families could be classified as high risk if they had few protective resources (such as income, education, social support) and would be more likely to have difficulty with normative transitions. Thus, there is no clear rule that competence in managing normative demands could not be characterized as resilience.

Generally, however, it is not likely that normative demands would fit the significant risk category, which is not meant to suggest they are not challenging. Rather, it means that the majority of families are competent in making these transitions. Furthermore, families who have adequate protective capacity (resiliency) are more likely to be competent in managing normative demands.

However, nonnormative demands, which are unexpected and many times traumatic, are more likely to fit the definition of significant risk. Clearly, there is a range of such events from natural disasters, such as floods and tornadoes, to the premature death of a parent or child. The diagnosis of a child's chronic illness and the ongoing strains of managing it have the potential to fit the significant risk category. Epidemiologic data related to the impact of a child's chronic condition on the family indicate twice the risk for psychological or behavioral problems in the target child (Lavigne & Faier-Routman, 1992; Pless, Power, & Peckham, 1993) or the siblings (Breslau, 1983), as well as a comparable risk for family problems (Wallander & Varni, 1998).

It is not uncommon that the child's chronic condition could trigger a chain of other risks and thereby move the family into high-risk status. The daily caregiving demands for some chronic conditions can lead to physical and emotional exhaustion in parents, which may contribute to depression or other psychological symptoms. In a study of medically fragile children living at home, 75% of the families had one or both of the parents scoring in the psychiatric case range on a standard symptom inventory (Patterson, Leonard, & Titus, 1992). In this same study, continuous hassles with insurers of their children's services and conflicts with professionals caring for their children in their homes also contributed to parental distress. Many families experienced social isolation, which was related to lack of time for social activities, the large effort required to arrange child care when going out, and the social stigma encountered if they tried to take their child with them to public places. In addition, many families reported loss of their prior social networks—former friends said or did insensitive things or avoided them (Patterson et al., 1992). Parental depression and social isolation are likely to contribute to additional risks, such as compromised parenting and/or increased marital dissatisfaction and conflict. Although all children with chronic health conditions do not have such high caretaking needs as those who are medically fragile, a comparable chain of risks is still quite plausible for many families engaged in daily caregiving for a vulnerable member. The likelihood is greater if there are insufficient capabilities or protective factors to help families meet these needs.

Family Protective Processes

The key to understanding family resilience is the identification of protective factors and processes that moderate the relationship between a family's exposure to significant risk and their ability to show competence in accomplishing family functions. As already noted, protective factors that contribute to competent family outcomes can emerge from within individual family members, from a family unit, and from multiple community contexts. Most scholars writing about family resilience or resiliency have focused on the relational processes within families as the primary basis for considering their resiliency (see, for example, McCubbin et al., 1995; Walsh, 1998). Two central aspects of these family relationship patterns are family cohesiveness and flexibility. These patterns are most protective when there is family agreement about the balance between closeness and distance and between change and stability. In addition, the quality of affective and instrumental communication patterns within a family usually is protective because it facilitates how families accomplish core functions.

These and many other family relational patterns are crucial in the ways families respond and adapt to stress. The authors just referenced have been careful to point out that racial, cultural and ethnic variation produce a wide range of family relational patterns that can contribute to family competence. It is important not to become too narrow in defining what these family patterns should be, which sometimes happens because so many methods for assessing family relationships have been developed and normed using primarily White, middle-class families. Fortunately, we have an extensive literature on diverse family strengths and protective processes, including a growing body of work on ethnic diversity in families (see McCubbin et al., 1995).

However, less attention has been given to the transactions between the multiple sources of protectors in the ecosystem (individual, family, and community contexts). We need to consider more fully the mechanisms that bring multiple protective factors in a family's ecological context into play and how they build on each other to create cascade or chain effects.

Nonnormative chronic stress has a way of pushing a family to the extremes of adaptation—either they decline in competence or they become even more competent (Hetherington, 1984). When stressors bring out greater than average strengths in families, this represents the inoculation or challenge model of resilience (Zimmerman & Arunkumar, 1994). In one study of families who have children with chronic health conditions, scores were higher than norms on standardized measures of child and family relational processes, suggesting that some families do get stronger from stress exposure (Patterson, 2000). Some families showed more cohesiveness, more affective communication, and clearer family role organization than families without children with chronic conditions. The families in the study were not representative of all families living with a chronic health condition, however. Most of the children lived in two-parent families, with middle-class family incomes and higher levels of parental education. They also lived in states where they had health and education services that were higher quality and more accessible than the national average. In other words, these families had resources that were protective at the individual (parent education and income), family (cohesiveness, communication skills) and community (health and education services) levels. There were transactions between these systems to make sure the needs of their children were met. Parents of children with special needs repeatedly tell stories of how they advocate for their children within school systems and health systems and among private and public payers of services to assure that they get the services guaranteed by law. This is an active process that emerges from families' commitment to their children (a family level resource), education and knowledge about their rights (individual resources), and support from other parents (community level resource) engaged in the same advocacy efforts. These are examples of how a chain of protective factors can be set in motion and contribute to family resiliency and resilience.

In the FAAR Model, coping is viewed as part of family capabilities and for the purposes of the present article, a component of protective factors associated with resiliency. In an earlier review of the literature examining resiliency in families who have children with disabilities, nine family coping strategies or processes were identified that seem to be protective for these families: (a) balancing the illness with other family needs, (b) maintaining clear family boundaries, (c) developing communication competence, (d) attributing positive meanings to the situation, (e) maintaining family flexibility, (f) maintaining a commitment to the family as a unit, (g) engaging in active coping efforts, (h) maintaining social integration, and (i) developing collaborative relationships with professionals (Patterson, 1991).

Several of these processes involve transactions between families and community systems. Maintaining clear family boundaries involves family protection of their integrity, sense of identity, values, routines and rituals from overdirectedness by health, education, and social service providers who are trying to help meet special family needs. Maintaining social integration is a reciprocal process between a community that is open and encouraging of involvement by persons with disabilities and family initiative to help reduce physical and psychological barriers that can isolate them. Similarly, collaborative relationships with professionals are reciprocal processes involving attitudes of mutual respect and skills for effective communication.

Included in the above list is the coping behavior, attributing positive meanings to the situation, which is a central process associated with family resilience. A family's ability to alter or make meaning from their significant risk experiences has been emphasized by many scholars (Antonovsky, 1987; McCubbin et al., 1995; Walsh, 1998). Families implicitly construct and share meanings at three levels: (a) about specific stressful situations, (b) about their identity as a family, and (c) about their view of the world (Patterson & Garwick, 1994).

For any given stressful situation, families implicitly evaluate how difficult it is or will be (primary appraisal). Their level of experienced stress is related to this subjective appraisal. Many sources of stress only exist by virtue of the expectation a family has (e.g., we are bad parents if our child has a birth defect). Each stressful situation also is appraised relative to a family's capabilities (secondary appraisal). Many capabilities are primarily subjective as well, such as a family's sense of mastery. This meaning making process influences how a family copes with stress. In a study of families with a medically fragile child, some families developed positive meanings about their situation as a way to cope (Patterson, 1993; Patterson & Leonard, 1994). Many parents emphasized the positive characteristics of their child (warmth, responsiveness, and the ability to endure pain), of their other children (empathy and kindness), of themselves as parents (assertiveness skills in dealing with service providers), and of their family (greater closeness and commitment to each other from facing the challenge together). Many of these families faced real limits in getting the services and help they needed because of the severity and extent of their child's medical needs. It was difficult, if not impossible, to achieve a balance between the accumulation of added strains and caretaking needs (demands) and resources to meet them. Thus, many families coped by changing the way they thought about their situation. They emphasized what they had learned and how they had grown as a family rather than the hardships they had experienced. Through the meaning making process, they increased their capabilities and reduced their demands.

A family's belief in their ability as a group to discover solutions and new resources to manage challenges may be the cornerstone of building protective mechanisms. Success in coping with one situation creates the foundation for this belief to generalize to other situations and ultimately to a set of meanings about the family unit, or what is referred to as a family's identity.

Families develop a shared identity from the spoken and unspoken values and norms that guide their relationships. Daily routines and rituals contribute to this process of building a sense of who a family is and how they are different from other families. For example, engaging in family rituals without the influence of alcoholic behavior has been identified as a major process protecting families from the intergenerational transmission of alcoholism after growing up with alcoholic parents (Steinglass, Bennet, & Wolin, 1987). On the other hand, routines and rituals can be disrupted when adversity such as chronic disease or other unpredictable risks strike a family. Steinglass (1998) emphasized that disruption of family routines and rituals, which regulate daily processes, threatens the development, maturation, and stability of families with members with chronic illnesses. With the ongoing stress of chronic disease, the family's valued routines and rituals may be subsumed by illness needs and if this pattern persists over time, there can be undesirable consequences. We found that parental coping that focused on balancing across family needs was associated with a better 10-year trend in pulmonary function (a key health status indicator) for children with cystic fibrosis (Patterson, Budd, Goetz & Warwick, 1993). Maintaining their own integrity about how to balance competing family demands is also an example of maintaining family boundaries discussed above.

A family's world view (the third level of meaning) can be instrumental in shaping day-to-day family functioning. A family's world view shapes their orientation to the world outside of the family and is often grounded in cultural or religious beliefs. In the aftermath of a major adversity, the family's world view may be changed as they reflect on the losses they have experienced. When a world view is shattered by a nonnormative experience like the death of a child, the family's ability to heal, grow, and move forward often involves reconstructing a new view of the world that allows them to make sense of such an event (Taylor, Kemeny, Reed, Bower, & Gruenewald, 2000). Hence, this meaning making process is a critical component of family resilience and is facilitated by group interaction within the family as well as through transactions in the community with other families experiencing similar circumstances.

Implications for Future Research on Family Resilience

The family resilience perspective has much to offer the family science discipline. Although, in many ways, the concepts that underlie it are already contained in family stress theory, a focus on resilience draws greater attention to family success and competence. The knowledge derived from family resilience studies can contribute to the resiliency approach being used in practice settings. However, greater understanding of how families remain or become competent following exposure to significant risk will require rigor and precision in the methodology employed to capture these dynamic processes in families. The following strategies are recommended:

Provide clear conceptual and operational definitions of key variables. It will be a major challenge to make the definitions of family outcomes indicating competence conceptually and operationally distinct from family protective processes. In this article, core family functions were suggested as one possible way to conceptualize meaningful family level outcomes but determining appropriate methods for measuring competence in fulfilling these functions will still be necessary. There well may be other meaningful ways to conceptualize family competence as an outcome that would be distinct from family relational processes that serve as protectors.

Develop and test conceptual models for risk and protective processes. These models should take account of the mechanisms by which risks or protectors accumulate and how the latter moderate risks and influence outcomes of family competence. The transactions between family risks and protectors and individual and community factors should be considered in models.

Study populations of families experiencing significant risk. The processes by which families succeed or fail will be more evident and sensitive to our measures if we examine more extreme situations of risk exposure, rather than the more normative challenges of daily life. Furthermore, it is only under conditions of significant risk that resilience as a process is operative. Such studies will help us discover which family relational processes are protective across a range of risk exposures and which are unique to specific adversities.

Conduct longitudinal studies. The only way to understand the dynamic processes associated with the cascade of risks and the cascade of protectors and the interactions between them is to follow families over time. Cross-sectional studies are limited in their ability to explain change processes given the unreliability of retrospective family reports about themselves. The nature of significant risk makes it difficult, if not impossible, to assess a family before the significant risk exposure, although this would be less of a problem for studying families characterized as high-risk status. In either case, the trajectory of the families' functioning can be assessed for change and factors and processes associated with improvement can be studied.

Include qualitative methods in research. Because family meaning-making processes are so important to family resilience and given the subjectivity of meanings, qualitative methods would help clarify how these processes unfold and the content of these meanings. We need to complement quantitative model testing with inductive approaches to understand the array of processes shaping family resilience.

A family's ability to be resilient in the face of normative or significant risk is related not only to their internal relational processes but also to risks or opportunities in the social systems in their ecological context. Living in poverty and in crime-ridden, violent neighborhoods place families at high risk and contribute to their inability to satisfactorily accomplish their core functions. Risk processes in the family (marital conflict, child abuse, etc.) are more likely to emerge under these social conditions. The absence of needed community resources to support families in fulfilling their core functions further undermines family resilience. Public programs and policies, societal norms and values, and other community institutions shape the style and degree to which families are able to fulfill their functions, as well as their ability to acquire and develop new capabilities when challenged. Successful functioning for the population of children and families living with chronic health conditions requires public policies and programs, and adequate funding of these, to assure full community integration and access to the resources all citizens enjoy, which contribute to a high quality of life.

Note

Preparation of this paper was supported by Grant MCJ000111 from the Maternal and Child Health Bureau.

References

Antonovsky, A. (1987). *Unraveling the mystery of health.* San Francisco: Jossey-Bass.

Boss, P. (2001). *Family stress management.* Newbury Park, CA: Sage.

Breslau, N. (1983). Family care: Effects on siblings and mothers. In G. Thompson et al. (Eds.), *Comprehensive management of cerebral palsy.* New York: Grune & Stratton.

Cassel, J. (1976). The contribution of the social environment to host resistance. *American Journal of Epidemiology, 104*(2), 107–123.

Corcoran, J. (1998). Consequences of adolescent pregnancy/parenting: A review of the literature. *Social Work in Health Care, 27*(2), 49–67.

Cowan, P., Cowan, C., & Schulz, M. (1996). Thinking about risk and resilience in families. In E. Hetherington & E. Blechman (Eds.), *Stress, coping, and resiliency in children and families* (pp. 1–38). Mahwah, NJ: Lawrence Erlbaum.

Hetherington, M. (1984). Stress and coping in children and families. In A. Doyle, D. Gold, & D. Moskowitz (Eds.), *Children in families under stress* (pp. 7–33). San Francisco: Jossey-Bass.

Hill, R. (1958). Generic features of families under stress. *Social Casework, 49,* 139–150.

Garmezy, N. (1991). Resilience and vulnerability to adverse developmental outcomes associated with poverty. *American Behavioral Scientist, 34,* 416–430.

Karpel, M. (1986). *Family resources: The hidden partner in family therapy.* New York: Guilford.

Lazarus, R., & Folkman, S. (1984). *Stress, appraisal, and coping.* New York: Springer.

Lavigne, J., & Faier-Routman, J. (1992). Psychological adjustment to pediatric physical disorders: A meta-analytic review. *Journal of Pediatric Psychology, 17,* 133–157.

Luthar, S., Cicchetti, D., & Becker, R. (2000). The construct of resilience: A critical evaluation and guidelines for future work. *Child Development, 71,* 543–562.

Mansour, M., Lanphear, B., & DeWitt, T. (2000). Barriers to asthma care in urban children: Parent perspectives. *Pediatrics, 106,* 512–519.

Masten, A. (1994). Resilience in individual development: successful adaptation despite risk and adversity. In M. Wang & E. Gordon (Eds.), *Educational resilience in inner-city America: Challenges and prospects* (pp. 3–25). Hillsdale, NJ: Lawrence Erlbaum.

Masten, A., & Coatsworth, J. (1998). The development of competence in favorable and unfavorable environments. *American Psychologist, 53*(2), 205–220.

McCubbin, H., Boss, P., Wilson, L., & Lester, G. (1980). Developing family vulnerability to stress: Coping patterns and strategies wives employ. In J. Trost (Ed.), *The family and change* (pp. 89–103). Sweden: International Library.

McCubbin, H., & McCubbin, M. (1988). Typologies of resilient families: Emerging roles of social class and ethnicity. *Family Relations, 37,* 247–254.

McCubbin, H., McCubbin, M., & Thompson, E. (1995). Resiliency in ethnic families: A conceptual model for predicting family adjustment and adaptation. In H. McCubbin, M. McCubbin, A. Thompson, & J. Fromer (Eds.), *Resiliency in ethnic minority families* (Vol. 1, pp. 3–48). Madison, WI: University of Wisconsin Press.

McCubbin, H., & Patterson, J. (1982). Family adaptation to crises. In H. McCubbin, A. Cauble, & J. Patterson (Eds.), *Family stress, coping and social support.* Springfield, IL: C.C. Thomas.

McCubbin, H., & Patterson, J. (1983). The family stress process: The double ABCX model of family adjustment and adaptation. *Marriage and Family Review, 6*(1–2), 7–37.

Ooms, T. (1996, July). *Where is the family in comprehensive community initiatives for children and families?* Paper presented at the Aspen Roundtable on Comprehensive Community Initiatives for Children and Families, Aspen, CO.

Patterson, J. (1988). Families experiencing stress: The family adjustment and adaptation response model. *Family Systems Medicine, 5*(2), 202–237.

Patterson, J. (1991). Family resilience to the challenge of a child's disability. *Pediatric Annals, 20,* 491–499.

Patterson, J. (1993). The role of family meanings in adaptation to chronic illness and disability. In A. Turnbull, J. Patterson, S. Behr, et al. (Eds.), *Cognitive coping research and developmental disabilities* (pp. 221–238). Baltimore: Brookes.

Patterson, J. (2000, October). *Resilience in families of children with special health needs.* Paper presented at Pediatric Grand Rounds, University of Washington Children's Medical Center, Seattle, WA.

Patterson, J., Budd, J., Goetz, D., & Warwick, W. (1993). Family correlates of a ten-year pulmonary health trend in cystic fibrosis. *Pediatrics, 91*(2), 383–389.

Patterson, J., & Garwick, A. (1994). Levels of family meaning in family stress theory. *Family Process, 33,* 287–304.

Patterson, J., Leonard, B. (1994). Caregiving and children. In E. Kahana, D. Biegel, & M. Wykle (Eds.), *Family caregiving across the lifespan* (pp. 133–158). Newbury Park, CA: Sage.

Patterson, J., Leonard, B., & Titus, J. (1992). Home care for medically fragile children: Impact on family health and well-being. *Journal of Developmental & Behavioral Pediatrics, 13,* 248–255.

Pless, I., Power, C., & Peckham, C. (1993). Long-term psychosocial sequelae of chronic physical disorders in childhood. *Pediatrics, 91,* 1131–1136.

Reiss, D. (1981). *The family's construction of reality.* Cambridge, MA: Harvard university Press.

Reiss, D. (1989). The represented and practicing family: Contrasting visions of family continuity. In A. Sameroff & R. Emde (Eds.), *Relationship disturbances in early childhood.* New York: Basic Books.

Reiss, D., Steinglass, P., & Howe, G. (1993). The family organization around the illness. In R. Cole & D. Reiss (Eds.), *How do families cope with chronic illness?* (pp. 173–213). Hillsdale, NJ: Lawrence Erlbaum.

Rutter, M. (1987). Psychosocial resilience and protective mechanisms. *American Journal of Orthopsychiatry, 57,* 316–331.

Seligman, M. E. P., & Csikszentmihalyi, M. (2000). Positive psychology. An introduction to special issue. *American Psychologist, 55*(1), 5–14.

Steinglass, P. (1998). Multiple family discussion groups for patients with chronic medical illness. *Family Systems Medicine, 16*(1–2), 55–70.

Steinglass, P., Bennet, L. A., Wolin, S. J. (1987). *The alcoholic family.* New York: Basic Books.

Stinnett, N., & DeFrain, J. (1985). *Secrets of strong families.* Boston: Little, Brown.

Taylor, S., Kemeny, M., Reed, G., Bower, J., & Gruenewaln, T. (2000). Psychological resources, positive illusions, and health. *American Psychologist, 55*(1), 99–109.

Wallander J., & Varni, J. (1998). Effects of pediatric chronic physical disorders on child and family adjustment. *Journal of Child Psychology & Psychiatry & Allied Disciplines, 39,* 29–46.

Walsh, F. (1998). *Strengthening family resilience.* New York: Guilford Press.

Wamboldt, F., & Wolin, S. (1989). Reality and myth in family life: Changes across generations. *Journal of Psychotherapy and the Family, 4,* 141–165.

Werner, E., & Smith, R. (1992). *Overcoming the odds.* Ithaca, NY: Cornell university Press.

Wolin, S., & Wolin, S. (1993). *The resilient self.* New York: Villard Books.

Zimmerman, M. A., & Arunkumar, R. (1994). Resiliency research: Implications for schools and policy. *Social Policy Report: Society for Research in Child Development, 8*(4), 1–17.

PART II

Family Stressors, Parenting, and Mental Health

CHAPTER **3**

Parenting Stress

Cui, M & Hong, P.
Ming Cui
Peipei Hong
Florida State University

Parental involvement in children's lives has changed dramatically throughout history. Parenting perspectives have evolved from providing minimal care and formal education, not maintaining close emotional ties, and regarding children as a good source of cheap labor in ancient Greece and Rome; to providing intensive care and educational investment and establishing lifelong parent-child attachments in the 20th century (Bigner, 2010). Parenting practice has shifted from stern discipline with physical punishment in European/Colonial America to various practices ranging from restrictive authoritarian styles advocated by John Watson to permissive parenting encouraged by Sigmund Freud and Benjamin Spock.

The theoretical framework of contemporary parenting was established by Baumrind (1967) and Maccoby and Martin (1983). Baumrind (1967) identified three distinct types of parents: authoritative, authoritarian, and permissive parenting. Extending Baumrind's work, Maccoby and Martin (1983), along the two dimensions of responsiveness and demandingness, added a fourth parenting style (neglectful parenting) and created a four-fold typology of parenting styles-authoritative, authoritarian, uninvolved/neglectful, and indulgent/permissive parenting.

Parenting has been a major focus in family research in the past several decades because of the critical role it plays in child development (Parke & Buriel, 1998). With parenting, all parents experience stress as they attempt to meet the challenges of raising their children. In this chapter of parenting stress, we introduce the definitions, theoretical frameworks, measurements, antecedents and consequences, and the resources and coping strategies. At the end, we also discuss the conclusions and implications.

Definitions

Moderate stress during parenthood is very common. Here are some examples. Although Amy enjoys being a mother most of the time, as a stay-at-home mother, she experiences exhaustion from caring for a toddler 24/7 and frustration when her toddler throws temper tantrums frequently. Amy spanks her child occasionally then feels guilty about it. Becky, a busy working mother of three, worries that her long work hours prevent her from meeting the many demands in mothering and that she is less involved in her children's lives as she would have hoped. Tom, a father of a child with ADHD, faces unique parenting challenges such as managing his child's difficult behaviors. Jennifer, a mother who seems to have it all (e.g., adequate income, housing, social resources), still feels distressed because her childrearing does not live up to her high expectations.

Indeed, regardless of socioeconomic status, race and ethnicity, age, gender, resources, health status, and many other factors, all parents experience parenting stress to some extent at one time or another, and some are chronically stressed (Deater-Deckard, 2008). Parenting stress has to do with not only absolute terms, but also subjective experiences. Further, parenting stress, tied specific to the role of parents, is distinct from stress arising from other roles and experiences.

Researchers have been trying to avoid research in parenting stress, as it is complex and difficult to define (Webster-Stratton, 1990). There are many definitions of parenting stress. According to Abidin (1992), each parent has an internal working model of himself or herself as a parent, and the results from self-appraisal of his or her role as a parent produce the level of stress that the parent experiences. Abidin suggests that, parenting stress, therefore, is *"the result of a series of appraisals made by each parent in the content of his or her level of commitment to the parenting role"* (1992: 410).

In his book of Parenting Stress, Deater-Deckard (2008) defines parenting stress as *"a set of processes that lead to aversive psychological and physiological reactions arising from attempts to adapt to the demands of parenthood"* (2008: 6). He further describes parenting stress as the "subjective experiences of distress such as emotional pain and anxiety" (2008: 1). According to Deater-Deckard, parenting stress also includes parents' thoughts, beliefs, and attributions – expectations about what is "normal," perceived lack of control, violation of expectations, and self-doubt.

Theoretical Perspectives

Similar to its definitions, parenting stress have been theorized in a number of ways (e.g., Abidin, 1992; Belsky, 1984; Crnic & Low, 2002; Deater-Deckard, 2008; Webster-Stratton, 1990). Based on the transactional model of stress (Lazarus & Folkman, 1984), Abidin (1992) proposes a parenting stress model as a specific application of Lazarus and Folkman's general theory. Specifically, parenting related stressors, such as work, daily hassles, life events, marital relationships, and parent and child characteristics, affect the appraisal of parenting role, which produces parenting stress (Abidin, 1992; Webster-Stratton, 1990).

The parent-child-relationship (P-C-R) theory (Crnic & Low, 2002; Deater-Deckard, 2008) suggests that there are three domains (i.e., parent domain, child domain, and parent-child relationship domain), and that parenting stress could arise from each of the domains (i.e., parenting stress from within the parent such as a parent's depression and anxiety, from the child such as a child's behavioral problems, or from parent-child relationship such as parent-child conflict). Parenting stress from these three domains subsequently affect parenting behavior (e.g., parental hostility) and child outcomes.

Different from the P-C-R theory which tends to focus on the parents or children with emotional or behavioral problems, the daily hassle theory (Crnic & Low, 2002; Deater-Deckard, 2008) focuses on stress on a daily basis. The daily hassles theory suggests that parenting stress occurs nearly every day, in small doses. The effects of minor daily stress, however, can accumulate and become persistent and powerful. These daily parenting hassles are not major stressors (e.g., divorce, unemployment), but are minor stressful events that occur frequently in many families and build over time, such as dealing with a child's minor misbehavior and navigating the complicated and usually conflicting family schedules. Such daily hassles lead to parenting stress.

It is important to note that these are just some of the theories of parenting stress. Further, they are not necessarily competing theories, but rather alternative and complementary perspectives about parenting stress and its causes and outcomes (Deater-Deckard, 2008).

Measurements

The Parenting Stress Index (PSI, Abidin, 1992) is probably the most widely used measurement of parenting stress. It screens for stress in the parent-child relationship, identifies dysfunctional parenting, and predicts parental behavior problems and child maladjustment. While the targeting population of this measure is parents of preschool children, the PSI can also be used with parents whose children are school age (12 years old). The full length PSI consists of over 100 items, which takes 20-25 minutes to complete. Upon obtaining the scores, a total score is created to yield a total parenting stress score.

A short-form of the PSI (PSI-SF, Abidin, 1995), which includes 36 items from the full-length PSI, is also available. Sample items include "I often find myself giving up more on my life to meet my children's needs than I ever expected," "Since having children, I feel that I am almost never able to do things that I like to do," and "Having children has caused more problems than I expected in my relationship with my spouse." The coding of this Likert scale measure ranges from 1 = *strongly agree* to 5 = *strongly disagree*. This PSI-SF measure has been used frequently and has proven reliability and validity (e.g., reliability alpha was .94 in Roggman, Moe, Hart, & Forthun, 1994; .96 in Abidin, 1995).

Other measures of parenting stress are also available. For example, Pearlin and Schooler (1978) developed a parental distress scale assessing distress related to being a parent (e.g., "When thinking of your role as a parent in the past week, how often have you felt frustrated?). Berry and Jones (1995) developed a parenting stress scale (e.g., "I sometimes worry whether I am doing enough for my child(ren).").

Antecedents

Many factors contribute to parenting stress, including external factors, interpersonal factors, and intrapersonal factors (Webster-Stratton, 1990). These factors could exist separately or jointly to produce parenting stress. Below we further discuss some major factors.

Low Socioeconomic Status (SES)

In general, research has suggested that, compared to their middle-class peers, parents of low SES are more likely to experience parenting stress and report parenting problems (Puff & Renk, 2014). For example, In Elder's pioneering research, "Children of the Great Depression" (1998), he found that parents with heavy financial losses were more likely to be less nurturant and more irritable compared to those who did not undergo financial losses. Several other studies have also reported that parents of low SES are particularly vulnerable to stressors and subsequently reported higher levels of stress as compared to those of higher SES (e.g., Lavee, Sharlin, & Katz, 1996; Pinderhughes, Dodge, Bates, Pettit, & Zellli, 2000).

Poverty is a powerful predictor of parenting stress, because it widens the gap between parenting demands and resources available to meet these demands (Deater-Deckard, 2008). Further, more recent studies revealed that differential SES is linked to different types of parenting stress. For example, a study suggested that parents with higher SES tend to have more demands or expectations for childrearing and experience more work-family conflict (Nomaguchi & Milkie, 2017).

Stressful Life Events (NLEs)

Major NLEs, as another major stressor, have been shown to be associated with more negative perceptions of parenting and child adjustment. In a study by Middlebrook and Forehand (1985), mothers experiencing more NLEs perceived their children's behavior as more deviant than mothers experiencing fewer NLEs. Others also found that NLEs were associated with punitive parenting behavior (Webster-Stratton, 1990), child abuse (Gelles & Straus, 1988), and attachment problems (Vaughn, Egeland, Sroufe, & Waters, 1979). Specific to parenting stress, in a study of 1,081 Swedish mothers, Östberg and Hagekull (2000) reported that NLEs were associated with more parenting stress.

Daily Hassles

Lazarus and Launier (1978) emphasize on the importance of daily hassles in understanding parenting stress. Studies have shown that an accumulation of minor day-to-day chronic life hassles is related to parenting stress and behavior problems (Crnic, Gaze, & Hoffman, 2005). Patterson (1983) reported that days that were characterized by high rates of minor hassles were typified by higher rates of irritability in mothers' interaction with their children.

Marital Problems

Marital problems, such as divorce, separation, and marital conflict are major familial stressors. Hetherington, Cox, and Cox (1982) reported that divorce and separation were associated with less parental involvement and greater punitiveness and irritability. Compared with divorce or separation, Emery and O'Leary (1982) argued that it is more important to examine the role of marital conflict, which has been demonstrated to undermine parental functioning (Cui & Conger, 2008). Particularly relevant to parenting stress, Webster-Stratton (1990) reported that low marital satisfaction was related to increased mothers' and fathers' report of parenting stress.

Parent Characteristics

Depressive symptoms. Parents' own psychological characteristics play a major part in causing parenting stress. Among them, depressive symptoms place parents at increased risks for parenting stress and parenting behavior issues (Gotlib & Goodman, 2002; Patterson, 1982). Depressed mothers were shown to report significantly higher levels of stress than nondepressed mothers on the Parenting Stress Index Parent Domain (Abidin, 1986), possibly due to self-blame, role restriction, and feeling of incompetence.

Drug and alcohol use. Drug and alcohol use is another factor found to be related to parenting issues (Patterson, 1986). In a study of mothers, Miller, Smyth, and Mudar (1999) reported an association between mothers' alcohol or other drug use and their punitiveness toward their children. Specific to parenting stress, studies have shown that parents' perceptions of parenting stress were influenced by alcohol and drug use (Webster-Stratton, 1990).

Personality. Individual differences in personality also predicts reactions to a stressor. Studies have shown that parents' personality is predictive of parenting beliefs and behaviors (e.g., Clark, Kochanska, & Ready, 2000). Specific to parenting stress, for example, it is suggested that parents who scored high on negative affectivity (e.g., sadness, anger, discomfort, difficulty in soothing) may be more vulnerable to parenting stress (Deater-Deckard, 2008). In a study of parents of children with spina bifida, Vermaes, Janssens, Mullaart, Vinck, and Gerris (2008) reported that extraversion among mothers and agreeableness among fathers were associated with less parenting stress.

Age. Studies have shown that parenting stress is greater among parents who are either very young or very old. For example, teenage mothers are more likely to experience greater parenting stress due to lack of resources (e.g., psychological maturity, income, education). At the other end of the age continuum, older first-time parents are also more likely to report parenting stress (Deater-Deckard, 2008; Östberg & Hagekull, 2000).

Gender. Research in parent gender and parenting stress is less clear. Some suggested that mothers tend to have more parenting stress because of their major role in parenting. For example, one study suggested that mothers are more susceptible to parenting issues and responsive to various types of stressors (Nair, Schuler, Black, Kettinger, & Harrngton, 2003). Others, however, suggested that fathers experience similar levels of parenting stress (see Webster-Stratton, 1990). Some also suggested that mothers and fathers respond to stressors differently (e.g., "tend and befriend" among mothers and "fight or flight" among fathers, see Deater-Deckard, 2008).

Child Characteristics

Research suggested that a "difficult" child causes more stress for parents (Bates, 1980). For example, Abidin (1986) reported that children who scored high in problems contributed considerable stress to their parents. In Webster-Stratton's (1990) study, parenting children with conduct problems were perceived by their parents as very stressful. Specifically, Webster-Stratton described these parents' experience of their child's repeated expulsion from daycare or schools, frequent distressful communications with frustrated teachers, the isolation from other parents and neighbors, and limited leisure time due to burnout sitters and fear of embarrassment in public. Indeed, the problems associated with child characteristics could be a major source of chronic parenting stress. Östberg and Hagekull (2000) reported that perceptions of the child being difficult was associated with more parenting stress. Kwok and Wong (2000) reported that parents who perceived their children as more demanding, less acceptable, and less reinforcing reported more parenting stress. Studies of parents of children with disabilities also supported similar findings (e.g., Estes, Munson, & Dawson, 2009; Hayes & Watson, 2013).

Summary of Antecedents

In sum, many external and internal factors, such as low SES, NLEs, daily hassles, marital problems, and parent and child characteristics, are predictive of parenting stress. Here two comments are made. First, it is important to note that these stressors usually happen simultaneously, as demonstrated by significant correlations among them. For example, depressed mothers also reported twice as many NLEs as compared with nondepressed mothers (Abidin, 1986). Parents with low SES were two to four times more likely to experience NLEs as compared to middle class parents (Roghmann, Hecht, & Haggerty, 1975). Divorce and separation were found to be associated with reduction of economic and social resources and changes in maternal employment, which aggravate parenting stress in mothers (Cooper, McLanahan, Meadows, & Brooks-Gunn, 2009). Together these factors may create a ripple effect or a negative cycle that lead to more stressors and subsequently parenting stress.

Second, it is also important to realize that many of the associations between these anteced-ents and parenting stress are bidirectional, meaning that the cause and effect could be reciprocal. With that in mind, we now turn to the consequences of parenting stress.

Consequences

Parenting. Higher levels of parenting stress lead to increased dysfunctional parenting. Studies have shown that parenting stress was negatively related to competent parenting and positively re-lated to dysfunctional parenting (e.g., irritable, critical, abusive, poor problem-solving, low nurtur-ance; see Abidin, 1992; Deater-Deckard, 2008). Such effect, however, may not be linear as very low level of parenting stress may suggest disengagement of the parent (Abidin, 1982).

Well-being of parents. Parenting stress has been shown to affect the well-being of parents. Lavee and colleagues (1996) reported that parenting stress was significantly related to parents' psychological distress and marital quality. Kwok and Wong (2000) also reported an association be-tween parenting stress and parents' mental health. Parenting stress has been shown to have a par-ticularly strong effect on parents' psychological well-being for those with children with disabilities (e.g., Hastings, 2002).

Well-being of children. Developmental psychologists have proposed and found that parent-ing stress affects child development. In a study of preschool children, parenting stress was found to be significantly associated with teachers' rating of child social competence, internalizing prob-lems, and externalizing problems (Anthony et al., 2005). Another study of families facing multiple difficulties and problems suggested that parenting stress was the strongest predictor of children's emotional and behavioral problems (Goldberg et al., 1997). In a study of homeless families, those parents with the highest levels of parenting stress had children with the highest levels of cognitive problems and social development problems (Danseco & Holden, 1998).

Once again, it is important to realize that these associations are most likely bidirectional, and that the problems in parenting, parents' well-being, and child problems could subsequently lead to more parenting stress.

Resources and Coping

Resources

Facing the same amount of stressors, some parents recover whereas others experience significant stress symptoms. Several individual and family factors have been shown to protect or buffer the effects of stressors.

Among them, social support is an important factor. Social support is defined as the availabil-ity of meaningful and enduring relationships that provide security and interpersonal commit-ment (Shonkoff, 1985). There has been increasing evidence suggesting that social support could buffer the effect of stressors on parental functioning (Belsky, 1984; Östberg & Hagekull, 2000). For example, social support is shown to alleviate the negative impact on stress among mothers of low SES (Turner & Noh, 1983) and among fathers who experienced unemployment (Gove &Zeiss, 1987).

Coping

Through cognitive appraisal, once a stressor is deemed as potentially stressful, there are several coping strategies that parents could use to minimize the stress reaction, including cognitive, emotional, and behavioral strategies (Deater-Deckard, 2008). Coping is a critical skill that determines why, facing the same situation, some parents are quite resilient showing minimal stress reaction, whereas others struggle.

Research has shown that parents who feel confident about their parenting abilities demonstrated more effective parenting and less parenting stress, as compared to those who are less self-efficacious (Coleman & Karraker, 2000). Also, parents who rely on passive, emotionally focused coping strategies were more likely to experience parenting stress (Barnett, Hall, & Barmlett, 1990). In contrast, parents who use problem-focused strategies were more likely to report less parenting stress (Miller, Gordon, Daniele, & Diller, 1992).

An important caveat to the general statements of coping strategies is that any specific coping strategy may only be effective for some parents, and that there is no "one size fits all" coping strategy for all parents in all situations (Deater-Deckard, 2008).

Conclusions and Implications

Although parenthood is mostly rewarding with substantial positive effects on parents, the cost of parenthood is also high (e.g., child-related financial cost, time cost, and psychological cost), and parenting stress is common (Fawcett, 1988; Pollmann-Schult, 2014). In this chapter, we discussed parenting stress-its definitions, theoretical frameworks, measurements, antecedents, consequences, and resources and coping strategies. Because parenting stress has important implications for the well-being of all family members, it is critical to develop and promote prevention and intervention programs that aim at reducing parenting stress.

Hasting and Beck (2004) proposed several interventions that have been used for reducing parenting stress, especially for parents of children with disabilities. Child-focused interventions aim at addressing child problems to reduce parenting stress (e.g., Wiggs & Stores, 2001). Parent-focused interventions aim at facilitating parent network to reduce parenting stress (e.g., Parent-to-Parent Movement, Santelli, Poyadue, & Young, 2001). Some interventions also include parents sharing experiences and learning about practical solutions form other parents and professional (Solomon, Pistrang, & Baker, 2001).

References

Abidin, R. R. (1982). Parenting stress and utilization of pediatric services. *Children's Health Care, 11*, 70–73.

Abidin, R. R. (1986). *Parenting Stress Index* (2nd Ed.). Charlottesville, VA: Pediatric Psychology Press.

Abidin, R. R. (1992). The determinants of parenting behavior. *Journal of Clinical Child Psychology, 21*, 407–412.

Abidin, R. R. (1995). *Manual for the Parenting Stress Index*. Odessa, FL: Psychological Assessment Resources.

Anthony, L. G., Anthony, B. J., Glanville, D. N., Naiman, D. Q., Waanders, C., & Shaffer, S. (2005). The relationships between parenting stress, parenting behavior and preschoolers' social competence and behavior problems in the classroom. *Infant and Child Development, 14*, 133–154.

Barnett, D. W., Hall, J. D., & Bramlett, R. K. (1990). Family factors in preschool assessment and intervention: A validity study of parenting stress and coping measures. *Journal of School Psychology, 28*, 13–20.

Bates, J. (1980). The concept of difficult temperament. *Merrill-Palmer Quarterly, 26*, 299–319.

Baumrind, D. (1967). Child care practices anteceding three patterns of preschool behavior. *Genetic Psychology Monographs, 75*, 43–88.

Belsky, J. (1984). The determinants of parenting: A process model. *Child Development, 5*, 83–96.

Berry, J. O., & Jones, W. H. (1995). The parental stress scale: Initial psychometric evidence. *Journal of Social and Personal Relationships, 12,* 463–472.

Bigner, J. J. (2010). *Parent-child relations: An introduction to parenting* (8th Ed.). New Jersey: Merril.

Clark, L. A., Kochanska, G., & Ready, R. (2000). Mothers' personality and its interaction with child temperament as predictors of parenting behavior. *Journal of Personality and Social Psychology, 79*, 274–285.

Coleman, P. K., & Karraker, K. H. (1998) Self-efficacy and parenting quality: Findings and future applications. *Developmental Review, 18*, 47–85.

Cooper, C. E., McLanahan, S. S., Meadows, S. O., & Brooks-Gunn, J. (2009). Family structure transitions and maternal parenting stress. *Journal of Marriage and Family, 71*, 558–74.

Crnic, K., Gaze, C., & Hoffman, C. (2005). Cumulative parenting stress across the preschool period: Relations to maternal parenting and child behavior at age 5. *Infant and Child Development, 14*, 117–132.

Crnic, K. A., & Low, C. (2002). Everyday stresses and parenting. In M. Bornstein (Ed.), *Handbook of parenting: Vol. 5. Practical issues in parenting* (2nd Ed., pp. 243–267). Mahwah, NJ: Earlbaum.

Cui, M., & Conger, R. D. (2008). Parenting behavior as mediator and moderator of the association between marital problems and adolescent maladjustment. *Journal of Research on Adolescence, 18*, 261–284.

Danseco, E. R., & Holden, E. W. (1998). Are there different types of homeless families? A typology of homeless families based on cluster analysis. *Family Relations: Journal of Applied Family and Child Studies, 47*, 159–165.

Deater-Deckard, K. (2008). *Parenting stress.* New Haven, CT: Yale University Press.

Elder, G. H. (1974). *Children of the Great Depression.* Chicago, IL: University of Chicago Press.

Emery, R. E., & O'Leary, K. D. (1982). Children's perceptions of marital discord and behavior problems of boys and girls. *Journal of Abnormal Child Psychology, 10*, 11–24.

Estes, A., Munson, J., Dawson, G., Koehler, E., Zhou, X., & Abbott, R. (2009). Parenting stress and psychological functioning among mothers of preschool children with autism and developmental delay. *Autism, 13*, 375–387.

Fawcett, J. T. (1978). The value of children and the transition to parenthood. *Marriage and Family Review, 12*, 11–34.

Gelles, R. J., & Straus, M. A. (1988). *Intimate violence: The definitive study of the causes and consequences of abuse in the American family.* New York, NY: Simon & Schuster.

Goldberg, S., Janus, M., Washington, J., Simmons, R. J., MacLusky, I., & Fowler, R. S. (1997). Prediction of preschool behavioral problems in healthy and pediatric samples. *Developmental and Behavioral Pediatrics, 18*, 304–313.

Gotlib, I. H., & Goodman, S. H. (2002). Introduction. In S. H. Goodman & I. H. Gotlib (Eds.), *Children of depressed parents: Mechanisms of risk and implications for treatment* (pp. 3–9). Washington, DC: American Psychological Association.

Gove, W. R., & Zeiss, C. (1987). Multiple roles and happiness. In F. Crosby (Ed.), *Spouse, parent, worker* (pp. 125–137). New Haven, CT: Yale University Press.

Hastings, R. P. (2002). Parental stress and behavior problems of children with developmental disability. *Journal of Intellectual and Developmental Disability, 27*, 149–160.

Hastings, R. P., & Beck, A. (2004). Stress intervention for parents of children with intellectual disabilities. *Journal of Child Psychology and Psychiatry, and Allied Disciplines, 45*, 1338–1349.

Hayes, S. A., & Watson, S. L. (2013). The impact of parenting stress: A meta-analysis of studies comparing the experience of parenting stress in parents of children with and without autism spectrum disorder. *Journal of Autism and Developmental Disorders, 43*, 629–642.

Hetherington, E. M., Cox, M., & Cox, R. (1982). Effects of divorce on parents and children. In M. Lamb (Ed.), *Nontraditional families* (pp. 233–288). Hillsdale, NJ: Erlbaum.

Kwok, S., & Wong, D. (2000). Mental health of parents with young children in Hong Kong: The roles of parenting stress and parenting self-efficacy. *Child & Family Social Work, 5*, 57–65.

Lavee, Y., Sharlin, S., & Katz, R. (1996). The effect of parenting stress on marital quality: An integrated mother-father model. *Journal of Family Issues, 17*, 114–135.

Lazarus, R. S., & Folkman, S. (1984). *Stress, appraisal, and coping.* New York, NY: Springer.

Lazarus, R. S., & Launier, R. (1978). Stress-related transactions between person and environment. In L. A. Pervin & M. Lewis (Eds.), *Perspectives in interactional psychology* (pp. 287–327). New York, NY: Plenum.

Maccoby, E. E., & Martin, J. A. (1983). Socialization in the context of the family: Parent-child interaction. In P. H. Mussen & E. M. Hetherington (Eds.), *Handbook of Child Psychology: Vol. 4. Socialization, personality, and social development* (4th Ed., pp. 1–101). New York: Wiley.

Middlebrook, J. L., & Forehand, R. (1985). Maternal perceptions of deviance in child behavior as a function of stress and clinic versus nonclinic status of the child: An analogue study. *Behavior Therapy, 16*, 494–502.

Miller, A. C., Gordon, R. M., Daniele, R. J., & Diller, L. (1992). Stress, appraisal, and coping in mothers of disabled and nondisabled children. *Journal of Pediatric Psychology, 17*, 587–605.

Miller, B. A., Smyth, N. J., & Mudar, P. J. (1999). Mothers' alcohol and other drug problems and their punitiveness toward their children. *Journal of Studies on Alcohol, 60*, 632–642.

Nair, P., Schuler, M. E., Black, M. M., Kettinger, L., & Harrington, D. (2003). Cumulative environmental risk in substance abusing women: Early intervention, parenting stress, child abuse potential and child development. *Child Abuse & Neglect, 27*, 997–1017.

Nomaguchi, K., & Milkie, M. (2017). Sociological perspectives on parenting stress: How social structure and culture shape parental strain and the well-being of parents and children. In K. Deater-Deckard & R. Panneton (Eds.), *Parenting stress and early child development: Adaptive and maladaptive outcome* (pp. 47–74). New York, NY: Springer.

Östberg, M., & Hagekull, B. (2000). A structural modeling approach to the understanding of parenting stress. *Journal of Clinical Child Psychology, 29*, 615–625.

Parke, R. D., & Buriel, R. (1998). Socialization in the family: Ethnic and ecological perspectives. In N. Eisenberg (Ed.), *Handbook of Child Psychology, Vol. 3: Social, emotional, and personality development* (5th Ed., pp. 463–552). New York, NY: Wiley.

Patterson, G. R. (1982). *Coercive family process.* Eugene, OR: Castalia.

Patterson, G. R. (1983). Stress: A change agent for family process. In N. Garmezy & M. Rutter (Eds.), *Stress, coping, and development in children* (pp. 235–264). New York, NY: McGraw-Hill.

Patterson, G. R. (1986). Performance models for antisocial boys. *American Psychologist, 41*, 432–444.

Pearlin, L. I., & Schooler, C. (1978). The structure of coping. *Journal of Health and Social Behavior, 22*, 337–356.

Pinderhughes, E. E., Dodge, K. A., Bates, J. E., Pettit, G. S., Zelli, A. (2000). Discipline responses: Influences of parents' socioeconomic status, ethnicity, beliefs about parenting, stress, and cognitive–emotional processes. *Journal of Family Psychology, 14*, 380–400.

Pollmann-Schult, M. (2014). Parenthood and life satisfaction: Why don't children make people happy? *Journal of Marriage and Family, 76*, 319–36.

Puff, J., & Renk, K. (2014). Relationships among parents' economic stress, parenting, and young children's behavior problems. *Child Psychiatry and Human Development, 45*, 712–727.

Roghmann, K., Hecht, P., & Haggerty, R. (1975). Coping with stress. In R. Haggerty, K. Roghmann, & I. Pless (Eds.), *Child health and the community* (pp. 54–66). New York, NY: Wiley.

Roggman, L., Moe, S., Hart, A., & Forthun, L. (1994). Family leisure and social support: Relations with parenting stress and psychological well-being in Head Start parents. *Early Childhood Research Quarterly, 9*, 463–480.

Santelli, B., Poyadue, F. S., & Young, J. L. (2001). *The parent to parent handbook connecting families of children with special needs.* Baltimore, MD: Paul H. Brookes.

Shonkoff, J. (1985). Social support and vulnerability to stress: A pediatric perspective. *Pediatric Annals, 14*, 550–554.

Solomon, M., Pistrang, N., & Barker, C. (2001). The benefits of mutual support groups for parents of children with disabilities. *American Journal of Community Psychology, 29*, 113–132.

Turner, R. J., & Noh, S. (1983). Class and psychological vulnerability among women: The significance of social support and personal control. *Journal of Health and Social Behavior, 24*, 2–15.

Vaughn, B., Egeland, B., Sroufe, L. A., & Waters, E. (1979). Individual differences in infant–mother attachment at twelve and eighteen months: Stability and change in families under stress. *Child Development, 50*, 971–975.

Vermaes, I. P., Janssens, J. M., Mullaart, R. A., Vinck, A., & Gerris, J. R. (2008). Parents' personality and parenting stress in families of children with spina bifida. *Child: Care, Health and Development, 34*, 665–674.

Webster-Stratton, C. (1990). Stress: A potential disrupter of parent perceptions and family interactions. *Journal of Clinical Child Psychology, 19*, 302–312.

Wiggs, L., & Stores, G. (2001). Behavioral treatment for sleep problems in children with severe intellectual disabilities and daytime challenging behavior: Effect on mothers and fathers. *British Journal of Health Psychology, 6*, 257–269.

CHAPTER 4

Families with Special Needs Children: Family Health, Functioning, and Care Burden

Carmen Caicedo[1]

O ver the past 30 years, advances in technology have improved survival rates for children with chronic conditions resulting from preterm births, congenital and genetic anomalies, diseases, or injuries (Cohen et al., 2011; Wise, 2012). Currently there are 11.2 million children with special health care needs (CSHCN) in the United States (Data Resource Center for Child and Adolescent Health, 2013) or one in five households caring for at least one special needs child. There is a small group of children who need continuous medical, nursing, and/or therapeutic services that enable them to survive and thrive, and it is growing in numbers.

The term *children with special health care needs* covers children with chronic conditions as well as children with disabilities ranging from mild to severe impairment. This latter subset includes medically complex and medical technology–dependent children. Caring for CSHCN poses challenges for parent caregivers and for family units (Kuo, Cohen, Agrawal, Berry, & Casey, 2011). Many CSHCN have developmental and intellectual delays, and/or functional limitations that require long-term assistance (Lollar, Hartzell, & Evans, 2012). They require health care that includes rehabilitative services, preventative, primary, specialty, emergent, and acute care services (Cohen et al., 2011; Oddy & da Silva Ramos, 2013). Parents must often perform tasks that are the usual purview of health care professionals, including administering medications or oxygen therapy, changing tracheostomy tubes, suctioning airways, passing nasogastric tubes or urinary

[1] Carmen Caicedo, PhD, RN, Florida International University, Miami, FL, USA

Carmen Caicedo, *Journal of the American Psychiatric Nurses Association*, vol. 20, issue 6. pp. 398–407, copyright © 2014 by SAGE Journals. Reprinted by Permission of SAGE Publications, Inc.

catheters, giving injections, or providing continuous and sometimes painful therapeutic regimes (Caicedo, 2013).

Caregiving for parents with children with complex medical conditions requires great attention and time, which can become burdensome and stressful (McCann, Bull & Winzenberg, 2012; Raphael, Zhang, Liu, & Giardino, 2010). It is not uncommon to find high stress levels in parent caregivers of CSHCN, which result in depression, fatigue, poor physical health, and social isolation (Carnevale, Alexander, Davis, Rennick, & Troini, 2006; Cousino & Hazen, 2013). In pediatric chronic conditions, the condition of the child as well as the treatment needs influence family health and functioning (American Academy of Pediatrics, 2003). A number of studies examined parent health-related quality of life (HRQOL) in parents of healthy children, parents from the community who may or may not have CSHCN, and parents of children with chronic diseases (Chen, Hao, Feng, Zhang, & Huang, 2011; Medrano, Berlin, & Davies, 2013; Panepinto, Hoffmann, & Pajewski, 2009; Scarpelli et al., 2008). Hatzmann, Heymans, Ferrer-i-Carbonell, van Praag, and Grootenhuis (2008) found parents of chronically ill children had lower HRQOL compared with parents of healthy children and who were at risk of impaired HRQOL. Varni, Sherman, Burwinkle, Dickinson, and Dixon (2004) measured HRQOL of parents with medically fragile children with complex chronic conditions who resided at home with their parents or in a long-term convalescent hospital facility and found that families with medically fragile children living at home had lower HRQOL or had more negative impact from the child's health than families with medically fragile children living in a residential facility. Understanding the effects of the pediatric chronic conditions on the physical and mental health of parent caregivers is important for providing care including mental health care to the families (Medrano et al., 2013; Panepinto et al., 2009).

The national goal in Healthy People 2010 (National Center for Health Statistics, 2012) proposed to have more CSHCN cared for at home because of high hospital costs, reduced payer reimbursement, the increased number of chronically ill children, and a recognition that prolonged hospital stays are detrimental to normal child development and family health and functioning (Namachivayam et al., 2012; Simon et al., 2010). However, little data are reported on the physical and mental health of parents who are primary caregivers or responsible for the care of children with medically complex and/or medical technology-dependent conditions (Toly, Musil, & Carl, 2012). Thus, the purpose of this study was to examine parent physical health (physical functioning), mental health (emotional, social, and cognitive functioning; communication; and worry), family functioning (daily activities and family relationships), and care burden (caregiver employment, caregiving time, travel time, health-related out-of-pocket expenditures) of parent caregivers of children with medically complex conditions and/or medical technology dependence over a 5-month period.

Method

Design and Sample

This longitudinal study used a convenience sample of parents caring for medically complex and/or medical technology–dependent children. Following institutional review board approval from Florida International University, families with CSHCN were recruited from local pediatric primary and specialty physician practices, medical day care settings, and long-term/residential care settings in South Florida. Recruitment and data collection occurred from March 2011 to March 2013.

Parent inclusion criteria: The participants were the primary caregiver or parent responsible for the care of CSHCN, 18 years or older who spoke English or Spanish.

Parent exclusion criteria: These included any major physical or mental disability that prevented them from participating in the study or completing the instruments.

CSHCN inclusion criteria: These included children 2 to 21 years old with a complex medical condition (chronic debilitating disease or condition involving one or more body systems that requires continuous monitoring of the child's symptoms; decision making on what tasks to do when the child's symptoms change such as airway suctioning, on when to stop or start tube feeding outside the scheduled times, on giving as needed medications for pain, respiratory distress, or seizures, etc., and maintaining the medical equipment) and CSHCN who were medically fragile (condition requiring dependence on medical technology devices such as ventilators, tracheotomies, gastrostomies, or procedures to maintain life, such as oxygen dependence, tube feedings, medication administration, urinary catheterizations; Kuo et al., 2011; Peterson-Carmichael & Cheifetz, 2012; Simon et al., 2010).

CSHCN exclusion criteria: These are CSHCN with only a single-system behavioral or mental health disorder, such as attention deficit/hyperactivity disorder or autism, without any other medical conditions.

Procedure

After approval from the institutional review board at Florida International University and permission and access from key administrators in the health care organizations, the principle investigator (PI) spoke with the designated site contacts. The study background, purpose, and study information sheet were discussed. Each site contact spoke with the parents who met study inclusion criteria and provided them with the study information sheet, consent forms, and contact information for the PI. Interested parents were asked if the PI could contact them by telephone. During that contact, a face-to-face home or site visit (where recruited) was scheduled with the PI to discussed the study purpose, answer their questions, and obtain the written consent from one parent (primary caregiver) from each family. Parent and child demographics, parent physical health, mental health, family functioning, and care burden data were collected during the meeting and monthly for 5 months by the PI. At the end of each face-to-face interview, which lasted 60 minutes, a tentative date for the next interview was scheduled with the same parent each month. Parents were called 1 to 3 days prior to the meeting in order to confirm their availability. Six parents who lived more than a 5-hour drive from the university requested telephone interviews, which the PI conducted, since the instrument was designed to be used as a written self-report or by telephone (Varni et al., 2004; Varni, Seid, & Kurtin, 2001; Varni, Seid, & Rode, 1999).

Instruments

Parent Physical, Mental Health, and *Family Functioning* were measured using the Pediatric Quality of Life (PedsQL) Family Impact Module, a 36-item questionnaire that measured the effect of pediatric chronic health conditions on parent physical health, mental health, and family functioning. *Physical health* includes problems with physical functioning, for example, feeling tired, getting headaches, feeling weak, and getting stomachaches (6 items). *Mental health* includes problems with emotional, social, and cognitive functioning as well as communication and worry. Emotional problems include anxiety, sadness, anger, frustration, helplessness, and hopelessness (5 items). Social problems include feeling isolated, difficulty getting support from others, and difficulty finding time or energy for social activities (4 items). Cognitive problems include difficulty maintaining attention, remembering things, and thinking quickly (5 items). Communication problems include others not understanding the family's situation and difficulty talking about their child's health condition and communicating with health professionals (3 items). Worry includes worrying about the child's condition, the effect of the illness on other family members and the child's future (5 items). *Family functioning* includes two subscales: problems with family daily activities taking more time and effort and difficulty finding time and energy to finish household chores (3 items), and family relationship problems, for example, communication, stress, conflict between family members, difficulty making decisions, and difficulty solving problems as a family (5 items). Parents were asked how much of a problem each item had been during the past month with the 5-point response scale, which was reversed scored (*never a problem* = 100, *almost never a problem* = 75, *sometimes a problem* = 50, *often a problem* = 25, and *always a problem* = 0). Higher scores indicated better functioning (Varni et al., 2004).

Three summary scores can be derived from the 36-item PedsQL Family Impact Module. *Total Family Impact Score* is computed by averaging all 36 items. *Parent HRQOL Summary Score* is computed by averaging the 20 items in Physical, Emotional, Social, and Cognitive Functioning subscales. *Family Functioning Summary Score* is computed by averaging 8 items in daily activities and family relationships subscales (Varni et al., 2004). Scale scores were computed as the sum of the items divided by the number of items answered. The reported scores are the means over the 5 months on each scale. This was done to obtain a more composite picture of the parent physical and mental health including emotional, social, and cognitive functioning; communication; worry; and family functioning versus data from a single time point. Higher scores reflect better functioning.

The Family Impact Module is reliable and valid for assessing the effects of the pediatric chronic conditions on parent HRQOL and family functioning (Scarpelli et al., 2008).

The internal consistency reliability for the Total Family Impact was .94, Parent HRQOL Summary scale was .92, and Family Functioning Summary scale was .82 in this study, which is consistent with findings from other studies (Chen et al., 2011; Medrano et al., 2013; Panepinto et al., 2009; Varni et al., 2004).

Care Burden. In this study, care burden was defined as lost employment time or missed work hours due to the CSHCN health condition, time invested in providing direct hands-on care for the CSHCN during the past week, time invested in care coordination during the past week, and time invested in transportation to and from health care appointments for the CSHCN, health-related out-of-pocket expenditures (copays, deductibles, medications, special foods, formula, adaptive clothing, durable equipment, home modifications, or any kind of therapy). Care burden was measured using questions from the Impact on the Family section from the 2005–2006 National Survey of Children with Special Health Care Needs (Blumberg et al., 2008). The means and minimum and maximum values over the 5 months are reported.

Demographics. The PedsQL Family Information Form was used to collect data on parent age, race/ethnicity, marital, educational, employment status, and relationship to the child (biological parent, other relative, or guardian).

Statistical Analysis

Descriptive statistics were used. Continuous variables are reported as means and standard deviations over the 5 months and categorical variables are reported as mean frequencies and percentages over the 5 months.

Results

Sample

A total of 84 parents or guardians caring for a medically complex and/or technology-dependent child were recruited. Characteristics of the parents are presented in Table 4.1. Most parents were biological mothers of the children with an average age of 40 years. Most parents were Hispanic and living with their spouse/partner for an average of 13 years. Most parents had greater than a high school education and were employed outside the home with 54% earning less than $39,000 per year. Most parents also received additional financial assistance (Supplemental Security Income; the Special Supplemental Nutrition Program for Women, Infants, and Children; or food stamps) and had Medicaid coverage for their CSHCN.

Characteristics of children are presented in Table 4.2. Fifty-nine percent of the children were 11 years of age or younger. Just over half the children were male and were severely disabled, but 66% were reported by parents to be in good to excellent health. As shown in Table 4.2, they had a range of chronic conditions, including seizure disorders, cerebral palsy, asthma, autism, and Down syndrome. More than half of the children had up to five different chronic conditions with a range of 1 to 16 different conditions as listed in the 2005/2006 NS-CSHCN (National Center for Health Statistics, 2012). As shown in Table 4.2, most children used more than one medical technology device, including tracheotomy, ventilator, oxygen, pulse oximetry, apnea monitor, suction machine, nebulizer for breathing treatments, gastrostomy feeding tube, feeding pump, humidifier, compression vest for chest physiotherapy, intravenous (IV) pump for intravenous medication administration, and continuous positive airway pressure masks. The vast majority of the children needed help or were dependent on help for activities of daily living because of physical or cognitive problems. Each week, about half of the children needed nursing home health services, physical therapy, and occupational therapy. Others also needed speech pathology and respiratory therapy. About one third of the parents reported their child needed treatment for emotional, developmental, or behavioral problems.

Parent Physical Health, Mental Health, Family Functioning, and Care Burden. Table 4.3 shows the descriptive statistics for parent physical health, mental health, family functioning and care burden.

Parent physical health. The majority of the parents in this study reported feeling tired during the day (87%, $n = 73$), feeling tired when they woke up (77%, $n = 65$), feeling too tired to do the things they like to do (63%, $n = 53$), feeling physically weak (50%, $n = 42$), feeling sick (33%, $n = 28$), and having headaches (67%, $n = 56$).

Parent mental health. In terms of *emotional health,* many parents reported feeling frustrated (82%, $n = 69$), anxious (66%, $n = 55$), sad (63%, $n = 53$), angry (52%, $n = 44$), and helpless or hopeless (44%, $n = 37$). In terms of *social activities,* parents reported problems finding time for social activities (64%, $n = 54$), not having energy for social activities (61%, $n = 51$), having trouble getting support from others (44%, $n = 37$), and feeling isolated (35%, $n = 29$). *Cognitively* they reported problems remembering what people told them (51%, $n = 43$), trouble remembering what they were just thinking (48%, $n = 40$), problems thinking quickly (44%, $n = 37$), and problems focusing their attention (36%, $n = 29$). In terms of *communication* (60%, $n = 50$), parents reported problems with

Table 4.1. *Characteristics of the Parents (N = 84).*

	% (*n*)
Age in years, *M (SD)*	40.2 (19.5)
	Range 22–64
Relationship to child	
Biological mother	75 (63)
Biological father	9 (8)
Grandmother	5 (4)
Guardian	6 (5)
Adoptive mother	5 (4)
Race/ethnicity	
Hispanic	47 (37)
White non-Hispanic	9 (8)
Black non-Hispanic	12 (10)
Other/mixed	9 (8)
Missing	25 (21)
Family structure	
Two-parent family	65 (55)
Single-parent family	35 (29)
Education	
<High school	9 (8)
High school	23 (19)
>High school	68 (57)
Employed	71 (60)
Work hours/week, M (SD)	35.8 (10.4)
Annual income, $	
<14,999	25 (18)
15,000–39,999	29 (21)
40,000–69,000	29 (21)
70,000+	17 (13)
Financial assistance	75 (63)
Insurance coverage	
Public (Medicaid)	88 (72)
Private	10 (8)
Both	2 (2)

others not understanding the family situation. They found it hard to talk about their child's health (41%, $n = 34$), and it was hard to tell doctors and nurses how they felt (23%, $n = 19$). These parents reported *worrying* much of the time. They worried about the child's future (86%, $n = 72$), about the side effects of medications and/or treatments (75%, $n = 63$), about how the medical treatments were working (67%, $n = 56$), about how others reacted to child's condition (58%, $n = 48$), and about how the child's condition was affecting other family members (52%, $n = 44$).

Table 4.2. *Characteristics of the Children (N = 84).*

	% (*n*)
Age in years	
2–5	35 (29)
6–1 1	24 (20)
12–17	22 (19)
18–21	19 (16)
Gender	
Male	56 (47)
Female	44 (37)
Chronic conditions	
Seizure disorders	29 (24)
Cerebral palsy	25 (21)
Asthma/respiratory problem	20 (17)
Autism	9 (8)
Down syndrome	8 (7)
More than one medical technology device	69 (58)
Tracheostomy	24 (20)
Ventilator	10 (8)
Oxygen	24 (20)
Pulse oximetry	29 (24)
Apnea monitor	17 (14)
Suction	42 (35)
Nebulizer	64 (54)
Gastrostomy tube	48 (40)
Feeding pumps	29 (24)
Chest compression vest	13 (11)
Intravenous medication	2 (2)
Continuous positive airway pressure	1 (1)
Need help with activities of daily life	89 (75)
General health	
Excellent	13 (11)
Very good	20 (17)
Good	33 (28)
Fair	23 (19)
Poor	11 (9)

Family functioning.   Most parents reported problems in *family daily activities*. They reported feeling too tired to finish household tasks (73%, *n* = 61) and had difficulty finding time to finish those household tasks (69%, *n* = 58). Almost half reported problems in *family relationships* with a lack of

Table 4.3. *Parent Physical Health, Mental Health, Family Functioning, and Care Burden.*

	M (SD)	Minimum-maximum
Physical health		
Tired during day	35.0 (30.5)	32.4–43.4
Tired when waking up	39.3 (33.2)	38.1–45.1
Too tired to do things they like to do	53.0 (35.7)	52.0–59.3
Physically weak	54.6 (33.4)	53.0–64.8
Feeling sick	62.4 (34.6)	62.4–64.8
Headaches	79.3 (26.7)	77.6–81.9
Mental health		
Emotional	60.9 (27.7)	45.8–67.8
Social	62.6 (31.7)	48.2–73.8
Cognitive	68.0 (27.9)	64.3–71.4
Communication	70.5 (23.5)	55.1–85.4
Worry	32.0 (32.1)	19.0–55.1
Family functioning		
Daily activities	33.0 (0)	27.1–39.8
Family relationships	67.9 (33.1)	66.3–69.5
Care burden		
Work hours per week		
Parent	35.8 (10.4)	35.3–37.1
Other family member	42.2 (14.5)	40.3–46.0
Missed work hours per week		
Parent	22.4 (13.1)	15.5–23.7
Other family member	17.4 (13.0)	14.9–23.7
Total time for appointments (minutes per month)	252.2 (224.7)	15–740
Travel time to routine care	37.5 (36.2)	27.8–37.2
Travel time to specialty care	67.6 (55.8)	37.1–98.2
Travel time to acute care	36.8 (36.3)	30.0–46.0
Travel time to urgent care	22.1 (13.2)	10.0–29.2
Travel time to emergency room	35.2 (30.7)	25.8–35.9
Hours/week providing direct care to children with special health care needs		
Parent	33.0 (30.4)	1–168
Other family member	14.7 (13.8)	2–72
Parent care coordination	6.6 (5.7)	1–33
Health-related out-of-pocket expenditures ($/month)	348.78 (623.34)	0–5,719.00
Summary scores		
Total family impact	52.5 (26.9)	49.6–56.3
Parent health-related quality of life	50.6 (26.9)	43.3–56.0
Total family functioning	47.3 (28.0)	40.5–57.6

communication (45%, *n* =38), difficulty solving family problems together (42%, *n* =35), stress or tension between family members, (42%, *n* = 35), conflicts between family members (37%, *n* = 31), and difficulty making decisions together (33%, *n* = 28).

Care burden.   The vast majority (81%, n = 68) of parents in this study reported that their work decisions were affected by their child's health condition. One third stopped working at some time to care full-time for their CSHCN. Parents reported that other immediate family member's employment decisions, (37%, *n* = 31) were also affected by the child's needs, and a smaller percentage (6%, *n* = 5) reported that family members had stopped working to help the parent care for the CSHCN. Employed parents worked on average 36 hours per week and missed on average 22 hours of work per week. The overall mean number of days parents missed work due to the CSHCN being sick in bed was 1.4 days (*SD* = 3.8) per month.

Caregiving Time invested in providing direct hands-on care for the CSHCN included time feeding, bathing, dressing, grooming, and toileting; mobility; administering medications; monitoring; and providing treatments. Parents provided direct care for their CSHCN an average 33 hours per week, and there was a considerable range from 1 hour to 168 hours. Other family members including older siblings, grandparents, and/or another relative also provided an average of 15 hours per week of direct care with a considerable range of 2 to 72 hours per week. Time invested in coordinating care included time spent calling health care providers for appointments and consultations, ordering durable medical equipment and supplies, contacting insurance providers regarding referrals and coverage, and consultations for legal issues. Care coordination time averaged about 7 hours per week with a considerable range of 1 to 33 hours per week.

Travel Time to and from appointments for routine care, specialty care, acute care, urgent care, emergency rooms and hospitals, therapy offices, or other health-related appointments averaged 4 hours (*SD* = 3.7) and ranged from 5 minutes to almost 12 hours per month.

Health-Related Out-of-Pocket Expenditures for the CSHCN included co-pays, deductibles, medications, special foods, formula, adaptive clothing, durable equipment, home modifications, or any kind of therapy. There was a considerable range of mean monthly expenditures, from $0/month to $5,719/month, with an average of approximately $350/month.

Summary Scores.   The *Total Family Impact Score* (mean of all 36 items in the PedsQL Family Impact Module) was 52.5 (*SD* = 26.9). The *Parent HRQOL Summary Score* (mean of 20 items in Physical, Emotional, Social, and Cognitive Functioning subscales) was 50.6 (*SD* = 26.9). The *Family Functioning Summary Score* (mean of all 8 items in the daily activities and family relationships subscales) was 47.3 (*SD* = 28.0).

Discussion

The present study provides a picture of the challenging experiences of parents (47% Hispanic) who have children aged 2 to 21 years who are medically complex and/or are medical technology–dependent. To put the findings in context, 89% of the children in our sample required help or were totally dependent on help with activities of daily living because of physical or cognitive problems, and 69% were using between two and six medical technology–dependent devices (e.g., tracheotomy, ventilators, oxygen, apnea monitors, suction machines, nebulizers, gastrostomy feeding tubes, and feeding pumps). Our findings suggest that parents who are primary caregivers of CSHCN have many unmet physical (e.g., fatigue, headaches) and mental (emotional, social, and cognitive functioning;

communication; and worry) health problems, compromised family functioning (daily activities and family relationships), and an enormous care burden (caregiver employment, caregiving time, travel time, health-related out-of-pocket expenditures).

Parents reported that fatigue was a major problem for them. They were tired when they woke up, were too tired to do the things they like to do, and had little energy for household chores or social activities. These findings are consistent with those of other studies. Hatzmann et al. (2008) found that parents with chronically ill children reported significant problems with daily functioning, vitality, and sleep compared to parents with healthy school-age children. Brehaut et al. (2011) reported that caregivers of children with complex medical conditions were more likely to report poorer physical health than caregivers of healthy children.

Emotionally, parents reported feeling emotionally frustrated, anxious, angry and that they felt helpless and hopeless. Socially they felt isolated, felt people did not understand their family situation, and felt it was hard to talk with others about the child and to talk with physicians and nurses. They had problems remembering and focusing on tasks. They worried a great deal about the child's medications, treatments, side effects, and the effect of the child's condition on other family members. And they worried about the child's future. Our findings are consistent with other studies but provide more richly descriptive data than those of similar reported studies. Hatzmann et al. (2008) reported that parents with chronically ill children had problems with emotions and with social functioning. In a qualitative study of families with ventilator-dependent children, Carnevale et al. (2006) reported that families with ventilator-dependent children felt a deep sense of isolation, and that their situation was unfair but that they had no alternative.

In terms of family functioning, 82% of parents reported problems in family daily activities. They felt too tired to finish household tasks and had difficulty finding the time to finish the tasks. Problems in family relationships included a lack of communication, difficulty solving family problems together, stress or tension between family members, conflicts between family members, and difficulty making decisions together. These findings are consistent with those of Lollar et al. (2012), who reported that caring for children with functional difficulties affected daily activities of the family.

The burden of care shouldered by parents in this study was substantial. Over 80% of study parents reported their employment decisions were affected by their child's health condition, with one third having stopped working at some point to care full-time for their CSHCN. In addition, other immediate family members' employment decisions were also affected by the child's needs. Parents provided on average 33 hours per week of direct care for their CSHCN, with other family members providing an average of 15 hours per week. This direct hands-on care included feeding, bathing, dressing, grooming, and toileting; mobility; administering medications; monitoring; and providing treatments. Kuo et al. (2011) reported that parents of CSHCN with complex care needs spent 11 to 20 hours per week providing direct hands-on care and about 1 to 6 hours per week providing care coordination. Children in the Kuo et al. study, however, had less complex care needs compared to children in the present study. Crowe and Michael (2011) reported that the need for constant supervision was one of the heaviest care burdens, and that time needed to care for the children reduces time from other parent activities, such as paid work outside the home, personal self-care, and social or leisure activities. In meeting the demands of providing care for others, many caregivers neglect their own physical and mental health (Gonzalez, Polansky, Lippa, Walker, & Feng, 2011). Hatzmann et al. (2008) reported lower HRQOL in parents caring for chronically ill children at home, including physical health, sleep, pain, vitality, social and cognitive functioning, and daily activities.

In the present study travel time to and from appointments for care averaged about 4 hours per month, adding to the care burden. Out-of-pocket expenditures for care of the CSHCN averaged about $350 per month, adding to the family's financial challenges. Lindley and Mark (2010) reported health-related out-of-pocket expenditures for CSHCN of $250 or more per month. Families perceived these expenses to be a financial burden.

Unfortunately, there are no national data to compare with the results from this study. However, we can compare our summary scores (total family impact, parent HRQOL, and family functioning) with scores from two other studies that used the PedsQL Family Impact Module. Better scores indicate less impact on the family, better parent HRQOL, and better family functioning. Varni et al.'s (2004) sample consisted of 23 parents (22 mothers, 1 father from home care) of medically fragile children with complex chronic health conditions including severe cerebral palsy and birth defects. They found that families caring for CSHCN at home (12 parents) reported lower physical and mental health and functioning than those families with CSHCN in the long-term care (LTC) residential facility (11 parents). Medrano et al. (2013) had a sample consisting of 929 community families who were neither recruited from health care organizations nor seeking medical care. Three hundred eighty three (41.2%) reported that one of their children had at least one chronic condition. They found that parents who had a child with a chronic condition had significantly poorer HRQOL than parents who did not report having a child with a chronic condition. The total family impact was greater (lower score) in our study ($M = 52.5$, $SD = 26.9$) compared to Varni et al. ($M = 81.0$, $SD = 17.1$, for those in long-term care; $M = 62.5$, $SD = 17.3$, for those at home), and Medrano (those with a chronic condition $M = 67.5$, $SD = 15.0$; those without a chronic condition $M = 73.2$, $SD = 13.6$). Our sample had a parent HRQOL score of $M = 50.6$, $SD = 26.9$, which was lower than that in the Varni sample ($M = 83.8$, $SD = 15.6$, for those in long-term care; $M = 62.9$, $SD = 19.8$, for those in home care) and the Medrano community sample ($M = 66.9$, $SD = 16.1$, for those with chronic conditions; $M = 71.2$, $SD = 14.9$, for those with no chronic conditions). Finally, the family functioning score in our sample was also lower at $M = 47.3$, $SD = 28.0$, than the Varni sample ($M = 84.3$, $SD = 20.5$, for those in long-term care; $M = 68.8$, $SD = 24.1$, for those in home care) and the Medrano community sample ($M = 62.5$, $SD = 18.3$, for those with chronic conditions; $M = 67.6$, $SD = 18.4$, for those with no chronic conditions).

Differences in the Total Family Impact Score, Parent HRQOL Summary Score, and Family Functioning Score between our study and the others may reflect the characteristics of the sample. The parent sample was largely Hispanic. Varni et al. (2004) did not report family or child demographics. The Medrano et al. (2013) sample was 83% White non-Hispanic. The present study differed in characteristics of the children. Varni's report was from 10 years ago. Today many of the advances in medical technology have improved the survival of children who may have died 10 years ago. In Medrano's community-based sample, parents not seeking any type of medical care (41%, $n = 383$) reported their children had a chronic condition that included less severe and less care-intensive conditions: asthma (11%), frequent headaches/migraines (7%), recurrent earaches (6%), attention deficit hyperactivity disorder (5%), nutritional problems (5%), sleep problems (5%), feeding problems (4%), recurrent abdominal pain (2%), depression (1%), and diabetes (0.3%). The lower Total Family Impact Score (greater total impact) in the current study may reflect the inclusion criteria of the medically complex and medical technology- dependent children with a higher condition severity and an increased parent involvement in the child's daily care.

Strengths and Limitations

Previous studies in this area report on largely White and Black samples of parents whereas the present study's sample was largely Hispanic. Most previous studies were cross-sectional, capturing data on parents at a single point in time that may have differed by a day, a week, or a month. The present study reported on parent experiences monthly for 5 months and reported means, thus providing a more complete picture of their experiences. In addition, most previous studies report on a very limited number of health and functioning outcomes of parents compared to the present study. The PedsQL Family Impact Module captures multiple ways in which the pediatric chronic condition can affect the parent. Such data are important since national trends indicate that more children who are medically complex and/or are medically technology–dependent are cared for by their parents in their homes. According to the American Academy of Pediatrics (2003), children's health and functioning outcomes are strongly influenced by how well their families function.

The present study used a convenience sample and may have resulted in self-selection. It is not known how many eligible families learned about the study but did not participate. The study had a small sample size and a 9.5% attrition rate. The attrition rate reported in other similar studies with quality-of-life scores range between 4% and 28% (Hewitt, Kumaravel, Dumville, & Torgerson, 2010; Smith, Williamson, Miller, & Schulz, 2011). There was no control group of families with children who did not have complex medical conditions, and therefore, it is difficult to know how physical and mental health, family functioning, and care burden compare to families with children without special health care needs. Future research would benefit from studies with larger samples of parents with greater diversity in the samples. Studies that follow families from the time of diagnosis of the child's complex medical condition over time would provide a profile of changes in the child's needed care, family coping, family physical and mental health, family care, and financial burden as the child's condition progresses.

Implications for Clinical Practice

Caring for CSHCN poses significant challenges for parent caregivers and for the family. Many CSHCN have developmental and intellectual delays and/or functional limitations that require long-term assistance. They require health care that includes rehabilitative, preventative, primary, specialty, emergent, and acute care services. Caregiving for parents with children with complex medical conditions requires great attention and time, which can become burdensome and stressful. Parents must often perform tasks that are the usual purview of health care professionals, which results in depression, fatigue, poor physical health, and social isolation. The health and functioning of parent caregivers and family functioning are clinically important to ensure optimal health and functioning of CSHCN. Any decline in parent physical and mental health indicates that their ability to provide quality care for their children may also be decreasing.

Advanced practice nurses are in a unique position to promote the parent's physical and mental health during the health care visit. Building a rapport with the parent may allow the parent to voice a concern or a need or to just communicate with someone willing to listen. Objective assessment should be performed routinely to detect risk for clinical depression in the parent caregiver and to assess challenges within the family unit. Appropriate referrals to community-based services for mental health problems, psychosocial needs, and even support needs at home should be considered for the parent, the CSHCN, and/or the family (Mesman, Kuo, Carroll & Ward, 2012; Toly, et al., 2012). These families may need a number of support services.

Advanced practice nurses are ideally prepared for the role of care coordination for medically complex, medical technology–dependent children and their families (Golden & Nageswaran, 2012). Research indicates that respite or temporary relief for the caregiver can be an effective intervention to decrease the stress that parents with CSHCN often experience (Doig, McLennan, & Urichuk, 2009). Over half (52%) of the families in this study had not had a vacation (away from home) in the past 4 years. Parents wanted to include the special needs child with the family on vacation. However, from anecdotal study data, the unpredictability of the child's condition, not having qualified help available, and the challenge of transportation made staying at home easier.

Conclusions

This study demonstrated the health and functioning challenges of parents of children who were medically complex and/or medical technology–dependent. These parents experienced fatigue and exhaustion, emotional problems ranging from frustration to hopelessness, and cognitive problems in remembering and focusing attention; had little time or energy for daily chores or social activities; and found it hard to talk about their child's health with others. Their caregiving included carrying out daily hygiene and medical procedures for the children and getting the children to and from health care appointments and facilities and resulted in changes in their own and their family members' employment decisions. At a time when national trends show more home care for CSHCN, failure to support parents through community-based services for mental health problems, psychosocial needs, even home support needs, or other respite services can only lead to a decrease in the parent caregiver's own physical and mental health. A decline in the parent caregivers' physical and mental health may result in a decreased ability to care for the CSHCN, and potentially a decrease in the CSHCNs health and functioning outcomes.

Acknowledgments

I would like to acknowledge Dr. Varni and colleagues for the use of the questionnaires.

Author's Note

The author is responsible for the content and writing of this article.

Declaration of Conflicting Interests

The author declared no potential conflicts of interest with respect to the research, authorship, and/or publication of this article.

Funding

The author disclosed receipt of the following financial support for the research, authorship, and/or publication of this article: Florida Nurses Foundation 2012 Undine Sams and Friends, Research Grant (District 5 Charitable Trust), and Florida International University, University Graduate School, Fall 2012, Doctoral Evidence Acquisition Fellowship.

References

American Academy of Pediatrics. (2003). Family pediatrics: Report of the Task Force on the Family. *Pediatrics, 111,* 11541–1571. Retrieved from http://pediatrics.aappublications.org/content/111/Supplement_2/1541.full.html

Blumberg, S. J., Welch, E. M., Chowdhury, S. R., Upchurch, H. L., Parker, E. K., & Skalland, B. J. (2008). *Design and operation of the National Survey of Children with Special Health Care Needs, 2005–2006* (Vital Health Statistics, Series 1, No. 45). Washington, DC: National Center for Health Statistics. Retrieved from http://www.cdc.gov/nchs/data/series/sr_01/sr01_045.pdf

Brehaut, J., Garner, R., Miller, A., Lach, L., KLassen, A., Rosenbaum, P., & Kohen, D. (2011). Changes over time in the health of caregivers of children with health problems: Growth-curve findings from a 10-year population-based study. *American Journal of Public Health, 101,* 2308–2316. doi:10.2105/AJPH.2011.300298

Caicedo, C. (2013). *Children with special health care needs: Comparison of the effects of home care settings, prescribed pediatric care settings, and long-term care settings on child and family health outcomes and health care service use* (Unpublished doctoral dissertation). Florida International University, Miami.

Carnevale, F., Alexander, E., Davis, M., Rennick, J., & Troini, R. (2006). Daily living with distress and enrichment: the moral experience of families with ventilator-assisted children at home. *Pediatrics, 117,* e48–e60.

Chen, R., Hao, Y., Feng, L., Zhang, Y., & Huang, Z. (2011). The Chinese version of the Pediatric Quality of Life Inventory (PedsQLTM) Family Impact Module: Cross-cultural adaptation and psychometric evaluation. *Health and Quality of Life Outcomes, 9*(16). Retrieved from http://www.hqlo. com/content/9/1/16

Cohen, E., Kuo, D., Agrawal, R., Berry, J., Bhagat, S., Simon, T., & Srivastava, R. (2011). Children with medical complexity: An emerging population for clinical and research initiatives. *Pediatrics, 127,* 529–538. doi:10.1542/peds.2010–0910

Cousino, M., & Hazen, R. (2013). Parenting stress among caregivers of children with chronic illness: A systematic review. *Journal of Pediatric Psychology, 38,* 809–828. doi:10.1093/jpepsy/jst049

Crowe, T., & Michael, H. (2011). Time use of mothers with adolescents: A lasting impact of a child's disability. *OTJR: Occupation, Participation and Health, 31,* 118–126.

Data Resource Center for Child & Adolescent Health. (2013). *2009–2010 National Survey of Children With Special Health Care Needs.* Retrieved fromhttp://www.child-healthdata.org/learn/NS-CSHCN

Doig, J., McLennan, J., & Urichuk, L. (2009). "Jumping through hoops": Parents' experiences with seeking respite care for children with special needs. *Child: Care, Health, and Development, 35,* 234–242. doi:10.1111/j. 1365-2214.2008.00922.x

Golden, S. L., & Nageswaran, S. (2012). Caregiver voices: Coordinating care for children with complex chronic conditions. *Clinical Pediatrics, 51,* 723–729. doi:10.1177/0009922812445920

Gonzalez, E., Polansky, M., Lippa, C., Walker, D., & Feng, D. (2011). Family caregivers at risk: Who are they? *Issues in Mental Health Nursing, 32,* 528–536. doi:10.3109/01612840.2011.573123

Hatzmann, J., Heymans, H., Ferrer-i-Carbonell, A., van Praag, B., & Grootenhuis, M. (2008). Hidden consequences of success in pediatrics: Parental health-related quality of life—results from the Care Project. *Pediatrics, 122,* e1030-e1038. doi:10.1542/peds.2008–0582

Hewitt, C. E., Kumaravel, B., Dumville, J. C., & Torgerson, D. J. (2010). Assessing the impact of attrition in randomized controlled trials. *Journal of Clinical Epidemiology, 63,* 1264–70. doi:10.1016/j. jclinepi.2010.01.010

Kuo, D., Cohen, E., Agrawal, R., Berry, J., & Casey, P. (2011). A national profile of caregiver challenges among more medically complex children with special health care needs. *Archives of Pediatric & Adolescent Medicine, 165,* 1020–1026. doi:10.1001/archpediatrics.2011.172

Lindley, L., & Mark, B. (2010). Children with special health care needs: Impact of health care expenditures on family financial burden. *Journal of Child and Family Studies, 19,* 79–89.

Lollar, D., Hartzell, M., & Evans, M. (2012). Functional difficulties and health conditions among children with special health needs. *Pediatrics, 129,* e714-e744. doi:10.1542/ peds.2011–0780

Mesman, G. R., Kuo, D. Z., Carroll, J. L., & Ward, W. (2012). The impact of technology dependence on children and their families. *Journal of Pediatric Health Care.* doi:10.1016/j. pedhc.2012.05.003

McCann, D., Bull, R., & Winzenberg, T. (2012). The daily patterns of time use for parents of children with complex needs: A systematic review. *Journal of Child Health Care, 16,* 26–52. doi:10.1177/1367493511420186

Medrano, G., Berlin, K., & Davies, H. (2013). Utility of the PedsQLTM Family Impact Module: Assessing the psychometric properties in a community sample. *Quality of Life Research, 22,* 2899–2907. doi:10.1007/ s11136-013-0422-9

Namachivayam, P., Taylor, A., Montague, T., Moran, K., Barrie, J., Delzoppo, C., & Warwick, B. (2012). Long-stay children in intensive care: Long-term functional outcome and quality of life from a 20-year institutional study. *Pediatric Critical Care, 13,* 520–528. doi:10.1097/PCC.013e31824fb989

National Center for Health Statistics. (2012). *Healthy People 2010: Final review—Publication No. (PHS)2012–1038*. Hyattsville, MD: Author. Retrieved from http://www.cdc. gov/nchs/data/hpdata2010/hp2010_final_review.pdf

Oddy, M., & da Silva Ramos, S. (2013). Cost effective ways of facilitating home based rehabilitation and support. *NeuroRehabilitation, 32,* 781–790. doi:10.3233/NRE-130902

Panepinto, J., Hoffmann, R., & Pajewski, N. (2009). The psychometric evaluation of the PedsQLTM Family Impact Module in parents of children with sickle cell disease. *Health and Quality of Life Outcomes, 7*(32). doi:10.1186/1477-75257-32

Peterson-Carmichael, S., & Cheifetz, I. (2012). The chronically critically ill patient: Pediatric considerations. *Respiratory Care, 57,* 993–1003. doi:10.4187/respcare.01738

Raphael, J. L., Zhang, Y., Liu, H., & Giardino, A. P. (2010). Parenting stress in US families: Implications for pediatric healthcare utilization. *Child: Care, Health and Development, 36,* 216–224. doi:10.1111/j.1365-2214.2009. 01052.x.

Scarpelli, A., Paiva, S., Pordeus, I., Varni, J., Viegas, C., & Allison, P. (2008). The Pediatric Quality of Life Inventory (PedsQLTM) family impact module: Reliability and validity of the Brazilian version. *Health and Quality of Life Outcomes,* 6(35). doi:10.1186/1477-7525-6-35

Simon, T., Berry, J., Feudtner, C., Stone, B., Sheng, X., Bratton, S.,...Srivastava, R. (2010). Children with complex chronic conditions in inpatient hospital settings in the United States. *Pediatrics, 126,* 647–655. doi:10.1542/peds.2009-3266

Smith, G. R., Williamson, G. M., Miller, L. S., & Schulz, R. (2011). Depression and quality of informal care: A longitudinal investigation of caregiving stressors. *Psychology and Aging, 26,* 584–591. doi:10.1037/a0022263

Toly, V., Musil, C., & Carl, J. (2012). A longitudinal study of families with technology-dependent children. *Research in Nursing & Health, 35,* 40–45.

Varni, J. W., Seid, M., & Kurtin. (2001). PedsQL 4.0: Reliability and validity of the Pediatric Quality of life version 4.0 generic core scales in healthy and patient populations. *Medical Care, 39,* 800–812.

Varni, J. W., Seid, M., & Rode, C. A. (1999). The PedsQL: Measurement model for the pediatric quality of life inventory. *Medical Care, 37,* 126–139.

Varni, J. W., Sherman, S., Burwinkle, T., Dickinson, P., & Dixon, P. (2004). The PedsQL Family Impact Module: Preliminary reliability and validity. *Health and Quality of Life Outcomes,* 2(55), 1–6. doi:10.1186/1477-7525-2-55

Wise, P. (2012). Emerging technologies and their impact on disability. *Future Child, 22,* 169–191.

CHAPTER 5

Mental Illness and Family Stress

Angie M. Schock-Giordano and Stephen M. Gavazzi

The terms *mental health* and *mental illness* fall on a continuum rather than reflect two distinct categories. On one end of the continuum, mental health is characterized by "successful performance of mental function, resulting in productive activities, fulfilling relationships with other people, and the ability to adapt to change and to cope with adversity," while on the opposite end, mental illness is described as "health conditions that are characterized by alterations in thinking, mood, or behavior associated with distress and/or impaired functioning," (U.S. Department of Health and Human Services, 1999, p. 4). This chapter will emphasize the experiences of individuals and their families as they cope with stressors associated with mental illness. Fortunately, our society is becoming more knowledgeable about identifying symptoms and is more willing to seek help from mental health professionals. Society is also becoming more sensitive to the fact that mental health and mental illness are family issues as well as individual concerns. Mental illness affects individuals of all ages; however, the family experience of coping with mentally unhealthy members can vary greatly based on which member is experiencing the impairment.

Facets of mental illness, such as the display and severity of symptoms, as well as the individual's and family's ability to cope with a disorder, are influenced by social, psychological, and biological factors. Therefore, understanding the impact of daily stressors and the ways in which individuals and family members cope with stress are topics that must be integrated into any discussion of mental illness. In this chapter, we present the most recent research findings related to the causes, courses, and treatment of mental illness as a family event. We discuss topics relevant to families coping with mentally ill members in reference to the ABC-X model of family stress, and we use personal narratives throughout the chapter to illustrate the links between family issues and components of the ABC-X model.

Family Stress Theory and Mental Illness

Walter is a 36-year-old married father of two young boys who recently returned from a 1-year tour of duty serving as a military officer in Iraq. Walter has been home for 7 months, but on a daily basis, he still talks to his wife, Rosa, about the overwhelming feelings of worry and guilt he has over the status of the war and the incidents that he saw take place; he has even displayed some uncharacteristic angry outbursts toward his two young sons. Walter sleeps only 2 to 3 hours per night due to reoccurring nightmares and has not been able to return to work at the military base. His recent condition has frightened Rosa, but she has not talked with her husband about this because she was raised in a family culture in which one does not discuss mental illness. Recently, Walter has begun spending his evenings meeting and talking with several officers in his unit who also have returned from Iraq and who have been experiencing similar problems.

Walter's situation appears to reflect symptoms associated with posttraumatic stress disorder (PTSD), a condition that may be an emerging problem in the near future among the many U.S. military men and women who have served recently in wars overseas. Many of the issues that Walter is facing correspond with the elements of the ABC-X model, and many of the topics that we discuss in this chapter can be illustrated through his story. For example, in the model, A refers to the stressor event, which is the family member's mental illness. For Walter, this would include the causes and symptoms of his PTSD. Thus, we discuss below the numbers of individuals in the United States who are affected by mental illness, with particular emphasis on the demographic characteristics (e.g., gender, age, socioeconomic status, and ethnicity) associated with mental illness. In addition, we review research related to the causes of mental illness, including genetic linkages, family environment contributions, and the combination of heredity and family relationships.

In the ABC-X model, B represents available resources that can exist within the individual, within the family system, and within the community. For Walter, his wife Rosa and the men's support group where he discusses his problems would be considered two main resources. In this chapter, we discuss family strengths and the positive outcomes that families can achieve by coping successfully with mental illness. We also discuss the community resources that exist for families coping with mental illness, such as treatment programs (e.g., psychoeducation), community-based organizations (e.g., the National Alliance for the Mentally Ill), Web-based support systems, and social policy efforts.

The C element in the family stress theory model refers to the family's perceptions of the family member's mental illness. In Walter's family, his wife Rosa has not addressed his symptoms, largely because her family of origin did not openly recognize or discuss mental illness. We review the literature pertaining to the concept of "expressed emotion," illustrating how family members' views of mental illness can translate into behaviors and attitudes that have a direct impact on the well-being of mentally ill family members. Another important issue discussed in this chapter is the notion of *subjective burden* (i.e., a family member's appraisal of the illness and/or the caregiving experience). For instance, a significant subjective burden for many families with mentally ill members involves the stigma attached to mental illness, both within the family and in society in general, which can be influenced by cultural and family belief systems.

Epidemiology of Mental Illness

Epidemiologists study disease patterns in given populations to determine how many people in those populations suffer from particular illnesses. Two terms from the field of epidemiology are used to estimate the occurrence of mental illness in a population: *incidence,* which refers to new cases of particular mental illnesses that occur during a set period of time, and *prevalence,* which refers to new and existing mental illnesses that have been observed during a set period or during one point in time (U.S. Department of Health and Human Services, 1999). Sometimes, however, it can be difficult to identify "cases." For example, although an individual may experience particular symptoms, the duration and/or intensity of the symptoms may not reach the threshold necessary for a diagnosis of mental illness (Kupfer, First, & Regier, 2002). In addition, most epidemiological studies survey members in households across the country and neglect to gather information from homeless persons or those living in institutions such as shelters, treatment centers, hospitals, and prisons (U.S. Department of Health and Human Services, 1999). Despite these limitations, current patterns of mental illness in the U.S. population can be described by using available information about the incidence and prevalence of various disorders.

As previously mentioned, the term *mental illness* is not entirely separate from *mental health* in that many people may experience mental health problems at some level of severity throughout life. Serious mental illnesses that can be officially diagnosed by mental health professionals using standard criteria often are classified into two groups of problem behaviors: internalizing disorders and externalizing disorders. Internalizing disorders involve a major disturbance in moods and emotions, and may include symptoms such as anxiety, sadness, worry, and guilt (although the features of these disturbances can vary widely). The two main types of internalizing disorders are mood disorders and anxiety disorders. Externalizing disorders, in contrast, are characterized by aggressive, impulsive, and/or delinquent behaviors, and can include a range of mild to severe acting-out behaviors. The two main types of externalizing disorders are disruptive behavior disorders and attention-deficit/hyperactivity disorders (McMahon & Estes, 1997; Zahn-Waxler, Klimes-Dougan, & Slattery, 2000).

Rates of Mental Illness in the U.S. Population

Mental illnesses are common in the United States. Nearly one in five U.S. adults lives with a mental illness (Merikangas et. al, 2010). Mental illnesses include many different conditions that vary in degree of severity, ranging from mild to moderate to severe. Any mental illness (AMI) is defined as a mental, behavioral, or emotional disorder. This can include disorders ranging from no impairment to severe impairment. Serious mental illness (SMI) is defined as a mental, behavioral, or emotional disorder resulting in serious impairment which substantially impacts life activities.

When assessing rates of mental illness in the U.S. population, it is important to review statistics on *lifetime prevalence rates* (i.e., the number of persons who will experience mental illness over the course of their lives), and *12-month prevalence rates* (i.e. the number of persons who have experienced the disorder in a given year).

According to Substance Abuse and Mental Health Services Administration (SAMHSA), there are an estimated 44.7 million adults aged 18 or older with some form of mental illness. This number represents 18.3% of all U.S. adults. Women are more likely to experience AMI (21.7%) than men (14.5%). Women are also more likely to seek treatment for mental illness (48.8%) than men (33.9%). Among the 44.7 million adult with AMI, an estimated 19.2 million received treatment in the past year (Merikangas et. al, 2010).

Data Source

Merikangas KR, He JP, Burstein M, Swanson SA, Avenevoli S, Cui L, Benjet C, Georgiades K, Swendsen J. Lifetime prevalence of mental disorders in U.S. adolescents: results from the National Comorbidity

Survey Replication--Adolescent Supplement (NCS-A). *I Am Acad Child Adolesc Psychiatry.* 2010 Oct; 49(10): 980–9.

Etiology of Mental Illness

Phillip is a 13-year-old boy who has recently been diagnosed with ADHD and bipolar disorder. His symptoms first surfaced at school when his grades dramatically dropped last year after experiencing severe distress over completing classroom assignments. He is also regularly getting into physical fights with other students on the playground. His mother, Shirley, is a stay-at-home mother, while, Jimmy, the father, is a full-time physician. Shirley and Jimmy have disagreed on the severity of Phillip's condition, and their many years of obvious marital discord now focuses daily on whether Phillip needs professional help. Shirley is especially distraught because she cannot convince her husband to attend family therapy. Also, she not only recognizes Phillip's aggressive behaviors in her husband, but Phillip is also echoing his father's defiance in not wanting to seek help for his symptoms. Just recently, Phillip came home from school complaining about the "mean kids" in his class who have been teasing him, and he told his mom that he "wants to die and never see them again."

Because all family members are a part of the family system, it is difficult to discuss the etiology (i.e., the causes or origins) of mental disorders in family members without adopting a family-oriented perspective. Moreover, it is necessary to understand the role of at least one parent (mother and/or father) in an individual's psychopathology since even molecular, genetic-based research studies have at their core the implication of family heritage.

The family-oriented view is consistent with the biopsychosocial model of disease (Engel, 1977), which contends that the causes, courses, and outcomes of all illnesses are influenced by interactions among biological predispositions, genetic and psychological vulnerability, and stressful family or life events. Thus, multiple factors play roles in the etiology of mental illness, and the relative importance of the various factors differs among individuals and across the stages of the life span. In Phillip's case, he may have inherited a predisposition for his condition from his father, and/or he may be displaying the effects of growing up surrounded by a family plagued with constant marital discord. In addition, Phillip is currently experiencing daily stress at school caused by his poor performance and fights with his peers. In sum, multiple factors have contributed to Phillip's condition and the feelings of hopelessness that have resulted.

Research on the etiology of mental illness parallels this biopsychosocial framework, such that studies utilizing a family-oriented perspective on mental disorders can be organized into three categories: (1) studies that examine how the presence of a mental disorder in a parent puts his or her offspring at risk and the contribution of shared genes on siblings' mental health outcomes (genetic linkage research), (2) studies that assess the relationship between various family environmental factors and the subsequent mental health status of family members (family environment research), and (3) studies that attempt to examine the simultaneous influence of both genetic linkage and family environment to the development of mental disorders.

Genetic Linkage Research

Genetic linkage research explores the relationship between the presence of a mental disorder in one family member and the concurrent or eventual manifestation of mental illness in other family members. To increase our understanding of how shared genes can cause mental illness among family members and to clarify the unique contributions of genetic influences and family environmental influences, researchers have implemented studies of twins and children who have been adopted. For example, researchers compare disorder rates among monozygotic twins (who share 100% of their genes) and dizygotic twins (who share only 50% of their genes) to evaluate the influence of heritability; if disorder rates are significantly higher among monozygotic twins, then heritability is deemed an important factor. Similarly, studies of adopted children generally compare adjustment/mental health similarities in twins who have been reared in separate environments. The results of twin and adoption studies suggest that genetic links are important elements in the onset of many different mental illnesses, such as personality disorders, mood disorders, autism, and substance abuse (Mash & Dozois, 1996). However, it is likely that the extent of genetic contributions may vary across specific disorders (Eley, 2001). Efforts in molecular genetics indicate that it may be useful to examine particular genes or genetic markers for links to mental illness (Plomin, DeFries, Craig, & McGuffin, 2003). Recent genetic research has focused on the relationships between genetic markers and anxiety (Eley, 2001), antisocial behavior (Eley, Lichtenstein, & Moffitt, 2003), and mood disorders (Morley, Hall, & Carter, 2004; Preisig, 2006).

Family Environment Research

Many family environmental factors have been shown to be related to the development of mental disorders, including family stressors, numerous family relationship variables (e.g., conflict, support, and relationship quality), and expressed emotion. Researchers have found interrelationships among particular family stressors, such as maternal physical and mental health, divorce, parental death, and everyday hassles (Forehand, Biggar, & Kotchick, 1998; Kahng, Oyserman, Bybee, & Mowbray, 2008; Sheeber, Hops, & Davis, 2001). For example, Forehand et al. (1998) found that half of the mothers in their sample of 285 families of adolescents (ages 11–15) reported experiencing two or more family stressors. Additionally, adolescents from those families with multiple stressors showed more depressive symptoms 6 years later compared with adolescents from less stressful family environments. In a more recent study, higher levels of parenting stress and lower levels of nurturing behaviors were positively associated with the level of symptom severity of mothers diagnosed with a serious mental illness (Kahng, Oyserman, Bybee, & Mowbray, 2008).

Family conflict, parenting approaches, and family members' relationship quality also have been associated with youth reports of mental illness. For example, family conflict, parental hostility, and harsh discipline have been related to adolescents' internalizing and externalizing disorders. Specifically, one longitudinal study found parent-adolescent disagreements during early adolescence predicted internalizing symptoms several years later among a sample of late adolescents (Reuter, Scaramella, Wallace, & Conger, 1999). Furthermore, high levels of negative parenting characteristics (e.g., using harsh discipline and feeling frustrated, angry, or impatient with their child) have been associated with antisocial behaviors in children (Larsson, Viding, & Plomin, 2008). Also, in a study of families with two siblings diagnosed with ADHD, results suggested that 40% of the siblings' impairment was accounted for by family conflict (Pressman, Loo, & Carpenter, 2006).

Several studies also suggest that family members' relationship quality and overall family environment are related to the mental health of children and adolescents. For instance, Sheeber, Hops, Alpert, Davis, and Andrews (1997) found that less supportive family environments and less facilitative behavior during problem-solving discussions were associated with adolescent depressive symptomatology, and Rowe and Liddle (2003) showed that low levels of family cohesion and poor attachment relationships were related to adolescent substance abuse. In addition, Puig-Antich et al. (1993) found that depressed adolescents reported poorer-quality relationships with parents and siblings than did nondepressed adolescents. When overall family environment has been assessed, it has been related to (a) boys' major depression, conduct disorder, ADHD, and alcohol use and (b) girls' major depression, conduct disorder, ADHD, operational defiant disorder, and posttraumatic stress disorder (Halloran, Ross, & Carey, 2002).

Research on Expressed Emotion

The research on expressed emotion (EE; see Brown, Birley, & Wing, 1972) has been very influential in the movement toward a family-oriented perspective on mental disorders. In addition, the concept of EE aligns with die C element in the ABC-X model of family stress, such that EE represents an individual's perceptions. Specifically, the concept of EE has traditionally been comprised of two factors: (1) the level of emotional (over)involvement among family members and (2) the degree to which family members display critical attitudes toward and/or make hostile comments about the family member who has a mental disorder (Vaughn & Leff, 1976). More recent studies have further identified behavior patterns within the emotional overinvolvement factor, noting the particular ways in which family members display inappropriate intrusiveness, distress, and self-sacrificing behaviors toward a mentally ill family member (Fredman, Baucom, Miklowitz, & Stanton, 2008).

Extensive research on EE has found that individuals suffering from a multitude of illnesses (e.g., schizophrenia, mood disorders, ADHD, panic disorders, eating disorders, posttraumatic stress disorder, alcohol abuse, Alzheimer's disease, and personality disorders) who live with high-EE (i.e., overinvolved, critical, or hostile) family members are more likely to experience relapse (i.e., another episode of symptoms) than are persons with the same illnesses who live with low-EE family members (Barrowclough & Hooley, 2003; Miklowitz, 2007).

Some researchers have attempted to gain a more complete understanding of exactly why EE is associated with psychiatric relapse. Barrowclough and Hooley (2003) note that growing evidence suggests that "high- and low-EE family members differ in the beliefs they hold about patients and the problem behaviors associated with the patient's illness" (p. 850) such that high-EE relatives tend to blame mentally ill family members for their abnormal behavior, whereas low-EE family members perceive the individual's behavior to be out of his or her control and a product of the illness. One implication of these research findings is the need to educate family members regarding the severity and origins of the patient's symptoms as a way of decreasing family EE levels. Lopez, Nelson, Snyder, and Minz (1999) contend that the goal of family treatment should be a "flexible attributional stance," in which family members neither attribute all aspects of the patient's behavior to factors beyond the patient's control nor assume that the patient could easily control his or her symptoms. Thus, the recognition that abnormal behaviors are distinct from the individual's personality and largely out of that person's control would increase the possibility that family members would act in a less critical fashion toward the patient (Fristad, Gavazzi, & Soldano, 1999).

Research Examining Both Genetic Linkage and Family Environment

In recent years, there has been a tremendous amount of growth in research combining genetic and environmental factors within the same study (Costello, Foley, & Angold, 2005; Jaffee, 2007). The biopsychosocial model emphasizes the value in combining genetic and environmental variables when studying the etiology of most mental disorders, such that heredity can provide an individual with a predisposition to a mental illness, but the likelihood that the illness will manifest is largely determined by environmental and family influences. Two directions have emerged in gene-environment research: (1) the gene-environment correlation approach focusing on the manner and extent that genetic factors shape family environmental variables (e.g., a parent's mental disorder creates a discordant marital relationship and family environment), and (2) the gene-environment interaction approach examining how the effects of one factor vary across levels of another factor (e.g., the impact of a negative family environment on a child's mental health is evident in only extremely unhealthy family situations) (Lau & Eley, 2008). Combined gene-environment research has been used to assess several different environmental factors in studies with twins and siblings with depressive symptoms (Lau & Eley, 2008) and externalizing behaviors (Button, Lau, Maughan, & Eley, 2001). Also, the gene-environment approach has been used when discussing the causes of anxiety disorder (Gregory & Eley, 2007) and specific antisocial behaviors (Larsson, Viding, & Plomin, 2008).

Assessment of Family Resources

Ron and Barbara are a middle-aged couple who have recently begun to care for Ron's mother, Lucille, who has been diagnosed with Alzheimer's disease. Since Lucille first moved in with Ron and Barbara, her condition has deteriorated rapidly, and she is now approaching the need for around-the-clock care, Ron and Barbara are struggling to pay for all of the medical treatment that Lucille needs, and the family is experiencing additional financial problems because Barbara had to quit her job to provide full-time care for her mother-in-low. Other adjustments the couple has had to make are also creating stress, and Barbara has limited her contact with friends in the neighborhood due to Lucille's occasional embarrassing behaviors. Although Ron and Barbara have been unsuccessful in locating local programs and resources for families caring for elders with Alzheimer's in their community, they have joined an online support group. Their search for resources on the Internet seems to have brought the couple closer to each other. They have grown to understand that many other couples who have sustained similar hardships involving family caretaking have found their relationships strengthened as a result. In addition, Ron and Barbara have decided to organize a support group at their local hospital for other families in their community who are caring for family members with Alzheimer's.

For Ron and Barbara, the stressors that are currently affecting the family include the financial burdens and daily tasks associated with caregiving; the stigma of the mental disorder, which has led Barbara to reduce contact with neighbors; and the lack of community resources available to help the family cope. However, as a result of their providing care for Ron's mother, the couple has discovered several family strengths, such as the improved quality of their relationship and their ability to organize a local support group.

Nearly three-fourths of patients released from mental hospitals following an illness episode return to live at home with family members (Shankar & Muthuswamy, 2007). As a result, it is imperative to understand the impact of mental disorders on families. Specifically, mental health professionals must have a reliable and valid understanding of what family members have and do not have at their disposal in terms of skills and resources for coping with and adapting to a member who is mentally ill. Because each individual family is different, it is important to recognize that the circumstance of caregiving may vary considerably as a result of a caregiver's "age, their years of caregiving experience, the stage of illness in the family member, the level of support the caregiver experiences, their stage in the family lifecycle, and their relationship to the care recipient" (Shankar & Muthuswamy, 2007, p. 303).

Scholars have argued that although families who provide care to a mentally ill family member do experience stress, many of these families also exhibit positive aspects and strengths as a result of their coping with mental illness (Doornbos, 1996; Hawley & DeHaan, 1996; Kramer, 1997; Morano, 2003; Walsh, 1996). One such strength is often referred to as *resiliency* in the family literature.

Other positive concepts are also discussed in the literature on caregiving, such as caregiver esteem (the extent to which participating in caregiving enhances an individual's self-esteem), uplifts of caregiving (caregiving events that evoke joy), caregiver satisfaction (benefits an individual receives as a result of his or her efforts at caregiving), caregiver gain (positive return received as a result of caregiving), and meaning through caregiving (finding higher levels of meaning through the caregiving experience) (Hunt, 2003).

In a nationwide study, Marsh et al., (1996) asked 131 family members of patients with serious mental illness to respond to a set of open-ended questions concerning the development of personal, family, and patient resilience. They found that 99.2% of their respondents reported the presence of some form of personal resilience, 87.8% reported family resilience, and 75.6% reported patient resilience. Examples of the resilience dimensions the respondents mentioned included family support/bonding, insight and caregiving competencies, and gratification through advocacy initiatives for constructive changes in the mental health system.

On the other hand, many scholars have focused on understanding the stressors related to family caregiving and mental illness. These stressors typically are described as the "burdens" associated with having a family member suffering from a mental disorder. These burdens have been characterized as being of two types: objective and subjective (Hunt, 2003). Objective burdens are the observable and tangible stressors or costs related to caregiving and mental illness (Jones, 1996), whereas subjective burdens are those based in individuals' perceptions about or appraisal of the illness and/or the caregiving experience (Nijober, Triemstra, Tempelaar, Sanderman, & Van den Bos, 1999).

Objective burdens usually are measured in terms of economic hardships faced by a family, often calculated as the amount of money the illness has cost the family in outright payment or copayment for medical expenses as well as lost wages. Objective burdens also include many other tangible family costs related to the care and treatment of an ill member, such as the costs of providing transportation, food, clothing, and insurance, and other disruptions to the household.

The amount of subjective burden a caregiver experiences is related to his or her perceptions about the family member and the mental illness. Research has shown that caregivers who experience high levels of subjective burden are at greatest risk for negative health outcomes, such as depression (Nijober et al., 1999). One of the most severe subjective burdens that families with mentally ill members experience is the stigma attached to mental disorders; this psychological burden can lead to lower self-esteem levels, reduced social contacts, job loss, and family relationship difficulties (Mittleman, 1985; Wahl & Harman, 1989). In addition, others have studied the health risks associated with caring for a mentally ill family member, revealing that nearly one-third of the sample of caregivers reported feeling stressed, frustrated, bored, easily upset, and mentally exhausted (Curtin & Lilley, 2001).

Community-Based Resources

Therapy

The family therapy profession has greatly influenced the family-oriented perspective regarding major mental disorders. Some of the earliest writings in the field of family therapy blamed families, directly and indirectly, for "causing" mental disorders in family members (Selvini Palazzoli & Prata, 1989). From this perspective, therapeutic interventions were designed to disrupt unhealthy family interactions in order to eliminate symptoms of the disorder.

Today, family-based treatment is considered to be any modality that involves family members as necessary participants in the course of treatment, and the combined use of family treatment and other forms of treatment (e.g., use of medications, cognitive therapy) is increasingly common. In a 10-year review of recent family-based treatments for a range of mental illnesses, Diamond and Josephson (2005) outline several challenges for the future study of family treatment, including the need (a) for empirically based treatment evaluations, (b) to match treatment approaches to respective mental disorders, (c) to implement multisystem-level approaches, (d) to identify which negative family behaviors are common across disorders, (e) to uncover the most effective basic tenets of treatment, and (f) to disseminate successful treatment models into the community.

Psychoeducational Approach

Most family therapists have moved away from positions of blame. Examples of this trend can be found in the work of those who utilize a psychoeducational approach when addressing mental disorders in a family context (McFarlane, 1991). A psychoeducational approach typically includes three elements: education, training in coping skills, and social support. The relative emphasis placed on each component varies, however (Marsh, 1998). Therapists using this approach encourage family members to learn all they can about the mental disorder, to become fully educated about the facts surrounding assessment and treatment. Nonblaming attributions about mental disorders and knowledge about the disorder's symptoms, course, and treatment are thought to be indicators of the effectiveness of psychoeducational programming (see Fristad, Gavazzi, & Mackinaw-Koons, 2003). In contrast to therapeutic approaches, which are designed to eliminate particular disorders, a psychoeducational approach largely seeks to prevent the *return* of a disorder as well as to alleviate the pain and suffering of family members.

Internet-Based Resources

Internet usage continues to expand as family members browse the Web to locate (a) information about mental illness symptoms and diagnoses, (b) agencies and organizations that provide family services in the community, and (c) online support groups and family networks that may be experiencing similar challenges when coping with mental illness (Weinberg, Schmale, Uken, & Wessell, 1995). In fact, online support groups appear to provide many of the same benefits as in-person resources (Bacon, Condon, & Fernsler, 2000) while offering the additional advantages of convenience and expediency (Salem, Bogar, & Reid, 1997). Given the recent estimate that approximately three-quarters of U.S. citizens with diagnosable mental disorders will never receive direct and necessary treatment (Norcross, 2000), Internet-based services may be the only resources available to many in need. It is still imperative, though, that one should receive an evaluation from a licensed professional when diagnosing mental illness.

Social Policy

In recent years, the most significant changes in Americans' social attitudes toward mental illness and in policymaking decisions surrounding mental disorders have come about as the result of the work of grassroots organizations such as the National Alliance for the Mentally Ill (NAMI) and its related affiliates. NAMI has the dual focus of (a) advocating for patient (and family) rights and (b) providing general public education about mental disorders (Howe & Howe, 1987). NAMI has a state organization in every state, along with more than 1,200 local affiliates. The organization also produces a magazine, the *Advocate,* and their Web site offers e-newsletters and a blog in their aggressive efforts to disseminate mental health information.

Recently, NAMI has published a comprehensive report that is "the first comprehensive survey and grading of state adult public mental healthcare Systems conducted in more than 15 years," that "includes tables that indicate each state's overall grade as well as its grade in each of four categories: infrastructure, information access, services, and recovery" (NAMI, 2006). Unfortunately, the report concludes that the overall national grade of a D is of poor quality, and that a higher quality of state mental health systems must include the following 10 characteristics: (1) comprehensive services and support, (2) integrated systems, (3) sufficient funding, (4) consumer- and family-driven systems, (5) safe and respectful treatment environments, (6) accessible information for consumers and family members, (7) access to acute care and long-term care treatment, (8) cultural competence, (9) health promotion and mortality reduction, and (10) an adequate mental health workforce.

Future Directions

In this chapter, we have applied concepts from the ABC-X model of family stress to organize our discussion of issues relevant to families coping with mentally ill family members. In particular, we have reviewed the characteristics of the stressor event (A, mental illness), such as demographic trends and potential causes of mental disorders. We have also outlined community resources (B) as we described current treatment approaches, supportive organizations, and policy initiatives aimed at improving family life. Finally, we have reviewed examples of family perceptions (C) through our discussion of family burdens and family attitudes/behaviors exhibited by family members toward the mentally ill member. Although great strides have been made with regard to these issues since earlier editions of *Families & Change* have been published, scholars today need to put forth a clear and detailed agenda to guide further work in this area.

Based on our analysis of the present situation, we offer the following suggestions concerning future research and intervention efforts. First, scholars need to continue to focus on mental illness prevalence rates in the population—in particular, on how mental illness may have disproportionate impacts on those persons in greatest need of assistance (e.g., children and elders, men in families, socioeconomically disadvantaged families, and ethnic families that still stigmatize the mentally ill). Similarly, it is important for professionals to develop more effective ways to deliver services and assistance to those groups most in need. Second, scholars need to identify strategies that will maximize family participation in community-based programs (Schock & Gavazzi, 2004) as well as techniques that will help researchers and practitioners to evaluate program effectiveness (Diamond & Josephson, 2005). Third, advances in technology will allow researchers to further disentangle the contributions of heredity and family environment to the development and continuance of mental illness. Finally, on a larger scale, we must continue to reduce the stigma attached to mental illness in American society and work to achieve a higher quality of mental health services that are easily available and affordable to all families in need.

Suggested Internet Resources

American Academy of Child and Adolescent Psychiatry: http://www.aacap.org
American Psychological Association: http://www.apa.org
National Alliance for the Mentally Ill: http://www.nami.org
National Institute of Mental Health: http://www.nimh.nih.gov
Office of the Surgeon General (site for the publication *Mental Health: A Report of the Surgeon General*): http://www.surgeongeneral.gov/library/mentalhealth/home.html

Suggested Readings

Costello, J. E., Foley, D. L., & Angold, A. (2005). 10-year research update review: The epidemiology of child and adolescent psychiatric disorders. *Journal of the American Academy of Child and Adolescent Psychiatry, 45,* 8–25.

Diamond, G., & Josephson, A. (2005). Family-based treatment research: A 10-year update. *Journal of the American Academy of Child & Adolescent Psychiatry, 44,* 872–887.

National Alliance on Mental Illness. (2007). *Mental illness: Facts and numbers.* Arlington, VA: National Alliance on Mental Illness.

National Institute of Mental Health. (2008.). *The numbers count: Mental disorders in America.* Retrieved April 8, 2008, from http://www.nimh.nih.gov/health/publications.

U.S. Department of Health and Human Services. (1999). *Mental health: A report of the surgeon general.* Rockville, MD: Author.

References

Alegria, M., Canino, G., Shrout, P. E., Woo, M., Duan, N., Vila, D., Torres, M., Chen, C., & Meng, X. (2008). Prevalence of mental illness in immigrant and nonimmigrant U.S. Latino groups. *American Journal of Psychiatry, 165, 359–369.*

Bacon, E. S., Condon, E. H, & Fernsler, J. I. (2000). Young widows' experience with an Internet self-help group. *Journal of Psychosocial Nursing, 38,* 24–33.

Barrowclough, C., & Hooley, J. M. (2003). Attributions and expressed emotion: A review. *Clinical Psychology Review, 23,* 849–880.

Breslau, J., Aguilar-Gaxiola, S., Kendler, K., Su, M., Williams, D., & Kessler, R. C. (2006). Specifying race-ethnic differences in risk for psychiatric disorder in a USA national sample. *Psychological Medicine, 36,* 57–68.

Brown, G. W., Birley, J. L. T., & Wing, J. K. (1972). Influence of family life on the course of schizophrenic disorders: A replication. *British Journal of Psychiatry, 121,* 241–258.

Button, T. M. M., Lau, J. Y. F., Maughan, B., & Eley, T. C. (2007). Parental punitive discipline, negative life events and gene-environment interplay in the development of externalizing behavior. *Psychological Medicine, 38,* 29–39.

Center for Multicultural Mental Health Research (2008). National Latino and Asian American Study: Background and aims of the NLAAS. Retrieved June 18, 2008, from http://www.multiculturalmentalhealth.org/nlaas.asp.

Centers for Disease Control and Prevention, National Center for Injury Prevention and Control. (2005). Web-Based Injury Statistics Query and Reporting System (WISQARS) [online]. Retrieved March 23, 2008, from http://www.cdc.gov/ncipc/wisqars.

Costello, J. E., Foley, D. L., & Angold, A. (2005). 10-year research update review: The epidemiology of child and adolescent psychiatric disorders. *Journal of the American Academy of Child and Adolescent Psychiatry, 45,* 8–25.

Curtin, T., & Lilley, H. (2001). *Caring across community 2000–2001: Carer education project for carers from culturally and linguistically diverse backgrounds.* Canberra, Australia: Carers Association of Australia.

Diamond, G., & Josephson, A. (2005). Family-based treatment research: A 10-year update. *Journal of the American Academy of Child & Adolescent Psychiatry, 44,* 872–887.

Doornbos, M. M. (1996). The strengths of families coping with serious mental illness. *Archives of Psychiatric Nursing, 10,* 214–220.

Eley, T. C. (2001). Contributions of behavioral genetics research: Quantifying genetic, shared environmental and nonshared environmental influences. In M. W. Vasey & M. R. Dadds (Eds.), *The developmental psychopathology of anxiety* (pp. 45–59). New York: Oxford University Press.

Eley, T. C., Lichtenstein, P., & Moffitt, T. E. (2003). A longitudinal behavioral genetic analysis of the etiology of aggressive and nonaggressive antisocial behavior. *Development and Psychopathology, 15,* 383–402.

Engel, G. L. (1977). The need for a new medical model: A challenge for biomedicine. *Science, 196,* 129–136.

Forehand, R., Biggar, H., & Kotchick, B. A. (1998). Cumulative risk across family stressors: Short- and long-term effects for adolescents. *Journal of Abnormal Child Psychology, 26,* 119–128.

Fredman, S. J., Baucom, D. H., Miklowitz, D. J., & Stanton, S. E. (2008). Observed emotional involvement and overinvolvement in families of patients with bipolar disorder. *Journal of Family Psychology, 22,* 71–79.

Friedman, R. M. (1996). *Prevalence of serious emotional disturbance in children and adolescents.* Unpublished manuscript, Center for Mental Health Services, Washington, DC.

Fristad, M. A., Gavazzi, S. M., & Mackinaw-Koons, B. (2003). Family psychoeducation: An adjunctive intervention for children with early onset bipolar disorder. *Biological Psychiatry, 53,* 1000–1008

Fristad, M. A., Gavazzi, S. M., & Soldano, K. W. (1999). Naming the enemy: Learning to differentiate mood disorder "symptoms" from the "self" that experiences them. *Journal of Family Psychotherapy, 10,* 81–88.

Gavazzi, S. M., Fristad, M. A., & Law, J. C. (1997). The Understanding Mood Disorders Questionnaire. *Psychological Reports, 81,* 172–174.

Gregory, A. M., & Eley, T. C. (2007). Genetic influences on anxiety in children: What we've learned and where we're heading. *Clinical Child and Family Psychology, 10,* 199–212.

Halloran, E. C., Ross, G. J., & Carey, M. P. (2002). The relationship of adolescent personality and family environment to psychiatric diagnosis. *Child Psychiatry & Human Development, 32,* 201–216.

Hawley, D. R., & DeHaan, L. (1996). Toward a definition of family resilience: Integrating life-span and family perspectives. *Family Process, 35,* 283–298.

Howe, C. W., & Howe, J. W. (1987), The National Alliance for the Mentally Ill: History and ideology. In A. B. Hatfield (Ed.), *Families of the mentally ill: Meeting the challenges* (pp. 23–42). San Francisco: Jossey-Bass.

Hunt, C. K. (2003). Concepts in caregiver research. *Journal of Nursing Scholarship, 35,* 27–33.

Hybels, C. F., & Blazer, D. G. (2003). Epidemiology of late-life mental disorders. *Clinics in Geriatric Medicine, 19, 663–696.*

Jaffee, S. R. (2007). Gene-environment correlations: A review of the evidence and implications for prevention of mental illness. *Molecular Psychiatry, 12,* 432–442.

Jones, S. (1996). The association between objective and subjective caregiver burden. *Archives of Psychiatric Nursing, 10,* 77–84.

Kahng, S. K., Oyserman, D., Bybee, D., & Mowbray, C. (2008). Mothers with serious mental illness: When symptoms decline does parenting improve? *Journal of Family Psychology, 22,* 162–166.

Kessler, R. C., Chiu, W. T., Demler, O., & Walters, E. E. (2005), Prevalence, severity, and comorbidity of 12-month *DSM-IV* disorders in the national comorbidity survey replication. *Archives of General Psychiatry, 62,* 617–709.

Kessler, R. C., McGonagle, K. A., Zhao, S., Nelson, C. B., Hughes, M., Eshleman, S., et al. (1994). Lifetime and 12-month prevalence of *DSM-III-R* psychiatric disorders in the United States. *Archives of General Psychiatry, 51,* 8–19.

Kessler, R. C., & Merikangas, K. R. (2004). The national comorbidity survey replication (NCS-R): Background and aims. *International Journal of Methods in Psychiatric Research, 13,* 93–121.

Kochanek, K. D., Murphy, S. L., & Anderson, R. N., & Scott, C. (2004). Deaths: Final data for 2002. *National Vital Statistics Report, 12,* 1–115.

Kramer, B. J. (1997). Gain in the caregiver experience: Where are we? What next? *Gerontologist, 37,* 218–232.

Kupfer, D. J., First, M. B., & Regier, D. A. (Eds.). (2002). *A research agenda for* DSM-V. Washington, DC: American Psychiatric Association.

Larsson, H., Viding, E., & Plomin, R. (2008). Callous-unemotional traits and anti-social behavior: Genetic, environmental, and early parenting characteristics. *Criminal Justice and Behavior, 35,* 197–211.

Lau, J. Y. F., & Eley, T. C. (2008). Disentangling gene-environment correlations and interactions on adolescent depressive symptoms. *The Journal of Child Psychology and Psychiatry, 49,* 142–150.

Lopez, S. R., Nelson, K. A., Snyder, K. S., & Minz, J. (1999). Attributions and affective reactions of family members and course of schizophrenia. *Journal of Abnormal Psychology, 108,* 307–314.

Marsh, D. T. (1998). *Serious mental illness and the family: The practitioner's guide.* New York: John Wiley.

Marsh, D. T., Lefley, H. P., Evans-Rhodes, D., Ansell, V. I., Doerzbacher, B. M., LaBarbera, L., et al. (1996). The family experience of mental illness: Evidence for resilience. *Psychiatric Rehabilitation Journal, 20,* 3–12.

Mash, E. J., & Barkley, R. A. (Eds.). (1996). *Child psychopathology.* New York: Guilford.

Mash, E, J., & Dozois, D. J. (1996). Child psychopathology: A developmental systems perspective. In E. J. Mash & R. A. Barkley (Eds.), *Child psychopathology* (pp. 3–63). New York: Guilford.

McFarlane, W. R. (1991). Family psychoeducational treatment. In A. S. Gurman & D. P. Kniskern (Eds.), *Handbook of family therapy* (Vol. 2, pp. 363–395). New York: Brunner/Mazel.

McMahon, R. J., & Estes, A. M. (1997). Conduct problems. In E. J. Mash & L. G. Terdal (Eds.), *Assessment of childhood disorders* (3rd ed., pp. 130–193). New York: Guilford.

Miklowitz, D. J. (2007). The role of the family in the course and treatment of bipolar disorder. *Association for Psychological Science, 16,* 192–196.

Minino, A. M., Arias, E., Kochanek, K. D., Murphy, S. L., & Smith, B. L. (2002). Deaths: Final data for 2000. Hyattsville, MD: National Center for Health Statistics.

Mittleman, G. (1985). First person account: The pain of parenthood of the mentally ill. *Schizophrenia Bulletin, 11,* 300–303.

Morano, C. (2003). Appraisal and coping: Moderators or mediators of stress in Alzheimer's disease caregivers? *Social Work Research, 27,* 116–128.

Morley, K. I., Hall, W. D., & Carter, L. (2004). Genetic screening for susceptibility to depression: Can we and should we? *Australian and New Zealand Journal of Psychiatry, 38,* 73–80.

Narrow, W. E. (1998). *One-year prevalence of depressive disorders among adults 18 and over in the U.S.: NIMH ECA prospective data.* Unpublished table.

National Alliance on Mental Illness. (2006). *Grading the states: A report on America's health care system for serious mental illness,* Arlington, VA: National Alliance on Mental Illness.

National Alliance on Mental Illness. (2007). *Mental illness: Facts and numbers.* Arlington, VA: National Alliance on Mental Illness.

National Institute of Mental Health. (1991). *Implementation of the national plan for research on child and adolescent mental disorders* (Publication No. PA-91-46). Washington, DC: U.S. Department of Health and Human Services.

National Institute of Mental Health. (2008.). *The numbers count: Mental disorders in America.* Retrieved April 8, 2008, from http://www.nimh.nih.gov/health/publications.

National Institute on Aging. (2005). *Progress report on Alzheimer's disease 2004–2005* (NIH Publication No. 05-5724). Bethesda, MD: National Institute on Aging.

Nijober, C., Triemstra, M., Tempelaar, R., Sanderman, R., & Van den Bos, G. (1999). Determinants of caregiving experiences and mental health of partners of cancer patients. *Cancer, 86,* 577–588.

Norcross, J. C. (2000). Here comes the self-help revolution in mental health, *Psychotherapy, 37,* 370–377.

Office of Applied Studies. (2007). *Results from the 2006 National Survey on Drug Use and Health: National findings* (DHHS Publication No. SMA 07-4293, NSDUH Series H-32). Rockville, MD: Substance Abuse and Mental Health Services.

Plomin, R., DeFries, J. C., Craig, I. W., & McGuffin, P. (2003). Behavioral genomics. In R. Plomin & J. C. DeFries (Eds.), *Behavioral genetics in the postgenomic era* (pp. 531–540). Washington, DC: American Psychological Association.

Preisig, M. (2006). Genetics of bipolar disorder: A review. *Schweizer Archiv fur Neurologie und Psychiatrie, 157,* 366–377.

Pressman, L. J., Loo, S. K., & Carpenter, E. M. (2006). Relationship of family environment and parental psychiatric diagnosis to impairment in ADHD. *Journal of the American Academy of Child & Adolescent Psychiatry, 45,* 346–354.

Puig-Antich, J., Kaufman, J., Ryan, N. D., Williamson, D. E., Dahl, R. E., Lukens, E., et al. (1993). The psychosocial functioning and family environment of depressed adolescents. *Journal of the American Academy of Child and Adolescent Psychiatry, 32,* 244–253.

Regier, D, A., Boyd, J. H., Burke, J. D., Jr., Rae, D. S., Myers, J. K., Kramer, M., et al. (1988). One month prevalence of mental disorders in the United States. *Archives of General Psychiatry, 45,* 977–986.

Regier, D. A., Burke, J. D., Jr., & Burke, K. C. (1990). Comorbidity of affective and anxiety disorders in the NIMH Epidemiologic Catchment Area Program. In J. D. Maser & C. R. Cloninger (Eds.), *Comorbidity of mood and anxiety disorders* (pp. 113–122). Washington, DC: American Psychiatric Press.

Reuter, M. A., Scaramella, L., Wallace, L. E., & Conger, R. D. (1999). First onset of depressive or anxiety disorders predicted by the longitudinal course of internalizing symptoms and parent-adolescent disagreements. *Archives of General Psychiatry, 56,* 726–732.

Roberts, R. E., Attkisson, C. C., & Rosenblatt, A. (1998). Prevalence of psychopathology among children and adolescents. *American Journal of Psychiatry, 155,* 715–725.

Rowe, C. L., & Liddle, H. A. (2003). Substance abuse. *Journal of Marital & Family Therapy, 29,* 97–120.

Salem, D. A., Bogar, G. A., & Reid, C. (1997). Mutual help goes on-line. *Journal of Community Psychology, 25,* 189–207.

Schock, A. M., & Gavazzi, S. M. (2004). A multimethod study of father participation in family-based programming. In R. D. Day & M. E. Lamb (Eds.), *Conceptualizing and measuring father involvement* (pp. 149–184). Mahwah, NJ: Lawrence Erlbaum.

Selvini Palazzoli, M., & Prata, G. (1989). *Family games: General models of psychotic processes in the family.* New York: W. W. Norton.

Shankar, J., & Muthuswamy, S. S. (2007). Support needs of family caregivers of people who experience mental illness and the role of mental health services. *Families in Society: The Journal of Contemporary Social Services, 88,* 302–310.

Sheeber, L., Hops, H., Alpert, A., Davis, B., & Andrews, J. (1997). Family support and conflict: Prospective relations to adolescent depression. *Journal of Abnormal Child Psychology, 25,* 333–344.

Sheeber, L., Hops, H., & Davis, B. (2001). Family processes in adolescent depression. *Clinical Child and Family Psychology Review, 4,* 19–35.

U.S. Department of Health and Human Services. (1999). *Mental health: A report of the surgeon general.* Rockville, MD: Author.

Vaughn, C. E., & Leff, J. P. (1976). The measurement of expressed emotion in the families of psychiatric patients. *British Journal of Social and Clinical Psychology, 15,* 157–165.

Wahl, O. F., & Harman, C. R. (1989). Family views of stigma. *Schizophrenia Bulletin, 15,* 131–139.

Walsh, F. (1996). The concept of family resilience: Crisis and challenge. *Family Process, 35,* 261–281.

Wang, P. S., Lane, M., & Olfson, M. (2005). Twelve-month use of mental health services in the United States: Results from the national comorbidity survey replication. *Archives of General Psychiatry, 62,* 629–640.

Weinberg, N., Schmale, J. D., Uken, J., & Wessell, K. (1995). Computer-mediated support groups. *Social Work With Groups, 17,* 43–54.

Weissman, M. M., Bland, R. G, Canino, G. J., Greenwald, S., Hwu, H. G., Joyce, P. R., et al. (1999). Prevalence of suicide ideation and suicide attempts in nine countries. *Psychological Medicine, 29,* 9–17.

Yeargin-Allsopp, M., Rice, C., Karapurkar, T., Doemberg, N., Boyle, C., & Murphy, C. (2003). Prevalence of autism in a U.S. metropolitan area. *Journal of the American Medical Association, 289,* 49–55.

Zahn-Waxler, C., Klimes-Dougan, B., & Slattery, M. J. (2000). Internalizing problems of childhood and adolescence: Prospects, pitfalls, and progress in understanding the development of anxiety and depression. *Development and Psychopathology, 12,* 443–466.

PART **III**

Family Stressors, Substance Abuse, Family Violence, and Trauma

CHAPTER 6

Families Coping with Alcohol and Substance Abuse

Judith Fischer, Kevin P. Lyness, and Rachel Engler

A prominent approach to the study of alcohol and families involves a biopsychosocial focus (Zucker, Boyd, & Howard, 1994). This perspective organizes the prediction of pathological alcohol involvement (and, by extension, more general substance abuse) through consideration of biological contributions, psychological factors, and social influences. Conjoining this model with the family stress and coping model (see McKenry & Price, 2005) acknowledges the contribution of these biopsychosocial factors at each juncture: stressor, resource, perception, coping, and managing. We pay particular attention to the mediating and moderating effects that intervene between two variables, such as those that occur when associations between parent drinking and offspring drinking are worked through (mediated) or altered (moderated) by other variables.

Some definitions are in order. *Substance use,* as we use the term in this chapter, includes both experimental and regular use. *Substance misuse* refers to the excessive consumption of a substance. *Substance abuse* and *substance dependence* are clinical designations involving serious and persistent problems with substances. The major distinction between abuse and dependence is in the level of use; that is, substance dependence includes spending a great deal of time using, unsuccessful attempts to control the substance use, and, for some, the presence of tolerance and withdrawal. If tolerance and withdrawal are present, the diagnosis is substance dependence with physiological dependence (American Psychiatric Association, 2000). Designations used in this chapter reflect those chosen by the authors cited.

In organizing the following literature review, we take a family developmental approach. Timing is an important part of the stress and coping model. Stressors may be time limited, but they may also extend over long periods. Particular situations may not be considered stressors at one developmental period but may be stressors at another. For example, Biederman, Faraone, Monuteaux, and Feighner (2000) found that *childhood* exposure to parental substance use disorders conferred a twofold risk on offspring, but *adolescent* exposure was associated with a threefold risk for the emergence of substance use disorders. Perceptions, resources, and problem solving may be greater or lesser depending on individual and family development. Coping that is effective in the short term may moderate the long-term impacts of a stressor or lead to a pileup of stressors over time. In any given family, the substance misuser may be the parents, the offspring, or both. Treatments vary depending on whether the child in the family or the adult is the presenting patient. And when intervening with an alcoholic parent, the ages of the children in the family need to be taken into account (Kelley & Fals-Stewart, 2008).

This review covers four topics within the context of families: (1) children and their parents coping with the challenges posed by substances, (2) adolescents who use and abuse substances, (3) bidirectional effects, and (4) intervention strategies. Throughout the chapter we put the emphasis on both the family stresses involved and the search for explanations of resilience in these situations of families coping with substance abuse. The chapter concludes with an illustrative vignette. Given limitations of space, we are unable to extend our discussion in this chapter beyond the contexts of families with children and adolescents. Information on other important topics related to families and substance misuse may be found in Arendt and Farkas (2007) for fetal alcohol spectrum disorder, Leonard and Eiden (2007) for adult couples, and Stelle and Scott (2007) for elders in families.

Children and Substance Abuse Problems

Most research on childhood substance abuse has focused on 8- to 11-year-olds. A number of scholars have documented the fact that children this young are using and even abusing substances (Griffin, Botvin, Epstein, Doyle, & Diaz, 2000; Loveland-Cherry, Leech, Laetz, & Dielman, 1996; McDermott, Clark-Alexander, Westhoff, & Eaton, 1999). According to McDermott et al. (1999), 18% of fifth graders may be described as active drinkers, having consumed alcohol in the previous 30 days. In 2007, almost 40% of eighth graders had consumed more than a few sips of alcohol (Johnston, O'Malley, Bachman, & Schulenberg, 2008).

Child Characteristics

Research on substance abuse prior to adolescence tends to focus on childhood predictors of *later* adolescent and adult use and abuse (cf., Zucker, 2008) rather than correlates of *actual* substance use in childhood. Early alcohol initiation is strongly predicted by the presence of conduct disorders (Sartor, Lynskey, Heath, Jacob, & True, 2006). A considerable body of literature suggests that behavioral undercontrol or behavioral disinhibition (failure to inhibit behavioral impulses) in childhood, especially among males, is an important precursor of later adolescent problems with substance use and abuse (Dubow, Boxer, & Huesmann, 2008; Zuclcer, 2008).

Cognitions (expectancies, beliefs, and values) about alcohol use appear in children as young as 3 to 6 years old (Zucker, Fitzgerald, Refior, Pallas, & Ellis, 2000), particularly among children in alcoholic families. Dunn and Goldman (1996) found that children 8 to 11 years old reported alcohol expectancies that were similar to those reported by adults. Children's favorable attitudes toward alcohol and intentions to use alcohol at age 10 are associated with a higher probability of drug abuse and dependency at age 21 (Guo, Hawkins, Hill, & Abbott, 2001). Examining young children's cognitions and behaviors is important to understanding childhood and later substance use and misuse. McDermott et al. (1999) have suggested that emphasizing health concerns as a reason not to use alcohol is likely to be ineffective with children, but it may be useful to correct children's misconceptions about alcohol-related norms and risks before they begin active use. Strong parental antialcohol norms have promoted more negative alcohol-related cognitions among seventh and eighth graders.

The child characteristics that scholars have found to be related to *childhood* substance use include a mix of behavioral and cognitive variables: less competence (Jackson, Henriksen, & Dickinson, 1997), more tolerance to deviance, more deviant self-image, more susceptibility to peer pressure, and greater reported peer use (Loveland-Cherry et al., 1996), In addition, childhood factors related to adolescent or young adult use include IQ and educational attainment (Dubow et al., 2008), children (age 10) living in a neighborhood with more trouble-making youth, antisocial friends, frequent alcohol use by best friends, frequent contact with antisocial friends, and high levels of bonding with antisocial friends (Guo et al., 2001). Childhood antisocial behavior is a recurring and important correlate of later use (Dubow et al., 2008; Fitzgerald, Puttler, Refior, & Zucker, 2007; Leonard & Eiden, 2007).

Parent Factors

Jacob and Johnson (1997) conceptualize parenting influence on children as alcohol-specific effects and non-alcohol-specific effects. *Alcohol-specific effects* involve the behaviors of the parents with respect to alcohol and how these parental behaviors are related to the child's behavior and cognition. Frequently studied are the effects of being a child of an alcoholic (COA). Weinberg, Dielman, Mandell, and Shope (1994) found that fifth and sixth graders had higher odds of current alcohol misuse and heavy alcohol use when there was greater mother or father drinking levels, a substance-specific influence. In general, parents' substance-specific influences on preadolescents have predictive utility for later adolescent and adult use and abuse (Dishion, Capaldi, & Yoerger, 1999). *Non-alcohol-specific effects* reflect the general aspects of the family environment that are related to children's deviant behavior, cognition, and substance use. Parenting practices and behaviors such as supervision, discipline, and nurturance of children; communication with children; and parental divorce and remarriage reflect the operation of non-substance-specific influences as do having clear family rules and monitoring (Guo et al., 2001).

Non-substance-specific factors are studied as operating alone, together with alcohol-specific factors, and as part of feedback loops. The non-substance-specific variables of low income, parental aggression, and low marital satisfaction have been found to be important correlates of child adjustment (Fals-Stewart, Kelley, Cooke, & Golden, 2003). In turn, childhood maladjustment is an important predictor of greater harmful drinking at age 42 (24% more) (Maggs, Patrick, & Feinstein, 2008). The combination of parental alcoholism (alcohol-specific) with parental antisocial behavior (non-alcohol-specific) has been shown to predict child externalizing behavior, itself a predictor of more harmful drinking as an adult (Fals-Stewart et al., 2003; Fitzgerald et al., 2007; Maggs et al., 2008). A number of studies have provided evidence that parent reactions to children's difficult behaviors are followed by additional child maladaptation (Dishion et al., 1999; Wong, Zucker, Puttler, & Fitzgerald, 1999). As well, parental divorce has been shown to be a lesser risk factor for preadolescents than for adolescents (Needle, Su, & Doherty, 1990).

In sum, children with conduct problems, particularly in stressful homes, are at high risk for later substance use problems. Parenting responses that emphasize increased monitoring may make child externalizing problems worse. Clearly, help for parents in dealing with difficult children is warranted. In addition, the problems seem to extend beyond parenting to parents' own issues with substances, their relationships with each other, and their relationships with society.

Adolescents and Youth and Substance Abuse Problems

In the United States, the period of adolescence, roughly ages 13 to 19, is characterized by dramatic increases in substance use. The period of youth or young adulthood, up to age 25, is generally the time during which substance use and abuse peak (National Institute on Alcohol Abuse and Alcoholism, 2000). Monitoring the Future's annual surveys of 50,000 students in the 8th, 10th, and 12th grades document the latest figures. "Nearly three quarters of students (72%) have consumed alcohol (more than just a few sips) by the end of high school. ... In fact, more than half (55%) of the 12th graders and nearly a fifth (18%) of the 8th graders in 2007 report having been drunk at least once in their life" (Johnston et al., 2008, p. 41).

From the late 1990s to 2007, substance use among adolescents generally declined. Despite this decline, however, data from the Monitoring the Future surveys show large shifts in behavior from those in the eighth grade to those in the twelfth grade. Scholars' attempts to account for these age-related changes, and to explain the use of substances in adolescence, have generated a substantial body of literature in which certain themes stand out. Researchers have looked at (a) adolescent characteristics, such as expectancies, achievements, moods, behaviors, stressors, personality, roles, and clinical diagnoses, as well as demographics of gender, ethnicity, school, and neighborhood; (b) substance-specific family characteristics, such as parent substance use and alcohol-specific parenting practices; and (c) non-substance-specific influences such as parenting styles, family dysfunction, family stressors, family socioeconomic status, and parent-adolescent communication. It should be noted that most of the research documents factors that are involved in greater risk. However, research on moderating variables highlights areas where there may be factors involved in resilience (doing well despite adversity).

Fitting primarily within the resources component of the stress and coping model, four important models link family history of alcoholism to adolescent pathological alcohol involvement: (1) positive affect regulation (produce positive feelings), (2) deviance proneness (demonstrate deficient socialization of which alcohol use is a part), (3) negative affect regulation (relieve negative emotions), and (4) pharmacological vulnerability (have physical sensitivity to the effects of alcohol) (Sher, Grekin, & Williams, 2005). In their research on moderators, scholars have sought to specify for whom and under what conditions associations hold between and among variables (Fischer & Wampler, 1994; Jacob & Johnson, 1997).

Adolescent Characteristics

Just as research has identified *childhood* behavioral disinhibition as an important factor in the prediction of early and later onset of substance use, there is a similar picture of the influence of *adolescent* behavioral disinhibition (Zucker, 2008). The relationship between high sensation seeking/impulsivity and substance use has been found to be moderated by gender, with a stronger association for males than for females (Baker & Yardley, 2002). The authors suggested that societal pressures and expectations placed upon females may help to explain this finding; such expectations may be protective for young women.

Researchers have examined problems related to both delinquency and substance use (deviance proneness) in adolescents over time, with mixed results (Mason & Windle, 2002). Mason and Windle found that early delinquency appeared to have enduring consequences in adolescence for boys, whereas Merline, Jager, and Schulenberg (2008) reported that later alcohol use disorders among women were related to earlier theft and property damage behaviors. Among girls, apparent links between drug use and delinquency were based on the shared influences of third variables such as conduct problems (Mason & Windle, 2002).

Evidence for a negative emotions or internalizing pathway is mixed. For example, in the research of Englund, Egeland, Olivia, & Collins (2008), children with internalizing problems at age 7 reported less alcohol use in adulthood; however, at age 11, children with internalizing problems reported more alcohol use during young and middle adulthood for both genders and, for males, more alcohol use during adolescence. Parenting is related to offspring depression that is, in turn, related to alcohol abuse in college men and women (Patock-Peckham & Morgan-Lopez, 2007).

Adolescent expectancies about the effects of substances are factors in substance use and misuse (Chen, Grube, & Madden, 1994). Research has found early expectancies to be predictive of later heavy drinking in boys but not in girls (Griffin et al., 2000). Neither mediating nor moderating effects of this association are well known. However, Barnow, Schuckit, and Lucht's (2002) research on German adolescents pulled together some of these threads. In their sample, adolescents with *alcohol problems* had more behavioral problems, more perceived parental rejection, less parental warmth, and more association with substance-using peers than did adolescents without alcohol problems. *Alcoholic* adolescents demonstrated all of these characteristics plus aggression/delinquency. Thus, adolescents lacking the self-control resource were more vulnerable to alcoholism. A review of general coping supports these conclusions: (1) Adolescent coping is enhanced by warm, close relationships with parents, and (2) self-regulation plays an important role in adolescent coping (see Aldwin, 2007).

Apart from adolescent delinquency, Windle (2000) found that a number of factors operated directly and indirectly on adolescent substance use over time. Stressful life events were related to drinking to cope and directly to adolescent alcohol problems. High activity levels and sociability of the adolescent were linked to substance use by peers and were thereby indirectly related to adolescent substance use and problems with alcohol. Adolescent self-control forms a link between parental monitoring and adolescent substance use (Chapple, Hope, & Whiteford, 2005). Regretfully, there is a reduced likelihood that stressed parents or those who themselves engage in deviant behavior will encourage or teach their children self-control.

Age of drinking onset in adolescence is a strong predictor of later alcohol abuse and disorder (Tyler, Stone, & Bersani, 2006); adolescents who began drinking at 12 years or younger were at increased risk for developing later abuse and dependence compared with adolescents who held off until age 16 or older. Males reported drinking before age 12 at a rate almost three times that of females. Other factors influencing early alcohol initiation are conduct disorders, externalizing disorders, attention-deficit/hyperactivity disorder (ADHD), parental alcohol dependence, and being male (Sartor et al., 2006). Associations between early drinking status and later problem behaviors remain even after controls are employed for a number of demographic and family variables (Ellickson, Tucker, & Klein, 2003). Findings such as these suggest that early drinking is an important risk in and of itself for later problems with alcohol.

Substance-Specific Parenting Factors

Many researchers have documented associations between parental drinking and adolescent drinking (Sher et al., 2005). Involved in these associations are all the elements of the stress and coping model. Not only is there greater risk for alcohol problems among children of alcoholics (COAs) and earlier initiation of drinking, but such children also show telescoped trajectories; that is, the interval from first using alcohol to the development of alcohol disorders is shorter (Hussong, Bauer, & Chassin, 2008).

Peak age for first signs of an alcohol disorder is age 18. Considering the important transitions that accompany this age period (graduating high school, employment, romantic involvements), experiencing an alcohol disorder could disrupt the timing and success of these events and relationships. Fischer and colleagues have documented pathways from alcohol misuse of parents both to young adults' difficulties with particular romantic relationships (e.g., Fischer et al., 2005) and to the initiation and maintenance of dating relationships in general (Fischer, Wiersma, Forthun, Pidcock, & Dowd, 2007).

Researchers have frequently found that a family history of alcoholism is an important element in adolescent development of substance use problems. Children are thought to imitate behaviors modeled by their parents, but such an effect has failed to appear in studies of adopted children (Sher et al., 2005), and in an offspring-of-twin research design, such effects were modest at best (Slutske et al., 2008). Although sibling substance use is also a significant predictor of adolescent substance use (Vakalahi, 2002), in line with the results of parent drinking, it may be that the sibling effect is less about modeling and more about social influence and availability. As Pandina and Johnson (1990) cautioned, a family history of alcoholism does not inevitably produce an offspring with alcohol abuse or other problems, and a family without alcoholism does not necessarily protect offspring from developing substance use problems. Furthermore, siblings from the same family may be concordant or discordant for alcohol use. Fischer and Wiersma (2008) reported that 18% of siblings were different in alcohol use, primarily in adolescence, and that this difference appeared to reflect a niche-seeking strategy when there was more parental drinking.

If parental use of alcohol is associated with adolescent use, then parental recovery from alcoholism or cessation of alcohol-related problems should deflect a reduction in family stress and an alteration in children's expectancies and alcohol-related behaviors. However, researchers have found mixed outcomes in the offspring of recovering alcoholics (e.g., Pidcock & Fischer, 1998). Family recovery is a stressful endeavor, and attention needs to be given to children when other family members go through recovery (Lewis & Allen-Byrd, 2007).

Mediators of associations between parental substance abuse and adolescent behavior identify mechanisms and processes in the transmission of adolescent alcoholism. Parenting styles represent one such mediator. Monitoring and supervision constitute one dimension of parenting style; warmth and support constitute another. When parents abuse substances, their ability to provide appropriate levels of monitoring and support may be compromised, thereby providing a mediating pathway to adolescent substance use and abuse (Barnes, Reifman, Farrell, & Dintcheff, 2000). Furthermore, because parents are regarded as sources of information for children, it is important to consider what parents tell their children about substance use and abuse (i.e., alcohol-specific parenting practices). Surveys indicate that parents do talk to their seventh- through twelfth-grade children about drugs, but their levels of communication vary for different substances: 70% discuss cigarettes, 66% discuss alcohol, and 53% discuss marijuana "a lot," but the proportion of parents who say they discuss Ecstasy "a lot" drops to just 24% ("Survey Finds," 2003). In addition, the effectiveness of parental communication about substance use varies. Although Chassin, Presson, Todd, Rose, and Sherman (1998) found that mothers' smoking-specific conversations with their adolescents were associated with lowered risk of adolescent smoking, Ennett, Bauman, Foshee, Pemberton, and Hicks (2001) indicated that for adolescents who were already using substances, parent-child communication on the topic actually made the situation worse. These researchers recommend that parents begin communicating with their children about substance use before the children initiate use.

Alcohol-specific parenting strategies could be a mechanism through which monitoring and other parenting practices work. Parental provision of alcohol and access to alcohol in the home increases the likelihood that adolescents will express greater intent to use as well as greater actual alcohol use (Komro, Maldonado-Molina, Tobler, Bonds, & Muller, 2007). Nonetheless, the findings have not been consistent from study to study, suggesting the presence of moderating effects.

Gender of the offspring and gender of the drinking parent are important moderators. Consistently, associations of predictors with drinking outcomes are stronger and more stable for males compared to females (Merline et al., 2008; Zucker, 2008). Greater male vulnerability may be genetic (Zucker, 2008). Maternal drinking is an often overlooked factor in offspring drinking but has been documented as playing an important role (Englund et al., 2008; White, Johnson, & Buyske, 2000). Tyler et al. (2006) attribute maternal influences to mothers' stronger role in child rearing.

Other moderating factors that have been found to alter the association between parental drinking and offspring outcomes include expectations, peer orientations, ethnicity, family functioning, family structure, family cohesion, parental support, personality of the offspring, and family roles of the offspring (Fischer & Lyness, 2005). However, buffering effects by one parent of the negative effects of the other parent's drinking has not been one of the moderators (Curran & Chassin, 1996), and parental support loses its effectiveness among adolescents with higher levels of undercontrol (King & Chassin, 2004). With respect to resilience, Fischer and Wampler (1994) investigated the buffering effects of personality and family roles (hero, mascot, scapegoat/lost child) on the associations between offspring alcohol misuse and both family history of addictions and family dysfunction. They found that personality was a moderator of the association of family addictions with offspring drinking for both males and females, but family roles such as hero buffered offspring drinking only with respect to family dysfunction. Other research points to the importance of avoiding the role of parentified child in families with parental alcohol misuse. Such avoidance was related to higher self-concept, an indication of more resilience in these particular 10- to 18-year-old children (Godsall, Jurkovic, Emshoff, Anderson, & Stanwyck, 2004). The kind of coping a child engages in, such as active coping, is important to adjustment (Smith et al., 2006); unfortunately, parental alcoholism is more likely to lead to children using avoidant coping, a tactic associated with poorer adjustment. Andrews, Hops, and Duncan (1997) concluded that although a good parent-child relationship is important to positive child adjustment, it may not always be protective in situations in which parents use substances.

Non-Substance-Specific Parenting Factors

Supervision and support are important parenting variables that operate regardless of parental substance use or abuse to influence adolescent outcomes. For example, based on their research on 9- to 17-year-olds, Coombs and Landsverk (1988) suggest that "for a youngster to remain free from substances, it is advantageous if parents set clear behavioral limits and maintain interpersonally satisfying relationships with their children" (p. 480). Among other benefits, these parenting practices may reduce stress, increase resources, and encourage active coping. Abstaining youth have parents who do not use punishment to maintain control but instead clarify appropriate behavior and reinforce that behavior; such parents also have warm relationships with their children. Increased family involvement, support, and bonding during adolescence are protective factors that predict less problem alcohol use in adulthood (Galaif, Stein, Newcomb, & Bernstein, 2001; Vakalahi, 2002). Maternal hostility toward their 24- to 42-month-old children predicted age 19 alcohol use for females although not for males (Englund et al., 2008). On the Other hand, White et al. (2000) failed to find an association of parental warmth/hostility in the adolescent period with later offspring adult drinking. The timing of the parenting behavior could be a factor in these differing findings.

Adolescent demands for autonomy may create parent-child stressors and disrupted parenting. Dishion and McMahon (1998) provide the following definition of parental monitoring: "[It] includes both structuring the child's home, school, and community environments, and tracing the child's behavior in those environments. ... [It] should be developmentally, contextually, and culturally appropriate" (p. 66). Good intentions are necessary but not sufficient to bring about successful parental monitoring practices. In a sample of high-risk adolescents, parental monitoring was a protective factor against alcohol and other drug use. However, for this protection to emerge, adolescents had to report that their parents *always* monitored them rather than just *sometimes* (Shillington at al., 2005).

Some scholars have theorized that single-parent family structure creates distress in adolescents that may lead to greater affect and mood alteration through substance use. In addition, the lower levels of supervision and availability of parents in single-parent households may also lead to greater substance experimentation and abuse. Reflecting the stress approach, Jeynes's (2001) research of nationally representative U.S. 12th graders found that adolescents who had experienced more recent parental divorce drank more alcohol. But other variables, including parent unavailability, family quality, peer acceptance/self-esteem, and deviant peer involvement, serve as mediators between parental divorce and adolescent alcohol use (Curry, Fischer, Reifman, & Harris, 2004). In addition to the absence of the nonresident father, factors such as weak attachment and limited monitoring are also associated with adolescent alcohol use (Jones & Benda, 2004). The association between single-parent homes and alcohol use may hold only during adolescence (Merline et al., 2008). Divorce is not the only family structure risk factor in that adolescents who transition from a single-parent family to a stepfamily increase their risk of initiating alcohol use (Kirby, 2006). There is some support, however, for the idea that instead of family structure, parent and peer relationships are better at explaining adolescent alcohol consumption (Crawford & Novak, 2008).

Regardless of intactness of family of origin, parental support is an important correlate of adolescent alcohol use, but the association is also mediated by other factors, such as religiosity, peer alcohol use, and school grades (Mason & Windle, 2002). Furthermore, students who received good grades elicited greater parental support. According to Bogenschneider, Wu, and Raffaelli (1998), mothers' responsiveness acted indirectly on adolescent alcohol use by helping to weaken adolescents' orientation to peers. Maternal depression, a condition that could reduce maternal support, contributed to adolescent and young adult problem drinking (Alati et al., 2005).

Wills and Cleary (1996) suggested that parent support buffers adolescent substance use by reducing the effects of risk factors and increasing the effects of protective factors. Family support moderates the effects of peers on adolescent substance use (Frauenglass, Routh, Pantin, & Mason, 1997). In a study of Hispanic eighth graders, Frauenglass et al. (1997) found that parent support was protective against the effects of peer modeling on tobacco and marijuana use. The combination of supervision and acceptance, an *authoritative* parenting style, has been identified as a particularly important factor, both concurrently and longitudinally, in the reduced use of substances (Adalbjarnardottir & Hafsteinsson, 2001). Among older adolescents, more indulgent and less controlling parents have been found to be related to substance abuse more often than have authoritative parents. Tucker, Ellickson, and Klein (2008) indicated that adolescents living in permissive homes were nine times more likely to drink heavily in the 9th grade and three times more likely to drink heavily in the 11th grade compared with children from nonpermissive homes. In general, the more the parent used alcohol, the more permissive were the alcohol rules for the adolescent.

The more permissive the alcohol rules, the more the adolescent drank. Despite living in a permissive home environment, there were factors predicting less heavy drinking for these adolescents: social influences, alcohol beliefs, and resistance self-efficacy (Tucker et al., 2008).

In addition to parenting style, the quality of parent-child communication is important. Kafka and London (1991) established the value of an adolescent's having at least one parent with whom the adolescent has "open" communication. They found reduced levels of substance use among high school-age adolescents who had such a parent. However, openness of communication may not be enough; Humes and Humphrey (1994) suggested that parents also need to be sensitive to adolescents' needs.

Trauma is another important pathway to adolescent problem behavior. Effects of trauma can be ameliorated by parenting behaviors of support and monitoring (Luster & Small, 1997). Adolescents in substance abuse treatment programs have reported more physical, sexual, and violent victimization compared with controls (National Institute on Alcohol Abuse and Alcoholism, 1997). The dual risks of COA status and sexual abuse in adolescence have been related to higher levels of adolescent problems, including chemical abuse, than that found in adolescents with only one risk factor (Chandy, Blum, & Resnick, 1996). Moreover, such experiences are related to lengthier periods of treatment and less treatment cooperation (Mulsow, 2007), Adolescents experiencing *current* abuse have been shown to have more problem behaviors, such as binge drinking, than adolescents with histories of *prior* abuse (Luster & Small, 1997), Employing a national data set, Kilpatrick et al. (2003) found connections between substance abuse and dependence during adolescence and (a) family alcohol problems, (b) having been a witness to violence, and (c) having been a victim of physical assault. Posttraumatic stress disorder (PTSD) occurred when sexual assault was added to the mix. Those who develop alcohol misuse subsequent to trauma are more at risk for future assault (Mulsow, 2007). The effects of secondhand abuse (i.e., childhood abuse of parents of substance-abusing adolescents) may also be at work through its association with greater parental alcohol dependence (Peters, Malzman, & Villone, 1994).

In sum, difficulties in making the transition from childhood to adolescence are compounded when alcohol and drugs enter the picture. Parents' use of substances gains added importance, creating stressors, influencing perceptions, detracting from resources, and hindering coping. Parents' flexibility in coping with adolescents' emerging needs for autonomy and independence should be gender sensitive, given that socialization pressures continue to differ for boys and girls. More resilient adolescents in the face of parental alcoholism, poorer parenting, and trauma tend to be female, less disinhibited, and more parentally supported and monitored.

Bidirectional Processes

Throughout this chapter, the studies we cited have primarily focused on a particular direction of effects from parent to child: alcohol abuse in parents *leads to* child and adolescent alcohol use and misuse; parenting practices help or hinder adolescent resistance to alcohol use. Other research suggests that bidirectional effects are at work. The title of one article put the issue as "Can your children drive you to drink?" (Pelham & Lang, 1999). A series of experimental studies documented an affirmative answer. Adoptive parents (Finley & Aguiar, 2002) of children whose biological parents had alcohol, antisocial, depressive, or other psychiatric disorders experienced double the risk of developing their own psychiatric or alcohol-related problems compared to adoptive parents of children without such a predisposition. Rather than parenting practices being a result of parental substance use disorders, parents' discipline was *elicited* by sons' neurobehavioral disinhibition (ND);

this ND was in turn related to sons' substance use disorders (Mezzich et al., 2007). Commenting on studies such as these, Leonard and Eiden (2007) stated, "Alcoholic parents are at higher risk for having children with behavior problems, and children's behavior problems may increase parental stress and lead to more drinking" (p. 299). Deater-Deckard (2004) suggested that parents may need family support, training in coping responses, and social policies such as parental leave to alleviate parenting stress.

Issues in Prevention and Treatment

Although we have focused on families coping with substance use and misuse in the discussion above, limiting prevention and treatment efforts to "the person" in the family with the substance use problem is not sufficient to address the multiple levels of factors that are implicated in a person's substance use problem. There is no one place to start. In fact, alcohol misuse in families can extend back generations (Garrett & Landau, 2007). The substance-abusing parent certainly needs help, but so do the children in the family. As the above review illustrates, the stress and coping model highlights the importance of all the components—stressors, perceptions, resources, problem-solving skills, coping skills, and bidirectional effects—found in families dealing with substance abuse. Helping parents to effectively manage a behaviorally disinhibited child may interrupt the negative sequence of events from childhood to young adulthood. But helping children cope with a substance-abusing parent is also critical. Prevention of both early onset of substance use and early conduct disorder problems is a key factor in positive youth development. Fitzgerald et al. (2007) suggested that children from antisocial alcoholic families would benefit from interventions that begin in infancy. Other pathways that children follow are sorted out in middle childhood, suggesting that interventions begin before this critical time. Bolstering the case for early intervention, Aldwin's (2007) developmental approach identifies coping as embedded in the social ecology of the family throughout the lifespan beginning with infant and even prenatal coping behaviors.

Although medicating children who have ADHD has been found to be effective in preventing later substance use, not all behaviorally disinhibited children have ADHD. Nor is medication the sole answer for multifaceted family problems. If children and adults are dually diagnosed (e.g., alcohol abuse/dependence with PTSD), it is important to treat both (Mulsow, 2007). It is also necessary to deal with such family background issues as stresses surrounding grief, loss, and trauma (Garrett & Landau, 2007) for which alcohol abuse is a symptom.

Effective programs aimed at treating or preventing substance abuse involve multiple components and multiple points of entry (Boyd & Faden, 2002). These programs may be expensive; they may require commitments of time, energy, and other resources from schools and communities as well as the dedication of skilled leaders. There is no "magic bullet" for treating or preventing substance abuse. Nor is there one for producing resilient children.

Currently in the United States, too many parents and children are in need of treatment services, but substance abuse treatment is expensive, and effective programs are scarce, particularly for those whose addiction issues have led to impoverishment and lack of insurance. At the societal level, reductions in access to treatment and program resources have contributed to a pileup of unmet needs (Etheridge, Smith, Rounds-Bryant, & Hubbard, (2001). Even when substance-abusing parents or children go into treatment and recovery, the relapse rates are discouraging (Alford, Koehler, & Leonard, 1991). For example, because an important concomitant of recovery is the disruption of family dynamics, programs need to address changes in family dynamics to prevent relapse and to prevent children in the family from experiencing additional difficulties (Lewis & Allen-Byrd, 2007). Fischer, Pidcock, and Fletcher-Stephens (2007) describe three evidence-based programs for alcohol-abusing adolescents that include the family as well as the adolescent. Dealing with family dynamics is only one goal of comprehensive intervention, however. As we noted in the earlier version of this chapter (Fischer & Lyness, 2005), to prevent relapse, programs must also consider settings and situations beyond the family itself, such as (a) effective aftercare services; (b) safe havens for children of addicted parents; (c) school, college, and community policies; (d) cultural and subcultural norms and behaviors; and (e) support for recovery, important for singly diagnosed and dually diagnosed alike.

Drawing on the general literature on coping and the effects of coping on mental health, Aldwin (2007) concludes: "Interventions that serve ... to enhance individual feelings of control (where appropriate) have been unequivocally demonstrated to have positive effects on both mental and physical health" (p. 208). In addition, Aldwin states that a key aspect of the development of positive coping is the focus on self-regulation that implies choice, consistency, and continuity, particularly in goal-directed coping. One implication of this self-regulation focus in coping in recent interventions has been in the development of *mindful coping* (Aldwin).

Conclusion

An encouraging aspect of recent studies examining how families cope with substance abuse is the inclusion of multiple variables, multiple perspectives, multiple waves of data collection spanning infancy to middle age, and sophisticated data analysis techniques. This very richness presents challenges to the scholars who report such research because the findings are embedded in complex webs of interrelated results. Studies that examine the changing nature of predictors across different developmental ages provide valuable information for prevention and risk reduction (e.g., Guo et al., 2001). With this information, programs can begin to focus on the key developmental periods specific to identified predictors.

With only a few exceptions, the literature we have reviewed in this chapter has largely reported on research with families of European heritage. However, the Monitoring the Future surveys repeatedly find lower rates of substance use among African American youth than among European American adolescents (Johnston, O'Malley, Bachman, & Schulenberg, 2008). Even when similar rates are reported across ethnic groups, as with marijuana use, researchers should not assume that predictors and pathways to substance use are analogous. Furthermore, the consequences of use are greater for African American than European American youth (Jones, Hussong, Manning, & Sterrett, 2008). Future research must reflect the diversity of families coping with substance abuse, not just in terms of ethnicity and culture but also in terms of emerging understandings of the broad spectrum of close relationships covered by the term *families*. We have included in this review research on families with children and adolescents that we believe illuminates family scholars' understandings of families coping with substance abuse.

—— Illustrative Vignette ——————————————————

Karl is a 13-year-old boy who has been getting into trouble for drinking at school. This is not Karl's first time in trouble—he is often disruptive and aggressive and seems to lack impulse control. When he was younger, his parents (at the urging of the school) had him tested for ADHD, but the results were inconclusive, and the psychiatrist did not recommend medication. Karl's parents are typically punitive and have been known to use physical punishment, and Karl has reported not feeling supported by his parents. Moreover, Karl's parents have been considering getting a divorce. His father is a heavy drinker, although he has never been diagnosed with a substance abuse problem. Karl sees his father come home from work each night and drink five to six beers as he complains about his day. Recently, his father reports that the stress of dealing with Karl has led to increased drinking in order to cope. Karl has never felt that he fits in very well with his peers, but this current group of friends seems more accepting of his impulsive nature. Karl has on older sister who has not gotten into trouble with substances, and who has always been more controlled and inhibited. The school has recommended that the family see a therapist.

The family therapist, knowing some of the literature on stress and coping as well as alcohol and substance abuse, engaged a multifaceted approach. The therapist first addressed parental behaviors and coping, including the quality of the marriage, parenting styles, and Karl's father's drinking, with a focus on increasing self-regulation capacities in both parents and in Karl. Partly as a result of increased self-awareness, Karl's father decided to cut down on his drinking and made a commitment to work on the marriage. Both parents agreed to specific behavioral interventions designed to interrupt Karl's disinhibited behavior patterns. The therapist also helped Karl find other, less maladaptive ways of coping, along with implementing interventions with Karl at the school that helped him develop a different peer group (particularly focusing on Karl's propensity for aggression). Finally, the therapist intervened with Karl directly about his drinking behavior, knowing that Karl's early onset of drinking places him at risk for later serious substance abuse problems. Karl was able to talk about using alcohol as a means of coping with rejection and reported some success with making new friends. The therapist also helped Karl by specifically focusing on self-regulation by developing positive goal structures and increasing his focus on choices he makes in coping. He still struggles with anger, but he is able to talk with his father about his choices at times. For all of the family members, the interventions focused on active coping and building in each a sense of control and mindfulness.

Suggested Internet Resources

National Institute on Alcohol Abuse and Alcoholism (an institute within the National Institutes of Health): http://www.niaaa.nih.gov

National Institute on Drug Abuse: http://www.drugabuse.gov

Monitoring the Future (information on adolescent substance use and abuse): http://www.monitoringthefuture.org

Harvard School of Public Health, College Alcohol Study (information on adolescent and young adult binge drinking in college): http://www.hsph.harvard.edu/cas

UNC Carolina Population Center, information about the National Longitudinal Survey of Adolescent Health): http://www.cpc.unc.edu/projects/addhealth

References

Adalbjarnardottir, S., & Hafsteinsson, L. G. (2001). Adolescents' perceived parenting styles and their substance use: Concurrent and longitudinal analyses. *Journal of Research on Adolescence, 11,* 401–423.

Alati, R., Kinner, S. A., Najman, J. M., Mamum, A. A., Williams, G. M., O'Callaghan, M., & Bor, W. (2005). Early predictors of adult drinking: A birth cohort study. *American Journal of Epidemiology, 162*(11), 1098–1107.

Aldwin, C. M. (2007). *Stress, coping, and development: An integrative perspective* (2nd ed.). New York: Guilford.

Alford, G. S., Koehler, R. A., & Leonard, J. (1991). Alcoholics Anonymous-Narcotics Anonymous model inpatient treatment of chemically dependent adolescents: A 2-year outcome study. *Journal of Studies on Alcohol, 52,* 118–126.

American Psychiatric Association. (2000). *Diagnostic and statistical manual of mental disorders* (4th ed., text rev.). Washington, DC: Author.

Andrews, J. A., Hops, H., & Duncan, S. C. (1997). Adolescent modeling of parent substance use: The moderating effect of the relationship with the parent. *Journal of Family Psychology, 11,* 259–270.

Arendt, R. E., & Farkas, K. J. (2007). Maternal alcohol abuse and fetal alcohol spectrum disorder: A life-span perspective. *Alcoholism Quarterly, 25*(3), 3–20.

Baker, J. R., & Yardley, J. K. (2002). Moderating effect of gender on the relationship between sensation seeking-impulsivity and substance use in adolescents. *Journal of Child and Adolescent Substance Abuse, 12*(1), 27–43.

Barnes, G. M., Reifman, A., Farrell, M. P., & Dintcheff, B. A. (2000). The effects of parenting on the development of adolescent alcohol misuse: A six-wave latent growth model. *Journal of Marriage and the Family, 62,* 175–186.

Barnow, S., Schuckit, M. A., & Lucht, M. (2002). The importance of a positive family history of alcoholism, parental rejection and emotional warmth, behavioral problems and peer substance use for alcohol problems in teenagers: A path analysis. *Journal of Studies on Alcohol, 63,* 305–312.

Biederman, J., Faraone, S. V., Monuteaux, M. C., & Feighner, J. A. (2000). Patterns of alcohol and drug use in adolescents can be predicted by parental substance use disorders. *Pediatrics, 106,* 792–797.

Bogenschneider, K., Wu, M., & Raffaelli, M. (1998). Parent influences on adolescent peer orientation and substance use: The interface of parenting practices and value. *Child Development, 69,* 1672–1688.

Boyd, G. M., & Faden, V. (2002). Overview. *Journal of Studies on Alcohol, 14*(Suppl.), 6–13.

Chandy, J. M., Blum, R. W., & Resnick, M. D. (1996). History of sexual abuse and parental alcohol misuse: Risk, outcomes and protective factors in adolescents. *Child and Adolescent Social Work Journal, 13,* 411–432.

Chapple, C. L., Hope, T. R., & Whiteford, S. W. (2005). The direct and indirect effects of parental bonds, parental drug use, and self-control on adolescent substance use. *Journal of Child & Adolescent Substance Abuse, 14*(3), 17–38.

Chassin, L., Presson, C. C., Todd, M., Rose, J. S., & Sherman, S. J. (1998). Maternal socialization of adolescent smoking: The intergenerational transmission of parenting and smoking. *Developmental Psychology, 34,* 1189–1201.

Chen, M., Grube, J. W., & Madden, P. A. (1994). Alcohol expectancies and adolescent drinking: Differential prediction of frequency, quantity, and intoxication. *Addictive Behaviors, 19,* 521–529.

Coombs, R. H., & Landsverk, J. (1988). Parenting styles and substance use during childhood and adolescence. *Journal of Marriage and Family, 50,* 473–482.

Crawford, L. A., & Novak, K. B. (2008). Parent-child relations and peer associations as mediators of the family structure-substance use relationship. *Journal of Family Issues, 29*(2), 155–184.

Curran, P. J., & Chassin, L. (1996). A longitudinal study of parenting as a protective factor for children of alcoholics. *Journal of Studies on Alcohol, 57*(3), 305–313.

Curry, L., Fischer, J., Reifman, A., &; Harris, K. (2004, March). *Family factors, self-esteem, peer involvement, and adolescent alcohol misuse.* Poster presented at the biennial meeting of the Society for Research on Adolescence, Baltimore.

Deater-Deckard, K. (2004). *Parenting stress.* New Haven, CT: Yale University Press.

Dishion, T. J., Capaldi, D. M., & Yoerger, K. (1999). Middle childhood antecedents to progressions in male adolescent substance use: An ecological analysis of risk and protection. *Journal of Adolescent Research, 14,* 175–205.

Dishion, T. J., & McMahon, R. J. (1998). Parental monitoring and the prevention of child and adolescent problem behavior: A conceptual and empirical formulation. *Clinical Child and Family Psychology Review, 1,* 61–75.

Dubow, E. F., Boxer, P., & Huesmann, L. R. (2008). Childhood and adolescent predictors of early and middle adulthood alcohol use and problem drinking: The Columbia County Longitudinal Study. *Addiction, 103*(Suppl. 1), 36–47.

Dunn, M. E., & Goldman, M. S. (1996). Empirical modeling of an alcohol expectancy memory network in elementary school children as a function of grade. *Experimental and Clinical Psychopharmacology, 4,* 209–217.

Ellickson, P. L., Tucker, J. S., & Klein, D. J. (2003). Ten-year prospective study of public health problems associated with early drinking. *Pediatrics, 111,* 949–955.

Englund, M. M., Egeland, B., Olivia, E. M., & Collins, W. A. (2008). Childhood and adolescent predictors of heavy drinking and alcohol use disorders in early adulthood: A longitudinal developmental analysis. *Addiction, 103*(Suppl, 1), 23–35.

Ennett, S. T., Bauman, K. E., Foshee, V. A., Pemberton, M., & Hicks, K. A. (2001). Parent-child communication about adolescent tobacco and alcohol use: What do parents say and does it affect youth behavior? *Journal of Marriage and Family, 63,* 48–63.

Etheridge, R. M., Smith, J. C., Rounds-Bryant, J. L., & Hubbard, R. L. (2001). Drug abuse treatment and comprehensive services for adolescents. *Journal of Research on Adolescents, 16,* 563–589.

Fals-Stewart, W., Kelley, M. L., Cooke, C. G., & Golden, J. C. (2003). Predictors of the psychosocial adjustment of children living in households of parents in which fathers abuse drugs: The effects of postnatal parental exposure. *Addictive Behaviors, 28,* 1013–1031.

Finley, G. E., & Aguiar, L. J. (2002). The effects of children on parents: Adoptee genetic dispositions and adoptive parent psychopathology. *Journal of Genetic Psychology, 163*(4), 503–506.

Fischer, J. L., Fitzpatrick, J. A., Cleveland, B., Lee, J.-M., McKnight, A., & Miller, B., (2005). Binge drinking in the context of romantic relationships. *Addictive Behaviors, 30,* 1496–1516.

Fischer, J. L., & Lyness, K. P. (2005). Families coping with alcohol and substance abuse. In P. S. McKenry & S. J. Price (Eds.), *Families and change: Coping with stressful events and transitions* (3rd ed., pp. 155–178). Thousand Oaks, CA: Sage.

Fischer, J. L., Pidcock, B. W., & Fletcher-Stephens, B. J. (2007). Family response to adolescence, youth and alcohol. In J. L. Fischer, M. Mulsow, & A. W. Korinek (Eds.), *Familial responses to alcohol problems* (pp. 27–41). Binghamton, NY: The Haworth Press.

Fischer, J. L., & Wampler, R. S. (1994). Abusive drinking in young adults: Personality type and family role as moderators of family-of-origin influences. *Journal of Marriage and the Family, 56,* 469–479.

Fischer, J. L., & Wiersma, J. D. (2008, November). *Patterns of sibling drinking in adolescence and young adulthood.* Presented at the National Council on Family Relations Annual Meeting, Little Rock, AR.

Fischer, J. L., Wiersma, J. D., Forthun, L. F., Pidcock, B. W., & Dowd, D. (2007, November). *Parent drinking, college student drinking, difficulties with friendships and difficulties with dating.* Presented at the National Council on Family Relations Annual Meeting, Pittsburg, PA.

Fitzgerald, H. E., Puttler, L. I., Refior, S., & Zucker, R. A. (2007). Family response to children and alcohol. In J. L. Fischer, M. Mulsow, & A. W. Korinek (Eds.), *Familial responses to alcohol problems* (pp. 11–25). Binghamton, NY: The Haworth Press.

Frauenglass, S., Routh, D. K., Pantin, H. M., & Mason, C. A. (1997). Family support decreases influence of deviant peers on Hispanic adolescents' substance use. *Journal of Clinical and Child Psychology, 26,* 15–23.

Galaif, E. R., Stein, J, S., Newcomb, M. D., & Bernstein, D. P. (2001). Gender differences in the prediction of problem alcohol use in adulthood: Exploring the influence of family factors and childhood maltreatment. *Journal of Studies on Alcohol and Drugs, 62,* 486–493.

Garrett, J., & Landau, J. (2007). Family motivation to change: A major factor in engaging alcoholics in treatment. In J. L. Fischer, M. Mulsow, & A. W. Korinek (Eds.), *Familial responses to alcohol problems* (pp. 65–83). Binghamton, NY: The Haworth Press.

Godsall, R. E., Jurkovic, G. J., Emshoff, J., Anderson, L., & Stanwyck, D. (2004). Why some kids do well in bad situations: Relation of parental alcohol misuse and parentification to children's self-concept. *Substance Use & Misuse, 39,* 789–809.

Griffin, K. W., Botvin, G. J., Epstein, J. A., Doyle, M. M., & Diaz, T. (2000). Psychosocial and behavioral factors in early adolescence as predictors of heavy drinking among high school seniors. *Journal of Studies on Alcohol, 61,* 603–606.

Guo, J., Hawkins, J. D., Hill, K. G., & Abbott, R. D. (2001). Childhood and adolescent predictors of alcohol abuse and dependence in young adulthood. *Journal of Studies on Alcohol and Drugs, 62,* 754–762.

Humes, D. L., & Humphrey, L. L. (1994). A multi-method analysis of families with a polydrug-dependent or normal adolescent daughter. *Journal of Abnormal Psychology, 103,* 676–685.

Hussong, A. M., Bauer, D., & Chassin, L. (2008). Telescoped trajectories from alcohol initiation to disorder in children of alcoholic parents. *Journal of Abnormal Psychology, 117,* 63–78.

Jackson, C., Henriksen, L., & Dickinson, D. (1997). The early use of alcohol and tobacco: Its relation to children's competence and parents' behavior. *American Journal of Public Health, 87,* 359–364.

Jacob, T., & Johnson, S. (1997). Parenting influences on the development of alcohol abuse and dependence. *Alcohol Health and Research World, 21,* 204–210.

Jeynes, W. H. (2001). The effects of recent parental divorce on their children's consumption of alcohol. *Journal of Youth and Adolescence, 30,* 305–319.

Johnston, L. D., O'Malley, P. M., Bachman, J. G., & Schulenberg, J. E. (2008). *Monitoring the Future national results on adolescent drug use: Overview of key findings, 2007* (NIH Publication No. 08–6418). Bethesda, MD: National Institute on Drug Abuse. Downloaded Nov. 21, 2008, from http://www.monitoringthefuture. org/pubs/monographs/overview2007.pdf

Jones, D. J., Hussong, A. M., Manning, J., & Sterrett, E. (2008). Adolescent alcohol use in context: The role of parents and peers among African American and European American youth. *Cultural Diversity and Ethnic Minority Psychology, 14*(3), 266–273.

Jones, K. A., & Benda, B. B. (2004). Alcohol use among adolescents with non-residential fathers: A study of assets and deficits. *Alcoholism Treatment Quarterly, 22,* 3–25.

Kafka, R. R., & London, P. (1991). Communication in relationships and adolescent substance use: The influence of parents and friends. *Adolescence, 26,* 587–597.

Kelley, M. L., & Fals-Stewart, W. (2008). Treating parental drug abuse using learning sobriety together: Effects on adolescents versus children. *Drug and Alcohol Dependence, 92*(1–3), 228–238.

Kilpatrick, D. G., Ruggiero, K. J., Acierno, R., Saunders, B. E., Resnick, H, S., & Best, C. L. (2003). Violence and risk of PTSD, major depression, substance abuse/dependence, and comorbidity: Results from the national survey of adolescents. *Journal of Consulting and Clinical Psychology, 71,* 692–700.

King, K. M., & Chassin, L. (2004). Mediating and moderated effects of adolescent behavioral undercontrol and parenting in the prediction of drug use disorders in emerging adulthood. *Psychology of Addictive Behaviors, 18,* 239–249.

Kirby, J. B. (2006). From single-parent families to stepfamilies: Is the transition associated with adolescent alcohol initiation? *Journal of Family Issues, 27*(5), 685–711.

Komro, K. A., Maldonado-Molina, M. M., Tobler, A. L., Bonds, J. R., & Muller, K. E. (2007). Effects of home access and availability of alcohol on young adolescents' alcohol use. *Addiction, 102,* 1597–1608.

Leonard, K. E., & Eiden, R. D. (2007). Marital and family processes in the context of alcohol use and alcohol disorders. *Annual Review of Clinical Psychology, 3,* 285–310.

Lewis, V., & Allen-Byrd, L. (2007). Coping strategies for the stages of family recovery. In J. L. Fischer, M. Mulsow, & A. W. Korinek (Eds.), *Familial responses to alcohol problems* (pp. 105–124). Binghamton, NY: The Haworth Press.

Loveland-Cherry, C. J., Leech, S., Laetz, V. B., & Dielman, T. E. (1996). Correlates of alcohol use and misuse in fourth-grade children: Psychosocial, peer, parental, and family factors. *Health Education Quarterly, 23,* 497–577.

Luster, T., & Small, S. A. (1997). Sexual abuse history and problems in adolescence: Explaining the effects of moderating variables. *Journal of Marriage and the Family, 59,* 131–142.

Maggs, J. L., Patrick, M. E., & Feinstein, L. (2008). Childhood and adolescent predictors of alcohol use and problems in adolescence and adulthood in the National Child Development Study. *Addiction, 103*(Suppl. 1), 7–22.

Mason, W. A., & Windle, M. (2002). Reciprocal relations between adolescent substance use and delinquency: A longitudinal latent variable analysis. *Journal of Abnormal Psychology, 111,* 63–76.

McDermott, R. J., Clark-Alexander, B. J., Westhoff, W. W., & Eaton, D. K. (1999). Alcohol attitudes and beliefs related to actual alcohol experience in a fifth-grade cohort. *Journal of School Health, 69,* 356–361.

McKenry, P. C., & Price, S. J. (2005). Families coping with change. In P. S. McKenry & S. J. Price (Eds.), *Families and change: Coping with stressful events and transitions* (3rd ed., pp. 1–24). Thousand Oaks, CA: Sage.

Merline, A., Jager, J., & Schulenberg, J. E. (2008). Adolescent risk factors for adult alcohol use and abuse: Stability and change of predictive value across early and middle adulthood. *Addiction, 103*(Suppl. 1), 84–99.

Mezzich, A. C., Tarter, R. E., Kirisci, L., Feske, U., Day, B., & Gao, Z. (2007). Reciprocal influence of parent discipline and child's behavior on risk for substance disorder: A nine-year prospective study. *American Journal of Drug and Alcohol Abuse, 33*(6), 851–867.

Mulsow, M. (2007). Treatment of co-morbidity in families. In J. L. Fischer, M. Mulsow, & A. W. Korinek (Eds.), *Familial responses to alcohol problems* (pp. 125–140). Binghamton, NY: The Haworth Press.

National Institute on Alcohol Abuse and Alcoholism. (1997). *Youth drinking: Risk factors and consequences* (Alcohol Alert 37). Retrieved December 20, 2004, from http://www.niaaa.nih.gov/publications/aa37.htm

National Institute on Alcohol Abuse and Alcoholism. (2000). Drinking over the life span: Issues of biology, behavior, and risk. In National Institute on Alcohol Abuse and Alcoholism, *Tenth special report to the U.S. Congress on alcohol and health: Highlights from current research.* Retrieved December 20, 2004, from http://www.niaaa.nih.gov/publications/10report/chap01.pdf

Needle, R. H., Su, S. S., & Doherty, W. J. (1990). Divorce, remarriage, and adolescent substance use: A prospective longitudinal study. *Journal of Marriage and the Family, 52,* 157–169.

Pandina, R. J., & Johnson, V. (1990). Serious alcohol and drug problems among adolescents with a family history of alcoholism. *Journal of Studies on Alcohol, 51,* 278–282.

Patock-Peckham, J. A., & Morgan-Lopez, A. A. (2007). College drinking behaviors: Mediational links between parenting styles, parental bonds, depression, and alcohol problems. *Psychology of Addictive Behaviors, 21*(3), 297–306.

Pelham, W. E., & Lang, A. R. (1999). Can your children drive you to drink Stress and parenting in adults interacting with children with ADHD. *Alcohol Research and Health, 23*(4), 292–298.

Peters, K. R., Malzman, I., & Villone, K. (1994). Childhood abuse of parents of alcohol and other drug misusing adolescents. *International Journal of the Addictions, 29*(10), 1259–1268.

Pidcock, B. W., & Fischer, J. L. (1998). Parental recovery as a moderating variable of adult offspring problematic behaviors. *Alcoholism Treatment Quarterly, 16,* 45–57.

Sartor, C. E., Lynskey, M. T., Heath, A. C., Jacob, T., & True, W. (2006). The role of childhood risk factors in initiation of alcohol use and progression to alcohol dependence. *Addiction, 102,* 216–225.

Sher, K. J., Grekin, E. R., & Williams, N. A. (2005). The development of alcohol use disorders. *Annual Review of Clinical Psychology, 1,* 493–523.

Shillington, A. M., Lehman, S., Clapp, J., Hovell, M. F., Sipan, C., & Blumberg, E. J. (2005). Prenatal monitoring: Can it continue to be protective among high-risk adolescents? *Journal of Child and Adolescent Substance Abuse, 15*(1), 1–15.

Slutske, W. S., D'Onofrio, B. M., Turkheimer, E., Emery, R. E., Harden, K. P., Heath, A. C., & Martin, N. G. (2008). Searching for an environmental effect of parental alcoholism on offspring alcohol use disorder: A genetically informed study of children of alcoholics. *Journal of Abnormal Psychology, 117*(3), 534–551.

Smith, C. L., Eisenberg, N., Spinrad, T. L., Chassin, L., Sheffield Morris, A., Kupfer, A., Liew, J., Cumberland, A., & Valiente, C. (2006). Children's coping strategies and coping efficacy: Relations to parent socialization, child adjustment, and familial alcoholism. *Development and Psychopathology, 18*, 445–469.

Stelle, C. D., & Scott, J. P. (2007). Alcohol abuse by older family members: A family systems approach. In J. L. Fischer, M. Mulsow, & A. W. Korinek (Eds.), *Familial responses to alcohol problems* (pp. 43–63). Binghamton, NY: The Haworth Press.

Survey finds parents unresponsive to Ecstasy threat. (2003, November 3). *Alcoholism and Drug Abuse Weekly.* Retrieved February 28, 2004, from http://www.drugfreeamerica.org

Tucker, J. S., Ellickson, P. L., & Klein, D. J. (2008). Growing up in a permissive household: What deters at-risk adolescents from heavy drinking? *Journal of Studies on Alcohol and Drugs, 69*, 528–534.

Tyler, K. A., Stone, R. T., & Bersani, B. (2006). Examining the changing influence of predictors on adolescent alcohol misuse. *Journal of Child and Adolescent Substance Abuse, 16*(2), 95–114.

Vakalahi, H. F. (2002). Family-based predictors of adolescent substance use. *Journal of Child and Adolescent Substance Abuse, 11*(3), 1–15.

Weinberg, N. Z., Dielman, T. E., Mandell, W., & Shope, J. T. (1994). Parental drinking and gender factors in the prediction of early adolescent alcohol use. *International Journal of the Addictions, 29*, 89–104.

White, H. R., Johnson, V., & Buyske, S. (2000). Parental modeling and parenting behavior effects on offspring alcohol and cigarette use: A growth curve analysis. *Journal of Substance Abuse, 12*(3), 287–310.

Wills, T. A., & Cleary, S. D. (1996). How are social support effects mediated? A test with parental support and adolescent substance use. *Journal of Personality and Social Psychology, 71*, 937–952.

Windle, M. (2000). Parental, sibling, and peer influences on adolescent substance use and alcohol problems. *Applied Developmental Science, 4*, 98–110.

Wong, M. M., Zucker, R. A., Puttler, L. I., & Fitzgerald, H. E. (1999). Heterogeneity of risk aggregation for alcohol problems between early and middle childhood: Nesting structure variations. *Development and Psychopathology, 11*, 727–744.

Zucker, R., Boyd, G., & Howard, J. (Eds.). (1994). *The development of alcohol problems: Exploring the biopsychosocial matrix of risk* (National Institute on Alcohol Abuse and Alcoholism Research Monograph No. 26). Rockville, MD: U.S. Department of Health and Human Services.

Zucker, R. A. (2008). Anticipating problem alcohol use developmentally from childhood into middle adulthood: What have we learned? *Addiction, 103*, 100–108.

Zucker, R. A., Fitzgerald, H. E., Refior, S. K., Pallas, D. M., & Ellis, D. A. (2000). The clinical and social ecology of childhood for children of alcoholics: Description of a study and implications for a differentiated social policy. In H. E. Fitzgerald, B. M. Lester, & B. S. Zuckerman (Eds.), *Children of addiction: Research, health, and policy issues* (pp. 109–141). New York: Routledge/Falmer.

CHAPTER 7

Family Influences on the Development of Aggression and Violence

Madelyn H Labella and Ann S Masten

Recent research confirms that many of the most salient risk and protective factors for the development of aggression and violence reside in the family system. Family-based risks begin before birth, encompassing genetic and epigenetic processes. Contextual stressors (*e.g.*, poverty, conflict) may impact development directly or indirectly through disrupted parenting behavior, including high negativity, low warmth, harshness, and exposure to violence. The family can also serve as a powerful adaptive system counteracting the risk of aggression and violence. Parents can promote healthy behavioral development through warmth, structure, and prosocial values, as well as by fostering adaptive resources in the child and community. Successful interventions often reduce aggression and violence by supporting parents and families. Recent insights and future directions for research and practice are discussed.

Address

Institute of Child Development, University of Minnesota, 51 East River Parkway, Minneapolis, 55455 MN, USA

Corresponding author: Labella, Madelyn H (label052@umn.edu)

The family is a critical context for child development, including the development of aggression and violence [1]. In developmental systems theory, individual development emerges from interactions across system levels, including interactions with the family, community, and physical environment [1–3]. Given the salience of family socialization, it is not surprising that many of the best-established risk and protective factors for the development of violence are located in the family system. This article examines recent evidence on family-based risk and protective factors for aggression and violence, describing how these influences cascade outward to affect children's adjustment at school, with friends, and in the community. Intervention efforts to reduce aggression and violence by targeting family processes are highlighted and future directions for multilevel research and interventions are discussed.

Risk Factors in the Family System

Family-based risk factors for aggression and violence begin before a child is born. In addition to genetic factors that may shape propensity to aggression, parents influence prenatal risk through the intrauterine environment. Fetal exposure to environmental toxins and maternal substance use have been linked to children's aggressive and antisocial behavior [4]. The family's psychosocial environment also influences fetal development, in part by shaping the stress response system. Extreme or chronic stress during pregnancy can lead to hyper-activation of the mother's hypothalamic-pituitary-adrenal (HPA) axis, producing high levels of the stress hormone cortisol, some of which permeates the placental barrier [5]. Prenatal maternal stress and cortisol exposure are associated with increased stress reactivity in utero, negativity emotionality, and behavior problems during infancy and beyond [5–7]. For example, prenatal (but not postnatal) intimate partner violence (IPV) predicted more mother-reported behavior problems and higher cortisol reactivity to an arm restraint task among one-year-old infants [8*]. Similar findings were demonstrated in middle childhood, suggesting long-term programming effects [9].

Accumulating evidence suggests that prenatal stress shapes development through epigenetic processes—for example, by decreasing expression of glucocorticoid receptors in the hippocampus, thereby slowing recovery from acute stress [5,6]. Alterations in HPA functioning may reflect conditional adaptations to a stressful postnatal environment that optimize survival at the cost of long-term health [5,10]. Chronic activation of a hyper-responsive stress system can lead to down-regulation of HPA reactivity, resulting in later failure to mobilize an adaptive stress response. Both hyper- and hypo-activation of the stress response system have been linked to violence and antisocial behavior [11,12].

Effects of prenatal stress are often compounded by ongoing adversity. Prenatal stressors, including maternal psychopathology and family strain, often persist in the postnatal period, fine-tuning the reactivity of the developing stress response system [7]. The impact of early stress on neurobehavioral development has major implications for etiological theories of violence. Several models of antisocial development identify vulnerabilities in neurobiology, temperament, and cognitive ability as risk factors for later aggression [4,12,13]. Because these individual differences are affected by stress in the family environment, they should not be interpreted as purely generic risks, but instead as co-acting genetic and environmental influences that shape development.

Children with individual vulnerabilities are particularly susceptible to adversity in the caregiving environment—as well as more likely to experience it. Parents who share genetic risk and provide stressful pre- and post-natal environments often struggle to parent effectively [12]. Furthermore, young children at neurobiological and temperamental risk are more difficult to parent, often eliciting frustration, low warmth, and harsh discipline [4,13]. Transactions between a difficult child and a pathogenic environment can compound and escalate individual risks. One influential developmental taxonomy [13] proposes that children with early neuropsychological risk factors (e.g., low verbal intelligence, attention problems) tend to evoke adverse care, initiating a stable trajectory of antisocial behavior across the lifespan. Recent refinements of this taxonomy acknowledge that early adversity directly shapes neurobiological vulnerability and that supportive caregiving environments may function to mitigate and/or delay the onset of antisocial behavior associated with such vulnerability [14**].

Family adversities linked to the development of aggression and violence include poverty, family stress, disorganization, single parenthood, large family size, and household conflict [15–20]. These adversities may shape the development of aggression and violence indirectly through parenting behavior and/or alterations in children's stress physiology [21*, 22]. Parental mental illness, substance abuse, and criminality are also associated with offspring aggression and violence [15–20, 23], These parental adjustment variables are likely linked to genetic risk, behavioral models of antisocial behavior, and disrupted parenting [22].

Ineffective parenting is one of the most consistently identified predictors of children's aggression and antisocial behavior. Trajectories of violence have been associated with high parental negativity and low parental warmth, as well as low cohesion and supportiveness in family relationships [21*, 22, 24, 25]. Emotionally unsupportive environments may heighten children's distress without facilitating emotion management, undermining the development of secure attachment and self-regulation. Harsh and inconsistent discipline has also been implicated in antisocial development [15–19]. For example, in a cohort of children at risk for aggressive behavior, socioeconomic risk and parental depression were linked to harsh and inconsistent parenting, which in turn predicted childhood conduct problems escalating to violent behavior in adolescence [26**]. The social interaction learning model proposes that inconsistent enforcement of behavioral expectations reinforces non-compliance, and intermittent harshness in response to misbehavior contributes to cycles of aggressive coercion, escalating antisocial development [27].

Harsh punishment may also cross the line into abuse. Robust associations between physical abuse and later aggression have been documented in studies using longitudinal and genetically-informed designs [28]. Research has identified genetic variations associated with greater vulnerability to antisocial behavior following physical abuse, although abuse operates as a risk factor regardless of genotype [29–31]. Other forms of maltreatment, such as neglect and sexual abuse, have also been linked to the development of aggression and violence. In a study of low-income families with or without maltreatment reports, repeated neglect and mixed-type maltreatment were uniquely associated with adulthood maltreatment perpetration, controlling for childhood demographics, adolescent risk behaviors, and adulthood well-being [32].

Abuse and neglect often co-occur with exposure to intimate partner violence (IPV) involving caregivers. Witnessing IPV is also known to predict aggressive and antisocial behavior [16, 19, 33, 34]. Cycle of violence theories propose that witnessing or experiencing violence undermines secure attachment, biases social information processes toward threat detection, and contributes to dysregulation of the stress response system [35]. According to social learning theory, children and adolescents who witness family violence may imitate aggressive behavior. In fact, family violence has been linked to bullying and fighting perpetration among middle schoolers [36], and adolescent conflict with best friends prospectively mediated links between witnessing inter-parental violence and involvement in dating violence [33]. Witnessing others engage in violence may also promote internalization of aggression as acceptable in the context of close relationships. Acceptance of aggression has been found to mediate links between IPV and antisocial outcomes, including children's self-reported externalizing behavior [37] and perpetration of dating violence [38].

Neighborhood factors, including concentrated poverty, disorganization, and community violence, also predict violent development [22, 39–41]. For example, cross-sectional and longitudinal studies have documented links between community violence exposure and increased aggressive behavior [25, 40, 41]. Because parents select young children's environments, exposure to violence in the broader community can reflect indirect family influences on children's behavioral development. Parents play a similarly critical role in structuring peer socialization. As children get older, dysfunctional behavior patterns acquired in the family can spread to other domains through processes described as developmental cascades [42]. Children with behavior problems at school entry are often rejected by mainstream peers, encouraging them to affiliate with deviant peers [4, 27]. Antisocial friend groups foster antisocial development, further contributing to the development of violence [16, 43].

Peer and community influences on violent behavior may be particularly important in adolescence, as autonomy increases and parental supervision decreases. Among urban adolescents, more time engaging in unstructured, unsupervised activities with friends was associated with more engagement in violent acts [25]. Unfortunately, early behavior problems predict less parental monitoring in adolescence, suggesting that parents may respond to the stress of chronic conflict by disengaging. Low parental monitoring predicts even greater adolescent delinquency, with cascading influences on violent behavior [22, 26**].

Family-based risk factors begin in utero and continue through adolescence and beyond. Risks tend to cluster together and exacerbate each other, and youth aggression escalates through reciprocal interactions with peer and family environments. Importantly, however, many children break the cycle, avoiding or desisting from violence. This evidence of resilience, defined as successful adaptation in the context of adversity, suggests that positive influences may offset or mitigate negative influences on children's behavioral development [3].

Protective and Promotive Factors in the Family System

Resilience science has converged on a common list of factors and processes associated with adaptive development [3]. These adaptive processes may serve promotive (*i.e.*, contributing similarly to positive outcomes regardless of level of risk) or protective functions (*i.e.*, contributing to positive outcomes especially in the context of increasing risk). Many of the most powerful adaptive processes occur in a family context. For example, parental warmth and sensitivity are often linked to less aggression and antisocial behavior [44*, 45]. Parental warmth has been found to buffer effects of family [17] and community violence [46] on children's externalizing behavior, consistent with a protective effect. Warm and responsive caregiving is believed to promote secure parent-child attachment, which has in turn been linked to lower behavior problems, particularly among low-income families [22].

Effective parents also provide structure, including routines, supervision, and consistent discipline [47]. These organizational factors have a powerful influence on behavioral outcomes, particularly as children grow older. In the Pittsburgh Youth Study, intensive supervision, consistent discipline, and child involvement in family activities predicted lower levels of youth violence [48]. Similarly, parental supervision protected participants of the Cambridge Study in Delinquent Development against the deleterious impact of child dishonesty on youthful convictions [49]. Parental monitoring may be particularly important for children at high risk of violence due to behavioral history and/or dangerous environments [22].

Prosocial parental values may also serve a protective role. In the Lehigh Longitudinal Study, parent (and peer) disapproval of violence predicted less self-reported violence and delinquency in adolescence, regardless of maltreatment history [50]. Parental values regarding education may also minimize antisocial behavior, perhaps by supporting children's achievement, motivation, and school engagement [49, 50]. Indeed, school attachment and educational aspirations have been linked to less delinquency in middle school [41] and violence in adulthood [51].

Positive family influences thus operate indirectly as well directly. Sensitive and stimulating parenting promotes the development of individual-level adaptive systems, including cognitive skills and self-regulation [3]. Furthermore, selecting high quality neighborhoods (*i.e.*, high cohesion, low crime) protects against the development of conduct problems in children at high sociodemographic or behavioral risk [22, 45]. Parents may also influence behavioral development through choices of quality housing and religious affiliation, both associated with lower youth violence [50, 51]. It is encouraging to note that these family processes are malleable rather than fixed, making them plausible targets for intervention.

Family-Focused Intervention Programs

Interventions often seek to leverage adaptive processes in the family to reduce youth violence. For example, the Parent Management Training: Oregon model emphasizes positive parental involvement and consistent behavioral consequences to avert coercive cycles of parent-child interaction. Evidence from randomized control trials suggests the intervention generates a positive developmental cascade, decreasing coercive parenting and increasing positive parenting, with downstream effects on decreasing child aggression and antisocial behavior [52]. Other prevention programs begin earlier, targeting families during prenatal and early childhood years to promote positive parenting behavior. A recent meta-analysis of such parenting programs found small to moderate reductions in child abuse, neglect, and associated risk factors (*e.g.,* harsh parenting), as well as improvements in positive parenting [53]. Several early childhood programs that target parenting (either alone or multi-modally) have demonstrated long-term impacts on preventing antisocial and criminal behavior [54, 55]. Prevention programs for older children and adolescents often employ a combination of parent management training, teacher training, and direct coaching of social skills and self-regulation [22, 56]. Any group engagement of antisocial peers in such interventions is handled with care given the potential for social contagion among deviant peers [57].

Multimodal interventions are also used to treat behavior problems that have already arisen. Multidimensional treatment foster care, which incorporates specialized training and therapy for foster and biological parents, has been shown to reduce antisocial and aggressive behavior among youth involved in child welfare; benefits are mediated through improved supervision and discipline, adult mentoring, and separation from deviant peers [55]. Outside of the foster care system, multisystemic therapy, an intensive family- and community-based treatment program, provides support to chronically violent adolescents at risk for out-of-home placement, with corresponding reductions in violent and non-violent offending [58].

Conclusions and Future Research Directions

Considerable progress has been made in understanding family-based influences on youth violence in recent years. Nonetheless, large knowledge gaps remain. Further research is needed to elucidate the roles of early experiences in shaping neurobehavioral development, including the effects of pre- and post-natal stress on the developing HPA axis and cognitive control skills. A better understanding of the biological embedding of early experience would clarify how aggressive behavior is transferred from one generation to the next, and identify opportunities to intervene.

Further research is needed on interventions and their developmental timing, including the best strategies for reducing stress in pregnant mothers and educating parents about developmentally appropriate monitoring of their older children and adolescents. These efforts would be greatly aided by public policies designed to reduce family stress and support positive development (*e.g.,* by improving access to high-quality foster care, early childhood education, and affordable housing). Information is also needed about who benefits from a given intervention. Provocative new research suggests that genetic variations may shape individual sensitivity to prevention programs, raising the possibility that interventions could be personalized to optimally match the needs of a given individual [59*]. Family and cultural factors may also influence treatment preference and response.

The future of the field requires rigorous research incorporating multiple systems and multiple-level designs, linking biological, behavioral, relational, and macrosocial processes, as well as longitudinal studies of developmental trajectories over the lifespan and across generations. Intervention research is needed to refine strategies, clarify optimal developmental timing, and tailor interventions to families' specific needs.

The family is a powerful context of human development. Interacting with multiple systems from genes to society, families may promote or prevent the development of aggression and violence in young people. Understanding these influences offers a promising avenue to cultivate resilience and reduce the risks for violence by harnessing one of the most powerful adaptive systems in a child's life: the family.

Conflict of Interest Statement

Nothing declared.

Acknowledgements

Preparation of this review paper was supported in part by a Graduate Research Fellowship awarded to M.L. from the University of Minnesota and by the Irving B. Harris and Regents Professorships to A.S.M. from the University of Minnesota.

References and Recommended Reading

Papers of particular interest, published within the period of review, have been highlighted as:
* of special interest
** of outstanding interest

1. Bronfenbrenner U, Morris PA: **The bioecological model of human development.** In *Handbook of Child Psychology,* vol. 1. Edited by Demon W, Lerner RM. **New Jersey: Wiley; 2006: 793–828.**
2. Gottlieb G: **Probabilistic epigenesis.** *Dev. Sci.* 2007, **10**: 1–11.
3. Masten AS: *Ordinary Magic: Resilience in Development.* New York: Guilford; 2014.
4. Dodge KA, Pettit GS: **A biopsychosocial model of the development of chronic conduct problems in adolescence.** *Dev. Psychol.* 2003, **39**: 349–371.
5. Meaney MJ, Szyf M, Seckl JR: **Epigenetic mechanisms of perinatal programming of hypothalamic-pituitary-adrenal function and health.** *Trends Mol. Med.* 2007, **13**: 269–277.
6. Sandman CA, Davis EP: **Neurobehavioral risk is associated with gestational exposure to stress hormones.** *Expert Rev. Endocrinol. Metab.* 2012, **7**: 445–459.
7. Monk C, Spicer J, Champagne FA: **Linking prenatal maternal adversity to developmental outcomes in infants: the role of epigenetic pathways.** *Dev. Psychopathol.* 2012, **24**: 1361–1376.
8. Levendosky AA, Bogat GA, Lonstein JS, Martinez-Torteya C. Muzik M, Granger DA, von Eye A: **Infant adrenocortical reactivity and behavioral functioning: relation to early exposure to maternal intimate partner violence.** *Stress* 2016, **19**: 37–44.
  * This novel study investigated hypothalamic-pituitary-adrenal axis reactivity among one-year-old infants, some of whom had been exposed to maternal intimate partner violence (IPV). Infants who had experienced prenatal (but not postnatal) IPV showed heightened cortisol reactivity to a laboratory stressor, providing support for a fetal programming hypothesis, and were rated by their mothers as having more behavior problems. Infant behavior problems were related to maternal mental health, but not to cortisol reactivity, contributing to growing literature about the disjunction between physiological stress responses and behavior.

9. Martinez-Torteya A, Bogat GA, Levendosky AA, von Eye A: **The influence of prenatal intimate partner violence exposure on hypothalamic-pituitary-adrenal axis reactivity and childhood internalizing and externalizing symptoms.** *Dev. Psychopathol.* 2016, **28:** 55–72.

10. Del Giudice M, Ellis BJ. Shirtcliff EA: **The adaptive calibration model of stress responsivity.** *Neurosci, Biobehav. Rev.* 2011, **35:** 1562–1592.

11. Puzzo I, Smaragdi A, Gonzalez K, Martin-Key N, Fairchild G: **Neurobiological, neuroimaging, and neuropsychological studies of children and adolescents with disruptive behavior disorders.** *Fam. Relat.* 2016, **65:** 134–150.

12. van Goozen SHM, Fairchild G, Snoek H, Harold GT: **The evidence for a neurobiological model of childhood antisocial behavior.** *Psychol. Bull.* 2007, **133:** 149–182.

13. Moffitt TE: **Adolescence-limited and life-course-persistent antisocial behavior: a developmental taxonomy.** *Psychol. Rev.* 1993, **100:** 674–701.

14. Fairchild G, van Goozen SHM, Calder AJ, Goodyer IM: **Research review: evaluating and reformulating the developmental taxonomic theory of antisocial behavior.** *J. Child Psychol. Psychiatry* 2013, **54:** 924–940.
   ** This comprehensive literature review synthesizes empirical research related to Moffitt's influential developmental taxonomic theory of life-course persistent vs. adolescent-limited antisocial behavior. The review offers a valuable reformulation of Moffitt's highly generative framework, noting evidence for childhood-limited conduct problems and persistent antisocial behavior with adolescent onset. The authors emphasize the role of the caregiving environment in moderating the expression of individual vulnerabilities (*e.g.*, delaying the onset of violent behavior until adolescence despite substantial individual-level risk).

15. Farrington DP, Gaffney H, Ttofi MM: **Systematic reviews of explanatory risk factors for violence, offending, and delinquency.** *Aggress. Violent Behav.* 2017, **33:** 91–106.

16. Costa BM, Kaestle CE, Walker A, Curtis A, Day A, Tombourou JW, Miller P: **Longitudinal predictors of domestic violence perpetration and victimization: a systematic review.** *Aggress. Violent Behav.* 2015, **24:** 261–272.

17. Fong VC, Hawes D, Allen JL: **A systematic review of risk and protective factors for externalizing problems in children exposed to intimate partner violence.** *Trauma Violence Abuse* 2017 http://dx.doi.org/10.1177/1524838017692383.

18. Frick PJ, Ray JV, Thornton L.C, Kahn RE: **Can callous-unemotional traits enhance the understanding, diagnosis, and treatment of conduct problems in children and adolescents? A comprehensive review.** *Psychol. Bull.* 2014, **140:** 1–57.

19. Jolliffe D, Farrington DP, Plquero AR, Loeber R, Hill KG: **Systematic review of early risk factors for life-course-persistent, adolescent-limited, and late-onset offenders in prospective longitudinal studies.** *Aggress. Violent Behav.* 2017, **33:** 15–23.

20. Paradis AD, Fitzmaurice GM. Koenen KC, Buka SL: **A prospective Investigation of neurodevelopmental risk factors for adult antisocial behavior combining official arrest records and self-reports.** *J. Psychiatr. Res.* 2015, **68:** 363–370.

21. Repetti RL, Robles TF, Reynolds B: **Allostatic processes in the family.** *Dev. Psychopathol.* 2011, **23:** 921–938.
   * This paper reviews pathways to anger and aggression among children from so-called 'risky families', characterized by chronic conflict and low warmth. Parental influences on psychosocial development are reviewed by developmental stage (infancy and early childhood, middle childhood, and adolescence), and biological processes related to allostasis are proposed as mechanisms for long-term effects of parenting on offspring health. Intermediate psychological and biological response patterns ('precursor outcomes') are identified, suggesting opportunities for targeted intervention, and physiological mechanisms of behavioral resilience are discussed.

22. Dodge KA, Cote JD, Lynam D: **Aggression and antisocial behavior in youth.** In *Handbook of Child Psychology,* vol. 3. Edited by Damon W, Lerner RM. New Jersey: Wiley: 2006: **719–788.**

23. Holmes MR, Yoon S, Berg KA: **Maternal depression and intimate partner violence exposure: longitudinal analyses of the development of aggressive behavior in an at-risk sample.** *Aggress. Behav.* 2017 http://dx.doi.org/10.1002/ab.21696.

24. Ibabe I, Bentler PM: **The contribution of family relationships to child-to-parent violence.** *J. Fam. Violence* 2016, **31:** 259–269.

25. Fagan AA, Wright EM, Pinchevsky GM: **The protective effects of neighborhood collective efficacy on adolescent substance use and violence following exposure to violence.** *J. Youth Adoiesc.* 2014, **43:** 1498–1512.

26. Dodge KA, Greenberg MT, Malone PS. The Conduct Problems Prevention Research Group: **Testing an idealized model of the development of serious violence in adolescence.** *Child Dev.* 2008, **79:** 1907–1927.
   ** Using data from the Fast Track Project, a multisite study on the development and prevention of conduct problems in children, the authors tested a complex dynamic cascade model of development. Consistent with theory, early social adversity predicted harsh and inconsistent parenting, which had cascading associations with children's social-cognitive deficits, early conduct problems, social and academic failure in elementary school, reduced parental modeling, affiliation with deviant peers, and adolescent violence. The authors emphasize transactional influences between parents and child over time and highlight opportunities for preventive interventions.

27. Patterson GR, Reid JB, Dishion TJ: *Antisocial Boys.* Eugene, OR: Castalia; 1992.

28. Cicchetti D, Toth SL: **Child maltreatment.** In *Handbook of Child Psychology and Developmental Science,* vol. 4. Edited by Lerner RM. **New Jersey: Wiley; 2015: 1–51.**

29. Caspi A, McClay J, Moffitt TE, Mill J, Martin J, Craig IW, Taylor A, Poulton R: **Role of genotype in the cycle of violence in maltreated children.** *Science* 2002, **297:** 851–853.

30. Jaffee SR, Caspi A, Moffitt TE, Polo-Tomas M. Taylor A: **Individual, family, and neighborhood factors distinguish resilient from non-resilient maltreated children.** *Child Abuse Negl.* 2007. **31:** 231–253.

31. Thibodeau EL, Cicchetti D, Rogosch FA: **Child maltreatment, impulsivity, and antisocial behavior in African American children: moderation effects from a dopaminergic gene index.** *Dev. Psychopathol.* 2015, **27:** 1621–1636.

32. Ben-David V, Jonson-Reid M, Drake B, Kohl PL: **The association between childhood maltreatment experiences and the onset of maltreatment perpetration in young adulthood controlling for proximal and distal risk factors.** *Child Abuse Negl.* 2015, **46:** 132–141.

33. Narayan AJ, Englund MM, Carlson EA, Egeland B: **Adolescent conflict as a developmental process in the prospective pathway from exposure to interparental violence to dating violence.** *J. Abnorm. Child Psychol.* 2014, **42:** 239–250.

34. Fleming PJ, McCleary-Sills J, Morton M, Levtov R, Heilman B, Barker G: **Risk factors for men's lifetime perpetration of physical violence against intimate partners: results from the International Men and Gender Equality Survey (IMAGES) in eight countries.** *PLoS One* 2015, **10:** e0118639.

35. Widom CS, Wilson HW: **Intergenerational transmission of violence.** In *Violence and Mental Health.* Edited by Lindert J, Levav I. Springer; 2015.

36. Espeiage DL, Low S, Rao MA, Hong JS, Little TD: **Family violence, bullying, fighting, and substance use among adolescents: a longitudinal mediation model.** *J. Res. Adolesc.* 2014, **24:** 337–349.

37. Jouriles EN, Vu ML, McDonald R, Rosenfield D: **Children's appraisals of conflict, beliefs about aggression, and externalizing problems in families characterized by severe intimate partner violence.** *J. Fam. Psychol.* 2014, **28:** 915–924.

38. Temple JR, Shorey RC, Tortolero SR, Wolfe DA, Stuart GL: **Importance of gender and attitudes about violence in the relationship between exposure to interparental violence and the perpetration of teen dating violence.** *Child Abuse Negl.* 2013, **37:** 343–352.

39. Van Horn P, Lieberman AF: **Early exposure to trauma: domestic and community violence.** In *The Cambridge Handbook of Environment in Human Development.* Edited by Mayes LC, Lewis M. New York, NY: Cambridge University Press; 2012: 466–479.

40. Margolin G, Gordis EB: **The effects of family and community violence on children.** *Annu. Rev. Psychol* 2000, **51**: 445–479.

41. Chen P, Voisin DR, Jacobson KC: **Community violence exposure and adolescent delinquency: examining a spectrum of promotive factors.** *Youth Soc.* 2016, **48**: 33–57.

42. **Editorial: developmental cascades [special issue].** Masten AS, Cicchetti D. 2010, **22**: 491–495.

43. Bond RM, Bushman BJ: **The contagious spread of violence through social networks in U.S. adolescents.** *Am. J. Public Health* 2017, **107**: 288–294.

44. Brurnley LD, Jaffee SR: **Defining and distinguishing promotive and protective effects for childhood externalizing psychopathology: a systematic review.** *Soc. Psychiatry Psychiatr. Epidemiol.* 2015, **51**: 803–815.
 * This systematic review paper synthesizes evidence on individual, family, and community level processes associated with lower childhood externalizing behavior. A subset of papers identified non-linear associations between adaptive processes and child outcomes using trichomotization (*i.e.*, comparing the middle half of the distribution to its upper and lower quartiles). The review further distinguished between evidence for promotive versus protective effects of family factors, for example, finding that parent-child relationship quality has been shown to be protective with respective to parental delinquency and stressful life events, but promotive in the context of peer substance use and neighborhood disadvantage.

45. Vanderbilt-Adriance E, Shaw DS, Brennan LM, Dishion TJ, Gardner F, Wilson MN: **Child, family, and community protective factors in the development of children's early conduct problems.** *Fam. Relat.* 2015, **64**: 64–79.

46. Ozer EJ, Lavi I, Douglas L, Wolf JP: **Protective factors for youth exposed to violence in their communities: a review of family, school, and community moderators.** *J. Clin. Child Adolesc. Psychol.* 2015: 1–26 http://dx.doi.org/10.1080/15374416.2015.1046178.

47. Masten AS, Monn AR: **Child and family resilience: a call for integrated science, practice, and professional training.** *Fam. Relat.* 2015, **64**: 5–21.

48. Jolliffe D, Farrington DP, Loeber R, Pardini D: **Protective factors for violence: results from the Pittsburgh Youth Study.** *J. Crim. Justice* 2016, **45**: 32–40.

49. Farrington DP, Ttofi MM, Piquero AR: **Risk, promotive, and protective factors in the Cambridge Study in Delinquent Development.** *J. Crim. Justice* 2016, **45**: 63–70.

50. Herrenkohl TI, Tajima EA, Whitney SD, Huang B: **Protection against antisocial behavior in children exposed to physically abusive discipline.** *J. Adolesc. Health* 2005, **36**: 457–465.

51. Dubow EF, Huesmann LR, Boxer P, Smith C: **Childhood and adolescent risk and protective factors for violence in adulthood.** *J. Crim. Justice* 2016, **45**: 26–31.

52. Patterson GR, Forgatch MS, DeGarmo DS: **Cascading effects following intervention.** *Dev. Psychopathol.* 2010, **22**: 941–970.

53. Chen M, Chan KL: **Effects of parenting programs on child maltreatment prevention: a meta-analysis.** *Trauma Violence Abuse* 2016, **17**: 88–104.

54. Olds DL: **The nurse-family partnership; an evidence-based preventive intervention.** *Infant Ment. Health J.* 2006, **27**: 5–25.

55. Schweinhart LJ, Barnes HV, Weikart DP: *Significant Benefits: The HighScope Perry Preschool Study Through Age 27.* Ypsilanti: HighScope Press; 1993.

56. Loeber A, Farrington DP (Eds): *Serious and Violent Juvenile Offenders: Risk Factors and Successful interventions.* Thousand Oaks, CA: Sage; 1998.

57. Dishion TJ, Tipsord JM: **Peer contagion in child and adolescent social and emotional development.** *Anna. Rev. Psychol.* 2011, **62**: 189–214.

58. Weisz JR, Kazdin AE (Eds): Evidence-based Psychotherapies for Children and Adolescents. New York: Guilford Press; 2010.

59. Brody GH, Chen YF, Beach SR: **Differential susceptibility to prevention: GABAergic, dopaminergic, and multilocus effects.** *J. Child Psychol. Psychiatry* 2013, **54**: 883–871.

* This innovative study combines data from two large prevention trials (Strong African American Families and Strong African American Families-Teen) to test associations among genetic variants implicated in alcohol use, intervention status, and longitudinal increases in delinquent behavior (*i.e.,* alcohol use). Variation in dopaminergic and GABA-ergic genes were associated with increases in alcohol use across two years, but only for youth whose families did not participate in the Strong African American Families intervention. Within the intervention group, alcohol use increased *less* for youth with more alcohol-associated genetic variants. This provides novel evidence that prevention programs can moderate genetic vulnerability and extends the differential susceptibility hypothesis, which proposes that some individuals are more genetically sensitive to environmental influences, both negative and positive (*i.e.,* the prevention program).

CHAPTER 8

An Update on Posttraumatic Stress Disorder in Children and Adolescents

Daniel F. Connor, MD[1], Julian D. Ford, PhD[1],
Amy F. T. Arnsten, PhD[2], and Carolyn A. Greene, PhD[1]

Recent violent tragedies in schools, universities, and in public spaces have focused increased attention on the symptoms and consequences of maladaptive traumatic stress and posttraumatic stress disorder (PTSD) in children and adolescents. Child maltreatment and its consequences continue to be prevalent in the United States. Recent changes to diagnosis in the *Diagnostic and Statistical Manual,* 5th edition (*DSM-5*) identify new criteria for PTSD in young children as well as in school-age children and adolescents. There is a growing body of knowledge about what psychological treatments are effective in children. Pediatricians are often the first to identify and treat traumatized children.[1] An update on this topic is relevant because data show that only 18% of primary care pediatricians' self-report adequate knowledge of childhood PTSDs, and only 10% report frequent experience in the assessment and treatment of posttraumatic stress symptoms.[2]

Epidemiology and Prevalence

Exposure to traumatic stress events including physical abuse, sexual abuse, violence, witnessing violence in the home or community, severe family dysfunction/psychopathology, natural disasters, severe accidents, and/or their own or their caregivers' life-threatening illness is not uncommon in children and adolescents. Estimates from epidemiological studies range from 25% of youths experiencing at least 1 traumatic event by age 16 years[3] to more than 60% by ages 16 to 18 years in the United States and

---

[1] University of Connecticut School of Medicine and Health Care Center, Farmington, CT, USA
[2] Yale University School of Medicine, New Haven, CT, USA

Daniel F. Connor, Julian D. Ford, Amy F.T. Arnsten et al, *Clinical Pediatrics*, vol. 54, issue 6, pp. 517–528, copyright © 2015 by SAGE Publications. Reprinted by Permission of SAGE Publications, Inc.

internationally.[4, 5] The Centers for Disease Control and Prevention reports that in 2010 more than 740 000 children and youths were treated in hospital emergency departments as a result of violence and that more than 3 million reports of child maltreatment are received each year by state and local agencies.[6]

Toxic stress in childhood may result from intense, frequent, or prolonged activation of the body's neurobiological stress systems in the absence of the buffering protection afforded by a supportive adult caregiving relationship and may result in physiologic, behavioral, and emotional stress-related vulnerabilities to a wide variety of physical and mental illnesses throughout the lifespan.[7] Risk factors for the development of clinically significant problems include exposure to multiple types of trauma (cumulative traumatization or polyvictimization)[8] in the context of a compromised family or extrafamilial social support system (eg, chronic poverty, parental mental illness or substance abuse, interpersonal isolation or affiliation with delinquent peers, multiple out-of-home placements), when children[3] or adolescents[4] experience psychological trauma(s). As the cumulative burden of childhood adversity increases, the likelihood of developing emotional and behavioral problems that persist into adulthood increases in a dose-response manner, including vulnerability to serious medical as well as mental health disorders.[9]

Most children experience transient psychological distress following exposure to traumatic events, which may manifest in the form of distinct changes in behavior (eg, regression, irritability) and physical complaints in young children[10, 11] or peritraumatic (ie, in the immediate wake of trauma exposure) states of distress, heightened arousal, or dissociation.[12]

Children with exposure to traumatic stressors may develop the syndrome of PTSD linked to a traumatic event and characterized by intrusive, avoidant, emotional numbing, and hyperarousal symptoms accompanied by pervasive negative changes in mood, cognition, and self-concept.[13] Associated symptoms may include depression, anxiety, impulsivity, aggression, hyperactivity, agitation, irritability, behavior problems, sleep difficulties, and attentional deficits that further impair daily functioning.[14, 15] The reported overall lifetime prevalence of PTSD in the general youth population is 3% to 9%[16, 17] and varies by gender with approximately 4% of male adolescents and 7% of female adolescents meeting full diagnostic criteria for PTSD.[4, 18] The 1-month posttrauma incidence of PTSD is 15.9%.[19] Least at risk appear to be boys exposed to noninterpersonal trauma (PTSD 1-month incidence of 8.4%). Most at risk for PTSD are girls exposed to interpersonal trauma (32.9%).[19]

It is important to note that a subgroup of youngsters develop persistent symptoms of traumatic stress that often extend beyond PTSD and may be quite varied, including anxiety/fears, anhedonic/dysphoric, angry/aggressive, and/or dissociative symptoms as well as problems with sleep, eating, concentration, substance use, sexuality (primarily following sexual trauma or interpersonal violence), reckless or avoidant behavior, self-harm, or suicidality.[20] In clinical pediatric samples, symptoms of traumatic stress have been found in approximately 90% of sexually abused children, 75% of children exposed to school violence, 50% of children who are physically abused, and in 35% of children exposed to community violence.[21] It is estimated that between 60% and 90% of children presenting for outpatient mental health treatment may have been exposed to at least 1 traumatic stressor.[21]

Trajectories of Posttraumatic Adaptation: Risk and Protective Factors

Outcomes for children after exposure to traumatic stress vary widely and often change over time. Trajectories of poor outcomes include severe initial reactions followed by persistent or episodic posttraumatic impairment (chronic PTSD) and mild to moderate initial reactions followed by severe impairment (delayed PTSD).[22] Delayed PTSD was considered rare until recent findings from prospective studies showed that as many as 2 in 10 youth, as well as adults, do not manifest clinically significant PTSD symptoms for several months or even years following initial exposure to traumatic stressors.[23]

Risk factors for chronic pediatric PTSD include *pretraumatic* psychiatric disorder, impaired caregivers/ family, poverty, low IQ, avoidant/anxious coping, and generalized arousal and negative affect, *exposure* to interpersonal traumatic stressors (eg, maltreatment, sexual assault, domestic violence) or cumulative (multiple type/polyvictimization or recurrent) traumatic stressors, *peritraumatic* distress (fear, perceived life threat, dissociation, acute PTSD), and *posttraumatic* low social support, social withdrawal, comorbid psychological problems, poor family functioning, and cognitive alterations (rumination, distraction, thought suppression, and attention bias toward threat).[4, 11, 20, 24]

On the other hand, many children are resilient and either are relatively asymptomatic following exposure to the adverse effects of trauma and able to adapt and preserve both functioning and development (resilient) or have moderate to severe initial reactions or early-onset PTSD (ie, within 3 months of exposure) but improve and regain normative functioning over time with or without treatment (recovery).[22] Resilience in the face of exposure to traumatic or other stressors and a capacity for posttraumatic growth is facilitated by protective factors such as individual self-control and problem-solving skills, and relational and environmental factors such as good schools, safe neighborhoods, positive relationships with supportive caregivers, socioeconomic advantage, religious faith, success at school and with peer friendships, and older age at time of traumatic exposure.[17, 25] Lower traumatic event frequency, number, and intensity of exposure also are important in determining resilient childhood posttraumatic outcomes. Individual capacity for adaptive resilience in the face of traumatic threat largely depends on human adaptive systems embedding the exposed child in a supportive caregiving web involving caregivers, families, friends, communities, and cultures.[26, 27]

Diagnostic Criteria for PTSD

In the fifth edition of the *Diagnostic and Statistical Manual of Mental Disorders* (*DSM-5*), PTSD is no longer considered an anxiety disorder, but instead is included in a new chapter on trauma- and stressor-related disorders. PTSD is a psychiatric disorder in which exposure to a traumatic or stressful event is explicitly required as part of the diagnosis and characteristic symptoms follow exposure to one or more traumatic events. For children aged 7 years and older, diagnostic criteria include 4 clusters of symptoms that emerge or are exacerbated following exposure to actual or threatened death, serious injury, or sexual violence through direct experience, witnessing an event, learning of a traumatic event occurring to a close family member or friend, or exposure to aversive details of a traumatic event (see Table 8.1). These symptoms must occur for duration of greater than 1 month and be associated with clinical distress and impairment in functioning.

For young children, there now exist explicit PTSD criteria, which include developmentally specific manifestations of symptoms. Acute stress disorder is diagnosed when traumatic stress or dissociative symptoms begin within 3 days of trauma exposure and resolve within 1 month.[13]

Table 8.1. *Posttraumatic Stress Disorder (PTSD) Diagnostic Criteria*[a]

A. Exposure to traumatic event(s) that involve actual or threatened death, serious physical injury, or sexual violation in one or more of the following ways (in children <6 years, exposure to actual or threatened death, serious injury, or sexual violence):
  1. Direct exposure to self (directly experiencing the traumatic events)
  2. Witness direct exposure to others (witnessing, in person, the event(s) as it occurred to others, especially primary caregivers)
  3. Learning of exposure by a close relative or close friend (learning that the traumatic event(s) occurred to a parent or caregiving figure)
  4. Repeated exposure to gruesome details of such exposures by others
B. Intrusive reexperiencing of traumatic event(s), including the following:
  1. Unwanted memories or distress related to reminders of traumatic event(s) (recurrent, involuntary, and intrusive distressing memories of the traumatic event(s). May be expressed as play reenactment)
  2. Nightmares of traumatic events or emotional distress (includes night terrors for children)
  3. Flashbacks (experiencing traumatic events as if they were occurring in the moment; dissociative reactions in which the child feels or acts as if the traumatic event(s) were recurring. Such trauma-specific reenactment may occur in play, derealization, depersonalization)
  4. Intense or prolonged psychological distress at exposure to trauma reminders
  5. Marked physiological reactions to reminders of the traumatic event(s)
C. Avoidance of stimuli (including people, places, conversations, activities, reminders, or bodily or emotional feelings) associated with the traumatic event(s)
  1. Avoidance of internal reminders of the traumatic event(s)
  2. Avoidance of external reminders of the traumatic event(s)
D. Negative alterations in cognitions and mood associated with the trauma
  1. Difficulty recalling important aspects of traumatic event(s)
  2. Persistent belief that the world is not safe or that oneself is irreversibly harmed or ruined
  3. Persistent distorted blame of self or others for traumatic event(s)
  4. Persistent negative emotion state(s) (substantially increased frequency of negative emotional states such as fear, guilt, sadness, shame, and confusion)
  5. Emotional numbing: inability to feel or express positive emotions (markedly diminished interest or participation in significant activities, including constriction of play)
  6. Detachment or withdrawal from relationships (socially withdrawn behaviors)
  7. Anhedonia (persistent reduction in expression of positive emotions)
E. Alterations in arousal and reactivity associated with the traumatic event
  1. Problems with anger or aggressive behavior (irritable behavior and angry outbursts [with little or no provocation], usually expressed as verbal or physical aggression toward people or objects—including extreme temper tantrums)
  2. Reckless, dangerously careless, or deliberately self-harming behavior
  3. Persistently feeling tense and on guard (hypervigilance)
  4. Easily startled (hyperarousal, exaggerated startle response)
  5. Difficulty in sustaining concentrated attention
  6. Problems falling or staying asleep (restless sleep)
F. Duration of symptoms (criteria B, C, D, and E) at least 30 days
G. The disturbance causes clinically significant distress or impairment in social, occupational, or other important areas of functioning
H. The disturbance is not attributable to the physiological effects of a medication or illicit substance or another medical condition

[a] Adapted from the *Diagnostic and Statistical Manual*, 5th edition (*DSM-5*) of the American Psychiatric Association. These criteria apply to adults, adolescents, and children older than 6 years. Criteria for children younger than 6 years appear in parentheses next to the older age criteria.

Evaluation of PTSD in Children

Pediatric providers cannot practically assess every type, let alone incident, of the potentially traumatic events that their patients may have experienced. However, careful listening and selective probing for details of recent or distal events that may have been traumatic is an efficient way to conduct ongoing surveillance when reviewing records or getting the history or progress updates from parents/caregivers and children.[28] It is helpful to refer to carefully constructed and thorough trauma-screening instruments (see Table 8.2 for examples) as a guiding framework for selective inquiry rather than as formal screening interview.[29-33] It is important to consider traumatic events that happen to others as well as directly to the child, especially those affecting the child's parents or caregivers, which the child witnessed or learned about (eg, domestic violence, severe injuries, or illnesses).

A complementary approach to pediatric surveillance of children's trauma history is careful observation and eliciting caregiver reports of children's symptoms consistent with PTSD. Children and caregivers may be unaware of or reluctant to disclose potentially traumatic events. Parents may not

Table 8.2. *Trauma History Screening Instruments for Children and Adolescents*

Measure	[a]Normed, [b]Validation, [c]Field-Tested Population	Description
Childhood Trauma Questionnaire–Short Form (CTQ-SF; Bernstein et al, 2003; www.psychcorp.com)[29]	[a,b,c]12- to 17-year-old psychiatric patients and community sample	28-item self-report questionnaire, subscales (emotional, physical, sexual abuse; emotional, physical neglect and validity minimization/denial)
Dimensions of Stressor Exposure (DOSE; Fletcher, 1996; kenneth.fletcher@umassmed.edu)[31]	[c]8- to 18-year-olds from psychiatric and community samples	50-item clinician-administered scale (26 items characterize each stressful event; 24 items specific to sexual abuse)
Traumatic Experiences Screening Instrument (TESI; Daviss et al, 2000; Ford, 2008; www.ncptsd. org)[30, 32]	[a,b]6- to 17-year-old psychiatric patients, emergency patients, and juvenile justice–involved youth [c]3- to 17-year-olds	15- to 24-item clinician-administered (age 3–17 years) or child self-report (age 11–17 years) measure of direct or witnessed exposure to noninterpersonal (accident, illness, disaster, loss) or interpersonal (abuse, neglect, family/community violence) traumatic victimization; probes for age(s) of onset, recency, risk factors, and Criterion A2 peritraumatic distress
UCLA Post Traumatic Stress Disorder Reaction Index (PTSD-RI; Steinberg et al, 2004; asteinberg@mednet.ucla.edu)[33]	[b,c]7- to 17-year-olds from psychiatric, school, child protection, medical, and community populations	13 self- or parent-rated items answered Yes-No (disaster, accident, medical trauma, assault, loss, abuse): "VERY SCARY, DANGEROUS, OR VIOLENT things that sometimes happen to children. These are times when someone was HURT VERY BADLY OR KILLED, or could have been."

know what has happened to their child, but they can identify abrupt changes or persistent deterioration in their child's behavior and functioning. With both young children and with older children and adolescents, such changes or deterioration in behavior or emotion are not exclusively the result of traumatic events but have been found to be associated with traumatic exposure.[10, 11] In addition, most children who experience potentially traumatic events do *not* develop lasting debilitating posttraumatic stress problems,[34] whereas other children develop PTSD despite their caregivers not being aware of any traumatic exposures.[35] Therefore, pediatric providers should be knowledgeable of brief systematic PTSD screening measures (see Table 8.3) in order to be able to detect symptoms or functional impairment that may be indicators of ptsd.[28, 30, 33, 36–40] Both parent/caregiver and child self-report versions of brief PTSD screening instruments have been validated and can be administered as a part of routine screening—or used by the pediatric provider as a framework and guide for conducting surveillance during history taking and at subsequent visits or checkups.

Table 8.3. *Validated Screening Measures for Child/Adolescent PTSD Symptoms (Ford et al, 2013)*[28]

Measure	[a]Normed, [b]Validation, [c]Field-Tested Population	Description
Symptoms of Traumatic Stress Child Version (SOTS-C; Ford, 2011)[38]	[b,c]5- to 17-year-olds in psychiatric or juvenile justice services	Clinician rating (7-point severity scale) of severity in past month of intrusive reexperiencing, avoidance, negative alterations in cognition and mood, hyperarousal, emotion, behavioral, and somatic dysregulation, dissociation, altered beliefs about self and the world, altered sexual functioning
UCLA Post Traumatic Stress Disorder Reaction Index (PTSD-RI; Steinberg et al, 2004); asteinberg@mednet.ucla.edu)[33]	[b,c]7- to 17-year-olds from psychiatric, school, child protection, medical, and community populations	Child self-report and parent/caregiver report of the frequency in an index month of the 17 (for *DSM-IV* version) or 20 (for *DSM-5* version) PTSD symptoms, 4 dissociative symptoms, and multidomain functional impairment
PTSD Checklist for Children/Parent Report (Daviss et al, 2000; Ford et al, 2000)[30, 39]	[b,c]5- to 17-year olds from psychiatric, medical, and community populations	Child self-report and parent/caregiver report of the severity of distress and impairment in an index month caused by the 17 *DSM-IV* PTSD symptoms
PTSD Symptom Scale for Children (Foa et al, 2001)[37]	[b,c]7- to 17-year olds from psychiatric, medical, and community populations	Child self-report and parent/caregiver report of the severity of distress and impairment in an index month caused by the 17 *DSM-IV* PTSD symptoms
Trauma Symptom Checklist for Children (TSCC) and Young Children (TSCYC) (Lanktree et al, 2008)[40]	[a,b,c]3- to 17-year-olds in schools, medical, child protection, and mental health services	Parent (TSCYC) and youth (TSCC) report of factor analysis–derived subscales for child posttraumatic stress, anxiety, depression, anger, dissociation, sexual symptoms. TSCC includes 2 validity scales.
Adolescent Dissociative Experiences Scale (ADES; Armstrong et al, 1997)[36]	[b,c]11- to 16-year olds in the community and in psychiatric services	20-item self-report (0–11 scale or 6-point Likert-type scale); with factor scores for dissociative absorption, depersonalization, amnesia, passive influence

Abbreviations: *DSM, Diagnostic and Statistical Manual of Mental Disorders*; PTSD, posttraumatic stress disorder.

Treatment

Psychosocial Therapies

Although childhood PTSD is highly impairing and has heterogeneous affective, anxiety, behavioral, somatic, and relational symptoms, it is a highly treatable condition. Over the past 20 years several empirically supported psychotherapies have been developed for both acute and chronic pediatric PTSD (see Table 8.4).[1, 41–52, 56]

Child traumatic stress treatment research is investigating specific therapeutic mechanisms that appear effective in trauma therapy with children and adolescents.[21, 53] Common treatment elements include (1) psychoeducation about PTSD, (2) relaxation and coping skills, (3) affect monitoring and emotion regulation skills, (4) cognitive processing of reactions to trauma, (5) helping the child construct a therapeutic trauma narrative, (6) in vivo exposure to trauma reminders and practicing of coping skills, (7) conjoint parent-child sessions, and (8) monitoring and enhancing individual safety.[53]

Evidence-based psychotherapy interventions for youngsters with PTSD and/or trauma exposure psychological symptoms have been developed for individual, group, and parent-child formats and delivered in therapist's offices, schools, and in the home or community.[54] When children (or their parents) are reluctant or unwilling to talk about specific trauma memories, there are evidence-based therapeutic options for either (a) preparing the child and parents to feel sufficiently safe, confident, and able to modulate distressing emotions so that the child is able to experience the trauma narrative portion of treatment successfully[55, 56] or (b) to enable the child and parent to develop cognitive-behavioral[57] and self-regulation[52] skills that address PTSD by reducing everyday traumatic stress reactivity and increasing emotion regulation, self-efficacy, and social support. A randomized controlled trial also supports the use of in vivo trauma exposure—carefully orchestrated encounters with cues in the youth's natural environment that are not traumatic but that are associated with past trauma—when coping skills are first taught to teenagers exposed to sexual abuse.[42]

Early identification of children who have experienced traumatic stressors and preventive intervention addressing risk factors for the development of PTSD is recommended but not as yet widely implemented or evidence based,[58, 59] with the positive exception of cognitive-behavioral interventions for traumatized children following disasters[60] or medical trauma.[61] Collaborative care strategies are indicated for integrated pediatric mental health treatment of traumatized children.[62] When pediatric and mental health providers explicitly share the responsibility for assisting traumatized children and their families to restore safety and recover from trauma-related behavioral and emotional problems, this can ensure the necessary continuity and coordination of care—as illustrated by 2 case vignettes. Note that all case materials are disguised to protect patients' privacy.

Case Vignette 1.   Alex is an 8-year-old boy who attends third grade at his neighborhood elementary school. Six months ago, he was riding his bike on the sidewalk in front of his house when he was hit by a car backing out of a nearby driveway. He suffered a broken arm, several bruised ribs, and severe lacerations. Prior to the accident, Alex was a friendly, outgoing boy who did well in school, had lots of friends, and enjoyed spending time with his younger brother and parents. Although his physical wounds have healed, Alex's parents have noticed several changes in his behavior since the accident. He climbs into their bed almost every night complaining of nightmares and he refuses to ride his bike or even play outside with the other neighborhood kids.

In fact, he mostly seems to keep to himself, declining invitations to play dates and birthday parties. Recently, Alex's parents suggested that they go on a family bike ride thinking that this would "help him get back out there." Alex immediately declined. When his parents gently urged him, he

Table 8.4. *Trauma-Focused Therapies[a]*

Intervention	[a]AHRQ Maltreatment, [b]AHRQ Other Trauma, [c]NREPP Evidence Base, [d]RCT *N*, Sample	Description
Trauma-Focused Cognitive-Behavioral Therapy (TFCBT)	[a,b,c,d]N = 507; age 3–18 years, male and female, sexual abuse, physical abuse, family violence, accidents	8- to 16-session individual/conjoint or group therapy with coping skills and (in some but not all cases) trauma narrative processing (Cohen et al, 2012; Mannarino et al, 2012)[45, 56]
Parent-Child Interaction Therapy (PCIT)	[a,c,d]N = 263; age 2–12 years, male and female, physical abuse,- family violence	14- to 20-week individual/conjoint therapy with behavior management and communication skills for parents aimed at preventing recurrent maltreatment (Chaffin et al, 2011)[41]
Child-Parent Psychotherapy (CPP)	[a,b,c,d]N = 141; age 1–5 years, male and female, sexual abuse, physical abuse, family or community violence	30- to 50-session (1 year) dyadic therapy focused on maternal and child attachment security, child behavior and traumatic stress symptoms (Lieberman et al, 2006)[44]
Trauma Affect Regulation: Guide for Education and Therapy (TARGET)	[b,c,d]N = 205; age 11 years to early adult, female, sexual abuse, physical abuse, family or community violence	10- to 12-session individual therapy with affect regulation, mindfulness, and trauma symptom–coping skills (Ford et al, 2011, 2012)[43,52]
Cognitive-Behavioral Intervention for Trauma in the School (CBITS)	[b,c,d]N = 121; age 10–15 years, male and female, violence	10 group sessions in school settings with coping skills and trauma memory disclosure (Stein et al, 2003)[46]
Child and Family Traumatic Stress Intervention (CFTSI)	[b,c,d]N = 61; age 3–15 years, male and female, family or community violence	4 conjoint/individual sessions for acute traumatic stress reactions and parent-child communication (Berkowitz et al, 2011)[48]
Cognitive Processing Therapy (CPT)	[b,d]N = 38; age 15–8 years old, incarcerated males, physical abuse or violence	12 individual sessions with coping and cognitive processing skills, trauma memory narrative processing (Ahrens and Rexford, 2002)[47]
Eye Movement Desensitization and Reprocessing (EMDR)	[b,d]N = 27; age 10–17 years male and female, motor vehicle accidents	4 individual sessions with coping and cognitive processing skills, trauma memory narrative processing (Kemp et al, 2010)[50]
Trauma and Grief Components Therapy for Adolescents (TGCT)	[b,d]N = 159; age 11–17 years male and female, war violence and traumatic loss	10 group sessions, 1 individual session, and 1 parent session with coping and cognitive processing skills, trauma memory narrative processing (Layne et al, 2008)[22]
Narrative Exposure Therapy (NET)	[b,c,d]N = 31; age 8–14 years male- and female, acute disaster/refugee trauma	6 individual sessions with coping and cognitive processing skills, trauma memory narrative processing (Catani et al, 2009)[49]
Prolonged Exposure Therapy (PET)	[a,d]N = 61; age 13–18 years all female, sexual abuse	14 individual sessions with coping skills and in vivo exposure to confront the trauma in real life (Foa etal, 2013)[42]

Abbreviations: AHRQ, Agency for Healthcare Research and Quality; NREPP, National Registry of Evidence-based Programs and Practices;

RCT, randomized controlled trial.

[a]See Ford and Courtois[1] for more detailed descriptions.

began to scream and cry, and locked himself in his room. His teachers have also noticed changes in Alex. They frequently have to repeat instructions to him several times, and even then he rarely finishes his school work. They often observe him staring out the window. At recess, Alex no longer climbs on the playscape or runs around with his friends as he used to, preferring instead to play quietly in the sand box or sit on a bench and read. On several occasions, he has burst into tears over small setbacks or frustration, or yelled at other kids for accidently bumping into him.

Case Vignette 2.   Danielle is a 16-year-old girl referred for treatment after her adoptive mother called emergency mobile psychiatric services because Danielle was unable to calm down following an argument. Danielle was removed from her biological mother's care at the age of 4 because of her mother's neglect, substance use, and domestic violence between her mother and her boyfriend. She was placed in a series of foster homes, moving frequently between placements because of tantrums and accusations that she was stealing food and hiding it under her bed. At the age of 6, her biological father gained custody of her, but she was removed from his care and placed in a foster home at the age of 9 because he and her stepmother were physically and emotionally abusive toward her. She was adopted by her foster mother when she was 11 years old. Initially, Danielle got along well with her adoptive mother and did well in school, where she was a friendly and hardworking student. However, about 3 years ago, she began to exhibit a number of concerning behaviors. She started smoking cigarettes and marijuana and engaged in self-injurious cutting. She began wearing suggestive clothing and spending more time with a group of older adolescents, including a 16-year-old boy she referred to as her boyfriend. She became easily angered when she was told she could not do something, and she and her adoptive mother began to have increasingly heated arguments, often culminating in Danielle running away. Her adoptive mother reported that she did not feel able to control Danielle or keep her safe. In the past 2 years, Danielle has been involved in several individual outpatient and intensive outpatient therapy programs. She has been taken to the emergency department 3 times for evaluation because of behavioral concerns and has been hospitalized in an inpatient unit once because of an attempted overdose of pills. Her teachers report that she appears angry much of the time and seems to have difficulty paying attention in class. She is frequently defiant toward authority figures, and she has been suspended twice for fighting with other students. She often skips classes and leaves school grounds without permission, and is at risk of failing several of her classes. Danielle frequently has trouble falling asleep and in recent months she has had repeated nightmares of being murdered.

Case Discussion

These 2 cases illustrate different characteristics in the presentation of pediatric PTSD and highlight different evidence-based therapeutic approaches to address the 2 individuals' different trajectories of posttraumatic adaptation, symptom presentation, developmental stage, number and type of traumas experienced, amount of social support, and level of current impairment.

In case 1, Alex is a typically developing school-aged child, with good attachment relationships, consistent social support, and a stable and safe home environment. He experienced acute PTSD with anxious and depressed symptoms (internalizing symptoms) after a single traumatic accident. After emergency department treatment of his broken bones and lacerations, he was referred for follow-up with his outpatient pediatrician. The role of the pediatrician is to recognize symptoms of traumatic stress in Alex, provide psychoeducation to the family, and recognize the need for and refer Alex to appropriate mental health treatment. The goals of mental health treatment are to address not only Alex's symptoms of traumatic stress but also associated internalizing symptoms. Trauma-focused cognitive-behavioral therapy (TF-CBT) is an evidence-based approach to addressing posttraumatic stress symptoms and internalizing symptoms in children.[45] TF-CBT involves a series of skill-based components presented to children and parents in parallel sessions, and culminates in conjoint sessions in which the child shares his or her "trauma story" with his or her parent(s).

Using this approach, the therapist first provided psychoeducation to both Alex and his mother about trauma and PTSD to help them understand Alex's symptoms and behaviors as common responses to stressful events. Next, Alex was taught relaxation skills to help him recognize, understand, and reduce the physiological reactivity he is experiencing. His parents were taught positive parenting techniques to help them address specific concerns and behaviors. Next, affective recognition and modulation (including feelings identification, intensity ratings, and positive self-talk) was addressed and then cognitive coping skills. Once Alex was able to effectively identify and express his feelings, regulate his emotions, and use cognitive coping skills to address distressing thoughts, his therapist told him that he was ready to create his trauma narrative, which could take the form of any developmentally appropriate undertaking that engaged him in thinking about his traumatic experience, including creation of a story, comic, or song. Alex chose to create a book about his life, his family, and the accident. Through exposure and therapist-guided cognitive processing, Alex increased his ability to tolerate thinking and talking about his accident and identified and altered unhelpful and inaccurate beliefs about what happened ("it was my fault"), himself ("I'm a bad boy"), and the world ("it's not safe to go outside"). When his trauma narrative was complete, Alex shared it with his parents, who had been carefully prepared by the therapist for this meeting, including engaging in role-plays of supportive and validating responses, praise, and feedback for Alex, thus providing the family the opportunity to practice talking about the trauma together, and simultaneously enhancing the parents' role as supportive and careful listeners for Alex. The therapist also kept track with Alex's mother of subsequent pediatric visits and provided the pediatrician with a brief summary of the therapy and Alex's progress prior to each visit. With this information, his pediatrician was able to efficiently check with Alex's mother about her perception of Alex's recovery and the therapy, and to observe how Alex was doing behaviorally in each visit.

By contrast, Danielle (case 2) is an adolescent girl who endured multiple interpersonal victimization events and traumatic losses throughout her early childhood, including emotional and physical abuse at the hands of both her mother and father, twice being removed from her biological parents' home, and multiple placements in foster homes. Although initially Danielle was relatively asymptomatic despite her significant trauma history, the onset of adolescence brought with it a delayed posttraumatic response. Danielle exhibited some of the more typical symptoms of PTSD, including intrusive reexperiencing (nightmares), avoidance of school, and hypervigilance (sleep and concentration problems), along with dysphoric, angry, and aggressive (externalizing) symptoms. Danielle had limited and inconsistent pediatric care until she was adopted, but her adoptive mother identified a pediatric practice that specialized in adolescent female health issues and scheduled regular checkup visits twice yearly to help Danielle develop better self-care and physical hygiene.

Danielle had been required to undergo emergency psychiatric treatment in several of her previous preadoptive placements. Danielle felt that none of these therapies had been helpful, because either the clinician seemed critical and "made me feel like there was something wrong with me, that I needed to be fixed" or the contact was only for a very limited time period and "as soon as I started to like [the therapists] I had to stop seeing them because I was moved to another group home or foster family." Danielle had been indifferent toward and unwilling to engage with 2 therapists who the Child Protective Services worker had required her to see, and her adoptive mother did not want to force Danielle to be in therapy. The adoptive mother talked privately about this dilemma with a nursing case manager in the pediatrics office, and the case manager then talked with both Danielle and her mother about what Danielle viewed as helpful in her positive past experiences with therapy and how they could identify therapists with a similar style and orientation whom Danielle could "audition" and then work with for as long as necessary without fear of untimely terminations. Danielle shifted from being unwilling to consider therapy to being skeptical but open to seeing if there was a therapist with whom she felt comfortable who could help—but not "fix"—her.

Danielle's therapist developed treatment goals that addressed the multiple domains of self-regulation and relatedness difficulties that were affected by the emotional and physical violence and the disruption of primary attachment bonds that occurred within the context of Danielle's developmental upbringing. In addition, addressing the strained relationship between Danielle and her adoptive mother, and helping her mother to provide consistent care, structure, and monitoring of Danielle's high-risk behaviors while also supporting Danielle's normative adolescent strivings for autonomy and privacy, were important components of her treatment. The therapist, with Danielle's knowledge and permission (and her mother's consent), updated the pediatric nurse case manager on a monthly basis about the progress, and setbacks, in Danielle's therapy. When Danielle had her next semiannual pediatric visit, the pediatrician and the nurse case manager were able to ask her and her mother what seemed helpful or not in the therapy, and how they each viewed Danielle's progress in dealing with emotional and behavioral challenges. With the preparation provided by the therapist's updates, this discussion was efficient and enabled the pediatric professionals to support Danielle's progress and her continued therapeutic involvement.

The mental health clinician used a combination of Parent Management Training and Trauma Affect Regulation: Guide for Education and Therapy (TARGET) to achieve these goals.[28] Danielle presented to therapy with the same defiant and angry presentation that her adoptive mother and teachers reported. She quickly told her therapist that she was "fine," that she would not talk about her past experiences, and that she did not need any therapy. She followed this up with the assertion that she had already been in lots of therapy and "it didn't help, anyway." Danielle's therapist reassured her that she would not have to talk about her worst memories unless she chose to do so, and that therapy would involve her and her mother learning about how coping with trauma turns on an alarm in the brain (the amygdala) that stays on even when it's not needed unless a trauma survivor knows how to reset it. Danielle liked the idea that her brain had become so proficient at protecting her when she was being abused that now it was stuck in a high alarm state, which was the source of her difficulty with anxiety and anger in relationships and school. As a result, now even small stressors were causing her brain to send out signals to prepare her body for extreme danger (the "fight-flight-freeze" response).

Danielle's therapist further explained to Danielle and her mother that therapy would help Danielle learn skills to deal with these extreme stress reactions by developing abilities that she already had—but had not known to apply to handle stress reactions—to think clearly and focus on her core values when she recognized that her brain and body were going back into "alarm mode." In subsequent sessions, Danielle (and her mother in parallel sessions) learned TARGET's mental focusing skills to help her clear her mind and think before acting, and started to identify the triggers that activated her brain's alarm response. Together, these 2 skills were the first steps in helping Danielle learn how to prepare for and manage her alarm reactions. Next, Danielle's therapist introduced TARGET skills aimed at helping Danielle to become aware of her emotions and thoughts in order to identify and differentiate those that were "reactive" (generated by her alarm) from those that reflect her "main" values, hopes, and goals (those that occur when her alarm is reset by focused thinking). Danielle then worked with her therapist to define her "main" goals and identify the choices and behaviors that would help her achieve them. Once Danielle was able to recognize and modulate what had seemed to be uncontrollable stress reactions, she began to recognize her strengths and the many positive qualities she had to offer. As a result, she was able to become closer with her adoptive mother, enjoy her company, and earn her respect and trust, and ultimately regain a stabilizing sense of hope and self-esteem. Although she still felt troubled and saddened by memories of trauma, her PTSD symptoms subsided.

Neurobiology of Psychotherapy

Neurobiological studies in animals have shown that a sense of control over a stressful situation is key for protecting higher brain functions and allowing top-down regulation of behavior, attention, and emotion by the dorsolateral prefrontal association cortex.[63, 64] When a subject feels out of control, the stress response is activated. High levels of catecholamine and cortisol release take the prefrontal cortex "off-line" while strengthening primitive brain circuits, producing unconscious, reactive behaviors and emotions, and loss of top-down executive control. In contrast, when a subject comes to feel in control of a stressful situation, the prefrontal cortex inhibits the stress response and stays "online" to thoughtfully guide behavior. Effective psychotherapy, which restores a sense of control and insight, likely acts by enhancing prefrontal cortical control over the stress response.[63, 65]

Psychopharmacology

Despite advances in psychotherapy, randomized psychopharmacology clinical trials are noticeably lacking for pediatric PTSD. *Selective serotonin reuptake inhibitors (SSRIs)* are considered to be first-line medications for adults with PTSD, and paroxetine and sertraline have a US Food and Drug Administration indication in adults. However, 2 independent controlled trials of sertraline in pediatric PTSD failed to demonstrate efficacy when compared with placebo.[66, 67] Pediatric PTSD is highly comorbid with other psychiatric disorders and SSRIs are effective for the treatment of pediatric anxiety disorders[68] and depression.[69] Adrenergic medications such as guanfacine extended release and prazosin may have a role in the adjunctive treatment of dysregulated behavior associated with pediatric traumatic stress.[70, 71] However, no randomized controlled trials have yet been completed to support their use for this condition.

Discussion

Recent and continuing community violence has focused attention on the symptoms and consequences of maladaptive traumatic stress and PTSD in children and adolescents. Children suffering from neglect and abuse are not uncommon in the population. Given high rates of traumatic stress exposure in children and adolescents primary care clinicians and pediatricians may increasingly be asked to identify disorders of posttraumatic stress in their treatment practices. *DSM-5* has new diagnostic PTSD criteria for children younger than 6 years. With these diagnostic changes, the prevalence of young child PTSD diagnoses may increase in the population and may increasingly present to the pediatrician for screening, evaluation, and referral.

Current standards-of-practice support TF-CBT as an evidenced-based first-line psychotherapeutic treatment for children with PTSD following abuse or community violence.[53, 66] Despite its overall efficacy, many children and parents decline therapy involving intensive discussion of traumatic experiences, between one quarter to one third of children do not respond to this type of treatment, and in community samples, up to 40% drop out before treatment is complete.[72] Although there is a national network of trained TF-CBT psychotherapists (http://www.nctsn.org), most mental health clinicians have not received TF-CBT training and certification, leading to long waiting lists for PTSD treatment in many mental health practices and clinics. As illustrated by the second case example, trauma-specific emotion regulation psychotherapy (eg, the TARGET intervention) is a viable evidence-based approach for older children and adolescents who either refuse trauma-narrative therapy or whose externalizing behavior problems interfere with therapeutic engagement.[57] Psychopharmacology remains adjunctive to evidence-based psychotherapies for pediatric PTSD.

Progress in the treatment of early-onset disorders of maladaptive traumatic stress is being facilitated by emerging knowledge of phenomenology, prognosis, risk and protective factors, and the neurobiology of stress. Ongoing research in this field offers hope to children and adolescents suffering from the effects of traumatic stress exposure in the developing years. By staying informed about the rapidly developing science and the expanding evidence-based clinical options for the treatment of children's posttraumatic behavioral and emotional disorders, pediatric professionals can respond efficiently and effectively to ensure that traumatized children in their practice receive timely, well-coordinated, and ultimately beneficial treatment.

Declaration of Conflicting Interests

The author(s) declared no potential conflicts of interest with respect to the research, authorship, and/or publication of this article.

Funding

The author(s) received no financial support for the research, authorship, and/or publication of this article.

References

1. Ford JD, Courtois CA, eds. *Treating Complex Traumatic Stress Disorders in Children and Adolescents: Scientific Foundations and Therapeutic Models.* New York, NY: Guilford Press; 2013.
2. Banh MK, Saxe G, Mangione T, Horton NJ. Physician-reported practice of managing childhood posttraumatic stress in pediatric primary care. *Gen Hosp Psychiatry.* 2008; **30:** 536–545.
3. Copeland-Linder N. Posttraumatic stress disorder. *Pediatr Rev.* 2008; **29:** 103–104.
4. McLaughlin KA, Koenen KC, Hill ED, et al. Trauma exposure and posttraumatic stress disorder in a national sample of adolescents. *J Am Acad Child Adolesc Psychiatry.* 2013; **52:** 815.e14-830.e14.
5. Seedat S, Nyamai C, Njenga F, Vythilingum B, Stein DJ. Trauma exposure and post-traumatic stress symptoms in urban African schools: survey in CapeTown and Nairobi. *Br J Psychiatry.* 2004; **184:** 169–175.
6. Centers for Disease Control and Prevention. Assault all injury causes nonfatal injuries and rates per 100,000, all races, both sexes, ages 0 to 24. 2010 (Web-based Injury Statistics Query and Reporting System (WISQARS) (2008). http://www.cdc.gov/injury/wisqars. Accessed December 7, 2011.
7. Shonkoff JP, Garner AS. The lifelong effects of early childhood adversity and toxic stress. *Pediatrics.* 2012; **129:** e232–e246.
8. Grasso DJ, Saunders BE, Williams LM, Hanson R, Smith DW, Fitzgerald MM. Patterns of multiple victimization among maltreated children in Navy families. *J Trauma Stress.* 2013; **26:** 597–604.

9. Felitti VJ, Anda RF, Nordenberg D, et al. Relationship of childhood abuse and household dysfunction to many of the leading causes of death in adults. The Adverse Childhood Experiences (ACE) Study. *Am J Prev Med.* 1998; **14:** 245–258.

10. Briggs-Gowan MJ, Carter AS, Clark R, Augustyn M, McCarthy KJ, Ford JD. Exposure to potentially traumatic events in early childhood: differential links to emergent psychopathology. *J Child Psychol Psychiatry.* 2010; **51:** 1132–1140.

11. Briggs-Gowan MJ, Ford JD, Fraleigh L, McCarthy K, Carter AS. Prevalence of exposure to potentially traumatic events in a healthy birth cohort of very young children in the northeastern United States. *J Trauma Stress.* 2011; **23:** 725–733.

12. Sugar J, Ford JD. Peritraumatic reactions and posttraumatic stress disorder in psychiatrically impaired youth. *J Trauma Stress.* 2012; **26:** 41–49.

13. American Psychiatric Association. *Diagnostic and Statistical Manual of Mental Disorders.* 5th ed. Washington, DC: American Psychiatric Association; 2013.

14. Ford JD, Fraleigh LA, Connor DF. Child abuse and aggression among seriously emotionally disturbed children. *J Clin Child Adolesc Psychol.* 2010; **39:** 25–34.

15. Strawn JR, Adler CM, Fleck DE, et al. Post-traumatic stress symptoms and trauma exposure in youth with first episode bipolar disorder. *Early Interv Psychiatry.* 2010; **4:** 169–173.

16. Breslau N, Davis GC, Andreski P, Peterson E. Traumatic events and posttraumatic stress disorder in an urban population of young adults. *Arch Gen Psychiatry.* 1991; **48:** 216–222.

17. Copeland WE, Keeler G, Angold A, Costello EJ. Posttraumatic stress without trauma in children. *Am J Psychiatry.* 2010; **167:** 1059–1065.

18. Kilpatrick DG, Ruggiero KJ, Acierno R, Saunders BE, Resnick HS, Best CL. Violence and risk of PTSD, major depression, substance abuse/dependence, and comorbidity: results from the National Survey of Adolescents. *J Consult Clin Psychol.* 2003; **71:** 692–700.

19. Alisic E, Zalta AK, van Wesel F, et al. Rates of post-traumatic stress disorder in trauma-exposed children and adolescents: meta-analysis. *Br J Psychiatry.* 2014; **204:** 335–340.

20. D'Andrea W, Ford JD, Stolbach B, Spinazzola J, Van der Kolk BA. Understanding interpersonal trauma in children: why we need a developmentally appropriate trauma diagnosis. *Am J Orthopsychiatry.* 2012; **82:** 187–200.

21. Schneider SJ, Grilli SF, Schneider JR. Evidence-based treatments for traumatized children and adolescents. *Curr Psychiatry Rep.* 2013; **15:** 332.

22. Layne C, Beck C, Rimmasch H, Southwick J, Moreno M, Hobfoll S. Promoting "resilient" posttraumatic adjustment in childhood and beyond. In: Brom D, Pat-Horenczyk R, Ford JD, eds. *Treating Traumatized Children: Risk, Resilience, and Recovery.* London, England: Routledge; 2008: 13–47.

23. Smid GE, Mooren TT, van der Mast RC, Gersons BP, Kleber RJ. Delayed posttraumatic stress disorder: systematic review, meta-analysis, and meta-regression analysis of prospective studies. *J Clin Psychiatry.* 2009; **70:** 1572–1582.

24. Briggs-Gowan MJ, Carter AS, Ford JD. Parsing the effects violence exposure in early childhood: modeling developmental pathways. *J Pediatr Psychol.* 2012; **37:** 11–22.

25. Kelly P. Posttraumatic stress disorder. *Pediatr Rev.* 2012; **33:** 382–383.

26. Betancourt TS, Newnham EA, McBain R, Brennan RT. Post-traumatic stress symptoms among former child soldiers in Sierra Leone: follow-up study. *Br J Psychiatry.* 2013; **203:** 196–202.

27. Masten AS, Narayan AJ. Child development in the context of disaster, war, and terrorism: pathways of risk and resilience. *Amu Rev Psychol.* 2012; **63:** 227–257.

28. Ford JD, Nader K, Fletcher KE. Clinical assessment and diagnosis. In: Ford JD, Courtois CA, eds. *Treating Complex Traumatic Stress Disorders in Children and Adolescents: Scientific Foundations and Therapeutic Models.* New York, NY: Guilford Press; 2013: 116–142.

29. Bernstein DP, Stein JA, Newcomb MD, et al. Development and validation of a brief screening version of the Childhood Trauma Questionnaire. *Child Abuse Negl.* 2003; **27:** 169–190.

30. Daviss WB, Mooney D, Racusin R, Ford JD, Fleischer A, McHugo G. Predicting post-traumatic stress after hospitalization for pediatric injury. *J Am Acad Child Adolesc Psychiatry.* 2000; **39:** 576–583.

31. Fletcher K. Psychometric review of Dimensions of Stressful Events (DOSE) Ratings Scale. In: Stamm BH, ed. *Measurement of Stress, Trauma, and Adaptation.* Lutherville, MD: Sidran Press; 1996: 144–151.

32. Ford JD. Diagnosis of traumatic stress disorders (DSM and ICD). In: Reyes G, Elhai JD, Ford JD, eds. *Encyclopedia of Psychological Trauma.* Hoboken, NJ: Wiley; 2008: 200–208.

33. Steinberg AM, Brymer MJ, Decker K, Pynoos RS. The University of California at Los Angeles Post-Traumatic Stress Disorder Reaction Index. *Curr Psychiatry Rep.* 2004; **6:** 96–100.

34. Copeland WE, Keeler G, Angold A, Costello EJ. Traumatic events and posttraumatic stress in childhood. *Arch Gen Psychiatry.* 2007; **64:** 577–584.

35. Kenardy JA, Spence SH, Macleod AC. Screening for posttraumatic stress disorder in children after accidental injury. *Pediatrics.* 2006; **118:** 1002–1009.

36. Armstrong JG, Putnam FW, Carlson EB, Libero DZ, Smith SR. Development and validation of a measure of adolescent dissociation: the Adolescent Dissociative Experiences Scale. *JNerv Ment Dis.* 1997; **185:** 491–497.

37. Foa EB, Johnson K, Feeny NC, Treadwell KR. The Child PTSD Symptom Scale: a preliminary examination of its psychometric properties. *J Clin Child Psychol.* 2001; **30:** 376–384.

38. Ford JD. Assessing child and adolescent complex traumatic stress reactions. *J Child Adolesc Trauma.* 2011; **4:** 217–232.

39. Ford JD, Racusin R, Ellis CF, et al. Child maltreatment, other trauma exposure, and posttraumatic symptomatology among children with oppositional defiant and attention deficit hyperactivity disorders. *Child Maltreat.* 2000; **5:** 205–217.

40. Lanktree CB, Gilbert AM, Briere J, et al. Multi-informant assessment of maltreated children: convergent and discriminant validity of the TSCC and TSCYC. *Child Abuse Negl.* 2008; **32:** 621–625.

41. Chaffin M, Funderburk B, Bard D, Valle LA, Gurwitch R. A combined motivation and parent-child interaction therapy package reduces child welfare recidivism in a randomized dismantling field trial. *J Consult Clin Psychol.* 2011; **79:** 84–95.

42. Foa EB, McLean CP, Capaldi S, Rosenfield D. Prolonged exposure vs supportive counseling for sexual abuse-related PTSD in adolescent girls: a randomized clinical trial. *JAMA.* 2013; **310:** 2650–2657.

43. Ford JD, Steinberg KL, Zhang W. A randomized clinical trial comparing affect regulation and social problem-solving psychotherapies for mothers with victimization-related PTSD. *Behav Ther.* 2011; **42:** 560–578.

44. Lieberman AF, Ghosh Ippen C, Van Horn P. Child- parent psychotherapy: 6-month follow-up of a randomized controlled trial. *J Am Acad Child Adolesc Psychiatry.* 2006; **45:** 913–918.

45. Mannarino AP, Cohen JA, Deblinger E, Runyon MK, Steer RA. Trauma-focused cognitive-behavioral therapy for children: sustained impact of treatment 6 and 12 months later. *Child Maltreat.* 2012; **17:** 231–241.

46. Stein BD, Jaycox LH, Kataoka S, et al. A mental health intervention for schoolchildren exposed to violence: a randomized controlled trial. *JAMA.* 2003; **290:** 603–611.

47. Ahrens J, Rexford L. Cognitive processing therapy for incarcerated adolescents with PTSD. *J Aggress Maltreat Trauma.* 2002; **6:** 201–216.

48. Berkowitz SJ, Stover CS, Marans SR. The Child and Family Traumatic Stress Intervention: secondary prevention for youth at risk of developing PTSD. *J Child Psychol Psychiatry.* 2011; **52:** 676–685.

49. Catani C, Kohiladevy M, Ruf M, Schauer E, Elbert T, Neuner F. Treating children traumatized by war and Tsunami: a comparison between exposure therapy and meditation-relaxation in North-East Sri Lanka. *BMC Psychiatry.* 2009; **9:** 22.

50. Kemp M, Drummond P, McDermott BM. A wait-list controlled pilot study of eye movement desensitization and reprocessing (EMDR) for children with post-traumatic stress disorder (PTSD) symptoms from motor vehicle accidents. *Clin Child Psychol Psychiatry.* 2010; **15:** 5–25.

51. Layne CM, Saltzman WR, Poppleton L, et al. Effectiveness of a school-based group psychotherapy program for war- exposed adolescents: a randomized controlled trial. *J Am Acad Child Adolesc Psychiatry.* 2008; **47**: 1048–1062.
52. Ford JD, Steinberg KL, Hawke J, Levine J, Zhang W. Randomized trial comparison of emotion regulation and relational psychotherapies for PTSD with girls involved in delinquency. *J Clin Child Adolesc Psychol.* 2012; **41**: 27–37.
53. Carrion VG, Kletter H. Posttraumatic stress disorder: shifting toward a developmental framework. *Child Adolesc Psychiatr Clin NAm.* 2012; **21**: 573–591.
54. American Academy of Child and Adolescent Psychiatry. Practice parameter for the assessment and treatment of children and adolescents with posttraumatic stress disorder. *J Am Acad Child Adolesc Psychiatry.* 2010; **49**: 414–430.
55. Matulis S, Resick PA, Rosner R, Steil R. Developmentally adapted cognitive processing therapy for adolescents suffering from posttraumatic stress disorder after childhood sexual or physical abuse: a pilot study. *Clin Child Fam Psychol Rev.* 2014; **17**: 173–190.
56. Cohen JA, Mannarino AP, Kliethermes M, Murray LA. Trauma-focused CBT for youth with complex trauma. *Child Abuse Negl.* 2012; **36**: 528–541.
57. Deblinger E, Mannarino AP, Cohen JA, Runyon MK, Steer RA. Trauma-focused cognitive behavioral therapy for children: impact of the trauma narrative and treatment length. *Depress Anxiety.* 2011; **28**: 67–75.
58. Kliem S, Kroger C. Prevention of chronic PTSD with early cognitive behavioral therapy. A meta-analysis using mixed-effects modeling. *Behav Res Ther.* 2013; **51**: 753–761.
59. Skeffington PM, Rees CS, Kane R. The primary prevention of PTSD: a systematic review. *J Trauma Dissociation.* 2013; **14**: 404–422.
60. Berger R, Gelkopf M. School-based intervention for the treatment of tsunami-related distress in children: a quasirandomized controlled trial. *Psychother Psychosom.* 2009; **78**: 364–371.
61. Kassam-Adams N, Garcia-Espana JF, Marsac ML, et al. A pilot randomized controlled trial assessing secondary prevention of traumatic stress integrated into pediatric trauma care. *J Trauma Stress.* 2011; **24**: 252–259.
62. Rousseau C, Measham T, Nadeau L. Addressing trauma in collaborative mental health care for refugee children. *Clin Child Psychol Psychiatry.* 2013; **18**: 121–136.
63. Arnsten AFT. Stress signaling pathways that impair prefrontal cortex structure and function. *Nat Rev Neurosci.* 2009; **32**: 267–287.
64. Arnsten A, Mazure CM, Sinha R. This is your brain in meltdown. *Sci Am.* 2012; **306**: 48–53.
65. Arnsten AF, Jin LE. Molecular influences on working memory circuits in dorsolateral prefrontal cortex. *Prog Mol Biol Transl Sci.* 2014; **122**: 211–231.
66. Cohen JA, Mannarino AP, Perel JM, Staron V. A pilot randomized controlled trial of combined trauma-focused CBT and sertraline for childhood PTSD symptoms. *J Am Acad Child Adolesc Psychiatry.* 2007; **46**: 811–819.
67. Robb AS, Cueva JE, Sporn J, Yang R, Vanderburg DG. Sertraline treatment of children and adolescents with posttraumatic stress disorder: a double-blind, placebo-controlled trial. *J Child Adolesc Psychopharmacol.* 2010; **20**: 463–471.
68. Rynn M, Puliafico A, Heleniak C, Rikhi P, Ghalib K, Vidair H. Advances in pharmacotherapy for pediatric anxiety disorders. *Depress Anxiety.* 2011; **28**: 76–87.
69. March J, Silva S, Petrycki S, et al. Fluoxetine, cognitive-behavioral therapy, and their combination for adolescents with depression: Treatment for Adolescents With Depression Study (TADS) randomized controlled trial. *JAMA.* 2004; **292**: 807–820.
70. Connor DF, Grasso DJ, Slivinsky MD, Pearson GS, Banga A. An open-label study of guanfacine extended release for traumatic stress related symptoms in children and adolescents. *J Child Adolesc Psychopharmacol.* 2013; **23**: 244–251.

71. Fraleigh LA, Hendratta VD, Ford JD, Connor DF. Prazosin for the treatment of posttraumatic stress disorder-related nightmares in an adolescent male. *J Child Adolesc Psychopharmacol.* 2009; **19:** 475–476.

72. Cohen JA, Mannarino AP, Iyengar S. Community treatment of posttraumatic stress disorder for children exposed to intimate partner violence: a randomized controlled trial. *Arch Pediatr Adolesc Med.* 2011; **165:** 16–21.

PART *IV*

Family Stressors among Vulnerable and Transitional Populations

Parenting in Poverty: Attention Bias and Anxiety Interact to Predict Parents' Perceptions of Daily Parenting Hassles

Eric D. Finegood, C. Cybele Raver, Meriah L. DeJoseph, and Clancy Blair
New York University

Parenting behaviors are multidetermined and emerge from a coordinated psychobiological caregiving system composed of parents' cognitive (Deater-Deckard, Wang, Chen, & Bell, 2012), affective (Belsky & Barends, 2002), neural (e.g., Swain, 2011), and physiological processes (e.g., Finegood et al., 2016; Gonzalez, Jenkins, Steiner, & Fleming, 2012). Research in areas focusing on risk and prevention to support parenting in the context of adversity highlights the ways that parents' own psychological and neurobiological resources work in concert with proximal interpersonal stressors as well as with the larger socioeconomic context (Belsky & Fearon, 2004). Building on this perspective, the following paper considers the respective roles that socioeconomic, interpersonal, and intrapsychic processes may play in predicting low-income parents' perceptions of their experiences in the parenting role. Specifically, this paper examines perceptions of daily parenting hassles, which constitute a significant part of the subjective parent experience and, at high levels, constitute a form of parenting stress with implications for family functioning and parent well-being (Crnic, Gaze, & Hoffman, 2005; Crnic & Greenberg, 1990).

Eric D. Finegood, C. Cybele Raver, Meriah L. DeJoseph, and Clancy Blair, Department of Applied Psychology, Steinhardt School of Culture, Education and Human Development, New York University.

This research was supported as part of the Buffering Children from Toxic Stress Consortium by Administration for Children and Families (ACF) Grant 90YR0057. The results of this study were presented at the 2016 ACF National Research Conference on Early Childhood in Washington, DC. The authors wish to thank Rachel McKinnon, doctoral student in the New York University Department of Applied Psychology, for her assistance with preparing the data for analysis.

Correspondence concerning this article should be addressed to Eric D. Finegood, Department of Applied Psychology, Steinhardt School of Culture, Education and Human Development, New York University, 627 Broadway, Floor 8, New York, NY 10012. E-mail: edf237@nyu.edu

Perceptions of Daily Hassles in the Parenting Role

Minor parenting hassles describe some of the day-to-day challenges that adults face in the process of caring for their children (Crnic & Greenberg, 1990). These include the normal but oftentimes frustrating occurrences faced by all parents, such as when children have difficulty at mealtimes or when children are resistant to or struggle with daily routines. These and other common minor stressors associated with parenting constitute some of the instances of difficulty that all parents face when raising children (Crnic & Low, 2002). The accumulation of these minor daily hassles over time, however, has been associated with increased parent distress, lowered satisfaction in the caregiving role, and increased child behavior problems (Creasey & Reese, 1996; Crnic & Greenberg, 1990), as well as with reductions in both the sensitivity of parents' behaviors and the positivity of parent-child dyadic interactions (Crnic et al., 2005). As such, perceived hassles in the parenting role constitute a means of understanding parenting stress processes that are highly relevant to parent well-being and family functioning. Certainly, at least some of the differences in parents' feelings of frustration and hassle may be due to child temperamental difficulty (Coplan, Bowker, & Cooper, 2003). But recent research suggests that at least some of the differences in how parents perceive the hassles of caregiving may also be due to factors that are not related to child behavior. Prior work suggests that those factors include the larger socioeconomic context in which families are embedded; a range of interpersonal factors that many parents navigate, such as interparental conflict; and intrapsychic factors, including parents' own affective and cognitive processes (Crnic & Low, 2002; Deater-Deckard, 2004).

Socioeconomic Predictors

Families are embedded within socioeconomic contexts that shape parents' well-being, family functioning, and child development (Conger & Donnellan, 2007; McLoyd, 1990). In the context of deep poverty, parents are at increased risk of experiencing anxiety, depression, negative life events, and reduced coping skills necessary for dealing with the significant and often daily stressors they confront (McLoyd, 1990). In turn, parents in poverty not only experience greater levels of financial hardship but also experience higher levels of parenting stress (Steele et al., 2016). Indeed, perceptions of greater material hardship predict parents' higher levels of psychological distress and less optimal parenting behaviors even when controlling for income levels (Gershoff, Aber, Raver, & Lennon, 2007). As yet, however, no studies to our knowledge have explicitly tested the extent to which financial or material hardship is associated with perceptions of minor parenting hassles above and beyond measured indicators of families' poverty levels.

While early work in the area of socioeconomic conditions and family processes has compared mean levels of parenting competence between low-income families and their middle- and high-income counterparts, more recent work has focused more closely on predictors of individual differences in parenting *among* samples of low-income parents (Burchinal, Vernon-Feagans, Cox, & Key Family Life Project Investigators, 2008; Raver, 2003). This increased attention to the predictors of family processes within groups of low-income parents has underscored that not all low-income families are alike in terms of the stressors that they face or in terms of their risk of parenting difficulty. These studies also offer to inform programs and policies that are means-tested, where an understanding of the mechanisms that alternately support or jeopardize low-income families' healthy functioning is of prime importance. In keeping with this more recent line of inquiry, this paper investigates key predictors of within-group differences in low-income parents' subjective experiences of hassles.

Interpersonal Predictors

In addition to socioeconomic factors, parents' perceptions of parenting hassles may be compounded by difficulties in interpersonal relationships outside the parent-child dyad. Interpersonal factors such as the perceived quality of the marital relationship have been consistently shown to be associated with perceptions of stress in the parent role as well as with parenting styles (Ponnet et al., 2013). Higher levels of marital conflict in particular have been shown across many studies to be associated with higher levels of distress in parents (Goldberg & Easterbrooks, 1984) and to be a robust predictor of more negative parenting behaviors with children (Krishnakumar & Buehler, 2000). Furthermore, exposure to intimate partner violence (IPV)—that is, to physical and/or sexual violence, threats of violence, and/or psychological abuse perpetrated by an intimate partner—may be a prominent contributor to parents' perceptions of difficulty in the parenting role. IPV is widespread—35% of women in the United States experience some exposure to IPV in their lifetime (Black et al., 2011). Perpetration and victimization of IPV are more prevalent in contexts characterized by deep poverty and concentrated disadvantage (Black et al., 2011) and are associated with increased prevalence of psychiatric disorders, physical health problems, and material hardship in these contexts (Tolman & Rosen, 2001). Especially important for the current investigation is that IPV has also been associated with increased parenting stress (Renner, 2009) and that forms of IPV particular to the parenting role have been positively associated with perceived parenting hassles (Ahlfs-Dunn & Huth-Bocks, 2016). Understanding the costs of IPV exposure for parents' perceptions of stress in the parenting role in contexts where it is highly prevalent thus remains a pressing public health priority.

Intrapsychic Predictors

Parents' own psychological characteristics also play an important role in how they perceive parenting in a more negative versus more positive light (Crnic & Low, 2002). Among the most widely studied parent characteristics are anxiety symptoms (e.g., Turner, Beidel, Roberson-Nay, & Tervo, 2003). Anxious parents experience more stress in the parenting role (e.g., Delvecchio, Sciandra, Finos, Mazzeschi, & Riso, 2015) and in general tend to experience parenting as more negative than nonanxious parents (Deater-Deckard, 2004). One framework in which to understand perceptions of stress in the parent role has to do with the appraisals or the cognitive evaluations that parents make about the difficulties and daily hassles of parenting (Crnic & Low, 2002; Mazur, 2006). Parents who exhibit negatively biased appraisals of their experience (who, for instance, take high amounts of responsibility for negative aspects of parenting or who selectively focus on the negative aspects of parenting) also tend to perceive higher frequencies of daily parenting hassles (Mazur, 2006). Yet the process by which parent characteristics such as mood and contextual risk factors such as material hardship come to influence parents' appraisals and perceptions of daily hassles is not well understood.

One neurobiologically anchored candidate mechanism for this process underlying parents' perceptions of hassles is that of adult attention. For instance, the process model of emotion posited by Gross (2014) highlights the ways in which individuals generate emotional and behavioral responses to a given situation or stimulus by first attending to that stimulus and then appraising it in a positive or negative light. The deployment of attention toward or away from specific aspects of the environment represents a coordinated set of neurocognitive processes (Petersen & Posner, 2012; Posner, 1994) that can become biased toward more positive or negative features of the environment. As such, attention processes serve as a "gate to engagement" (Petersen & Posner, 2012) and may influence, quite literally, what parents see in themselves, their children, and their successes versus difficulties in the parenting role. Past research on attention bias among adults and children suggests not only that humans are particularly good at attending extremely quickly to emotional (e.g., LoBue & DeLoache, 2008) and to threatening (Bublatzky & Schupp, 2012) stimuli in their environment but also that environmental exposure to acute stressors may "tune" attentional processes over time to be biased toward threating information, serving as a nonconscious neuropsychological survival mechanism to protect an individual from harm in the context of high stress (Bar-Haim, Lamy, Pergamin, Bakermans-Kranenburg, & van IJzendoorn, 2007; Pollak, Vardi, Putzer Bechner, & Curtin, 2005).

Such attentional biases to threat may confer vulnerabilities to individuals, and to parents in particular, to the extent that they increase perceptions of difficulty or stress in the parenting role. This hypothesis is supported by a vast prior literature suggesting that negative attentional bias increases the effect of other psychosocial and experiential vulnerabilities on individual functioning (Bar-Haim et al., 2007). This is evident within developmental studies of children and adolescents, for example, where it has been shown that behaviorally inhibited children are more likely to develop later life anxiety symptomatology if they display a pattern of attentional bias to threat (Perez-Edgar et al., 2010). Findings in adults suggest that highly anxious individuals display heightened attentional biases to threat, which maintains anxiety disorders across time (Bar-Haim et al., 2007; Mathews & MacLeod, 2005) and may also interact with individual vulnerability factors to predict emotional difficulty (Osinsky, Losch, Hennig, Alexander, & MacLeod, 2012). Furthermore, among individuals who are exposed to trauma, those who show negative attentional bias are at risk of developing psychiatric problems, including posttraumatic stress symptomatology, as seen among combat veterans (Iacoviello et al., 2014) and among women exposed to IPV (DePierro, D'Andrea, & Pole, 2013). Despite this strong foundation, little to no prior research has focused on the extent to which attentional biases in parents—or the interactions of attentional biases with socioeconomic, interpersonal, and other intrapsychic factors—represent significant predictors of perceptions of daily parenting hassles in parents of young children living in conditions of poverty.

The Present Study

To address these questions, the primary goal of this study was to test the extent to which financial hardship, exposure to IPV, symptoms of anxiety, and attentional biases toward threat are associated independently and interactively with parents' appraisals of hassles in the parenting role. These questions are particularly pressing for families in poverty. While prior research has underscored the ways that parents' cognitive resources may be depleted by the challenges of "trying to make ends meet" with low incomes and few material assets, few studies have quantitatively examined the ways in which mounting financial, interpersonal, and psychological pressures may be independently and jointly predictive of perceptions of the parenting role for parents in the context of poverty (Edin & Lein, 1997; Mullainathan & Shafir, 2013). In addition, while new research has begun to test models of neurocognitive processes and parenting in the contexts of poverty, few studies to our knowledge have extended those questions to include Latino/a families living in urban areas of concentrated disadvantage. Doing so is important, given that this group increasingly represents a large fraction of families facing poverty in the United States (Lopez & Cohn, 2011). Latino/a families in the United States are at significant risk of experiencing higher levels of adversity, given their ethnic minority status, their lower access to public services, and for some, greater barriers to social inclusion based on language and immigrant status (Coburn, Gonzales, Luecken, & Crnic, 2016; Yoshikawa & Kalil, 2011). Yet few studies have tested multivariate models predicting individual differences in Latino/a parents' vulnerability versus resilience in their perceptions of the parenting role (Parke et al., 2004). In the following analyses, we aimed to contribute to these theoretically important and policy-relevant questions.

Consistent with prior research on parenting daily hassles, we expect perceptions of financial hardship, exposure to IPV, anxiety, and attentional bias toward threat to be each uniquely associated with low-income parents' increased reports of daily hassles in the parenting role. Furthermore, given prior literature suggesting that higher proneness to negative attentional bias may exacerbate the role of other psychosocial vulnerabilities, such as anxiety, in predicting adults' appraisals, we expect that parents' attentional biases toward negative stimuli may serve as a key moderator of the other risks examined in this study. More specifically, we expect that parents whose attentional biases are directed toward threatening stimuli (i.e., displaying a more negative attention bias) and who are also experiencing high amounts of anxiety, financial hardship, and exposure to IPV will endorse higher amounts of daily hassles in the parenting role.

Method

Participants

In order to oversample families below the poverty line, 190 families were recruited from seven social service programs providing federally funded Early Head Start home-visiting services (where eligibility is largely determined by very low family income) to families with children 0–3 years of age. Additional families ($n = 77$) were recruited from the waiting rooms of three public hospital-affiliated pediatric clinics in the same neighborhoods as those social service agencies in order to increase the range of family incomes represented in the sample.

The data used in this analysis come from 185 parents who had nonmissing data on the analysis variables. The majority of primary caregivers and respondents were mothers (92.4%). 7.6% of respondents were fathers, and 0.5% were grandparents. The average age of the respondents was 31 years ($SD = 7$). Thirty-five percent of parents spoke English as a primary language; 65% of parents spoke Spanish as a primary language. The mean age of children in the sample was 24 months ($SD = 9$); 55% of children were female and 45% were male. The majority of families were Hispanic or Latino. The majority of families were low income—68% of the analysis sample reported an annual total household income of less than $21,000.

Procedure

Parent respondents were assessed in the home by an ethnically diverse, bilingual team of trained assessors recruited from New York University and the greater New York City community. Written and informed consent was obtained from the primary caregiver. Assessors collected survey and observational data on the mother and child during visits that lasted approximately 2 hr. Survey data were collected in either Spanish or English (depending on parental preference) via paper as well as laptops, and observational data were collected via digital video for later coding. All measures and procedures were approved by the Institutional Review Board (IRB) of New York University (IRB 13-9818).

Measures

Generalized anxiety disorder. The Generalized Anxiety Disorder 7-Item (GAD-7) Scale (Spitzer, Kroenke, Williams, & Lowe, 2006) was used to assess symptoms and severity of anxiety based on the *DSM-IV* (American Psychiatric Association [2000]) diagnostic criteria for generalized anxiety disorder (GAD). This seven-item scale has demonstrated strong internal consistency and test-retest reliability as well as convergent, construct, criterion, procedural, and factorial validity for the diagnoses of GAD (Kroenke, Spitzer, Williams, Monahan, & Lowe, 2007). Parents indicated how often they had been bothered by symptoms of anxiety in the last 2 weeks, rated on a 4-point Likert-type scale (0 = *not at all sure,* 1 = *several days,* 2 = *over half the days,* 3 = *nearly every day*). Mean scores were calculated among respondents who answered at least five of the seven items (Cronbach's α = .85); higher scores indicated more anxiety symptoms in the last 2 weeks.

Conflict Tactics Scale. A seven-item short form of the Conflict Tactics Scale (Straus & Douglas, 2004) was used to assess IPV. Evidence for reliability and validity across gender and diverse ethnic groups is prevalent (Straus, 1979; Straus & Douglas, 2004). In keeping with the definition of IPV by the Centers for Disease Control and Prevention (2016) that emphasizes "physical, sexual, or psychological harm inflicted by someone who is a current or former spouse or dating partner", respondents indicated how often physical and psychological acts of violence occurred within their intimate relationship (from 0 [*never*] to 4 [*all the time*]). Physical violence items included *my partner or I pushed, shoved, or slapped each other* and *my partner or I hit or tried to hit him/her/you with something.* Psychological items included *my partner or I insulted, swore, shouted, or yelled at each other*; *my partner or I sulked or refused to talk about an issue*; and *my partner or I threatened to hit or throw something at him/her/you.* The two positively rated items in the scale were not included in our analyses. For descriptive analyses, exposure to any physical violence and exposure to psychological conflict at moderate levels or higher were calculated. For analyses predicting parenting daily hassles, a mean score of IPV was calculated among all participants in the analytic sample (Cronbach's α = .72); higher scores indicated higher instances of IPV.

Parenting daily hassles. The Parenting Daily Hassles (PDH) Scale (Crnic & Greenberg, 1990) was completed to assess parents' appraisals of everyday hassles and inconveniences associated with parenting. This measure has been shown to be reliable, with strong concurrent validity (Crnic & Greenberg, 1990). It consists of 20 items rated on a 5-point Likert-type scale for frequency of occurrence (1 = *rarely,* 2 = *sometimes,* 3 = *a lot,* 4 = *constantly*), with an added frequency score of 0 (*never*). Example items include *the kids won't listen, the kids won't do what they are asked without being nagged, having to change your plans because of an unpredieted child need,* and *the kids get dirty several times a day, requiring changes of clothes.* In its original form, the PDH Scale is composed of both a frequency rating scale and an intensity rating scale; however, for the purposes of this study, only the frequency rating scale was used. Mean scores were calculated among respondents who answered at least 15 of the 20 items (Cronbach's α = .88); higher scores on the parenting daily hassles measure indicated higher perceptions of hassles in the caregiving context.

Financial hardship. Financial hardship was assessed using a total of eight parent-reported items, four of which asked about difficulty paying bills and whether or not utilities have been shut off in the past 12 months, and four of which asked whether or not parents are currently receiving (or have ever received) welfare or lived in public housing. Responses were dichotomized in terms of whether or not parents reported difficulty or endorsed each item, and all eight items were averaged using standard practice.

Attentional bias.   Attentional bias toward threat was assessed using a computerized dot-probe task, a widely used measure of attention bias to emotional cues. In this task, participants are asked to identify the position of a target dot (asterisk) after a brief presentation of emotionally neutral (e.g., book, lamp), positive (e.g., kittens), or negative (e.g., weapon, threatening dog) pairs of images drawn from the International Affective Picture System (Lang, Bradley, & Cuthbert, 1999). Each trial began with a fixation cross presented for 500 ms at the center of the screen. After this, one neutral and one positive or negative picture (or two neutral pictures) are presented side by side for 250 ms. Immediately following the picture pair presentation, a target dot appears on the left or right side of the screen. Parents were instructed to indicate as quickly as possible whether the dot was on the right or left side using laptop keys that corresponded to the location on the computer screen. The dot remained on the screen until the participant responded. If the participant did not respond within 5,000 ms, the next trial began automatically. Seventy-two trials were presented in a semirandom order that was held constant across all participants.

Accuracy and response time for each trial were recorded and aggregated using standard practice to calculate a set of six variables. Mean response latencies were calculated for each trial type if at least 60% of trials were valid. Attention bias toward threat was calculated by subtracting the mean latency to respond to congruent trials (negative image and dot appear on the same side of the screen) from the mean latency to respond to incongruent trials (negative image and dot appear on opposite sides of the screen). If participants preferentially attend to the threat-related image, latencies will be faster for congruent displays and longer for incongruent displays, creating attentional bias scores that are large and positive. Conversely, if participants are less distracted by the threatening image, the difference between the latencies is shorter and the difference is smaller.

Covariates.   In addition to the aforementioned variables, covariates were modeled, including parent report of the highest level of education attained as well as a dummy code for whether the parent reported an annual total household income of at least $21,000. All continuous variables were standardized via z-score transformation prior to regression analyses.

Data Analysis Plan

We first conducted a series of preliminary analyses that included descriptive statistics as well as zero-order correlations of the analysis variables. To address our primary research aim—the prediction of daily hassles from parents' levels of financial hardship, exposure to IPV, anxiety, and attentional biases—we conducted a series of ordinary least squares (OLS) regression models using Mplus 7 software (Muthén & Muthén, 1998–2012).

Model 1 regressed parent reports of daily hassles onto a vector of independent variables that included parents' reports of IPV, financial hardship, anxiety symptoms, and their attentional bias toward threat exhibited during the dot-probe task. Additionally, there were two covariates in this model, the first of which was a dummy code for whether families reported a total annual household income of more than $21,000 (1) or not (0). The second covariate included was parents' highest level of education attained. These covariates were included in the model on an a priori basis. Three subsequent models were built to test the extent to which parents' attentional biases interacted with their levels of anxiety, experiences of financial hardship, and exposure to domestic violence. Specifically, Model 2 was the same as Model 1 with the addition of an Anxiety X Attentional

Bias interaction. Model 3 was the same as Model 1 with the addition of a Financial Hardship X Attentional Bias interaction. Model 4 was the same as Model 1 with the addition of a Domestic Violence X Attentional Bias interaction.

Results

Preliminary Analyses

Table 9.1 displays descriptive statistics of the analysis variables. As shown in Table 9.1, parents reported a moderate amount of daily parenting hassles ($M = 1.46$, $SD = 0.57$, minimum of 0.35, maximum of 3.35); that is, parents felt hassled in the parenting role between *rarely* and *sometimes,* on average, although there was considerable spread in the distribution of hassles reported. Mothers in the sample reported feeling bothered by symptoms of anxiety between *not at all* and for *several days* of the past 2 weeks ($M = 0.52$, $SD = 0.58$). Based on symptom scores established using this measure, approximately 21% of mothers met criteria for mild anxiety, 5% met criteria for moderate anxiety, and 3% met criteria for severe anxiety. Mothers in our sample experienced a moderate amount of IPV ($M = 0.42$, $SD = 0.50$, minimum of 0.00, maximum of 3.2). A mean of 0.42 indicates parents reported that IPV occurrences happened between *never* and *rarely* on average. Notably, 16.7% of the mothers in our sample reported some physical violence (i.e., reported a score of 1 or greater on any of the physical violence items), and 65.7% of mothers reported some psychological conflict (i.e., reported a score of 1 or greater on any of the psychological conflict items). In our sample, 52% of mothers endorsed at least one of the financial hardship items, suggesting a significant amount of economic strain and difficulty in making ends meet. Approximately 68% of families in the sample reported an annual household income of less than $21,000. The highest level of education attained by mothers in the sample was a GED on average. Approximately 37% of mothers in the sample had not graduated high school, and 11% had completed a bachelor's degree or higher.

Table 9.2 displays zero-order correlations between the analysis variables. Daily parenting hassles were positively associated with parent-reported anxiety symptoms, $r = .47$, $p < .01$, financial hardship, $r = .21$, $p < .01$, and reports of IPV, $r = .25$, $p < .01$. Attentional bias toward threat was not associated with daily hassles, nor was parent education or household income. As noted in Table 9.2, there was a modest positive correlation between financial hardship and anxiety symptoms, $r = .18$, $p < .05$, and between exposure to IPV and anxiety symptoms, $r = .27$, $p < .01$.

Table 9.1 *Descriptive Statistics of the Analysis Variables (N = 185)*

Variable	*MI%*	*SD*	Minimum	Maximum
Parenting daily hassles	1.46	.57	.35	3.35
Anxiety	.52	.58	.00	2.57
IPV	.42	.50	.00	3.20
Financial hardship	.12	.14	.00	.63
Dot-probe attentional bias to threat	.94	46.64	−159.00	128.20
Household income <$21,000 (% yes)	68%	—	—	—
Parent education	3.46	1.67	1.00	7.00

Note. IPV = intimate partner violence.

Table 9.2 Zero-Order Correlations Among the Analysis Variables (N = 185)

Variable	1	2	3	4	5	6	7
1. IPV	1	—	—	—	—	—	—
2. Anxiety	.27**	1	—	—	—	—	—
3. Parent education	.03	.00	1	—	—	—	—
4. Income	.00	−.04	.26**	1	—	—	—
5. Attentional bias	−.03	−.03	.21**	.00	1	—	—
6. Financial hardship	−.06	.18*	−.00	−.20**	−.11	1	—
7. Parenting hassles	.25**	.47**	.02	−.05	.01	.21**	1

Note. IPV = intimate partner violence.

* $p < .05$. ** $p < .01$.

Primary Analyses

Results of OLS regression models predicting parenting hassles are displayed in Table 9.3. Model 1 of Table 9.3 displays the unique main effects of anxiety symptoms, financial hardship, IPV, attentional bias toward threat, and the covariates on parenting hassles. Anxiety was the largest predictor of hassles included in the model ($b = 0.23$, $SE = 0.03$, $p < .001$) net of the other predictors included in the model. In terms of effect size, a 1 SD increase in anxiety symptomatology was associated with a 0.40 SD increase in reported daily hassles. Greater financial hardship was also modestly predictive of higher levels of parent-reported hassles ($b = 0.08$, $SE = 0.03$, $p < .05$), with a 1 SD increase in financial hardship associated with a 0.15 SD increase in hassles net of the other predictors in the model. Exposure to IPV was also modestly associated with parent-reported hassles ($b = 0.09$, $SE = 0.04$, $p < .05$). In terms of effect size, a 1 SD increase in exposure to IPV was associated with a 0.15 SD increase in reported hassles. No statistically significant association was found between attentional bias toward threat and daily hassles or between parents' education or household income and daily hassles. Model 1 explained 26.6% of the variance in parents' reports of daily hassles in the parenting role.

Model 2 of Table 9.3 is identical to Model 1 with the addition of an Anxiety Symptoms × Attentional Bias Toward Threat interaction. The interaction between anxiety symptoms and attentional bias toward threat was a significant predictor of daily hassles ($b = 0.07$, $SE = 0.03$, $p < .05$), suggesting that the relation between anxiety symptoms and reports of hassles in the parenting role is moderated by parents' attentional biases toward threat. As shown in Figure 9.1, attentional bias exacerbated the relation between anxiety and daily hassles such that those parents who display a high attentional bias toward threat and who also experience high amounts of anxiety report the most daily hassles in the parenting role. Adding this interaction to the model explained an additional 1.9% of the variance in parenting hassles.

Models 3 and 4 of Table 9.3 are identical to Model 1 with the addition of interactions between financial hardship and attention bias and the addition of an interaction between exposure to IPV and attention bias. Neither the interaction between financial hardship and attention bias nor the interaction between IPV and attention bias were statistically significantly associated with parenting hassles, and these additions to the model did not explain any more variance in parenting daily hassles. In subsequent analyses, we reran each model excluding primary caregivers who were not

Table 9.3 *Regressions Predicting Daily Hassles (N = 185)*

Variable	Model 1			Model 2			Model 3			Model 4		
	b	SE	β	b	SE	β	b	SE	β	b	SE	β
Intercept	1.47			1.47			1.47			1.46		
Education	.00	.02	.01	.00	.02	.01	.00	.02	.01	.00	.02	.01
Income	−.01	.08	−.01	−.01	.08	−.01	−.01	.08	−.01	−.01	.08	−.01
Anxiety	.23	.03	.40**	.22	.03	.38**	.23	.03	.41**	.23	.03	.40**
Financial hardship	.08	.03	.15*	.09	.03	.17**	.08	.03	.15*	.08	.03	.15*
IPV	.09	.04	.15*	.10	.04	.16*	.09	.04	.15*	.09	.04	.15*
Attentional bias	.02	.03	.05	.02	.03	.03	.02	.03	.03	.02	.03	.04
Anxiety × Bias				.07	.03	.14*						
Financial Hardship × Bias							.02	.03	.05			
IPV × Bias										−.01	.05	−.01
Total R^2		.266			.285			.269			.266	

Note. Education = parent education; income = indicator for total annual household income >$21,000; IPV = intimate partner violence; bias = attentional bias toward threat.

* $p < .05$. ** $p < .01$.

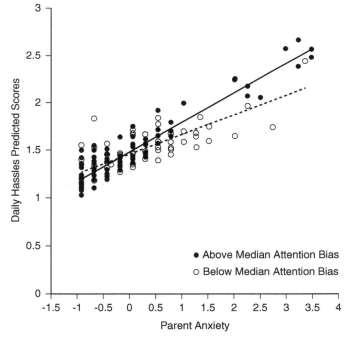

Figure 9.1. *The association between parent-reported anxiety symptoms and parenting daily hassles is moderated by attentional bias toward threat. The solid line is the trend line between anxiety and hassles for those individuals above the median on attention bias toward threat (solid black circles). The dotted line is the trend line between anxiety and hassles for those individuals below the median on attention bias toward threat (white circles).*

mothers (14 fathers and one grandparent) to assess the extent to which parameter estimates were robust in a sample of only mothers. Under these constraints, parameter estimates did not change meaningfully from what they were in the full analysis sample. As a further robustness check, we reran each model using full information maximum likelihood as a missing data treatment and assessed any changes in the estimates. Parameter estimates did not change in a meaningful way except for the estimate of the interaction between attention bias and anxiety, which under these specifications was no longer significant at $p < .05$ but remained significant at trend level ($b = 0.058$, $SE = 0.03, p = .09$).

Discussion

How do low-income parents cognitively represent the daily challenges involved in caring for their infants and toddlers while also managing a range of economic, interpersonal, and psychosocial stressors? Our descriptive analyses of parents' reports of daily hassles are heartening: On the whole, low-income parents in four neighborhoods in New York City reported relatively low amounts of daily hassles overall. The mean level of daily hassles among the parents in our sample is similar to that found among low-income Mexican American women surveyed during the prenatal period, who also reported lower rather than higher levels of everyday hassles on average (Coburn et al., 2016). With this in mind, we were also able to examine the ways that some parents reported much more negative appraisals regarding the challenges of parenting—with a substantial fraction of parents reporting a high frequency of hassles.

Evidence for the Roles of Parental Anxiety and Attention

What accounts for these individual differences in perceptions of daily parenting hassles among the adult respondents in our sample? Our analyses highlight the roles of adults' self-reported anxiety symptoms and neurobiologically anchored attention processes in predicting parents' perceptions of hassles. Specifically, parents who reported higher levels of anxiety (including persistent feelings of nervousness, worry, and restlessness) reported significantly higher amounts of hassles in the parenting role on average. This finding is in keeping with prior research with clinical and non-clinical samples, where difficulty modulating feelings of anxiety has been argued to exert a debilitating effect on adults' cognitions about parenting and their parenting behavior (Möller, Majdandžić, & Bögels, 2015).

Importantly, this study extends emerging neuropsychological research to also consider the ways in which parents' nonconscious attentional biases toward more negatively versus positively valenced stimuli may exacerbate the role of anxiety in tuning subjective experiences of parenting (Bar-Haim et al., 2007). To capture the potential role of adult attention, we adapted the dot-probe paradigm, a standardized neurocognitive assessment of attention that is often used in lab contexts, for laptop administration with low-income Latino/a parents in home visits. Our results suggest that parents' attentional biases toward negative stimuli appear to moderate the relation between anxiety and parents' perception of hassles—parents experiencing high levels of attention bias in combination with high levels of anxiety reported significantly more daily hassles in the context of caregiving. Findings from the current study provide a window into the of adult information processing and emotion regulation and have implications for parenting prevention programs, as we discuss in the following sections.

Expanding Models of Parental Cognition to Include Interpersonal and Economic Contexts

The results of this study also point to ways that experiences of high levels of adversity both inside and outside the household likely play a significant contributing role in shaping or tuning adults' perceptions of their children, the tasks of parenting, and themselves as parents. Past research has clearly highlighted the importance of the relationship between parents and their adult romantic partners (e.g., Krishnakumar & Buehler, 2000). Experiences of acute forms of conflict and violence with one's partner (including hostility, denigration, and other forms of psychological and physical harm) have also recently been found to be significantly associated with adults' more biased attention to threatening stimuli, more negative cognitions, and maladaptive styles of coping (DePierro et al., 2013). Based on those recent findings, we expected that greater IPV exposure might not only be related to parents' more negative attention bias but that IPV and attention bias might work jointly as well as independently in predicting parents' perceptions of daily parenting hassles.

Our descriptive analyses suggest that reports of experiences of physical violence and psychological conflict were high among the low-income Latino/a parents in our sample, with 16.7% of parents reporting experiencing at least one type of physical violence and with over half of the sample reporting experiences of at least some psychological conflict in their relationships with their spouses or romantic partners. Results of our analyses suggest that parents' reports of higher levels of interparental violence were predictive of more parenting hassles, even after statistically taking into account parents' levels of anxiety and attention bias; that is, parents who reported experiencing higher numbers of episodes involving physical harm or psychological conflict with their partners also reported feeling significantly more demoralized and frustrated with parenting.

Finally, we also considered the role of larger socioeconomic factors such as financial strain for parents' perceptions of hassles, drawing upon over two decades of research on what has been termed the family stress model of parenting in the contexts of poverty and income inequality (e.g., Conger & Donnellan, 2007). Our analyses suggest that Latino/a families experiencing higher levels of financial hardship reported higher levels of parenting hassles, even after statistically controlling for higher versus lower family income as well as the psychological and interpersonal factors discussed previously. This is in keeping with recent analyses that highlight the corrosive role that material hardship plays for maternal mental health, linking those stressful experiences to subsequent compromises in parenting behavior (Shelleby et al., 2014). In summary, this study contributes to a small but rapidly growing area of research on the ways that cognitive representations of parenting among low-income families in urban areas of concentrated disadvantage may be shaped by socioeconomic and interpersonal contexts as well as by parents' own psychological resources (see Kim et al., 2010). These findings help inform both neurobiologically based and ecologically based models of early parenting for families facing high levels of adversity and illustrate the ways that those models can be integrated in applied developmental science.

Limitations and Future Directions

While this study makes several empirical contributions to our understanding of parenting among low-income families, the findings are constrained by several limitations. First, we were surprised to not be able to detect a statistical association between parents' attention bias and their experiences of IPV, given prior findings in the adult and child literatures. This may indicate that our measured indicators were less precise, particularly given our use of shortened measures of IPV and field-based assessments of attention bias using a laptop-administered dot-probe paradigm in families' homes. The implication of this imprecision in measurement is that our analyses yielded conservative estimates of the associations between parents' neurobiologically anchored resources, environmental exposures to adversity, and their perceptions of parenting hassles. We look forward to refining these methodological challenges in future field- and laboratory-based research with families facing a range of psychosocial stressors. While our supplementary analyses suggested that the findings were generally robust to different model specifications, we note the need to interpret findings from the current study with caution given the small effect sizes reported.

Second, this study's design was a cross-sectional one and does not allow us to make inferences regarding temporal precedence or causal mechanism. Prior research regarding adults' experiences of negatively valenced cognitions, their symptoms of anxiety, and their experiences of higher versus lower levels of adversity suggests that relations among individuals' negative thoughts, mental health difficulties, and vulnerabilities to experiences of victimization are bidirectional and transactional in nature. In extant research on maternal anxiety and depression, for example, negative cognitions are understood to be a main feature of clinically diagnosed mothers' psychiatric difficulty and may serve as antecedents or primes to biases in how adults deploy their attention (Holden et al., 2012). We look forward to future longitudinal research using observational and experimental designs (in our own laboratory as well as in others' laboratories) to address questions of temporal precedence and causal mediation.

Implications for Prevention and Policy

Our findings have several clear implications for prevention and policies that target the well-being of low-income families. For example, policy leaders have increased investment in a range of family support services targeting parenting as a key foundation for children's early brain development, as illustrated by the U.S. Senate's recent reauthorization of $800 million for the Maternal, Infant and Early Childhood Home Visiting Program (Mongeau, 2015). Our findings suggest that those leaders and practitioners who are designing, implementing, and delivering programs would benefit from considering both parents' thoughts and beliefs about parenting from a multidetermined and neuroscientifically and clinically informed perspective. Given that just over one fifth of the low-income parents in our sample reported mild levels of anxiety (and 8% of parents reported moderate to severe levels of anxiety), this domain of psychological vulnerability is an important domain for family-serving agencies to identify and address as those agencies strive to support positive parenting. This also suggests that benefits in domains of parenting may also be reaped when community initiatives such as NYC Thrive, a recent comprehensive public mental health effort targeting adult mental health, are implemented (City of New York, 2016).

Similarly, our findings suggest that policies and programs that promote low-income parents' safety and financial security are likely to offer substantial additional payoffs in terms of supporting their parenting beliefs and practices in the early years. Our findings highlight the corrosive nature of financial strain and IPV for the ways that young parents see themselves, their young children, and the challenges of caregiving. These and other findings from our colleagues serve as a clear call to embed parenting programs in a comprehensive policy safety net emphasizing reductions in both poverty and violence. Policies to support parents in poverty that are neurobiologically and ecologically informed may provide the most benefit to parents and children and may have wide-ranging positive impacts on family functioning, well-being, and physical and psychological health.

References

Ahlfs-Dunn, S. M., & Huth-Bocks, A. C. (2016). Intimate partner violence involving children and the parenting role: Associations with maternal outcomes. *Journal of Family Violence, 31,* 387–399. http://dx.doi.org/10.1007/s10896-015-9791-x

American Psychiatric Association. (2000). *Diagnostic and statistical manual of mental disorders* (4th ed., text rev.). Washington, DC: Author.

Bar-Haim, Y., Lamy, D., Pergamin, L., Bakermans-Kranenburg, M. J., & van IJzendoorn, M. H. (2007). Threat-related attentional bias in anxious and nonanxious individuals: A meta-analytic study. *Psychological Bulletin, 133,* 1–24. http://dx.doi.org/10.1037/0033-2909.133.L1

Belsky, J., & Barends, N. (2002). Personality and parenting. In M. H. Bornstein (Ed.), *Handbook of parenting: Volume 3: Being and becoming a parent* (2nd ed., pp. 415–438). Mahwah, NJ: Erlbaum.

Belsky, J., & Fearon, R. M. P. (2004). Exploring marriage-parenting typologies and their contextual antecedents and developmental sequelae. *Development and Psychopathology, 16,* 501–523. http://dx.doi.org/10.1017/S095457940400464X

Black, M. C., Basile, K. C., Breiding, M. J., Smith, S. G., Walters, M. L., Merrick, M. T., … Stevens, M. R. (2011). *The National Intimate Partner and Sexual Violence Survey (NISVS): 2010 Summary Report.* Atlanta, GA: National Center for Injury Prevention and Control and Centers for Disease Control and Prevention.

Bublatzky, F., & Schupp, H. T. (2012). Pictures cueing threat: Brain dynamics in viewing explicitly instructed danger cues. *Social Cognitive and Affective Neuroscience, 7,* 611–622. http://dx.doi.org/10.1093/scan/nsr032

Burchinal, M., Vernon-Feagans, L., Cox, M., & Key Family Life Project Investigators. (2008). Cumulative social risk, parenting, and infant development in rural low-income communities. *Parenting: Science and Practice, 8,* 41–69. http://dx.doi.org/10.1080/15295190701830672

Centers for Disease Control and Prevention. (2016). *Intimate partner violence: Definitions.* Retrieved from http://www.cdc.gov/violenceprevention/intimatepartnerviolence/definitions.html

City of New York. (2016). *Thrive NYC: A roadmap for mental health for all.* New York, NY: Author. Retrieved from https://thrivenyc.cityofnewyork.us/wp-content/uploads/2016/03/ThriveNYC.pdf

Coburn, S. S., Gonzales, N. A., Luecken, L. J., & Crnic, K. A. (2016). Multiple domains of stress predict postpartum depressive symptoms in low-income Mexican American women: The moderating effect of social support. *Archives of Women's Mental Health, 19,* 1009–1018. http://dx.doi.org/10.1007/s00737-016-0649-x

Conger, R. D., & Donnellan, M. B. (2007). An interactionist perspective on the socioeconomic context of human development. *Annual Review of Psychology, 58,* 175–199. http://dx.doi.org/10.1146/annurev.psych.58.110405.085551

Coplan, R. J., Bowker, A., & Cooper, S. M. (2003). Parenting daily hassles, child temperament, and social adjustment in preschool. *Early Childhood Research Quarterly, 18,* 376–395. http://dx.doi.org/10.1016/S0885-2006(03)00045-0

Creasey, G., & Reese, M. (1996). Mothers' and fathers' perceptions of parenting hassles: Associations with psychological symptoms, nonparenting hassles, and child behavior problems. *Journal of Applied Developmental Psychology, 17,* 393–406. http://dx.doi.org/10.1016/S01933973(96)90033-7

Crnic, K. A., Gaze, C., & Hoffman, C. (2005). Cumulative parenting stress across the preschool period: Relations to maternal parenting and child behaviour at age 5. *Infant and Child Development, 14,* 117–132. http://dx.doi.org/10.1002/icd.384

Crnic, K. A., & Greenberg, M. T. (1990). Minor parenting stresses with young children. *Child Development, 61,* 1628–1637.

Crnic, K., & Low, C. (2002). Everyday stresses and parenting. In M. H. Bornstein (Ed.), *Handbook of parenting: Volume 5: Practical issues in parenting* (2nd ed., pp. 243–267). Mahwah, NJ: Erlbaum.

Deater-Deckard, K. (2004). *Parenting stress.* New Haven, CT: Yale University Press. http://dx.doi.org/10.12987/yale/9780300103939.001.0001

Deater-Deckard, K., Wang, Z., Chen, N., & Bell, M. A. (2012). Maternal executive function, harsh parenting, and child conduct problems. *Journal of Child Psychology and Psychiatry, 53,* 1084–1091. http://dx.doi .org/10.1111/j.1469-7610.2012.02582.x

Delvecchio, E., Sciandra, A., Finos, L., Mazzeschi, C., & Riso, D. D. (2015). The role of co-parenting alliance as a mediator between trait anxiety, family system maladjustment, and parenting stress in a sample of non-clinical Italian parents. *Frontiers in Psychology, 6,* 1177. http://dx.doi.org/10.3389/fpsyg.2015.01177

DePierro, J., D'Andrea, W., & Pole, N. (2013). Attention biases in female survivors of chronic interpersonal violence: Relationship to trauma-related symptoms and physiology. *European Journal of Psychotraumatology, 4,* 1–10. http://dx.doi.org/10.3402/ejpt.v4i0.19135

Edin, K., & Lein, L. (1997). Work, welfare, and single mothers' economic survival strategies. *American Sociological Review, 62,* 253–266. http:// dx.doi.org/10.2307/2657303

Finegood, E. D., Blair, C., Granger, D. A., Hibel, L. C., Mills-Koonce, R., & Family Life Project Key Investigators. (2016). Psychobiological influences on maternal sensitivity in the context of adversity. *Developmental Psychology, 52,* 1073–1087. http://dx.doi.org/10.1037/ dev0000123

Gershoff, E. T., Aber, J. L., Raver, C. C., & Lennon, M. C. (2007). Income is not enough: Incorporating material hardship into models of income associations with parenting and child development. *Child Development, 78,* 70–95. http://dx.doi.org/10.1111/j.1467-8624.2007.00986.x

Goldberg, W. A., & Easterbrooks, M. A. (1984). Role of marital quality in toddler development. *Developmental Psychology, 20,* 504–514. http:// dx.doi.org/10.1037/0012-1649.20.3.504

Gonzalez, A., Jenkins, J. M., Steiner, M., & Fleming, A. S. (2012). Maternal early life experiences and parenting: The mediating role of cortisol and executive function. *Journal of the American Academy of Child & Adolescent Psychiatry, 51,* 673–682. http://dx.doi.org/10.1016/ j.jaac.2012.04.003

Gross, J. J. (2014). Emotion regulation: Conceptual and empirical foundations. In J. J. Gross (Ed.), *Handbook of emotion regulation* (pp. 3–20). New York, NY: Guilford Press.

Holden, K. B., Hall, S. P., Robinson, M., Triplett, S., Babalola, D., Plummer, V., … Bradford, L. D. (2012). Psychosocial and sociocultural correlates of depressive symptoms among diverse African American women. *Journal of the National Medical Association, 104*(11–12), 493–504. http://dx.doi.org/10.1016/ S0027-9684(15)30215-7

Iacoviello, B. M., Wu, G., Abend, R., Murrough, J. W., Feder, A., Fruchter, E., … Charney, D. S. (2014). Attention bias variability and symptoms of posttraumatic stress disorder. *Journal of Traumatic Stress, 27,* 232–239. http://dx.doi.org/10.1002/jts.21899

Kim, P., Leckman, J. F., Mayes, L. C., Feldman, R., Wang, X., & Swain, J. E. (2010). The plasticity of human maternal brain: Longitudinal changes in brain anatomy during the early postpartum period. *Behavioral Neuroscience, 124,* 695–700. http://dx.doi.org/10.1037/a0020884

Krishnakumar, A., & Buehler, C. (2000). Interparental conflict and parenting behaviors: A meta-analytic review. *Family Relations, 49,* 25–44. http://dx.doi.org/10.1111/j.1741-3729.2000.00025.x

Kroenke, K., Spitzer, R. L., Williams, J. B., Monahan, P. O., & Lowe, B. (2007). Anxiety disorders in primary care: Prevalence, impairment, comorbidity, and detection. *Annals of Internal Medicine, 146,* 317–325. http://dx.doi.org/10.7326/0003-4819-146-5-200703060-00004

Lang, P. J., Bradley, M. M., & Cuthbert, B. N. (1999). *International Affective Picture System (IAPS): Instruction manual and affective ratings.* Gainesville, Florida: Center for Research in Psychophysiology, University of Florida.

LoBue, V., & DeLoache, J. S. (2008). Detecting the snake in the grass: Attention to fear-relevant stimuli by adults and young children. *Psychological Science, 19,* 284–289.

Lopez, M. H., & Cohn, D. (2011). *Hispanic poverty rate highest in new supplemental census measure.* Retrieved from http://www.pewhispanic .org/2011/11/08/ hispanic-poverty-rate-highest-in-new-supplemental- census-measure/

Mathews, A., & MacLeod, C. (2005). Cognitive vulnerability to emotional disorders. *Annual Review of Clinical Psychology, 1,* 167–195. http://dx .doi.org/10.1146/annurev.clinpsy.1.102803.143916

Mazur, E. (2006). Biased appraisals of parenting daily hassles among mothers of young children: Predictors of parenting adjustment. *Cognitive Therapy and Research, 30,* 161–175. http://dx.doi.org/10.1007/s10608-006-9031-z

McLoyd, V. C. (1990). The impact of economic hardship on black families and children: Psychological distress, parenting, and socioemotional development. *Child Development, 61,* 311–346. http://dx.doi.org/10.2307/1131096

Möller, E. L., Majdandžić, M., & Bogels, S. M. (2015). Parental anxiety, parenting behavior, and infant anxiety: Differential associations for fathers and mothers. *Journal of Child and Family Studies, 24,* 2626–2637. http://dx.doi.org/10.1007/s10826-014-0065-7

Mongeau, L. (2015). *Home-visiting, children's health insurance programs reauthorized.* Retrieved from http://blogs.edweek.org/edweek/early_years/2015/04/us_senate_passes_medicare_access_and_chip_reauthorization.html

Mullainathan, S., & Shafir, E. (2013). *Scarcity: Why having too little means so much.* New York, NY: Holt.

Muthen, L. K., & Muthen, B. O. (1998–2012). *Mplus user's guide* (7th ed.). Los Angeles, CA: Author.

Osinsky, R., Losch, A., Hennig, J., Alexander, N., & MacLeod, C. (2012). Attentional bias to negative information and 5-HTTLPR genotype interactively predict students' emotional reactivity to first university semester. *Emotion, 12,* 460–469. http://dx.doi.org/10.1037/a0026674

Parke, R. D., Coltrane, S., Duffy, S., Buriel, R., Dennis, J., Powers, J., ... Widaman, K. F. (2004). Economic stress, parenting, and child adjustment in Mexican American and European American families. *Child Development, 75,* 1632–1656. http://dx.doi.org/10.1111Zj.1467-8624.2004.00807.x

Pérez-Edgar, K., Bar-Haim, Y., McDermott, J. M., Chronis-Tuscano, A., Pine, D. S., & Fox, N. A. (2010). Attention biases to threat and behavioral inhibition in early childhood shape adolescent social withdrawal. *Emotion, 10,* 349–357. http://dx.doi.org/10.1037/a0018486

Petersen, S. E., & Posner, M. I. (2012). The attention system of the human brain: 20 years after. *Annual Review of Neuroscience, 35,* 73–89. http://dx.doi.org/10.1146/annurev-neuro-062111-150525

Pollak, S. D., Vardi, S., Putzer Bechner, A. M., & Curtin, J. J. (2005). Physically abused children's regulation of attention in response to hostility. *Child Development, 76,* 968–977. http://dx.doi.org/10.1111/j.1467-8624.2005.00890.x

Ponnet, K., Mortelmans, D., Wouters, E., Van Leeuwen, K., Bastaits, K., & Pasteels, I. (2013). Parenting stress and marital relationship as determinants of mothers' and fathers' parenting. *Personal Relationships, 20,* 259–276. http://dx.doi.org/10.1111/j.1475-6811.2012.01404.x

Posner, M. I. (1994). Attention: The mechanisms of consciousness. *Proceedings of the National Academy of Sciences of the United States of America, 91,* 7398–7403. http://dx.doi.org/10.1073/pnas.91.16.7398

Raver, C. C. (2003). Does work pay psychologically as well as economically? The role of employment in predicting depressive symptoms and parenting among low-income families. *Child Development, 74,* 1720–1736. http://dx.doi.org/10.1046/j.1467-8624.2003.00634.x

Renner, L. M. (2009). Intimate partner violence victimization and parenting stress: Assessing the mediating role of depressive symptoms. *Violence Against Women, 15,* 1380–1401. http://dx.doi.org/10.1177/1077801209346712

Shelleby, E. C., Votruba-Drzal, E., Shaw, D. S., Dishion, T. J., Wilson, M. N., & Gardner, F. (2014). Income and children's behavioral functioning: A sequential mediation analysis. *Journal of Family Psychology, 28,* 936–946. http://dx.doi.org/10.1037/fam0000035

Spitzer, R. L., Kroenke, K., Williams, J. B., & Lowe, B. (2006). A brief measure for assessing generalized anxiety disorder: The GAD-7. *Archives of Internal Medicine, 166,* 1092–1097. http://dx.doi.org/10.1001/archinte.166.10.1092

Steele, H., Bate, J., Steele, M., Dube, S. R., Danskin, K., Knafo, H., ... Murphy, A. (2016). Adverse childhood experiences, poverty, and parenting stress. *Canadian Journal of Behavioural Science, 48,* 32–38.

Straus, M. A. (1979). Measuring intrafamily conflict and violence: The Conflict Tactics (CT) Scales. *Journal of Marriage and the Family, 41,* 75–88. http://dx.doi.org/10.2307/351733

Straus, M. A., & Douglas, E. M. (2004). A short form of the Revised Conflict Tactics Scales, and typologies for severity and mutuality. *Violence and Victims, 19,* 507–520. http://dx.doi.org/10.1891/vivi.19.5.507 .63686

Swain, J. E. (2011). The human parental brain: In vivo neuroimaging. *Progress in Neuro-Psychopharmacology & Biological Psychiatry, 35,* 1242–1254. http://dx.doi.org/10.1016Zj.pnpbp.2010.10.017

Tolman, R. M., & Rosen, D. (2001). Domestic violence in the lives of women receiving welfare: Mental health, substance dependence, and economic well-being. *Violence Against Women, 7,* 141–158. http://dx .doi.org/10.1177/1077801201007002003

Turner, S. M., Beidel, D. C., Roberson-Nay, R., & Tervo, K. (2003). Parenting behaviors in parents with anxiety disorders. *Behaviour Research and Therapy, 41,* 541–554. http://dx.doi.org/10.1016/ S0005- 7967(02)00028-1

Yoshikawa, H., & Kalil, A. (2011). The effects of parental undocumented status on the developmental contexts of young children in immigrant families. *Child Development Perspectives, 5,* 291–297. http://dx.doi.org/ 10.1111/j.1750-8606.2011.00204.x

CHAPTER 10

Stress among Immigrant Families

Fiorella L. Carlos Chavez[1] University of Missouri
Joseph G. Grzywacz[2] Florida State University

Introduction

Immigration imposes various stressors on individuals and families considering relocating from one country to another, and adjusting to such a move. Some families flee their home country due to poverty or violence (e.g., Guatemala, El Salvador, Honduras), oppression or political unrest (Bohra-Mishra & Massey, 2011; Sasin & McKenzie, 2007; Shellman & Stewart, 2007), and still others because of terrorism or war (e.g., Syria, South Sudan, Afghanistan). Other families are not fleeing but are drawn to another country by hopes of getting ahead or providing a better future for their children. Yet other families move to another country out of job re-assignment or career advancement. Regardless of the reason, immigrant families frequently pay a "price" through the form

Correspondence concerning this book chapter should be addressed to Fiorella L. Carlos Chavez, 410 Gentry Hall, Columbia, MO USA 65211. E-mail: carloschavezf@missouri.edu Phone: 573-882-1108

---

[1] Human Development and Family Science, College of Human Environmental Sciences, University of Missouri, 410 Gentry Hall, Columbia, MO 65211. MO USA
[2] Family and Child Sciences Department, College of Human Sciences, Florida State University, Tallahassee, FL USA

of *stressors* encountered during and following migration. The unique stressors immigrant families face are complex phenomenon and poorly understood. Indeed, the shared and unique immigration experiences of individual family members shape the family's stressors; and the family's stressors in and through immigration often differ by a myriad of forces contributing to migration (e.g., persecution, failing economy), migration process (e.g., whole family at once versus one person first and the rest of the family follows later), and their sequela (e.g., authorized or not, destination country). Poor understanding of the nuances and uniqueness of immigrant families' stressors is concerning given that over 258 million individuals left some vestige of family and community for international migration (Office of the United Nations High Commissioner for Human Rights, 2018).

Investigators from a diverse array of disciplines have produced a large and expansive body of results from research studies on stressors related to immigration. For example, the field of social work frequently focuses on the availability of social or community supports for immigrants (Aranda, Castaneda, Lee, & Sober, 2001) and how to best meet those support needs with social services (Negi, Maskell, Goodman, Hooper, & Roberts, 2018; Reitz, 2018). Sociologists commonly view new immigrants as being placed on the margins of society (Ayon, 2018; Wenhong & Kaichun, 2008) and the consequences of that marginalization on immigrants life satisfaction, experiences of discrimination (Safi, 2010) and health inequality (Brown, 2018). On the other hand, psychologists frequently study the cultural underpinnings of identity, sense of self, and personal value – each of which has implications for immigrant mental health (Kim, Schwartz, Perreira, & Juang, 2018), including sources of resilience (Motti-Stefanidi, 2018). This high-level overview of other bodies of research is, by necessity, course; but nevertheless, captures the predominant discipline-specific themes on stress-related research among immigrants. That is, psychologists tend to focus on cognitive and emotional response to, or about, immigration, whereas sociologists view immigration as a vehicle for understanding how systems of social stratification are maintained and perpetuated, and those systems affect immigrants. Social work frequently transcends these areas of focus by remaining attentive to both individuals' responses to stressors and the social systems in place to eliminate or attend to those individual responses to immigration-related stressors.

Family scientists also study immigration-related stressors, but largely in the context of the families. Family scientists emphasize both structural features of families, like differential documentation status of parents and children (Zapata-Roblyer & Grzywacz, 2015), as well as family processes, like the implications of being physically separated from family (Suarez-Orozco, Todorova, Louie, 2002) or intra-family conflict resulting from different family members' experiences in the host country, and their subsequent similar or diverging embracing or shunning of those experiences. The chapter elaborates the stressors that are prevalent, perhaps unique, to immigrant families. {Readers interested in individual-level stressors confronted by immigrants or the individual-level consequences of those stressors are encouraged to read other key summaries (Antman, 2010; Moskal, 2015; Orellana, Thorne, Chee, & Lam, 2001).

The primary goal of this chapter is to provide the reader with a solid contextual understanding of stress among immigrant families. To achieve this goal, the chapter covers two primary topics. First, we present basic foundations for studying immigrant families, including definitions of key concepts, descriptions of immigration from a global and U.S. context, and the role of legal authorization to reside and work (or the lack thereof) in the lives and realities of immigrants families. Second, following a short overview of the transactional model of stress, we delineate stressors that are common among immigrant families differentiating those that are intrapersonal, but given differential meaning in the context of family, from those that are familial or interpersonal. Particularly, in this final section we highlight the marital, parent-child, and intergenerational relationship stressors among immigrant families.

Basic Foundations

Definitions and Salient Concepts

Despite widespread use of the terms in everyday conversation, terms like "immigrant," "migrant" and "migrate" are often inappropriately used interchangeably. The United Nations (UN) uses the terms "immigrant" and "international migrant" interchangeably to refer to an individual *"who lives temporarily or permanently in a country where he or she was not born, and has acquired some significant social ties to this country"* (United Nations Educational Scientific and Cultural Organization [UNESCO], 2018, para. 1). Under this umbrella, migrating, or the process of relocating from one country to another, is presumed to involve a decision-making process on the part of every immigrant. Immigrants are widely seen as being "free" to choose when and how they will leave their country, as well as their final destination (UNESCO, 2018, para. 3). Unlike immigrate which connotes a sense of permanence, to migrate means to move from one place to another (i.e., from one country to another, or from a region of a country to another region of the same country) for a period of time but not for purposes of settlement. This idea is often invoked to characterize "migrants" or a group of people who move from place to place, oftentimes for employment (e.g., "migrant farmworker"). As such, it can be understood that not all "immigrants" are migrants because they typically do not move from place to place, but all "migrants"–provided there was an international relocation–are immigrants.

However, what can be said about refugees? Are they immigrants, migrants, or both? Refugees are a special group of people living in unique circumstances: they did not "choose" to leave their home countries voluntarily, they were forced to because of "persecution, war, or violence" (United Nations High Commissioner for Refugees [UNHCR], 2018, para 1). In addition, refugees, unlike immigrants and migrants, are protected by international law. Their host countries are primarily (84%) among the developed countries of the world (Edmond, 2017). As such, refuges may be more likely to have fewer choices and opportunities about the regions and countries (e.g., developed nations vs developing nations) to relocate, but they have protections and supports in those receiving countries that immigrants (i.e., non-refugees) frequently are not offered.

Finally, there is a significant group of people who relocate internationally because of job assignment or career advancement. Expatriates are a unique group of people living and working outside their country of origin by virtue of special employment assignment. Unlike immigrants, migrants, and refugees who are often targeted by negative stereotypes, expatriates are often viewed in more favorable terms because they are generally well-educated or highly trained and they gain entrée to the country via a major or well-known organization. It is possible that the "poor connotation" assigned to immigrants and migrants (Nash, 2017) plays a key role on how individuals and families on the move see themselves in comparison to others in the global area. However, we suggest that, regardless of the nature of the family (i.e., immigrant, migrant, refugee, or expatriate) the decision to migrate creates vulnerabilities (de Genova, 2002) that can create or exacerbate stressors among immigrant families.

Prevalence of Families as "Immigrants" in the United States

The U.S. holds the largest immigrant population in the world (Lopez, Bialik, & Radford, 2018). From 1960 to 2015, the immigrant population in the U.S. increased from 9.7 million to 43.2 million, thus currently constituting 13.4% of the U.S. population (Lopez, Bialik, & Radford, 2018). Indeed, the number of immigrant families has increased rapidly, and the distribution of those settlements has shifted to include a variety of "new arrival destinations" (Migration Policy Institute [MPI], 2016) that are increasingly located in remote and small communities that historically experienced little or no in-migration (Zapata Roblyer, Carlos, Merten, Gallus, Grzywacz, 2017). Most immigrants in the U.S. (41.4%) are from Latin American (i.e., Mexico, Central America, and South America), with a strong and growing group of immigrants (close to 26.9%) from South and East Asia (Radford & Budiman, 2018; Lopez, Bialik, & Radford, 2018). There is wide variability in how the general U.S. population views or perceived immigrants from different regions of the world. Over four-in-ten Americans hold optimal views of European (44%) and Asian (47%) immigrants, while 25% of Americans expressed similarly optimal views Latino and African immigrants (Lopez, Passel, & Rohal, 2015).

Immigrants profile.   Immigrants tend to have lower levels of education than U.S.-born individuals: estimates from the Pew Research Center indicate the number of immigrants without high school degree tripled (29%) that of US-born individuals (9%) (Lopez, Bialik, & Radford, 2018). Nevertheless, immigrants in the U.S. are "as likely as the U.S. born to obtain a college degree or more" (Krogstad & Radford, 2018). The dominant preferred language among immigrants is Spanish (Radford & Budiman, 2018); nevertheless, other common languages spoken by immigrants include Chinese, Hindi, Filipino/Tagalog, French, and Vietnamese (Lopez, Bialik, & Radford, 2018).

Immigrants in the U.S. are anticipated to help offset the market exit of a substantial proportion of the labor force due to baby boomers' retirement (Passel & Cohn, 2017). Immigrants in the U.S. work a diverse range of occupations and industries, and have been described as having strong work ethics (Dinan, 2006) and being work harders (Pew Research Center, 2017). Indeed, immigrants with a work-authorization, visa, or green card can be found in professional, managerial and technical occupations across industries, while undocumented immigrants are concentrated in the service, construction, and agricultural sectors (Lopez, Bialik, & Radford, 2018).

Currently, 51% of children of immigrant families (at least one parent who is a non-US born; National Center for Children in Poverty [NCCP]) live in low-income families while 38% of children (20.3 million) of US-born parents live in low-income families (Koball & Jiang, 2018). In addition, approximately 4.2 million children of immigrant parents face poverty (Wight, Thampi, & Chau 2011; Wight, Chau, & Aratani, 2011). In contrast to children of US-born parents living in poverty, children in immigrant families living in poverty are less likely to have access to food stamps, have lower access to health services, and have at least one parent working a full-time job (Wight, Thampi, & Chau, 2011). Circumstances such as these highlight the role of documentation status – particularly the ability to obtain legal employment – in producing stressors like poverty that are common, albeit not unique to, immigrants.

Intrapersonal Stressors

The translational model is the primary foundation for thinking about "stress" in the context of immigrant families. The transactional model contends the stress process has three fundamental components; (1) the stressor or the demand placed upon the individual psychologically (i.e., intrapersonal demands), socially (i.e., interpersonal demands), or environmentally (i.e., cultural or socio-structural demands); (2) the appraisal of the stressor relative to the resources available for accommodating or adapting to the stress; and (3) the stress response which has cognitive, affective, and physiological components (Lazarus, 1999). The individual's appraisal of the stressor and the evaluation of the personal and social resources for accommodating or adapting to the stressor shapes the intensity and severity of the stress response (Hovey & Seligman, 2006).

Visa and Documentation Status: Implications for Immigrant Families

Legal migration requires documentation for each migrating individual that allows temporary or permanent authorization to reside, and possibly work, in the host country. Currently, about one-fourth of immigrants (24%) in the U.S. do not have legal authorization to reside to work (Lopez, Bialik, & Radford, 2018; Passel & Cohn, 2016). According to the U.S. Department of Homeland Security (DHS) a total of 1.1 million immigrants received a green card in 2016 and were granted the status of lawful permanent resident (LPR) which allows the green card holder to switch employers without restriction; a situation that "empowers the immigrant to seek and secure the most satisfying work arrangement available" (Grzywacz, Gopalan, & Carlos Chavez, 2017, p. 459). Likewise, immediate family members of an immigrant with a green card are not only admitted to the U.S., but are eligible to become a lawful permanent resident. Even though the process takes time, the spouses of immigrant green card holders may pursue job opportunities and have their children go to school (Grzywacz et al., 2017).

The salient role for immigrant families of their family members' authorization to reside and work in the host country cannot be overstated. Legal authorization to reside or work in a host country (e.g., temporary work visa, legal permanent resident) is salient because only a small number of authorizations are granted each year. In the U.S., only about 226,000 family-sponsored visas and only about 140,000 employment-based permanent visas are issued each year (USCIS, 2015). Moreover, the number of visas issued each year varies by country of origin, such that common waiting times span 10–15 years before family members are allowed legal permanent residence in the U.S. Immigrant families with permanent visas, those with pending permanent visa applications, and those with temporary authorizations face relatively "manageable" stressors when compared to immigrant families who are undocumented in the U.S. The lack of legal authorization to reside in the country makes individuals vulnerable to deportation, whereas the lack of legal authorization to work places substantial barriers to employment and the income necessary to purchase basic needs like shelter and food.

The number of immigrants who lack legal authorization to live and work in the U.S. remains unknown. In 2014, the Pew Research Center estimated that approximately 11.1 million undocumented (i.e., unauthorized) immigrants lived in the U.S. (Passel & Cohn, 2014). Other estimates suggest that 25% of U.S. immigrants are undocumented, most of whom are from Mexico (52% as of 2012), yet unauthorized immigrants from Canada, South America, Europe, and Asia are increasing in number (Passel & Cohn, 2014). Family members of undocumented immigrants face the threat of family separation due to one or more family members' forced deportation (Grzywacz et al., 2017). In the 2016 fiscal year alone, over one-third of a million immigrants were deported from the U.S.– many leaving U.S. born children behind. In the summer of 2018 the world watched how the Trump administration handled the separation of parents and children at the US-Mexico Border. Although stunning, the media spectacle that followed these cases overlooks the parallel but less sensational reality that approximately 4 million U.S. children face the potential of family fragmentation because one or more parents lack legal authorization to be in the country (NCCP, 2018). The risk of family fragmentation can lead parents to withdraw their children from school or avoid going to their children's schools out of fear that schools may be cooperating with police officers or Immigration and Customs Enforcement (ICE) agents. As such, immigrant families, particularly those who are undocumented, are more likely to be vulnerable to documentation stressors that affect the whole family. Moreover, these families may be more inclined to separate themselves from known and bigger social networks, and communities enclaves which can compromise health and impede resilience (Martinez, Ruelas, & Granger, 2018).

Interpersonal Stressors

The Marital Relationship

Earlier studies identified a set of stressors common to immigrant couples (Ben-David & Lavee, 1994). First, immigrant couples see an intensification of in their interpersonal relationship because they lose vestiges of strong, often taken-for-granted support networks. Whether lost support networks provided basic household assistance (Meintel et al., 1984) including child care because "family always comes first" (Yu, 2015) or more emotive forms of support, the bottom line remains the same—mutual dependence for needs increases as external supports decrease, thereby creating greater opportunity for strain (Guruge et al., 2010). Second, immigrant couples experience shifts in structural elements of daily life, chief among them are frequently increased opportunities for wives' employment and associated time demands and shifts in home-based responsibilities to accommodate those time demands (Grzywacz et al., 2007; Lim, 1997; Min, 2001). A related challenge someone specific to immigrant couples is loss of socioeconomic status and earnings potential because accumulated educational and occupational experience may not be *transferred* (Muruthi & Lewis, 2017). Third, immigrant couples frequently come to learn that established forms of conflict resolution may not be appropriate in the western countries that often receive immigrants (Ben-David & Lavee, 1994). For example, clearly gender-based divisions of labor are neither sustainable nor interpreted as acceptable by many immigrant wives, especially if they are working (Grzywacz et al., 2007; Lim, 1997; Min, 2001), so simple conflict resolution resting on "this is the way it is always done" quickly becomes insufficient (Benjamin & Barash, 2004; Darvishpour, 2002; Yu, 2011).

Acculturative stressors. Like all families, immigrant families confront a myriad of interpersonal stressors. However, the process of immigration poses distinctive—perhaps unique—stressors for immigrant families because taken-for-granted elements of daily life like the fundamental meaning of "husband" or "daughter," or prescriptions of how individuals in different roles like "husband and wife" should interact with one another can be challenged by a new culture. Acculturation represents the cultural and psychological changes that occur due to contact between different cultural groups and individual members (Berry, 2005). Because the pace and depth of acculturation can differ among family members (Bostean & Gillespie, 2018), acculturation gaps can emerge whereby values and practices consistent with the heritage culture oppose or conflict with values and practices of the hosting culture (Telzer 2011). The "cultural clashes" or "acculturative stressors" (Berry, 2005) experienced by immigrants reflect a unique variety of interpersonal stressors that do not exist for non-immigrant families. The remainder of this section highlights common interpersonal acculturative stressors in the context of three discrete elements of family life: the marital relationship, the parent-child relationship, and the intergenerational—oftentimes transnational—relationship.

Acculturation and related stressors are frequently associated with poorer marital outcomes. Differences in acculturation between husbands and wives has been associated with greater marital distress (Negy & Snyder, 2000), and poorer marital outcomes like appraisals of warmth and relationship satisfaction (Cruz et al., 2014). Similarly, Helms and colleagues (2014) contended that navigating the inconsistencies between cultural values from the country of origin and the host country, along with situational stressors like economic hardship, impede marital quality. Wheeler and colleagues (2010) noted that differential acculturation strategies among wives and husbands contributed to poorer marital relations among immigrants. They described, for example, that wives who embraced more American values reported greater marital negativity, less love and poorer marital satisfaction than wives who adhered more closely to their traditional values perhaps because of differences in conflict resolution styles. Similarly, others contend that differences in how husbands and wives acculturate can contribute to conflict and marital instability (Cruz et al., 2014; Lavee & Krivosh, 2012).

Although acculturation is commonly believed to pose stressors to marriages and other intimate relationships, some contend that focusing on "acculturation" is too broad because it does not offer insight into specific cultural values or practices held by immigrants that are threatened by dominant cultural values (Hunt, Schneider & Comer, 2004). Toward this, researchers have begun to focus on more specific forms of acculturation that may create stress. Grzywacz and colleagues (2007), for example, argued that immigrant women's employment and her greater contributions to household earnings created direct threats to men's culturally-enforced power advantage in the home. Among the threats to men's power was women's expectations of equal involvement in financial decision-making given her role in contributing to household earnings, and priorities for childrearing and more general family roles. Basic challenges to men's power by women immigrants' employment have been documented among Chinese (Yu, 2011), Korean (Lim, 1997; Min, 2001), and Arabic (Darvishpour, 2002) immigrants in diverse receiving countries (Hengstebeck et al., 2015; Hyman et al., 2008; Meintel et al., 1984; Shirpak et al., 2011).

Gender roles. Underlying many of the acculturative stressors that impede marital outcomes among immigrants are constructions of gender and appropriate behaviors for men and women. Indeed, several researchers outline how immigration frequently and ultimately affects fundamental understandings of "gender" and associated social artifacts. Yu (2015), for example emphasizes the role of women's employment in the U.S. as a fundamental experience that challenges the "male as breadwinner" and "female as homemaker" traditional models that dominate family life in China. Similarly, Lim (1997) argued women's employment challenged power differentials in the home enabled by broader Confucian ideals that demanded patriarchal authority in the home, and Hondagneu-Sotelo (1992) characterized women's employment as a vehicle for "overcoming patriarchal constraints" for Mexican immigrant women.

Beyond employment, though, immigration resulted in other experiences that redefine the meaning of gender and appropriate behavior. Shirpak and colleagues (2011) describe how some changes in women's dress and behavior as a consequence of "westernization" was viewed as problematic by Iranian men, whereas Iranian women viewed "westernized" men as indecisive because "real" Iranian men would never seek women's input on basic family issues. Gupta (2005), using a case study of an elderly Asian Indian couple filing for divorce after 27 years of marriage, commented on the woman's loss of identity when her children "left the nest," a problem exaggerated by the absence of a work authorization that precluded her from obtaining employment and accumulating marketable skills. Moreover, as an immigrant, her extended family remained in India, thereby limiting her ability to support other members of her family. Finally, although subsequent sections of this chapter discusses parent-child relations among immigrant families, basic decisions about parenting styles and strategies to be used in the home – including decisions about the extent to which extended family like grandparents, aunts, and uncles are allowed to participate in parenting – can become a stressor for immigrant couples.

The Parent-Child Relationship

We focus on the first generation (i.e., foreign-born children and their immigrant parents) as well as second generation (i.e., US born children from immigrant parents) (Rumbaut, 2004) immigrants to address the parent-child relationship stressors among immigrant families. We highlight that for these two generations, the importance of income generation as a means of financial duty and love manifests through financial remittances. In addition, we address three main areas that are most salient among in the immigrant literature and that are likely to influence the parent-child relationship: levels of acculturation, language brokerage, and familial duties and responsibilities among immigrant families.

Income. In 2017 alone, developing and underdeveloped countries received a total of 450 billion US dollars in remittances (Boulanger Martel, Pelling, Wadensjo, 2018). Immigrants who remit money back home do so when they 1) have the financial capacity to remit money, and 2) have the desire to remit money (Carling, Erdal & Horst, 2012). However, the ability or inability to send money home is far from being the motor driving parents to generate income. Indeed, immigrant parents are known for send remittances to their "left behind" children and extended kin. To understand how income plays out in a parent-child relationship, we must first remember that at the heart of sending remittances back to the home country to "take care of" the children's needs (e.g., food, clothing, education, health) is the expression of human care and reciprocity. Possibly, parents unconsciously hope that one day these children may also provide financial remittances for them in old age. Second, in an effort to keep family relations and presence in their children's lives, the immigrant parent(s) may send monthly remittances to their families back home, not simply as a "financial transaction" but with the hopes to "establish intimacy across borders" (Parreñas, 2005, p. 324). Indeed, the lack of parent-child physical proximity between immigrant parent(s) and the children at the home country may be perceived as a loss (i.e., the loss of being together as a family; the loss of not being home for the holidays or birthdays). This may be particularly salient among Latino immigrant families whereby parents come to the U.S. to work at the expense of an emotional toll; that of homesickness and longing for the loss of family proximity and kin support (Solheim, Zaid, & Ballard, 2016).

Although the immigration rate of mothers for work abroad has increased, it is still the father who migrates regionally or internationally to generate income for the family (Foner & Dreby, 2011). When mothers do immigrate, they may be making more income and taking on the "breadwinner" role for the home, yet they are not excused from their "familial duties" on the parent-child domain. In other words, income can provide, to a certain extent, *comfort* and *flexibility*, yet it does not liberate immigrant mothers from their role as caregivers for their children and the home. In fact, immigrant mothers may "overcompensate" for their physical absence in the home country (Hays, 1996) by financially covering for the household's expenses and engaging in *long-distance nurturing* (Hondagneu-Sotelo & Avila, 1997) with their children. A clear example of this can be seen among Filipino families. Immigrant Pilipino mothers who are away from home and contribute higher financial earnings to the home than their husbands challenge the conventional gender role on the family (Parreñas, 2005). However, the father's neglect of "caring responsibilities in the family" further contributes to the default of traditional gender roles whereby the immigrant mother has to make up for lack of parent-child nurturance (Parreñas, 2005, p. 333). If we add that immigrant and US born children living in immigrant families may also experience simultaneous *within* stressors due to their interaction with the mainstream culture (e.g., school, neighborhood, and peers) and maintenance of their family's traditional values and expectations, we have a recipe for *emotional turmoil* and [di] stress. We suggest that parent-child's differences in acculturation, interdependence, and family's expectations of son or daughter may further lead to stressors that are unheard of or unrealistic among mainstream families. Here we introduce such unique stressors within the parent-child relationship among immigrant families.

Levels of acculturation. Briefly, we highlight some of the downside that differences in levels of acculturation represents for immigrant families. For example, acculturative stress, which is the stress-reaction in the face of situations that challenge the way people live their lives (Berry, 2006) may delineate how parents and children perceive their day-to-day interactions as stressful.

For example, the pressures to speak English and acculturate to the U.S. mainstream culture, while simultaneously experiencing pressures to speak the heritage language and enculturation (i.e., pressure against acculturation) can further exacerbate the parent-child relationship among immigrant families. An example of this can be seen in immigrant Mexican families who try to hold on to their Mexican culture while adapting to U.S. culture (Cuellar, Arnold, Maldonado, 1995).

Indeed, what do you do when your core values as an immigrant parent are threatened by having your kid participating in mainstream's values? What do children do when their beliefs and traditions are challenged outside the home? It is not unusual for immigrant families to live under *the same roof* yet be living in very different ways. However, the downside to poor acculturation, confronted with mom or dad's disapproving views' on the child "newly acquire" behaviors and customs, can manifest in poor health outcomes among Latino and Asian children in immigrant families (Lui, 2015). Particularly on the children's mental health such as externalized behaviors and depressive symptoms (Kim et al. 2017) and poor academic performance (Castillo et al., 2008). Besides acculturation gaps that may put "tension" on the parent-child relationship, the role children play in assisting their immigrant parents as language brokers could lead them to "hot and cold" feelings on the extra roles these children *must take on* in order to assist their immigrant parents. Again, this may conflict with the parental expectations of children's service to the family and the new "acquire" freedom these children may mimic from their peers.

Language brokerage.   The majority of youth (over 70%) in immigrant families usually take on the role of a language broker by translating for their non-English speaker parents (Chao 2006) thus becoming key intermediaries between their parents and the mainstream society (Kim, Hou, Gonzalez, 2017). Language brokering may be seen as a stressor when the child perceives it to be a burden (Kim et al., 2018) with potential negative consequences on mental health outcomes (i.e., depressive symptoms) for adolescents in Chinese American households (Kim, Wang, Deng, Alvarez, & Li, 2011) and perceived stress in Latino immigrant families (Anguiano, 2018). However, we suggest that not all language brokerage is a stressor. For example, among Latino, Chinese, and Korean immigrant families, youth may not only feel high levels of efficacy about being the intermediary for their parents but also a stronger sense of identity which can strengthen the parent-child relationship quality (Kim, et al. 2017; Shen et al. 2014). When language brokerage becomes a stressor, it is possible that the experience of being a *language broker* vary based on the broker's gender (Kim et al., 2018). True, previous research has shown that female language brokers are highly involved in language brokerage for the home (Buriel, Perez, De Ment, Chavez, Moran, 1998), as well as outside the home (Villanueva & Buriel, 2010). In addition, in the case of Mexican American youth, boys tend to have better English skills than their female counterparts (Weisskirch, 2005). This alone may explain why boys in immigrant households may feel more comfortable and confident when brokering for their parents than girls do (Kim et al., 2018). In addition, children's experiences with brokering for their parents may also vary based on the parent's gender. Indeed, previous research has shown that immigrant mothers are the ones who use language brokering the most (Shen & Dennis, 2018) and turn to female brokers (i.e., daughters) for their translating rather than their sons (Sy, 2006). Therefore, we could argue that adolescents in immigrant families may be conflicted due to the burdensome yet necessary task they take on when brokering for their mothers (perhaps a less acculturated family member) than their fathers, especially when their brothers are not expected nor required to take on that role.

Chinese or Latino immigrant children in the U.S. who engage in language brokerage do so to "save their parents' face," (Reynolds & Orellana, 2009) and as a sign of respect and care for the immigrant parent (e.g., Garcia-Sanchez, 2018). Nevertheless, it is necessary to remember that language brokerage is not unique to the U.S. In fact, language brokerage is a common phenomenon and practice among immigrant families with similar underpins and motifs of action. For example, Morrocan immigrant children in Spain actively take on the role of language brokers as a way to alleviate their parents' inadequacy (Schieffelin & Cochran-Smith, 1985). Moreover, a child's role as language broker shape the internal resourcefulness they can bring about in relation to inter-generational differences and permissiveness among adult–child relationships (Garcia-Sanchez, 2018). Although language brokerage may be seen as unique stressors salient among immigrant families, it may also play a dual role; that of preparing the child for his or her future responsibilities of *caregiver* toward his/her immigrant parents in old age as well as shaping the habit of stepping up into a *provider's role* not only for the spouse and children, but also for the elderly parents and elderly relatives.

Familial duties and responsibilities. Most of the immigrant families who relocate in the U.S. come from collectivistic backgrounds (Davis, Carlo, Streit, Schwartz, Unger, Baezconde-Garbanati, & Szapocznik, 2018; Phinney, Ong, Madden, 2000). Collectivism puts emphasis on family interde-pendence and group harmony (Triandis, 1995) which can be used as a *safety net* among immigrant families and their children. However, it is possible that the family (i.e., group) solidarity that col-lectivism fosters may clash with more acculturated children of immigrants as well as financially vulnerable immigrant parents. From the child's perspective, we identify three core familial duties and responsibilities among immigrants' families; they include: 1) being a tutor, 2) being an ad-vocate, and 3) being a surrogate parent (Valenzuela, 1999). First, as previously mentioned, chil-dren engage in language brokerage for their parents and act as "the middle person" between their parents and government authorities (e.g., teachers, officials), as well as interpreters of day-to-day activities (e.g., the news, ordering food) (Valenzuela, 1999). Second, children in immigrant fami-lies, based on the "heat" of political climates, may have to advocate on behalf of their parents or siblings as needed. In other words, in the face of injustice, and discriminatory acts, children from immigrant families may step in as act as the "mediator" in conversations with mainstream culture and authorities. Third, based on the parents' work-schedules, some children may see the need to become a pseudo-parent. This role may be assigned or expected from the older sibling(s) whereby the sibling is responsible for taking care of the household chores (e.g., cooking, cleaning) as well as taking care of the younger siblings (e.g., baby-sitting, dressing, and bathing) (Valenzuela, 1999). As such, it is no surprise to find immigrant parents consulting with the pseudo-parent child regarding household income distribution and home responsibilities (Parreñas, 2005).

However, these core family duties/responsibilities among immigrant families can be embedded in the immigrant family parenting style' psyche and cultural expectations. For example, among Asian and Latino parents, an authoritarian [tiger] parenting (Kim, Wang, Orozco-Lapray, Shen, Murtuza, 2013), (although stressful from the child's perspective), may be perceived as a unique strategy to help the child navigate the environmental demands (e.g., academic success) from the mainstream society, especially if coming from an ethnic minority background (Garcia Coll et al. 1996). On the other hand, a more "no-nonsense" parenting approach that includes harsh-and-au-thoritarian parenting (White, Zeiders, Gonzales, Tein, & Roosa, 2013) may be applied to youth in high-risk neighborhoods (White, Liu, Gonzales, Knight, & Tein, 2016). For Latino immigrant, how-ever, this type of parent-child relationship may work on their favor. That is, cultural values such as *respeto* (e.g., respect for elder, hierarchy) and *familismo* (e.g., concern for family priorities first) may further align with authoritative parenting (White, Zeiders, Gonzales, Tein, & Roosa, 2013) yet cre-ate tension among parents and children due to the "family requirements" from the children's part.

However, from the immigrant parents' perspective, there is the family responsibility and the expectation to be a caregiver for older family members (Connelly & Maurer-Fazio, 2016; Antman, 2011; Antman, 2010). This implies, asking for as little help as possible from government assis-tance or retirement homes that may jeopardize family privacy, interdependence, and filial piety (i.e., respect for elders, being good to one's parents; Kwan, 2000) (Qi, 2018). However, when the children *fail* to take care of their aging parents or family members, this may provoke feelings of embarrassment and shame from part of the elderly parents (Guo, Sabbagh Steinberg, Dong, & Tiwari, 2018). As such, an immigrant parent may see his/her children's neglect toward them as *their failure as a parent* because the child did not fulfil his/her responsibilities as a son or daughter. Nonetheless, it is worth mentioning that, cultural values and expectations among families do not necessarily vanish from one generation to the next (Sy & Romero, 2008). Among immigrant families, especially those of Latino origin, both sons and daughters continue their loyalty toward the family even at the expense of their own personal needs (Sy & Romero, 2008). True, there is a potential contradiction whereby relieving the family financials burdens lays on "the youth' shoulders" as such, feeling the pressure to succeed not only for themselves but for the family (Sy & Romero, 2008). Yet whether familial duties and responsibilities are seen as stressors is debatable. Perhaps it is not so much of a burden the responsibility youth in immigrant families feel toward their parents (Toro, Schofield, Calderon-Tena, & Farver, 2018) but rather an *expression of care* resulting from cultural socialization that prioritizes family before the self (Gloria & Castellanos, 2012). This type of care is more prevalent in the intergenerational relationship among immigrant families.

The Intergenerational Relationship

When immigrant families relocate, it is likely that they either take their children with them or leave them behind under the supervision of extended families such as parents, aunts, uncles or siblings in the home country (Parreñas, 2005). However, children are not the only family members left behind, elderly parents of migrant adults are also *left behind* (Connelly & Maurer-Fazio, 2016; Antman, 2010). Traditionally, children of migrant workers would stay with their grandparents at the home country (He & Ye, 2014). However, lately, due to the emotional toll family separation has on children (Dreby 2010), migrant parents and immigrant parents are bringing their children with them to the city or country where they are relocating to for greater work and educational opportunities (Qi, 2018). For example, for undocumented immigrants who work in the U.S., their family separation is linked to the family's long-term economic success (Boehm 2008). That is, their work abroad serves various purposes, including that of saving money to improve their quality of lives at their home country (Chavez, 2012) thus potentially avoiding migration for work in old age. Their income may also secure enough resources for their minor children coming to the U.S. (Rojas, Grzywacz, Zapata Roblyer, Crain, & Cervantes, 2016). As such, more and more elderly parents are left at the home country; a phenomenon that knows no borders. For example, the elderly in China (82.0%), count with the financial support of the migrant children who leave their rural communities to pursue nonagricultural jobs in the city (Connelly & Maurer-Fazio, 2016). While the "left behind" parents of Mexican immigrants in the U.S. are likely to suffer poor health (e.g., mental, physical) by having an adult child working abroad, away from home (Antman, 2010).

Remembering Elderly Parents

Immigrant families hold dear feelings of closeness that are exemplified in intergenerational relations, which provide both emotional and financial support (Swartz, 2009). Intergenerational support is rooted in filial obligations and family reciprocity (De Vries, Kalmijn, & Liefbroer, 2009; Gans & Silverstein, 2006); parents took care of and provided for children when they were little, now older children provide and take care of their elderly parents. In their attempt to keep some ties in the home country and to be remembered by the family members who stayed, immigrant families maintain "here–there" bonds (Waldinger, 2008). This may be particularly salient among immigrants' parents who could not bring their elderly parents with them and feel the moral responsibility to send financial remittances and keep frequent *long-distance* communication and financial support. It is widely known that, immigrant families, especially those of Latino origin, continue to support their extended family members and are taken into account on key and day-to-day family decisions despite the distance (Parra-Cardona, Bulock, Imig, Villarruel, & Gold, 2006). However, the uncertainty on whether the immigrant parents would be reunited with their elderly parents and family members has an emotional *price* that can manifest through stress. As such, immigrant families and families who stay at the home country are "trapped," living in a constant *limbo* (Falicov, 2005); unable to return home due to the potential risk of stopping financial remittances for their elderly parents. This, *uncertainty* alone and the potential inability to physically take care of aging parents in sickness or in health (Solheim, Zaid, & Ballard, 2016) further delineate the unique intergenerational relationship stressors among immigrant families.

Indeed, being away from the home country implies some type of "loss" from part of the immigrant (Solheim, Zaid, & Ballard, 2016). Whether he/she loses a "layer" from of his/her close niche, traditions, language, or extended family members' physical-closeness, it is the family members that remain at the home country who also loose the presence or role the immigrant family member had prior leaving home (Antman, 2011). Perhaps immigrant adult children do not realize what they lose when they first leave home and vice versa. The reader may be aware by now that *family* may have a very different meaning depending of the immigrant family's background. Apart from providing for one's nuclear family (i.e., spouse and children), immigrant families may be also providing for their parents as well as elderly kin family members. Therefore, continuing with the intergenerational relationship in an individualistic society such as the U.S. poses challenges for recent and older cohorts of immigrant families. Nevertheless, immigrant families' concern for extended kin back at the home country is likely to continue despite the distance. That is, immigrants, especially adult children, would try to find the means to fulfill their expression of care and familial duty not only toward the children or spouse left behind but also toward the elderly mother or father who is unable to join the immigration journey.

Conclusion

We have made efforts to present an overview of the stressors immigrant families face as well as the unique characteristics and definitions that pertain to this population. We acknowledge that there are other potential stressors immigrant families face such as work-related stressors yet we decided to focus on the family component to better understand the cultural nuances that may be rooted in immigrant families' realities. Indeed, immigration and stress are interviewed; they can be seen as together-but-separate phenomenon among immigrant families. As mentioned in this chapter, the delineation of these phenomena are in great part due to cultural aspects from the immigrant family and their experiences in the settlement country (Motti-Stefanidi & Salmela-Aro, 2018). Without diminishing the individual stressors, we have focused on the stressors that pertain to immigrant families. It is inevitable to point out that competitive world-demands require competitive measures to keep up with work-related expectations. Such competitive arena (i.e., globalization) may be potentially pushing individuals/families away from home countries to find work abroad and to get ahead in life at the expense of family separation. In years to come, the immigrant families we discussed in this chapter would continue to face the *flux* of their gender roles and re-construction of identities of what it means to be a father, a mother, as well as a "breadwinner" and "caregiver" for the home and for others. Perhaps, this is one of the greatest challenges immigrant families are yet to accept, that of learning to live in the proximity of feminine and masculine roles as a way of "survival" for their offspring and for themselves.

Stress is inevitable and as living beings, we are doomed to experience it at some point of our lives. Indeed, everybody and anybody are capable of experiencing stressors that challenge their way of living and being in the world. However, immigrant families may be *worse of* or *unequipped* enough to face the marital, parent-child, and intergenerational relationship stressors of resettling in a new country. We suggest that more attention could be placed on the "family left behind" (e.g., elderly parents, siblings, grandparents) at the home country after a son/daughter's migration. To date, there is limited knowledge on the effects of adult child migration and the elderly parents' wellbeing at the home country. Previous research has shown that international migration of adult Mexican children "shakes" the commonly known living arrangements in the household (i.e., multi-generational household) thus leading to elderly parent(s) living alone (Kanaiaupuni, 2000). We may agree that remittances play a vital role in the lives of transnational immigrant families, particularly because adult children immigration has "trade-offs," in the availability of resources parents have access to due to their children's work abroad (Waidler, Vanore, Gassmann, & Siegel, 2016). Nevertheless, it is possible that elderly parents grieve the loss as well as the physical absence from their children based on the immigration circumstances (i.e., documented vs undocumented). Yet it is the immigration status that dictates whether the immigrant children may or may not return to their home countries to be with/take care of their parents (Grant, Falkingham, & Evandrou, 2009). However, it is also possible that an adult child working abroad is financially sustaining their parents and/or siblings back home whereby his/her absence does not imply that parents are not receiving other means of support from their other children (Zimmer & Knodel, 2013). Although research has found that families wherein the siblings of migrants who leave home for work are likely to stay close to the parents to be their physical caregivers (Waidler et al., 2016), there is still much to learn from the reality of immigrants who may never return to their home countries, grandparents who may never know their grandchildren, and families who may not have kin siblings to fill their caregiving roles. Despite these threats to immigrant families' well-being, we believe these families are resilient and have the strength as well as the courage to make the best of their situation and reformulate the narratives of their own lives and that of their loved ones.

References

Anguiano, R. M. (2018). Language brokering among latino immigrant families: Moderating variables and youth outcomes. *Journal of Youth and Adolescence, 47*(1), 222–242. doi:10.1007/s10964-017-0744-y

Antman, F. M. (2010). How does adult child migration affect the health of elderly parents left behind? Evidence from Mexico. *American Economic Review Papers and Proceedings.* 2010; 100(2). doi: 10.2139/ssrn.1578465

Antman, F. M. (2012). Elderly care and intrafamily resource allocation when children migrate. *Journal of Human Resources, 47*(2), 331–363.

Aranda, M. P., Castaneda, I., Lee, P. J., & Sobel, E. (2001). Stress, social support, and coping as predictors of depressive symptoms: Gender differences among Mexican Americans. *Social Work Research, 25*(1), 37–48. doi: 10.1093/swr/25.1.37

Ayón, C. (2018). Unpacking immigrant health: Policy, stress, and demographics. *Race and Social Problems, 10*(3), 171–173. doi: 10.1007/s12552-018-9243-3

Ben-David, A., & Lavee, Y. (1994). Migration and marital distress: The case of Soviet immigrants. *Journal of Divorce & Remarriage, 21*(3–4), 133–146. doi: 10.1300/J087v21n03_07

Benjamin, O., & Barash, T. (2004). "He thought I would be like my mother": The silencing of Mizrachi women in Israeli inter- and intra-marriages. *Ethnic and Racial Studies, 27*(2), 266–289. doi: 10.1080/0141987042000177333

Berry, J. W. (2006). Acculturative stress. In *Handbook of multicultural perspectives on stress and coping* (pp. 287–298). Springer, Boston, MA.

Bohra-Mishra, P., & Massey, D. S. (2011). Individual decisions to migrate during civil conflict. *Demography, 48*(2), 401–424. doi: 10.1007/s13524-011-0016-5

Boulanger Martel, S. P., Pelling, L., & Wadensjö, E. (2018). *Economic Resources, Financial Aid and Remittances* (No. 11552). IZA Discussion Papers.

Brown, T. H. (2018). Racial stratification, immigration, and health inequality: A life course intersectional approach. *Social Forces, 96*(4), 1507–1540. doi: 10.1093/sf/soy013

Buriel, R., Perez, W., De Ment, T. L., Chavez, D. V., & Moran, V. R. (1998). The relationship of language brokering to academic performance, biculturalism, and self-efficacy among Latino adolescents. *Hispanic Journal of Behavioral Sciences, 20*(3), 283–297. doi:10.1177/07399863980203001

Carling, J., Erdal, M. B., & Horst, C. (2012). How does conflict in migrants' country of origin affect remittance-sending? Financial priorities and transnational obligations among Somalis and Pakistanis in Norway. *International Migration Review, 46*(2), 283–309. doi:10.1111/j.1747-7379.2012.00888.x

Castillo, L. G., Cano, M. A., Chen, S. W., Blucker, R. T., & Olds, T. S. (2008). Family conflict and intragroup marginalization as predictors of acculturative stress in Latino college students. *International Journal of Stress Management, 15*(1), 43. doi: 10.1037/10725245.15.1.43

Chao, R. K. (2006). The prevalence and consequences of adolescents' language brokering for their immigrant parents. In M. H. Bornstein, L. R. Cote, M. H. Bornstein & L. R. Cote (Eds.), *Acculturation and parent-child relationships: Measurement and development* (pp. 271–296). Mahwah, NJ: Erlbaum.

Cruz, R. A., Gonzales, N. A., Corona, M., King, K. M., Cauce, A. M., Robins, R. W., ... Conger, R. D. (2014). Cultural dynamics and marital relationship quality in Mexican-origin families. *Journal of Family Psychology, 28*(6), 844–854. doi: 10.1037/a0038123

Connelly, R., & Maurer-Fazio, M. (2016). Left behind, at-risk, and vulnerable elders in rural China. *China Economic Review, 37*, 140–153. doi: 10.1016/j.chieco.2015.10.005

Cuellar, I., Arnold, B., & Maldonado, R. (1995). Acculturation rating scale for Mexican Americans-II: A revision of the original ARSMA scale. *Hispanic journal of behavioral sciences, 17*(3), 275–304. doi: 10.1177/07399863950173001

Chavez, L. (2012). Shadowed lives: Undocumented immigrants in American society. Boston, MA: Cengage Learning

Darvishpour, M. (2002). Immigrant women challenge the role of men: How the changing power relationship within Iranian families in Sweden intensifies family conflicts after immigration. *Journal of Comparative Family Studies, 33*(2), 270–296.

Davis, A. N., Carlo, G., Streit, C., Schwartz, S. J., Unger, J. B., Baezconde-Garbanati, L., & Szapocznik, J. (2018). Longitudinal associations between maternal involvement, cultural orientations, and prosocial behaviors among recent immigrant Latino adolescents. *Journal of Youth and Adolescence, 47*(2), 460–472. doi: 10.1007/s10964-0170792-3

De Genova, N. P. (2002). Migrant "illegality" and deportability in everyday life. *Annual review of anthropology, 31*(1), 419–447. doi: 10.1146/annurev.anthro.31.040402.085432

Department of Homeland Security [DHS]. (2018). Yearbook if immigration statistics 2017. Retrieved from https://www.dhs.gov/immigration-statistics/yearbook/2017

Dinan, K. A. (2006). Young Children in Immigrant Families The Role of Philanthropy. *New York: National Center for Children in Poverty.*

Dreby, J. (2010). Divided by borders: Mexican migrants and their children. Univ of California Press.

De Vries, J., Kalmijn, M., & Liefbroer, A. C. (2009). Intergenerational transmission of kinship norms? Evidence from siblings in a multi-actor survey. *Social Science Research, 38*(1), 188–200. doi: 10.1016/j.ssresearch.2008.09.005

Edmond, C. (2017, June 20). 84% of refugees live in developing countries. World Economic Forum. Retrieved from https://www.weforum.org/agenda/2017/06/eighty-four-percent of-refugees-live-in-developing-countries/

Falicov, C. J. (2005). Emotional transnationalism and family identities. *Family Process, 44*(4), 399–406. doi: 10.1111/j.1545-5300.2005.00068.x

Foner, N., & Dreby, J. (2011). Relations between the generations in immigrant families. *Annual Review of Sociology, 37,* 545–564. doi: 10.1146/annurev-soc-081309-150030

Gans, D., & Silverstein, M. (2006). Norms of filial responsibility for aging parents across time and generations. *Journal of Marriage and Family, 68*(4), 961–976. doi: 10.1111/j.17413737.2006.00307.x

Garcia Coll, C. G., Crnic, K., Lamberty, G., Wasik, B. H., Jenkins, R., Garcia, H. V., & McAdoo, H. P. (1996). An integrative model for the study of developmental competencies in minority children. *Child development, 67*(5), 1891–1914. doi:10.2307/1131600

García-Sánchez, I. M. (2018). Children as interactional brokers of care. *Annual Review of Anthropology,* (0). doi: 10.1146/annurev-anthro-102317-050050

Gloria, A. M., & Castellanos, J. (2012). Desafíos y bendiciones: A multiperspective examination of the educational experiences and coping responses of first-generation college Latina students. *Journal of Hispanic Higher Education, 11*(1), 82–99. doi:10.1177/1538192711430382

Grant, G., Falkingham, J., & Evandrou, M. (2009). The impact of adult children's migration on wellbeing in later life: voices from Moldova. *Centre for Research on Aging Discussion Paper,* (0902).

Grzywacz, J. G., Rao, P., Gentry, A., Marín, A., & Arcury, T. A. (2009). Acculturation and conflict in Mexican immigrants' intimate partnerships: The role of women's labor force participation. *Violence Against Women, 15*(10), 1194–1212. doi: 10.1177/1077801209345144

Grzywacz, J. G., Gopalan, N., Carlos Chavez, F. L. (2018). Work and family among immigrants. In Shockley, K. M., Shen, W., & Johnson, R. C. (Eds.). *The Cambridge Handbook of the Global Work–Family Interface* (pp. 454–478). New York, NY: Cambridge University Press.

Guo, M., Steinberg, N. S., Dong, X., & Tiwari, A. (2017). A cross-sectional study of coping resources and mental health of Chinese older adults in the United States. *Aging & mental health,* 1–8. doi: 10.1080/13607863.2017.1364345

Gupta, R. (2005). Acculturation and Marital Problems Among South Asian Immigrants: Implications for Practitioners. *Clinical Gerontologist: The Journal of Aging and Mental Health, 29*(1), 71–77. doi: 10.1300/J018v29n01_06

Guruge, S., Shirpak, K. R., Hyman, I., Zanchetta, M., Gastaldo, D., & Sidani, S. (2010). A Meta synthesis of Post-migration Changes in Marital Relationships in Canada. *Canadian Journal of Public Health-Revue Canadienne De Sante Publique, 101*(4), 327–331.

Hays, S. (1996). The cultural constructions of motherhood. *New Haven.*

He, C., & Ye, J. (2014). Lonely sunsets: impacts of rural–urban migration on the left-behind elderly in rural China. *Population, Space and Place, 20*(4), 352–369.

Helms, H. M., Supple, A. J., Su, J., Rodriguez, Y., Cavanaugh, A. M., & Hengstebeck, N. D. (2014). Economic pressure, cultural adaptation stress, and marital quality among Mexican-origin couples. *Journal of Family Psychology, 28*(1), 77–87. doi: 10.1037/a0035738

Hengstebeck, N. D., Helms, H. M., Wood, C. A., & Rodriguez, Y. (2018). Mexican-origin husbands' work contexts and spouses' marital quality. *Journal of Latina/o Psychology, 6*(1), 64–78. doi: 10.1037/lat0000083

Hondagneu-Sotelo, P. (1992). Overcoming patriarchal constraints: The reconstruction of gender relations among Mexican immigrant women and men. *Gender & Society, 6*(3), 393–415. doi: 10.1177/089124392006003004

Hondagneu-Sotelo, P., & Avila, E. (1997). "I'm here, but I'm there" the meanings of Latina transnational motherhood. *Gender & Society, 11*(5), 548–571. doi: 10.1525/california/9780520225619.003.0015

Hovey, J. D., & Seligman, L. D. (2006). The mental health of agricultural workers. *Agricultural Medicine,* 282–299.

Hunt, L. M., Schneider, S., & Comer, B. (2004). Should "acculturation" be a variable in health research? A critical review of research on US Hispanics. *Social Science & Medicine (1982), 59*(5), 973–986. doi: 10.1016/j.socscimed.2003.12.009

Hyman, I., Guruge, S., & Mason, R. (2008). The impact of migration on marital relationships: A study of Ethiopian immigrants in Toronto. *Journal of Comparative Family Studies, 39*(2), 149–163.

Kanaiaupuni, S. M. (2000). *Leaving parents behind: migration and elderly living arrangements in Mexico*. Center for Demography and Ecology, University of Wisconsin-Madison.

Kim, S. Y., Schwartz, S. J., Perreira, K. M., & Juang, L. P. (2018). Culture's influence on stressors, parental socialization, and developmental processes in the mental health of children of immigrants. *Annual Review of Clinical Psychology, 14,* 343–370.

Kim, S. Y., Hou, Y., & Gonzalez, Y. (2017). Language brokering and depressive symptoms in Mexican-American adolescents: Parent–child alienation and resilience as moderators. *Child Development*, 88, 867–881. doi: 10.1111/cdev.12620.

Kim, S. Y., Wang, Y., Weaver, S. R., Shen, Y., Wu-Seibold, N., & Liu, C. H. (2014). Measurement equivalence of the languagebrokering scale for Chinese American adolescents and their parents. *Journal of Family Psychology*, 28, 180–192. doi: 10.1037/a0036030.

Kim, S. Y., Wang, Y., Orozco-Lapray, D., Shen, Y., & Murtuza, M. (2013). Does "tiger parenting" exist? Parenting profiles of Chinese Americans and adolescent developmental outcomes. *Asian American Journal of Psychology*, 4(1), 7. doi: 10.1037/a0030612

Kim, S. Y., Wang, Y., Deng, S., Alvarez, R., & Li, J. (2011). Accent, perpetual foreigner stereotype, and perceived discrimination as indirect links between English proficiency and depressive symptoms in Chinese American adolescents. *Developmental Psychology*, 47(1), 289. doi: 10.1037/a0020712

Koball, H., Jiang, Y. (2018). Basic facts about low-income children. Children under 18 years, 2016. National Center for Children in Poverty [NCCP]. Retrieved from http://www.nccp.org/publications/pdf/text_1194.pdf

Krogstad, J. M. & Radford, J. (2018). Education levels of U.S. immigrants are on the rise. Pew Research Center. Retrieved from http://www.pewresearch.org/facttank/2018/09/14/education-levels-of-u-s-immigrants-are-on-the-rise/

Kwan, K. L. K. (2000). Counseling Chinese peoples: Perspectives of filial piety. *Asian Journal of Counseling*, 7(1), 23–41.

Lazarus, R. S. Stress and Emotion: A New Synthesis. New York: Springer, 1999.

Lavee, Y., & Krivosh, L. (2012). Marital stability among Jewish and mixed couples following immigration to Israel from the former Soviet Union. *European Psychologist*, 17(2), 158–167. doi: 10.1027/1016-9040/a000112

Lim, I.-S. (1997). Korean immigrant women's challenge to gender inequality at home: The interplay of economic resources, gender and family. *Gender & Society*, 11(1), 31–51. doi: 10.1177/089124397011001003

Lopez, G., Bialik, K., Radford, J. (2018). Key findings about U.S. immigrants. Pew Research Center. Retrieved from http://www.pewresearch.org/fact-tank/2018/09/14/key-findingsabout-u-s-immigrants/

Lopez, M. H., Passel, J., & Rohal, M. (2015). Modern immigration wave brings 59 million to US, driving population growth and change through 2065. Views of immigration's impact on U.S. society mixed. Pew Research Center. Retrieved from http://www.pewresearch.org/wp-content/uploads/sites/5/2015/09/2015-09-28_modernimmigration-wave_REPORT.pdf

Lui, P. P. (2015). Intergenerational cultural conflict, mental health, and educational outcomes among Asian and Latino/a Americans: Qualitative and meta-analytic review. *Psychological Bulletin*, 141(2), 404. doi: 10.1037/a0038449

Martínez, A. D., Ruelas, L., & Granger, D. A. (2018). Household fear of deportation in relation to chronic stressors and salivary proinflammatory cytokines in Mexican-origin families post-SB 1070. *SSM-Population Health*. doi: 10.1016/j.ssmph.2018.06.003

Meintel, D., Labelle, M., Turcotte, G., & Kempineers, M. (1984). Migration, wage labor, and domestic relationships: Immigrant women workers in Montréal. *Anthropologica*, 26(2), 135–169. doi: 10.2307/25605162

Migration Policy Institute [MPI]. (2016). Children in U.S. immigrant families. Retrieved from https://www.migrationpolicy.org/programs/data-hub/charts/children-immigrant-families

Min, P. G. (2001). Changes in Korean immigrants' gender role and social status, and their marital conflicts. *Sociological Forum*, 16(2), 301–320. doi: 10.1023/A:1011056802719

Moskal, M. (2015). 'When I think home I think family here and there': Translocal and social ideas of home in narratives of migrant children and young people. *Geoforum*, *58*, 143–152. doi: 10.1016/j.geoforum.2014.11.011

Motti-Stefanidi, F. (2018). Resilience among immigrant youth: The role of culture, development and acculturation. *Developmental Review*. doi: 10.1016/j.dr.2018.04.002

Motti-Stefanidi, F., & Salmela-Aro, K. (2018). Challenges and Resources for Immigrant Youth Positive Adaptation.

Nash, K. (2017, January 20). The difference between an expat and an immigrant? Semantics. Retrieved from http://www.bbc.com/capital/story/20170119-who-should-be-called-an expat

Negy, C., & Snyder, D. K. (1997). Ethnicity and acculturation: Assessing Mexican American couples' relationships using the Marital Satisfaction Inventory—Revised. *Psychological Assessment*, *9*(4), 414–421. doi: 10.1037/1040-3590.9.4.414

Negi, N. J., Maskell, E., Goodman, M., Hooper, J., & Roberts, J. (2018). Providing social services in a new immigrant settlement city: A qualitative inquiry. *American Journal of Orthopsychiatry*, *88*(1), 16. doi: 10.1037/ort0000276

Office of the United Nations High Commissioner for Human Rights. (2018). Migration and human rights. Retrieved from https://www.ohchr.org/EN/Issues/Migration/Pages/MigrationAndHumanRightsIndex.aspx

Orellana, M. F., Thorne, B., Chee, A., & Lam, W. S. E. (2001). Transnational childhoods: The participation of children in processes of family migration. *Social Problems*, *48*(4), 572–591. doi: 10.1525/sp.2001.48.4.572

Parreñas, R. (2005). Long distance intimacy: class, gender and intergenerational relations between mothers and children in Filipino transnational families. *Global Networks*, *5*(4), 317–336. doi: 10.1111/j.1471-0374.2005.00122.x

Parra-Cardona, J. R., Bulock, L. A., Imig, D. R., Villarruel, F. A., & Gold, S. J. (2006). "Trabajando duro todos los dias": Learning from the life experiences of Mexican-origin migrant families. *Family Relations*, *55*(3), 361–375. doi: 10.1111/j.17413729.2006.00409.x

Passel, J. S. & Cohn, D. V. (2014). Unauthorized immigrant total rise in 7 states, fall in 14. Decline in those from Mexico fuels most state decreases. Pew Research Center. Retrieved from http://www.pewhispanic.org/2014/11/18/unauthorized-immigrant-totals-rise-in-7states-fall-in-14/

Passel, J. S., Cohn, D.V. (2016). Overall Number of US Unauthorized Immigrants Holds Steady since 2009: Decline in share from Mexico mostly offset by growth from Asia, Central America and Sub-Saharan Africa. Pew Research Center. Retrieved from http://www.pewhispanic.org/wp-content/uploads/sites/5/2016/09/PH_2016.09.20_Unauthorized_FINAL.pdf

Passel, J. S. & Cohn, D. V. (2017). Immigration projected to drive growth in U.S. working-age population through at least 2035. Pew Research Center. Retrieved from http://www.pewresearch.org/fact-tank/2017/03/08/immigration-projected-to-drive growth-in-u-s-working-age-population-through-at-least-2035/

Pew Research Center [PEW]. (2017). The partisan divide on political values grows even wider. Retrieved from http://www.people-press.org/2017/10/05/the-partisan-divide-on-politicalvalues-grows-even-wider/

Phinney, J. S., Ong, A., & Madden, T. (2000). Cultural values and intergenerational value discrepancies in immigrant and non-immigrant families. *Child development*, *71*(2), 528–539. doi: 10.1111/1467-8624.00162

Qi, X. (2018). Floating grandparents: Rethinking family obligation and intergenerational support. *International Sociology*, 0268580918792777. doi: 10.1177/0268580918792777

Radford, J & Budiman, A. (2018). Facts on U.S. immigrants, 2016. Statistical portrait of the foreign-born population in the United States. Pew Research Center. Retrieved from http://www.pewhispanic.org/2018/09/14/facts-on-u-s-immigrants/

Reitz, J. G. (2018). Warmth of the welcome: The social causes of economic success in different nations and cities. Routledge.

Reynolds, J. F., & Orellana, M. F. (2009). New immigrant youth interpreting in white public space. *American Anthropologist*, *111*(2), 211–223. doi: 10.1111/j.15481433.2009.01114.x

Rojas, S. M., Grzywacz, J. G., Zapata Roblyer, M. I., Crain, R., & Cervantes, R. C. (2016). Stressors among Hispanic adults from immigrant families in the United States: Familismo as a context for ambivalence. *Cultural Diversity and Ethnic Minority Psychology, 22*(3), 408. doi: 10.1037/cdp0000082

Rumbaut, R. G. (2004). Ages, life stages, and generational cohorts: decomposing the immigrant first and second generations in the United States 1. *International Migration Review, 38*(3),1160–1205. doi: 10.1111/j.1747-7379.2004.tb00232.x

Sasin, M. J., & McKenzie, D. (2007). *Migration, remittances, poverty, and human capital: conceptual and empirical challenges.* The World Bank. doi: 10.1596/1813-9450-4272

Schieffelin, B. B., Cochran-Smith, M. (1985). Learning to read culturally: literacy before schooling. In *Awakening to Literacy,* ed. H Goelman, AA Oberg, F Smith, pp. 3–23. Exeter, NH: Heinemann Educ.

Shalabi, D., Mitchell, S., & Andersson, N. (2015). Review of Gender Violence Among Arab Immigrants in Canada: Key Issues for Prevention Efforts. *Journal of Family Violence, 30*(7), 817–825. doi: /10.1007/s10896-015-9718-6

Swartz, T. T. (2009). Intergenerational family relations in adulthood: Patterns, variations, and implications in the contemporary United States. *Annual Review of Sociology, 35,* 191–212. doi: 10.1146/annurev.soc.34.040507.134615

Shen, Y., Kim, S. Y., Wang, Y., & Chao, R. K. (2014). Language brokering and adjustment among Chinese and Korean American adolescents: A moderated mediation model of perceived maternal sacrifice, respect for the mother, and mother–child open communication. *Asian American Journal of Psychology, 5,* 86–95. doi: 10.1037/a0035203.

Shen, J. J., & Dennis, J. M. (2018). The family context of language brokering among Latino/a young adults. *Journal of Social and Personal Relationships,* 0265407517721379. doi: 026540751772137

Shirpak, K. R., Maticka-Tyndale, E., & Chinichian, M. (2011). Post Migration Changes in Iranian Immigrants' Couple Relationships in Canada. *Journal of Comparative Family Studies, 42*(6), 751–770.

Solheim, C., Zaid, S., & Ballard, J. (2016). Ambiguous loss experienced by transnational Mexican immigrant families. *Family Process, 55*(2), 338–353. doi: 10.1111/famp.12130

Suarez-Orozco, C., Todorova, I. L., & Louie, J. (2002). Making up for lost time: The experience of separation and reunification among immigrant families. *Family Process, 41*(4), 625–643. doi: 10.1111/j.1545-5300.2002.00625.x

Sy, S. R. (2006). Family and work influences on the transition to college among Latina adolescents. *Hispanic Journal of Behavioral Sciences, 28*(3), 368–386. doi: 10.1177/0739986306290372

Sy, S. R., & Romero, J. (2008). Family responsibilities among Latina college students from immigrant families. *Journal of Hispanic Higher Education, 7*(3), 212–227. doi: 10.1177/1538192708316208

Triandis, H. C. (1995). Individualism and collectivism. Bouler, CO: Westview.

Toro, R. I., Schofield, T. J., Calderon-Tena, C. O., & Farver, J. M. (2018). Filial Responsibilities, Familism, and Depressive Symptoms Among Latino Young Adults. *Emerging Adulthood,* doi: 10.1177/2167696818782773

United Nations Educational Scientific and Cultural Organization [UNESCO]. (2018). Learning to live together. Retrieved from http://www.unesco.org/new/en/social-and-human sciences/themes/international-migration/glossary/migrant/

United Nations High Commissioner for Refugees [UNHCR]. (2018). What is a refugee? Retrieved from https://www.unrefugees.org/refugee-facts/what-is-a-refugee/

U.S. Citizenship and Immigration Services [USCIS]. (2015). Visa availability and priority dates. Retrieved from https://www.uscis.gov/greencard/visa-availability-priority-dates

Valenzuela Jr, A. (1999). Gender roles and settlement activities among children and their immigrant families. *American Behavioral Scientist, 42*(4), 720–742. doi: 10.1177/0002764299042004009

Villanueva, C. M., & Buriel, R. (2010). Speaking on behalf of others: A qualitative study of the perceptions and feelings of adolescent Latina language brokers. *Journal of Social Issues, 66*(1), 197–210. doi: 10.1111/j.1540-4560.2009.01640.x

Waidler, J., Vanore, M., Gassmann, F., & Siegel, M. (2017). Migration and the multi dimensional well-being of elderly persons in Georgia. *Journal of Population Ageing*, 1–22. doi: 10.1007/s12062-017-9176-4

Waldinger, R. (2008). Between "here" and "there": Immigrant cross-border activities and loyalties. *International Migration Review*, *42*(1), 3–29. doi: 10.1111/j.17477379.2007.00112.x

Weisskirch, R. S. (2005). The relationship of language brokering to ethnic identity for Latino early adolescents. *Hispanic Journal of Behavioral Sciences*, *27*(3), 286–299. doi: 10.1177/0739986305277931

Wenhong, Z., & Kaichun, L. (2008). The Urban New Immigrants' Social Inclusion: Internal structure, present situation and influential factors [J]. *Sociological Studies*, *5*, 117–41.

Wight, V. R., Chau, M., Aratani, Y. (2011). Who are America's poor children? The official story. National Center for Children in Poverty [NCCP]. Retrieved from http://www.nccp.org/publications/pdf/text_1001.pdf

Wight, V. R., Thampi, K., & Chau, M. (2011). Poor children by parents' nativity: What do we know? National Center for Children in Poverty [NCCP]. Retrieved from http://nccp.org/publications/pub_006.html

White, R., Zeiders, K. H., Gonzales, N. A., Tein, J. Y., & Roosa, M. W. (2013). Cultural values, US neighborhood danger, and Mexican American parents' parenting. *Journal of Family Psychology*, *27*(3), 365.

White, R. M., Liu, Y., Gonzales, N. A., Knight, G. P., & Tein, J. Y. (2016). Neighborhood qualification of the association between parenting and problem behavior trajectories among Mexican-origin father–adolescent dyads. *Journal of Research on Adolescence*, *26*(4), 927–946. doi: 10.1111/jora.12245

Wheeler, L. A., Updegraff, K. A., & Thayer, S. M. (2010). Conflict resolution in Mexican-origin couples: Culture, gender, and marital quality. *Journal of Marriage and Family*, *72*(4), 991–1005. doi: 10.1111/j.1741-3737.2010.00744.x

Yu, Y. (2011). Reconstruction of gender role in marriage: Processes among Chinese immigrant wives. *Journal of Comparative Family Studies*, *42*(5), 651–668.

Yu, Y. (2015). The Male Breadwinner/Female Homemaker Model and Perceived Marital Stability: A Comparison of Chinese Wives in the United States and Urban China. *Journal of Family and Economic Issues*, *36*(1), 34–47. doi: 10.1007/s10834-014-94170

Zapata Roblyer, M. I., & Grzywacz, J. G. (2015). "We thought we had a future": Diversity and resilience in mixed-status families. In A. Schueths & J. Lawston (eds.), *Living Together, Living Apart: Mixed Status Families and US Immigration Policy* (pp. 70–84). University of Washington Press

Zapata Roblyer, M. I., Carlos, F. L., Merten, M. J., Gallus, K., & Grzywacz, J. G. (2017). Psychosocial factors associated with depressive symptoms among Latina immigrants living in a new arrival community. *Journal of Latina/o Psychology*, *5*(2), 103. doi: 10.1037/lat0000068

Zimmer, Z., & Knodel, J. (2013). Older-Age Parents in Rural Cambodia and Migration of Adult Children: A case study of two communes in Battambang province. *Asian Population Studies*, *9*(2), 156–174. doi: 10.1080/17441730.2013.797297

Culture's Influence on Stressors, Parental Socialization, and Developmental Processes in the Mental Health of Children of Immigrants

Su Yeong Kim,[1] Seth J. Schwartz,[2] Krista M. Perreira,[3] and Linda P. Juang[4]

Prevalence of Mental Health Problems in Children of Immigrants

The mental health of immigrants has most often been framed in terms of the immigrant paradox, in which immigrants experience better mental health than their native-born counterparts despite the lower socioeconomic status of immigrants (Marks et al. 2014). This paradox has also been termed the healthy immigrant effect (Castañeda et al. 2015). The assumption is that the most healthy immigrants are selecting themselves to migrate, and unhealthy immigrants are returning to their country of origin (salmon bias) (Arenas et al. 2015), thus making the immigrant pool more healthy overall. At present, though, due to lack of cross-country data, a full and rigorous test of these assumptions has not been fully realized. Moreover, we currently lack a national epidemiological study to ascertain levels of psychiatric diagnoses by nativity for children of immigrants. We therefore use national epidemiological data sets on adults, along with data related to nativity, age of arrival, and years of residence in the United States, to ascertain information relevant for understanding mental health functioning in children of immigrants. We also turn to prominent studies that have sampled adolescents in the United States and have also included an assessment of nativity to make more direct inferences about the mental health of children of immigrants, acknowledging that such studies typically assess mental health functioning in terms of symptoms rather than as psychiatric diagnoses.

Large-scale epidemiological surveys generally support the notion of an immigrant paradox for psychiatric diagnoses among adults, using criteria from the *Diagnostic and Statistical Manual of Mental Disorders*, fourth edition (DSM-IV) (Am. Psychiatr. Assoc. 1994). Using DSM-IV criteria, Breslau et al. (2007) found a health advantage for adult immigrants relative to native-born individuals for various classes of psychiatric disorders in the National Comorbidity Survey Replication (NCS-R). Also using DSM-IV criteria, Alegría et al. (2007) and Takeuchi et al. (2007) found that this nativity advantage was replicated in the National Latino and Asian American Study (NLAAS) for lifetime prevalence of psychiatric diagnoses (depressive disorders, anxiety disorders, substance use disorders) among Latinos and Asian Americans in the United States.

The age of an immigrants' arrival can provide information on whether developmental status at the time of migration can influence immigrants' future mental health. The NCS-R and NLAAS on adults suggest that migration before adolescence puts immigrants at a risk level for psychiatric diagnoses similar to that of native-born individuals, whereas migration as an adult provides a mental health advantage (Alegría et al. 2007, Breslau et al. 2007, Takeuchi et al. 2007).

Acculturation is a construct that is central to understanding the mental health of immigrants (Schwartz et al. 2010). Acculturation refers to the culture change that occurs when immigrants settle in a destination culture. In large epidemiological studies, acculturation is often studied using English fluency or years of residence in the United States as a proxy (Schwartz et al. 2010). Whether acculturation relates to better or worse mental health is unclear, as findings have been generally inconsistent. In the NLAAS, for example, higher English proficiency related to disadvantaged mental health status in Latinos, whereas the pattern was the opposite for Asian American men (Alegría et al. 2007, Takeuchi et al. 2007).

The evidence is also mixed on whether the initial immigrant mental health advantage dissipates over time. The NCS-R showed that the incidence of psychiatric disorders among immigrants increased Math longer time spent in the United States, until levels of impulse control, substance use, and mood disorders reached those seen among native-born individuals (Breslau et al. 2007). In contrast, the NLAAS showed no consistent pattern and no significant effect of longer time spent in the United States on psychiatric diagnoses after accounting for age (Alegría et al. 2007, Takeuchi et al. 2007). However, because the NLAAS was conducted in 2002–2003, more recent statistics are needed. The Hispanic Community Health Study/Study of Latinos (HCHS/SOL), conducted between 2008 and 2011, provides more recent data on the mental health of immigrants, but it does not include measures of psychiatric disorders (Perreira et al. 2015). Nonetheless, the HCHS/SOL does find evidence that, among Latinos, there are higher rates of moderate to severe psychological distress, depression, and anxiety with longer exposure to US culture (Perreira et al. 2015).

The national epidemiological studies we review above were based on information provided by adult participants; however, it is also important to examine the rates of mental health problems in child and adolescent populations directly. We anchor our review using data from the National Longitudinal Study of Adolescent to Adult Health (Add Health), one of the most prominent national studies of adolescents in the United States. Across studies, there is evidence for both immigrant advantage and disadvantage in internalizing problems, whereas our review on suicidal behaviors, externalizing problems, and substance use generally points to immigrant advantage among children of immigrants.

For internalizing problems, the evidence for immigrant advantage in children of immigrants is mixed. The Add Health study found that the adolescent immigrant health advantage of lower depressive symptoms was initially not apparent but became apparent after accounting for protective factors such as family support and parental supervision (Harker 2001). Another prominent study, the Project on Human Development in Chicago Neighborhoods, found an opposite pattern, in which first- and second-generation Latino children had higher levels of internalizing problems relative to third-generation children, but this disadvantage was no longer significant after accounting for neighborhood characteristics (Lara-Cinisomo et al. 2013). In a review of 35 studies published between the years 2009 to 2013, Kouider et al. (2015) identified children of immigrants in the United States with an Asian background as being particularly at risk for internalizing problems.

For suicidal behavior, the immigrant health advantage is more apparent. The risk of suicide is lower in the first generation and increases in second- and third-generation adolescents in both the Latino and the Asian American samples of Add Health (Duldulao et al. 2009, Peña et al. 2008). Although the risk of suicidal behavior is lower among first-generation children, a review of 18 studies showed that immigrant children were at greater risk of being victims of bullying, peer aggression, and violence; the risk was especially high among those whose heritage language was not English (Pottie et al. 2015).

For externalizing problems and substance use, we again find a consistent pattern: an immigrant advantage that dissipates over time spent living in the United States. The National Survey on Drug Use and Health found evidence of an immigrant health advantage, especially among 15- to 17-year-olds, for externalizing problems such as crime, violence, and drug misuse (Salas-Wright et al. 2016). They also found that later age of arrival and fewer years spent in the United States functioned as protective factors for externalizing problems. Such findings were replicated in two other national studies, for alcohol use among Latinos in Add Health (Bacio et al. 2013) and for substance use in the National Household Survey on Drug Abuse (Gfroerer & Tan 2003).

The mental health of undocumented children, unaccompanied minors, and refugee children deserves special mention because of the often traumatic circumstances, such as war, violence, or other natural disasters, that they face both before migration and in their transit to the United States and because of the lack of legal status that can continually undermine children's mental health. Despite some evidence of first-generation children in the United States having an advantage in terms of their mental health, children who are undocumented, unaccompanied, or refugees are at elevated risk for mental health problems (Takeuchi 2016). Indeed, in a survey of first-generation immigrant adolescents, relative to documented adolescents, undocumented adolescents were at elevated risk for anxiety, and adolescents in mixed-status families showed both greater anxiety and marginally greater risk for depressive symptoms (Potochnick & Perreira 2010). Unauthorized parental legal status can be particularly detrimental; for example, relative to those with documented parents, Mexican children in Los Angeles with mothers who were unauthorized showed elevated rates of internalizing and externalizing problems (Landale et al. 2015). Another special case in which children are at higher risk of mental health problems occurs when the family is involuntarily transnational, and children are maintaining contact with parents who lack legal status and have therefore been deported from the United States back to their country of origin (Dreby 2012a).

The number of unaccompanied minors has grown precipitously in the United States in recent years, swelling from 24,000 in 2012 to over 67,000 in 2014; this growth is mostly attributable to the northern triangle consisting of El Salvador, Guatemala, and Honduras (Roth & Grace 2015). Unaccompanied minors are often fleeing gang violence in their country of origin and show high rates of mental health problems because of the trauma that they experienced in their country of origin as well as during their journey to the United States (Ciaccia & John 2016). Refugee children also show high rates of posttraumatic stress disorder, both on arrival and in the United States post-migration, due to the continuing acculturative stressors they face (Lincoln et al. 2016).

Studies on the mental health of immigrants often argue that accounting for stressors, such as the discrimination facing immigrants, may explain nativity differences found in mental health (e.g., Lau et al. 2013, Perreira et al. 2015). It is therefore important to understand the predictors, mechanisms, and conditions through which such stressors affect the mental health of children of immigrants. In. the next section, we review how both culture-specific and transcultural stressors influence the mental health of children of immigrants.

Developmental Processes

Children of Asian and Latino immigrants are likely to be exposed to a heritage language other than English at home, and a body of research has identified a bilingual advantage for these children, as well as development processes, such as ethnic identity, that can be a source of both risk and protection in terms of the mental health of children of immigrants.

The term bilingual advantage refers to cognitive advantages that come with being proficient in two or more languages (Bialystok 2015). Bilingualism comes with some costs, such as smaller receptive vocabulary (Luk & Bialystok 2013). However, bilingualism generally confers advantages across the life span when it conies to nonverbal executive functioning cognitive tasks, such as superior performance in working memory and sometimes in inhibitory control relative to monolinguals (Bialystok 2011, Luk & Bialystok 2013). Studies with adults indicate that being bilingual is associated with better physical and mental health relative to those who are proficient only in English or proficient only in the heritage language (Schachter et al. 2012). The positive effect of bilingualism on mental health can be partially explained by socioeconomic status and family support but not by acculturation, discrimination, or health behaviors (Schachter et al. 2012). Studies with children also demonstrate a bilingual advantage for mental health. Relative to monolinguals, who show faster growth in problem behaviors, Asian bilingual children of immigrants show low levels of growth in externalizing and internalizing behaviors over time (Han & Huang 2010).

A central developmental task of adolescence is developing a sense of identity. Research on identity in children of Asian and Latino immigrants in the United States has largely focused on the role of ethnic identity in their mental health. A strong sense of ethnic identity among children of immigrants is generally considered to be a protective factor for adolescent mental health. Ethnic identity affect (positive feelings about one's ethnicity), in particular, is linked with robust positive effects on a range of mental health outcomes (e.g., depressive symptoms, internalizing and externalizing problems) among children of immigrants (Neblett et al. 2012, Rivas-Drake et al. However, there is some research indicating that there exist conditions under which ethnic identity may also function as a risk factor. In fact, a stressor such as discrimination relates to more delinquent behaviors, and this relationship can be exacerbated or mitigated depending on the dimension of ethnic identity under examination. In a sample that included low-income Latino boys, Williams et al. (2014) found that, when adolescents are faced with discrimination, high ethnic identity affirmation (sense of belonging to one's ethnic group) can be a protective factor, as it does not relate significantly to delinquency, whereas low ethnic identity affirmation is significantly related to delinquency. However, ethnic identity achievement (exploring and committing to one's ethnic identity) can be a risk factor exacerbating the link between discrimination and delinquency (Williams et al. 2014).

The Role of Physiology in the Mental Health of Children of Immigrants

The current research on the mental health of children of immigrants has relied mainly on reports of perceived stressors, especially discrimination. An emerging body of research is demonstrating the ways in which such stressors can get under the skin to influence physiological changes, such as changes in hypothalamic-pituitary-adrenal axis functioning. Perceived discrimination related to greater overall cortisol output in a sample of Mexican American adolescents (Zeiders et al. 2012), and it also related to flatter diurnal slope in ethnic minority young adults, both of which indicate more dysfunctional cortisol rhythms (Zeiders et al. 2014). Psychological stressors experienced early in the life course (e.g., poverty, discrimination) can also result in inflammation, as evidenced by elevated levels of C-reactive protein, which is considered a precursor of depression and cardiovascular disease (Goosby et al. 2015., Miller et al. 2011). As dysregulated cortisol functioning and inflammation can relate to a range of health disparities, including in mental health functioning, an important avenue for future research would be understanding the physiological underpinnings of stressors commonly experienced by children of immigrants to deliver the most effective interventions (McEwen 2004, Miller et al. 2011).

One construct related to ethnic identity in children of Asian and Latino immigrants is bicultural identity integration, which refers to the degree to which individuals living in a bicultural setting perceive their two cultural identities as compatible rather than as oppositional (Benet-Martínez & Haritatos 2005). Bicultural identity integration relates to positive mental health (Chen et al. 2008) and positive youth development (self-esteem, optimism, prosocial behaviors, parental involvement, parent-adolescent communication, and family communication) (Schwartz et al. 2015a) in both Asians and Latinos (see the sidebar tided The Role of Physiology in the Mental Health of Children of Immigrants).

Evidence-Based Interventions for Children of Immigrants

The studies reviewed above highlight the risk and protective factors that can impact the mental health of children of immigrants. Identification of such factors is important, as they can represent key program components in interventions. In this section, we highlight various types of evidence-based intervention programs (family-based interventions, a developmentally focused intervention on ethnic identity, and an intervention specific to refugee children) that show efficacy in reducing mental health problems in children of immigrants.

Examples of efficacious family-based interventions have core program components that are culture specific or are both culture specific and transcultural. Entre Dos Mundos is a culture-specific bicultural skills training program designed for Latino adolescents and parents. The program focuses on mediating the negative impact of parent-child conflict and perceived discrimination while increasing familism and biculturalism in parents and adolescents (Bacallao & Smokowski 2005). Attending more sessions was predictive of fewer externalizing problems, such as child aggression and oppositional defiant disorder, along with gains in family adaptability and bicultural identity integration (Smokowski & Bacallao 2009). Familias Unidas is another family-based intervention program that includes culture-specific components such as educating parents about US culture and biculturalism (Pantin et al. 2003). The program also includes transcultural elements, such as increasing communication and negotiation skills to reduce family conflict and distance and fostering connections between the family and other important systems, such as peers and schools, to improve Latino parents' investment in their adolescents' lives (Pantin et al. 2003). Program effects indicate increases in parental investment and decreases in adolescent problem behaviors, although there were no significant program effects for school achievement (Pantin et al. 2003).

Examples of efficacious family-based interventions can also have core program components that are more transcultural in focus, but with culturally responsive adaptations. Parent Training (PT) is a program for high-risk Chinese immigrant parents that augments content by addressing the cultural challenges facing these parents (Lau et al. 2011). Sessions target a transcultural component, namely improving multiple parenting skills (e.g., logical consequences, cognitive restructuring, communication training, positive and proactive parental involvement) (Lau et al. 2011). Examples of cultural adaptations in these sessions would be group leaders eliciting parental views on potential cultural and practical barriers to implementing the skills being taught in the sessions or facilitating a discussion with parents about the identified barriers and how the skills being taught can achieve parenting goals. PT has been shown to be effective in reducing negative discipline and increasing positive parenting in Chinese American families and in reducing externalizing and internalizing problems in Chinese American children (Lau et al. 2011).

Another family-based intervention, Bridges, has core program components that are transcultural and is also culturally responsive to Mexican American families (Gonzales et al. 2014). The program has three components: parent sessions (emphasizing effective parenting practices), adolescent sessions (emphasizing coping efficacy), and family sessions (emphasizing family cohesion). It is culturally responsive because its core program components were adapted to recognize the processes more germane to low-income Mexican American families. For example, given that low-income Mexican American parents have a poor understanding of US schools and are less prepared to monitor their children's academic challenges, parenting sessions emphasize positive parenting practices, such as monitoring of schoolwork (Gonzales et al. 2014). Bridges is delivered in middle school and has been shown to be effective in increasing school engagement as a primary mediating mechanism to reduce internalizing symptoms, substance use, and school dropout (Gonzales et al. 2014).

The Identity Project is an evidence-based identity intervention that focuses on increasing adolescents' identity exploration and resolution, based on empirical evidence for the positive impact of ethnic identity on adolescent mental health (Umaña-Taylor et al. 2017). It is designed as an 8-week, intervention for delivery in a school-based setting. Initial results indicate that increasing exploration of adolescents' ethnic identity improves ethnic identity resolution for youths in the treatment condition. Because ethnic identity resolution can relate to positive mental health, the initial results of this intervention suggest that it shows promise as an evidence-based intervention to reduce mental health problems in children of immigrants.

Because refugees are a special population, we also highlight an intervention that may specifically reduce mental health problems in children in this population. Project SHIFA (Supporting the Health of Immigrant Families and Adolescents) is a multitiered intervention program for Somali refugee youth. It has three main components: resilience building in the community, school-based intervention for those at risk, and direct trauma therapy for those reporting significant levels of psychological distress (Ellis et al. 2013). Program results showed effectiveness in reducing symptoms of depression and post-traumatic stress disorder among refugee adolescents.

Policies for Children of Immigrants

Government policies and programs are one way to reduce mental health problems in children of immigrants. Programs such as Medicaid, Children's Health Insurance Program (CHIP), Supplemental Nutrition Assistance Program (SNAP), and Temporary Assistance to Needy Families (TANF) provide important financial, health, and nutritional assistance for low-income families in the United States (Perreira et al. 2012). Despite their greater need for these services, low-income immigrant families have less access to these programs because of strict eligibility requirements and barriers that result in lower usage of these benefits (Perreira et al. 2012). These Arriva barriers include the complexity of the application and eligibility rules, administrative burdens, language and cultural barriers, transportation and other logistical issues, and fear and mistrust of government authorities (Perreira et al. 2012). Moreover, although many children in immigrant families are US-born and are thus eligible for government services, many do not access them, especially when parents are undocumented (Torres & Young 2016). In addition, increased risk of deportation can decrease use of public services such as Medicaid (Vargas 2015).

Lack of legal status is a major obstacle to being eligible for government programs. Government policies such as the 2012 Deferred Action for Child Arrivals (DACA), which provided temporary relief from deportation and renewable work permits for undocumented children of immigrants, have shown positive consequences for mental health (Venkataramani et al. 2017). Specifically, relative to DACA-ineligible individuals, those who were DACA eligible showed lower levels of psychological distress (Venkataramani et al. 2017). For this reason, it is important to implement programs such as DACA to improve the mental health of children of immigrants in die future.

Despite some favorable government policies (e.g., DACA) for undocumented children in the United States, between 2003 and 2013, over 3.7 million immigrants were deported from the United States (Koball et al. 2015). The majority (91%) of these deportees are men, and up to 25% are parents of US-born children (Koball et al. 2015). Deportation of undocumented immigrant parents can have disastrous consequences for families. For example, children may be left in foster care, mothers may become single parents if fathers are deported, parents may lose custody of their US-born children, children may begin to fear law enforcement, children may begin to view being an immigrant as the same as being illegal, and children may begin to associate their immigrant and heritage background with stigma (Dreby 2012b). Among other recommendations, government policies to improve access to benefits, better coordination with child welfare caseworkers, and short-term financial assistance are useful strategies for improving the lives of families affected by the deportation of a family member (Koball et al. 2015).

Unaccompanied minors, in particular, are a group of undocumented immigrant children who have received recent media attention. The peak of arrivals of unaccompanied minors to the United States occurred in 2014, with the largest number coming from Honduras, followed by Guatemala, El Salvador, and Mexico. These children are often apprehended and detained at the border (Am. Immigr. Counc. 2015). The Office of Refugee Resettlement, an agency of the US Department of Health and Human Services, is then responsible for finding them shelter and directing their legal proceedings (Pierce 2015). The vast majority of unaccompanied minors stay with a parent, relative, or friend in the United States while awaiting the settlement of their cases in the US immigrant courts (Pierce 2015). The length of the process, which can take years, means that unaccompanied minors become further integrated into the United States while awaiting the results of their court proceedings. Typically, after their cases are heard, 97% of unaccompanied minors remain unauthorized

(Pierce 2015). They may be given informal relief but not legal status in the United States, which means they have limited access to social programs. Given the strong link between undocumented status and poor mental health (Potochnick & Perreira 2010), providing a better avenue for achieving legal status may go a long way toward improving the mental health of unaccompanied minors.

Conclusion

The United States is a country founded by immigrants and is expected to increase its immigrant population, from today's 14% of the US population to 18% in 2065. In fact, immigrants and their children are projected to comprise 36% of the US population in 2065 (Pew Res. Cent. 2015). With these future trends in mind, we have reviewed the ways in which transcultural and culture-specific stressors, parental socialization, and developmental processes influence the mental health of children of immigrants. We have also identified risk factors that can be reduced, and protective factors that can be promoted, to improve the mental health of children of immigrants. Given the many obstacles immigrants and their children face, implementing the evidence-based interventions and policies identified in this review would go a long way toward bolstering the mental health of a growing population, specifically children of immigrants, who represent a large proportion of the US population and our future workforce.

Summary Points

1. Among both Asian Americans and Latinos, individuals who migrate before adolescence are at similar risk for psychiatric disorders as US-born individuals.
2. Asian children of immigrant backgrounds in the United States are particularly at risk for internalizing problems.
3. Relative to documented adolescents, undocumented adolescents and children in mixed status families are at elevated risk for anxiety.
4. Parental experiences of discrimination relate to adolescent delinquency and depressive symptoms via increased paternal depressive symptoms and parental hostility toward adolescents.
5. Parent-child dyads with matching acculturation levels experience more supportive parenting and fewer adolescent depressive symptoms, whereas dyads with mismatched acculturation report less supportive parenting and more depressive symptoms.
6. Asian bilingual children of immigrants show slower growth in internalizing and externalizing problems over time relative to monolingual children.
7. Ethnic identity affirmation has a robust relationship with positive mental health and can mitigate the negative effects of discrimination.
8. Relative to DACA-ineligible individuals, those who were DACA eligible showed lower levels of psychological distress.

Future Issues

1. An up-to-date national study to ascertain the prevalence or psychiatric diagnoses in a US adolescent sample by nativity is needed.
2. Relative to studies of Latino children of immigrants, there are fewer studies of Asian children of immigrants in the United States. As the number of Asian Americans is expected to surpass

the number of Latino immigrants in the future, more research attention to this population is needed.

3. Migration stressors related to the context, of exit from the country of origin and entrance into the United States have been studied in reference to refugee children and unaccompanied minors, hut we know less about the role of these experiences in the development of immigrant children more generally.

4. Children of immigrants are faced with both transcultural and culture-specific challenges, and real-time interventions targeting changes in these stress responses may be most fruitful in improving their mental health.

5. The exact mechanisms through which bilingual advantage, characterized by enhanced executive functioning, relates to better mental health need to be identified.

6. Longitudinal studies that follow immigrant children from their experiences in their countries of origin, to their experiences journeying to the United States, to their post settlement experiences are needed to understand their mental health prospectively.

7. More long-term follow-up is needed for intervention studies that have targeted children of immigrants into adulthood to incorporate life-course perspectives on health and the potential cumulative impact of interventions over time on the mental health of children of immigrants.

8. An immigration policy allowing a path to citizenship in the United States for undocumented children and their parents will allow them to realize a more secure future, free from the fear of deportation, and will improve their long-term mental health.

Disclosure Statement

K.M.P. is a board member of the Population Association of America and a coinvestigator of the Hispanic Community Health Study, supported by the National Heart, Lung, and Blood Institute (contract N01-HC65233).

Acknowledgments

This work was supported by grants to S.Y.K. from the National Science Foundation, Division of Behavioral and Cognitive Sciences (1651128 and 0956123), and the Eunice Kennedy Shriver National Institute of Child Health and Human Development (5R03HD060045-02 and 5R03HD051629-02), and by grants to the Population Research Center at the University of Texas at Austin from the Eunice Kennedy Shriver National Institute of Child Health and Human Development (2P2CHD042849-16).

References

Aiken LS, West SG. 1991. *Multiple Regression: Testing and Interpreting Interactions*. Thousand Oaks, CA: Sage

Alegría M, Mulvaney-Day N, Torres M, Polo A, Cao Z, Canino G. 2007. Prevalence of psychiatric disorders across Latino subgroups in the United States. *Am. F. Public Health* **97**: 68–75.

Am. Immigr. Counc. 2015. *A Guide to Children Arriving at the Border: Laws, Policies, and Responses*. Washington, DC: Am. Immigr. Counc.

Am. Psychiatr. Assoc. 1994. *Diagnostic and Statistical Manual of Mental Disorders*. Washington, DC: Am. Psychiatr. Assoc. 4th ed.

Arenas E, Goldman N, Pebley AR, Teruel G. 2015. Return migration to Mexico: Does health matter? *Demography* **52**: 1853–68.

Armenta BE, Lee RM, Pituc ST, Jung K-R, Park IJK, et al. 2013. Where are you from? A validation of the Foreigner Objectification Scale and the psychological correlates of foreigner objectification among Asian Americans and Latinos. *Cult. Divers. Ethn. Minor. Psychol.* **19**: 131–42.

Bacallao ML, Smokowski PR. 2005. "Entre Dos Mundos" (Between Two Worlds): bicultural skills training with Latino immigrant families. *F. Prim. Prev.* **26**: 485–509.

Bacio GA, Mays VM, Lau AS. 2013. Drinking initiation and problematic drinking among Latino adolescents: explanations of the immigrant paradox. *Psychol. Addict. Behav.* **27**: 14–22.

Benet-Martínez V, Haritatos J. 2005. Bicultural identity integration (BII): components and psychosocial antecedents. *F. Personal.* **73**: 1015—50.

Benner AD, Kim SY. 2009a. Experiences of discrimination among Chinese American adolescents and the consequences for socioemotional and academic development. *Dev. Psychol.* **45**: 1682–94.

Benner AD, Kim SY. 2009b. Intergenerational experiences of discrimination in Chinese American families: influences of socialization and stress. *F. Marriage Pam.* **71**: 862–77.

Berry JW, Phinney JS, Sam DL, Vedder P. 2006. *Immigrant Youth in Cultural Transition: Acculturation, Identity, and Adaptation Across National Contexts.* Mahwah, NJ: Erlbaum.

Bialystok E. 2001. *Bilingualism in Development: Language, Literacy, and Cognition.* Cambridge, UK: Cambridge Univ. Press.

Bialystok E. 2011. Reshaping the mind: the benefits of bilingualism. *Can. F. Exp. Psychol.* **65**: 229–35.

Bialystok E. 2015. Bilingualism and the development of executive function: the role of attention. *Child Dev. Perspect.* **9**: 117—21.

Blakemore S-J, Mills KL. 2014. Is adolescence a sensitive period for sociocultural processing? *Annu. Rev. Psychol.* **65**: 187–207.

Breslau J, Aguilar-Gaxiola S, Borges G, Kendler KS, Su M, Kessler RC. 2007. Risk for psychiatric disorder among immigrants and their US-born descendants: evidence from the National Comorbidity Survey Replication. *F. Nerv. Ment. Dis.* **195**: 189–95.

Calzada EJ, Huang K-Y, Anicama C, Fernandez Y, Brotman LM. 2012. Test of a cultural framework of parenting with Latino families of young children. *Cult. Divers. Ethn. Minor. Psychol.* **18**: 285–96.

Case A, Fertig A, Paxson C. 2005. The lasting impact of childhood health and circumstance. *F. Health Econ.* **24**: 365–89.

Castañeda H, Holmes SM, Madrigal DS, De Trinidad Young M-E, Beyeler N, Quesada J. 2015. Immigration as a social determinant of health. *Annu. Rev. Public Health* **36**: 375–92.

Chan EYY, Mercer SW, Yue C, Wong S, Griffiths SM. 2009. Mental health of migrant children. *Int. F. Ment. Health* **38**: 44–52.

Chao RK. 1994. Beyond parental control and authoritarian patenting style: understanding Chinese parenting through the cultural notion of training. *Child Dev.* **65**: 1111–19.

Chao RK. 2006. The prevalence and consequences of adolescents' language brokering for their immigrant parents. In *Acculturation and Parent–Child Relationships: Measurement and Development,* ed. MH Bornstein, LR Cote, pp. 271–96. Mahwah, NJ: Erlbaum.

Chen SX, Benet-Martínez V, Bond MH. 2008. Bicultural identity, bilingualism, and psychological adjustment in multicultural societies: immigration-based and globalization-based acculturation. *F. Personal.* **76**: 803–38.

Ciaccia KA, John RM. 2016. Unaccompanied immigrant minors: where to begin. *F. Pediatr. Health Care* **30**: 231–40.

Collins LM, Lanza ST. 2010. *Latent Class and Latent Transition Analysis: With Applications in the Social, Behavioral, and Health Sciences.* Hoboken, NJ: Wiley.

Conger RD, Conger KJ. 2002. Resilience in Midwestern families: selected findings from the first decade of a prospective, longitudinal study. *F. Marriage Fam.* **64**: 361–73.

Connor P, Lopez G. 2016. 5 facts about the U.S. rank in worldwide migration. *Factank: News in the Numbers,* May 18.

Crouter AC, Davis KD, Updegraff K, Delgado M, Fortner M. 2006. Mexican American fathers' occupational conditions: links to family members' psychological adjustment. *F. Marriage Fam.* **68**: 843–58.

Darling N, Steinberg L. 1993. Parenting style as context: an integrative model. *Psychol. Bull.* **113**: 487–96.

Drachman D. 1992. A stage-of-migration framework for service to immigrant populations. *Soc. Work* **37**: 68–72.

Dreby J. 2012a. The burden of deportation on children in Mexican immigrant families. *F. Marriage Fam.* **74**: 829–45.

Dreby J. 2012b. *How Today's Immigration Enforcement Policies Impact Children, Families, and Communities: A View from the Ground.* Washington, DC: Cent Am. Prog.

Dreby J, Adkins T. 2012. The strength of family ties: how US migration shapes children's ideas of family. *Child. Glob. F. Child Res.* **19**: 169–87.

Duldulao AA, Takeuchi DT, Hong S. 2009. Correlates of suicidal behaviors among Asian Americans. *Arch. Suicide Res.* **13**: 277–90.

Ellis BH, MacDonald HZ, Klunk-Gillis J, Lincoln A, Strunin L, Cabral HJ. 2010. Discrimination and mental health among Somali refugee adolescents: the role of acculturation and gender. *Am. F. Orthopsychiatry* **80**: 564–75.

Ellis BH, Miller AB, Abdi S, Barrett C, Blood EA, Betancourt TS. 2013. Multi-tier mental health program for refugee youth, *F. Consult. Clin. Psychol.* **81**: 129–40.

Flannery WP, Reise SP, Yu J. 2001. An empirical comparison of acculturation models. *Personal. Soc. Psychol. Bull.* **27**: 1035–45.

Garcia Coll C, Lamberty G, Jenkins R, McAdoo HP, Cmic K, et al. 1996. An integrative model for the study of developmental competencies in minority children. *Child Dev.* **67**: 1891–914.

Gartner M, Kiang L, Supple A. 2014. Prospective links between ethnic socialization, ethnic and American identity, and well-being among Asian-American adolescents. *F. Youth Adolesc.* **43**: 1715–27.

Gfroerer JC, Tan LL. 2003. Substance use among foreign-born youths in the United States: Does the length of residence matter? *Am. F. Public Health* **93**: 1892–95.

Gil AG, Wagner EF, Vega WA. 2000. Acculturation, familism and alcohol use among Latino adolescent males: longitudinal relations. *F. Community Psychol.* **28**: 443–58.

Goldbach JT, Berger Cardoso J, Cervantes RC, Du an L. 2015. The relation between stress and alcohol use among Hispanic adolescents. *Psychol. Addict. Behav.* **29**: 960–68.

Gonzales NA, Coxe S, Roosa MW, White RMB, Knight GP, et al. 2011. Economic hardship, neighborhood context, and parenting: prospective effects on Mexican-American adolescent's mental health. *Am. F. Community Psychol.* **47**: 98–113.

Gonzales NA, Dumka LE, Millsap RE, Gottschall A, McClain DB, et al. 2012. Randomized trial of a broad preventive intervention for Mexican American adolescents. *F. Consult. Clin. Psychol.* **80**: 1–16.

Gonzales NA, Wong JJ, Toomey RB, Millsap R, Dumka LE, Mauricio AM. 2014. School engagement mediates long-term prevention effects for Mexican American adolescents. *Prev. Sci.* **15**: 929–39.

Goosby BJ, Malone S, Richardson EA, Cheadle JE, Williams DT. 2015. Perceived discrimination and markers of cardiovascular risk among low-income African American youth. *Am. F. Hum. Biol.* **27**: 546–52.

Greene ML, Way N, Pahl K. 2006. Trajectories of perceived adult and peer discrimination among Black, Latino, and Asian American adolescents: patterns and psychological correlates. *Dev. Psychol.* **42**: 218–36.

Han W-J, Huang C-C. 2010. The forgotten treasure: bilingualism and Asian children's emotional and behavioral health. *Am. F. Public Health* **100**: 831–38.

Harker K. 2001. Immigrant generation, assimilation, and adolescent psychological well-being. *Soc. Forces* **79**: 969–1004.

Hernandez DJ, Denton NA, Blanchard VL. 2011. Children in the United States of America: a statistical portrait by race-ethnicity, immigrant origins, and language. *Ann. Am. Acad. Political Soc. Sci.* **633**: 102–27.

Hou Y, Kim SY, Hazen N, Benner AD. 2017. Parents' perceived discrimination and adolescent adjustment in Chinese American families: mediating family processes. *Child Dev.* **88**: 317–31.

Hou Y, Kim SY, Wang Y. 2016. Parental acculturative stressors and adolescent adjustment through inter-parental and parent-child relationships in Chinese American families. *F. Youth Adolesc.* **45:** 1466–81.

Huemer J, Karnik NS, Voelkl-Kemstock S, Granditsch E, Dervic K, et al. 2009. Mental health issues in unaccompanied refugee minors. *Child Adolesc. Psychiatry Ment. Health* **3:** 13.

Hughes D, Hagelskamp C, Way N, Foust MD. 2009. The role of mothers' and adolescents' perceptions of ethnic-racial socialization in shaping ethnic-racial identity among early adolescent boys and girls. *F. Youth Adolesc.* **38:** 605–26.

Hughes D, Rodriguez J, Smith, EP, Johnson DJ, Stevenson HC, Spicer P, 2006. Parents' ethnic-racial socialization practices: a review of research and directions for future study. *Dev. Psychol.* **42:** 747–70.

Juang LP, Alvarez AA. 2010. Discrimination and adjustment among Chinese American adolescents: family conflict and family cohesion as vulnerability and protective factors. *Am. F. Public Health* **100:** 2403–9.

Juang LP, Shen Y, Kim SY, Wang Y. 2016. Development of an Asian American parental racial-ethnic socialization scale. *Cult. Divers. Ethn. Minor. Psychol.* **22:** 417–31.

Kam JA, Lazarevic V. 2014. The stressful (and not so stressful) nature of language brokering: identifying when brokering functions as a cultural stressor for Latino immigrant children in early adolescence. *F. Youth Adolesc.* **43:** 1994–2011.

Kam JA, Marcoulides KM, Merolla AJ. 2017. Using an acculturation-stress-resilience framework to explore latent profiles of Latina/o language brokers. *F. Res. Adolesc.* **27:** 842–61.

Kessler RC, Berglund P, Demler O, Jin R, Merikangas KR, Walters EE. 2005. Lifetime prevalence and age-of-onset distributions of DSM-IV disorders in the National Comorbidity Survey Replication. *Arch. Gen. Psychiatry* **62:** 593—602.

Kia-Keating M, Ellis BH. 2007. Belonging and connection to school in resettlement: young refugees, school belonging, and psychosocial adjustment *Clin. Child Psychol. Psychiatry* **12:** 29–43.

Kim SY, Chen Q, Wang Y, Shen Y, Orozco-Lapray D. 2013a. Longitudinal linkages among parent-child acculturation discrepancy, parenting, parent-child sense of alienation, and adolescent adjustment in Chinese immigrant families. *Dev. Psychol.* **49:** 900–12.

Kim SY, Gonzales NA, Stroh K, Wang JJ-L. 2006. Parent-child cultural marginalization and depressive symptoms in Asian American family members. *F. Community Psychol.* **34:** 167–82.

Kim SY, Hou Y, Gonzalez Y. 2017. Language brokering and depressive symptoms in Mexican-American adolescents: parent-child alienation and resilience as moderators. *Child Dev.* **88:** 867–81.

Kim SY, Wang Y, Deng S, Alvarez R, Li J. 2011. Accent, perpetual foreigner stereotype, and perceived discrimination as indirect links between English proficiency and depressive symptoms in Chinese American adolescents. *Dev. Psychol.* **47:** 289–301.

Kim SY, Wang Y, Orozco-Lapray D, Shen Y, Murtuza M. 2013 b. Does "tiger parenting" exist? Parenting profiles of Chinese Americans and adolescent developmental outcomes. *Asian Am. F. Psychol.* **4:** 7–18.

Kim SY, Wang Y, Shen Y, Hou Y. 2015. Stability and change in adjustment profiles among Chinese American adolescents; the role of parenting. I. *Youth Adolesc.* **44:** 1735–51.

Kim SY, Wang Y, Weaver SR, Shen Y, Wu-Seibold N, Liu CH. 2014. Measurement equivalence of the language-brokering scale for Chinese American adolescents and their parents. *F. Fam. Psychol.* **28:** 180–92.

Kline RB. 2016. *Principles and Practice of Structural Equation Modeling.* New York: Guilford Press.

Koball H, Capps R, Perreira K, Campetella A, Hooker S, et al. 2015. *Health and Social Service Needs of US-Citizen Children with Detained or Deported Immigrant Parents.* Washington, DC: Urban Inst/Migr. Policy Inst.

Kouider EB, Koglin U, Petermann F. 2015. Emotional and behavioral problems in migrant children and adolescents in American countries: a systematic review. *F. Immigr. Minor. Health* **17:** 1240–58.

Landale NS, Hardie JH, Oropesa RS, Hillemeier MM. 2015. Behavioral functioning among Mexican-origin children: Does parental legal status matter? *F. Health Soc. Behav.* **56:** 2–18.

Lara-Cinisomo S, Xue Y, Brooks-Gunn J. 2013. Latino youth's internalising behaviours: links to immigrant status and neighbourhood characteristics. *Ethn. Health* **18**: 315–35.

Lau AS, Fung JJ, Ho LY, Liu LL, Gudiño OG. 2011. Parent training with high-risk immigrant Chinese families: a pilot group randomized trial yielding practice-based evidence. *Behav. Tber.* **42**: 413–26.

Lau AS, McCabe KM, Yeh M, Garland AF, Wood PA Hough RL. 2005. The acculturation gap-distress hypothesis among high-risk Mexican American families. *F. Fam. Psychol.* **19**: 367–75.

Lau AS, Tsai W, Shih J, Liu LL, Hwang W-C, Takeuchi DT. 2013. The immigrant paradox among Asian American women; Are disparities in the burden of depression and anxiety paradoxical or explicable? *F. Consult. Clin. Psychol.* **81**: 901–11.

Lee EH, Zhou Q, Ly J, Main A, Tao A, Chen SH. 2014. Neighborhood characteristics, parenting styles, and children's behavioral problems in Chinese American immigrant families. *Cult. Divers. Ethn. Minor. Psychol.* **20**: 202–12.

Lewis TT, Cogburn CD, Wiliams DR. 2015. Self-reported experiences of discrimination and healtii: scientific advances, ongoing controversies, and emerging issues. *Annu. Rev. Clin. Psychol.* **11**: 407–40.

Lincoln AK, Lazarevic V, White MT, Ellis BH. 2016. The impact of acculturation style and acculturative hassles on the mental health of Somali adolescent refugees. *F. Immigr. Minor. Health* **18**: 771–78.

Liu LL, Lau AS. 2013. Teaching about race/ethnicity and racism, matters: an examination of how perceived ethnic racial socialization processes are associated with depression symptoms. *Cult. Divers. Ethn. Minor. Psychol.* **19**: 383–94.

Liu LL, Lau AS, Chen AC-C, Dinh KT, Kim SY. 2009. The influence of maternal acculturation, neighborhood disadvantage, and parenting on Chinese American adolescents' conduct problems: testing the segmented assimilation hypothesis. *F. Youth Adolesc.* **38**: 691–702.

Lopez MH, Passel J, Rohal M. 2015. Modem immigration wave brings 59 million to U.S., driving population growth and change through 2065: views of immigration's impact on U.S. society mixed. *Pew Research Center Hispanic Trends*, Sept. 28.

Lorenzo-Blanco El, Unger JB, Oshri A, Baezconde-Garbanati L, Soto D. 2016. Profiles of bullying victimization, discrimination, social support, and school safety: links with Latino/a youth acculturation, gender, depressive symptoms, and cigarette use. *Am. F. Orthopsychiatry* **86**: 37–48.

Lui PP. 2015. Intergenerational cultural conflict, mental health, and educational outcomes among Asian and Latino/a Americans: qualitative and meta-analytic review. *Psychol. Bull.* **141**: 404–46.

Luk G, Biaiystok E. 2013. Bilingualism is not a categorical variable: interaction between language proficiency and usage. *F. Cogn. Psychol.* **25**: 605–21.

Lustig SL, Kia-Keatmg M, Knight WG, Geltman P, Ellis H, et al. 2004. Review of child and adolescent refugee mental health. *F. Am. Acad. Child Adolesc. Psychiatry* **43**: 24–36.

Marks AK, Ejesi K, Coll CG. 2014. Understanding the U.S. immigrant paradox in childhood and adolescence. *Child Dev. Perspect.* **8**: 59–64.

McEwen BS. 2004. Protection and damage from acute and chronic stress: allostasis and allostatic overload and relevance to the pathophysiology of psychiatric disorders. *Ann. N. Y. Acad. Sci.* **1032**: 1–7.

Miller GE, Chen E, Parker KJ. 2011. Psychological stress in childhood and susceptibility to the chronic diseases of aging: moving toward a model of behavioral and biological mechanisms. *Psychol. Bull.* **137**: 959–97.

Mistry RS, Benner AD, Tan CS, Kim SY. 2009. Family economic stress and academic well-being among Chinese-American youth: the influence of adolescents' perceptions of economic strain. *F. Fam. Psychol.* **23**: 279–90.

Nair RL, White RMB, Roosa MW, Zeiders KH. 2013. Cultural stressors and mental health symptoms among Mexican Americans: a prospective study examining the impact of the family and neighborhood context. *F. Youth Adolesc.* **42**: 1611–23.

Neblett EW Jr., Rivas-Drake D, Umaña-Taylor AJ. 2012. The promise of racial and ethnic protective factors in promoting ethnic minority youth development. *Child Dev. Perspect.* **6**: 295–303.

Nguyen A-MD, Benet-Martínez V. 2013. Biculturalism and adjustment: a meta-analysis. *J. Cross-Cult Psychol.* **44:** 122–59.

Ortega J, Huang S, Prado G. 2012. Applying ecodevelopmental theory and the theory of reasoned action to understand HIV risk behaviors among Hispanic adolescents. *Hisp. Health Care Int.* **10:** 42–52.

Pantin H, Coatsworth JD, Feaster DJ, Newman FL, Briones E, et al. 2003. Familias Unidas: the efficacy of an intervention to promote parental investment in Hispanic immigrant families. *Prev. Sci.* **4:** 189–201.

Park IJK, Wang L, Williams DR, Alegría M. 2017. Coping with racism: moderators of the discrimination-adjustment link among Mexican-origin adolescents. *Child Dev.* In press, https://doi.org/10.1111/cdev.12856/

Pascoe EA, Smart Richman L. 2009. Perceived discrimination and health: a meta-analytic review. *Psychol. Bull.* **135:** 531–54.

Passel J, Cohn DV. 2017. Immigration projected to drive growth in U.S. working-age population through at least 2035. *Factank: News in the Numbers,* March 8.

Passel JS. 2011. Demography of immigrant youth: past, present, and future. *Future Child.* **21:** 19–41.

Peña JB, Wyman PA, Brown CH, Matthieu MM, Olivares TE, et al. 2008. Immigration generation status and its association with suicide attempts, substance use, and depressive symptoms among Latino adolescents in the USA. *Prev. Sci.* **9:** 299–310.

Perreira KM, Crosnoe R, Fortuny K, Pedroza J, Ulvestad K, et al. 2012. *Barriers to immigrants' access to health and human services programs.* ASPE Res. Brief, Off. Assist. Seer. Plan. Eval, Washington, DC.

Perreira KM, Gotman N, Isasi CR, Arguelles W, Castaneda SF, et al. 2015. Mental health and exposure to the United States: key correlates from the Hispanic Community Health Study of Latinos. *F. Nerv. Ment. Dis.* **203:** 670–78.

Pew Res. Cent. 2015. Immigration's impact on past and future U.S. population change. *Pew Research Center Hispanic Trends,* Sept. 28.

Pierce S. 2015. *Unaccompanied child migrants in US communities, immigration court, and schools.* Policy Brief, Migr. Policy Inst., Washington, DC.

Potochnick SR, Perreira KM. 2010. Depression and anxiety among first-generation immigrant Latino youth. *F. Nerv. Ment. Dis.* **198:** 470–77.

Pottie K, Dahal G, Georgiades K, Premji K, Hassan G. 2015. Do first generation immigrant adolescents face higher rates of bullying, violence and suicidal behaviours than do third generation and native born? *F. Immigr. Minor. Health* **17:** 1557–66.

Prado G, Huang S, Maldonado-Molina M, Bandiera F, Schwartz SJ, et al. 2010. An empirical test of ecodevelopmental theory in predicting HIV risk behaviors among Hispanic youth. *Health Educ. Behav.* **37:** 97–114.

Pumariega AJ, Rothe E, Pumariega JB. 2005. Mental health of immigrants and refugees. *Community Ment. Health F.* **41:** 581–97.

Rivas-Drake D, Hughes D, Way N. 2009. A preliminary analysis of associations among ethnic racial socialization, ethnic discrimination, and ethnic identity among urban sixth graders. *F. Res. Adolesc.* **19:** 558–84.

Rivas-Drake D, Syed M, Umaña-Taylor A, Markstrom C, French S, et al. 2014. Feeling good, happy, the proud: a meta-analysis of positive ethnic-racial affect and adjustment. *Child Dev.* **85:** 77–102.

Romero AJ, Martinez D, Carvajal SC. 2007. Bicultural stress and adolescent risk behaviors in a community sample of Latinos and non-Latino European Americans. *Ethn. Health* **12:** 443–63.

Romero AJ, Roberts RE. 2003. Stress within a bicultural context for adolescents of Mexican descent. *Cult. Divers. Ethn. Minor. Psychol.* **9:** 171–84.

Rosenbloom SR, Way N. 2004. Experiences of discrimination among African American, Asian American, and Latino adolescents in an urban high school. *Youth Soc.* **35:** 420–51.

Roth BJ, Grace BL. 2015. Falling through the cracks: the paradox of post-release services for unaccompanied child migrants. *Child. Youth Serv. Rev.* **58:** 244–52.

Salas-Wright CP, Vaughn MG, Schwartz SJ, Cordova D. 2016. An "immigrant paradox" for adolescent externalizing behavior? Evidence from a national sample. *Soc. Psychiatry Psychiatr. Epidemiol.* **51:** 27–37.

Schachter A, Kimbro RT, Gorman BK. 2012. Language proficiency and health status: Are bilingual immigrants healthier? *F. Health Soc. Behav.* **53:** 124–45.

Schofield TJ, Parke RD, Kim Y, Coltrane S. 2008. Bridging the acculturation gap: parent-child relationship quality as a moderator in Mexican American families. *Dev. Psychol.* **44:** 1190–94.

Schwartz SJ, Unger JB, Baezconde-Garbanati L, Benet-Martínez V, Meca A, et al. 2015a. Longitudinal trajectories of bicultural identity integration in recently immigrated Hispanic adolescents: links with mental health and family functioning. *Int. F. Psychol.* **50:** 440–50.

Schwartz SJ, Unger JB, Baezconde-Garbanati L, Zamboanga BL, Córdova D, et al. 2016. Testing the parent-adolescent acculturation discrepancy hypothesis: a five-wave longitudinal study. *F. Res. Adolesc.* **26:** 567–86.

Schwartz SJ, Unger JB, Baezconde-Garbanati L, Zamboanga BL, Lorenzo-Bianco El, et al. 2015b. Trajectories of cultural stressors and effects on mental health and substance use among Hispanic immigrant adolescents. *F. Adolesc. Health* **56:** 433–39.

Schwartz SJ, Unger JB, Lorenzo-Bianco El, Des Rosiers SE, ViUamar JA, et al. 2014. Perceived context of reception among recent Hispanic immigrants: conceptualization, instrument development, and preliminary validation. *Cult. Divers. Ethn. Minor. Psychol.* **20:** 1–15.

Schwartz SJ, Unger JB, Zamboanga BL, Szapocznik J. 2010. Rethinking the concept of acculturation: implications for theory and research. *Am. Psychol.* **65:** 237–51.

Smokowski PR, Bacallao M. 2009. Entre Dos Mundos/Between Two Worlds: youth violence prevention for acculturating Latino families. *Res. Soc. Work Pract.* **19:** 165–78.

Sue S, Okazaki S. 1990. Asian-American educational achievements: a phenomenon in search of an explanation. *Am. Psychol.* **45:** 913–20.

Takeuchi DT. 2016. Vintage wine in new bottles: infusing select ideas into the study of immigration, immigrants, and mental health. *J. Health Soc. Behav.* **57:** 423–35.

Takeuchi DT, Zane N, Hong S, Chae DH, Gong F, et al. 2007. Immigration-related factors and mental disorders among Asian Americans. *Am. F. Public Health* **97:** 84—90.

Telzer EH. 2011. Expanding the acculturation gap-distress model: an integrative review of research. *Hum. Dev.* **53:** 313–40.

Torres JM, Young M-ED. 2016. A life-course perspective on legal status stratification and health. *SSM Popul. Health* **2:** 141–48.

Torres L, Driscoll MW, Voell M. 2012. Discrimination, acculturation, acculturative stress, and Latino psychological distress: a moderated mediational model. *Cult. Divers. Ethn. Minor. Psychol.* **18:** 17–25.

Trentacosta CJ, McLear CM, Ziadni MS, Lumley MA, Artken CL. 2016. Potentially traumatic events and mental health problems among children of Iraqi refugees: the roles of relationships with parents and feelings about school. *Am. F. Orthopsychiatiy* **86:** 384–92.

Umaña-Taylor AJ, Douglass S, Updegraff KA, Marsiglia FF. 2017. A small-scale randomized efficacy trial of the Identity Project: promoting adolescents' ethnic-racial identity exploration and resolution. *Child Dev.* In press, https://doi.org/10.llll/cdev.12755.

Umaña-Taylor AJ, O'Donnell M, Knight GP, Roosa MW, Berkel C, Nair R. 2014a. Mexican-origin early adolescents' ethnic socialization, ethnic identity, and psychosocial functioning. *Couns. Psychol.* **42:** 170–200.

Umaña-Taylor AJ, Quintana SM, Lee RM, Cross WE, Rivas-Drake D, et al. 2014b. Ethnic and racial identity during adolescence and into young adulthood: an integrated conceptualization. *Child Dev.* **85:** 21–39.

Unger JB, Thing J, Soto DW, Baezconde-Garbanati L. 2014. Associations between ethnic labels and substance use among Hispanic/Latino adolescents in Los Angeles. *Subst. Use Misuse* **49:** 1007–16.

Vargas ED. 2015. Immigration enforcement and mixed-status families: the effects of risk of deportation on Medicaid use. *Child. Youth Serv. Rev.* **57:** 83–89.

Venkataramani AS, Shah SJ, O'Brien R, Kawachi I, Tsai AC. 2017. Health consequences of the U.S. Deferred Action for Childhood Arrivals (DACA) immigration programme: a quasi-experimental study. *Lancet Public Health* **2:** e175–81.

Wang Y, Benner AD. 2016. Cultural socialization across contexts: family—peer congruence and adolescent well-being. *F. Youth Adolesc.* **45:** 594–611.

Weaver SR, Kim SY. 2008. A person-centered approach to studying the linkages among parent-child differences in cultural orientation, supportive parenting, and adolescent depressive symptoms in Chinese American families. *F. Youth Adolesc.* **37:** 36–49.

White RMB, Liu Y, Gonzales NA, Knight GP, Tein JY. 2016. Neighborhood qualification of the association between parenting and problem behavior trajectories among Mexican-origin father—adolescent dyads. *F. Res. Adolesc.* **26:** 927–46.

White RMB, Liu Y, Nair RL, Tein J-Y. 2015. Longitudinal and integrative tests of family stress model effects on Mexican origin adolescents. *Dev. Psychol.* **51:** 649–62.

White RMB, Roosa MW, Weaver SR, Nair RL. 2009. Cultural and contextual influences on parenting in Mexican American families. *F. Marriage Fam.* **71:** 61–79.

White RMB, Zeiders KH, Gonzales NA, Tein J-Y, Roosa MW. 2013. Cultural values, U.S. neighborhood danger, and Mexican American parents' parenting. *F. Fam. Psychol.* **27:** 365—75.

Williams JL, Aiyer SM, Durkee MI, Tolan PH. 2014. The protective role of ethnic identity for urban adolescent males facing multiple stressors. *F. Youth Adolesc.* **43:** 1728–41.

Witkow MR, Huynh V, Fuligni AJ. 2015. Understanding differences in college persistence: a longitudinal examination of financial circumstances, family obligations, and discrimination in an ethnically diverse sample. *Appl. Dev. Sci.* **19:** 4—18.

Yip T. 2015. The effects of ethnic/racial discrimination and sleep quality on depressive symptoms and self-esteem trajectories among diverse adolescents. *F. Youth Adolesc.* **44:** 419–30.

Zeiders KH, Doane LD, Roosa MW. 2012. Perceived discrimination and diurnal cortisol: examining relations among Mexican American adolescents. *Horm. Behav.* **61:** 541–48.

Zeiders KH, Hoyt LT, Adam EK 2014. Associations between self-reported discrimination and diurnal cortisol rhythms among young adults: the moderating role of racial-ethnic minority status. *Psychoneuroendocrinology* **50:** 280–88.

Zeiders KH, Roosa MW, Knight GP, Gonzales NA. 2013. Mexican American adolescents' profiles of risk and mental health: a person-centered longitudinal approach. *F. Adolesc.* **36:** 603–12.

Related Resources

Migration Policy Institute website: **http://wmv.migrationpolicy.org/.** Provides up-to-date information on migration policy and its impact on Americans.

Pacione L, Measbam T, Rousseau C. 2013. Refugee children: mental health and effective interventions. *Curr. Psychiatry Rep.* **15:** 341–41.

Pew Research Center Hispanic Trends website: **http://www.pewhispanic.org/.** Provides timely information on a wide range of social issues facing US Latinos.

Weisskirch RS. 2017. *Language Brokering in Immigrant Families: Theories and Contexts.* New York: Routledge.

Yoshikawa H, Suárez-Orozco C, Gonzales RG. 2017. Unauthorized status and youth development in the United States: consensus statement of the Society for Research on Adolescence. *F. Res. Adolesc.* **27:** 4—19.

Zhou Q, Tao A, Chen SH, Main A, Lee E, et al. 2012. Asset and protective factors for Asian American children's mental health adjustment. *Child Dev. Perspect.* **6:** 312–19.

PART V

Caregiving Stressors, End of Life Challenges, and Resilient Families

An Expanded Review of the Challenges and Experiences of Informal Caregivers: Families, Factors, and Frameworks

Gregory J. Harris[1] *Florida State University*

Introduction

Family members have historically provided the bulk of care for older or ill family members; making informal or unpaid care for older, ill, or disabled family members a stressful and often burdensome task for many U.S. families (Houtven & Norton, 2004). These potential stressors and strains are anticipated to increase among older and minority populations, which will create a substantial need for more family caregivers to assist with basic activities of daily living, particularly those providing dementia related care (Cox, 2005; Langa et al., 2001; Spillman & Pezzin, 2000; U. S. Census Bureau,

Correspondence concerning this manuscript should be addressed to Gregory J. Harris 120 Convocation Way, Sandels Building, Room 207-E, Tallahassee, FL USA 32306. E-mail: gjharris@ fsu.edu. Phone: 850-644-2694

[*] An earlier version of this paper was published from my dissertation:

Harris, G. J. (2009). Caregiver well-being: Factors influencing positive outcomes in the informal caregiving process (Doctoral dissertation). Retrieved from http://diginole.lib.fsu.edu/islandora/object/fsu%3A182404
[1] Family and Child Sciences Department, College of Human Sciences, Florida State University Tallahassee, FL USA

2000; Wolf & Kasper, 2006). Further, these demands are expected to intensify as older, frail, or ill family members live longer and suffer from more chronic and debilitating illnesses and diseases (Crimmins, 2001; Stone, Cafferata, & Sangl, 1987; Kanwar, Singh, Lennon, Ghanta, McNallan, & Roger, 2013). While informal caregivers are the preferred source of long-term care for most people; the psychological, physiological and financial costs to the overall well-being of caregivers can be compromised (Chappell & Reid, 2002; Kramer, 1997; Lawton, Moss, Kleban, Glicksman, & Rovine, 1991).

Recent studies have indicated that not all informal caregivers experience negative outcomes in the care process, and many often express satisfaction or gain with the challenges of caregiving (Foley, Tung, & Mutran, 2002; Kinney & Stephens, 1989; Kinney, Stephens, Franks, & Norris, 1995; Kramer, 1993, 1997; Roth, Dilworth-Anderson, Huang, Goss, & Gitlin, 2015). Many researchers have noted the need for more positive approaches to studying the multidimensional aspects of family caregiving, especially the contextual impacts of race on positive well-being (Dilworth-Anderson, Williams, & Cooper, 1999; Dilworth-Anderson, Williams, & Gibson, 2002; Kramer, 1997; Lloyd, Patterson, Muers, 2014; Walker, Pratt, & Eddy, 1995). Stressors, strains, and burdens associated with the caregiving role often place families, and particularly women, at a disadvantage. Nonetheless, some racial groups report satisfaction and in some cases, a much higher functioning level in the caregiving role (Boss, 1988; Dilworth-Anderson et al., 2002; Radina, 2007; Stull, Kosloksi, & Kercher, 1994). Since not all caregivers denote the care process as negative, attention should focus on the more positive, proactive, and satisfying aspects of caregiving while understanding the contextual influences of race in the caregiving process (Foley, Tung, & Mutran, 2002; Kramer, 1997). Therefore, investigating factors within the context of race, such as intensity of care demands, use of formal and informal resources, and caregiver manageability/mastery will provide a better understanding of why some caregivers experience positive well-being (Dilworth-Anderson, et al., 1999; Dilworth-Anderson et al., 2002).

As family members age, become ill, or disabled, the intensity of care demands can increase and the need to use more formal and informal coping resources may be necessary for caregivers to deal with the challenges of caregiving and avoid or delay institutionalization (George, 1987, George & Gwyther, 1988; George, Blazer, Winfield-Laird, Leaf, & Fischbach, 1988). Likewise, caregivers will need to feel prepared or competent to undertake this role and its associated demands with a sense of manageability/mastery (Pearlin, Mullan, Semple, & Skaff, 1990). Successful responses to the stresses and strains associated with this anticipated increase in caregiving will ultimately impact whether caregivers experience positive or negative outcomes (Aneshenel, Pearlin, Mullan, Zarit, & Whitlatch, 1995; Dilworth-Anderson et al., 2002; Radina, 2007; Stull et al., 1994).

An earlier study of the National Alliance for Caregiving and American Association of Retired Persons (2004, 2015), estimated that 83% of U.S. families were providing care to a family member or spouse and more recently, estimated that there are 34.2 million adult family members who provided care to a family member age 50 or older in the past year (NAC/AARP, 2015). The value of this care has been estimated at 257 billion dollars annually as a potential cost-savings to society, however, that cost has increased to about 470 billion in recent years (Arno, 2002; Haley, 2003; Reinhard, Feinberg, Choula, & Huser, 2015). An estimated 43.5 million caregivers age 18 and older who provided unpaid care to an adult family member or friend who was also 18 years or older in the past year (NAC/AARP, 2015). While caregivers make enormous contributions to their families and society; the emotional, physical, and financial impact they often face is of critical importance to caregivers' well-being. Several studies have documented that the mere presence or absence of willing family members to provide this care has been linked to the decision to institutionalize older family members, which can also increase the stress levels of caregivers and the care recipient (Lyons, Zarit, Sayer, & Whitlatch, 2002).

Caring for an aging parent or spouse can be very demanding on individuals in families, as well as the family unit as a whole. These family demands can be internalized as physical, emotional, and financial stressors and strains and are often referred to as family demands (McCubbin, 1998). Several researchers have documented the impact of these caregiving demands on the caregiver and the family (Stull et al., 1994). Caregiving stressors are events or situations that arise out of the caregiving process that place the caregiver or caregiving family at-risk.

Intensity of care demands are considered one of those stressors associated with caregiving. It consists partially of the number of activities of daily living (ADLs) such as bathing, dressing, and the need for overall supervision and instrumental activities of daily living (IADLs) characterized as managing finances, using the telephone and general coordination, and the time devoted to these tasks (NAC & AARP, 1997; 2004). Additionally, the number hours of care provided also contribute to the intensity of care within the caregiving context (NAC/AARP, 2004, 2009, 2015). When taken together, all of these factors add to the stress, strain, and burden experienced by the caregiver and the caregiving family (Donelan, Hill, Hoffman, Scoles, Feldmen, Levin, & Gould, 2002; Lawton et al., 1991; Pearlin et al., 1990; Zarit & Zarit, 1986). For example, caregivers who provide care for recipients suffering from dementia and other mental illnesses and those that are wheel-chair bound or physically disabled may require a great deal of intense care and supervision (George et al, 1988). Caregivers who provide care under these types of conditions often find that their own emotional, physical, and financial well-being is at stake. Often the mental health condition issues of the care recipient can induce fear and discomfort in the care environment among adult children, thus placing a burden on the primary caregiver. Disease, health conditions, and lack of control over the situation along with disruptive behaviors have been noted to be the most critical in the intensity of care demand context (Horowitz, 1985).

Another area of concern in caregiving is the use of formal coping resources. Several factors are thought to influence coping and resiliency among family caregivers. Formal coping resources are defined as the caregiver's ability to seek and use outside assistance or formal professional networks and support to aid them in the caregiving process (NAC & AARP, 2004, 2009). Such resources are amount, availability, and degree to which there are other resources that could be used in the care situation such as: information about how to get financial assistance, availability of support groups, access to Adult Day Care, recreational programs or camps, access to Meals on Wheels, and outside transportation services (Dilworth-Anderson et al., 2002; Montgomery & Kosloski, 1994; NAC & AARP, 2004; Zarit, Stephens, Townsend, & Greene, 1998). Resources of this nature may serve as coping and adaptation strategies for the caregiver when professional care services are needed as higher levels of family care are required, and the informal networks have either become strained or limited (Cox, 2005). It should be noted that formal support services do not diminish the use of or need for informal support by family members, but some functions may merely shift (Horowitz, 1985).

There are also informal coping resources that caregivers can use in order to better respond to the demands and stressors of caregiving. Such personal resources are characterized as communicating with or seeking advice from friends or relatives; exercising or working out; medication assistance; talking to spiritual or professional counselors; praying; searching for information on the internet; and reading about caregiving in books or other materials. Resources of this type and nature serve as coping and adaptation mechanisms within the caregiver's informal networks. The receipt of emotional support from family has been associated with decreased feelings of depression or burden (Aneshenal et al., 1995; Franks & Stephens, 1996). Like formal coping, informal coping allows the caregivers greater adaptability in the care process considering the associated demands of caregiving. Informal coping can also be conceptualized as both coping resources and coping strategies (Folkman & Lazarus, 1980; Pratt, Schmall, Wright, & Cleland, 1985; Segall & Wykle, 1988; & Vaux & Wood, 1987). When analyzed together, formal and informal coping resources may provide a general understanding of why some caregivers cope well and others do not. A recent national study found that 84% of African American caregivers coped with caregiving stress by praying and talking with professional or spiritual counselors versus 71% of whites, and 50% of Asians (NAC & AARP, 2004). This phenomenon may further help clarify the factors that promote adaptation and resiliency levels of some racial groups compared to others.

Coupled with the intensity of care demands and associated coping resources; it is difficult to understand the effects of caregiving without taking into consideration factors which may impact the manner in which caregivers perceive or appraise the care situation (Lazarus & Folkman, 1984). The caregivers' sense of manageability or mastery in the provision of care is paramount to their perceptions of sense of control, self-esteem, competence, gain, self-loss, and their capacity to continue to provide care (Foley et al., 2002; Kinney & Stephens, 1989, 1995; Kramer, 1997: Lawton et al., 1989; Lazarus & Folkman, 1984; Pearlin et al., 1990; Skaff, Pearlin, & Mullan, 1996). Stress has been known to impact the psychological and physiological well-being of caregivers in the care role as positive or negative. The caregivers' perception of the caregiving demands, stressors, and their available coping resources may impact perceptions of their ability to maintain, or carry out the caregiving role with the least amount of emotional, physical, or financial deterioration (Lazarus & Folkman, 1984).

It is therefore, important to link the perceptions of unmet needs caregivers identify and face in the care role as areas in which they evaluate their sense of manageability/mastery (NAC & AARP, 2004). Too many unmet needs can ultimately lead to a weak sense of manageability/mastery and control over the care situation which can be noted as sense of coherence (Antonovsky, 1979) or a lack of mastery (Pearlin et al., 1990; Siegal, Raveis, Houts, & Mor, 1991). Additionally, implicit in unmet needs is a sense of whether the caregiver has the ability, knowledge and the confidence required to continue to meet the needs of the care recipient before falling into a state of physical, emotional, or financial distress and disorganization. Several key components of the manageability/mastery of unmet caregiver needs have been identified as important to understanding how the caregiving role can be positively or negatively impacted without intervention or assistance. For example, caregivers often have to make important decisions about the care of the recipients as their health or mental status deteriorates or improves. Some of those decisions focus on whether or not to transfer the person to an assisted living facility, a nursing home, or another type of care agency (NAC & AARP, 2004; Pearlin et al., 1990; Zarit & Zarit, 1986). Management or mastery issues may focus on decisions to manage the person due to psychological issues, such as wandering, safety, or joint activities that can be shared between the caregiver and the care recipient in order to enrich the caregiving situation (NAC & AARP, 2004; Pearlin et al., 1990; Zarit & Zarit, 1986). According to the NAC & AARP (2004) study, other components of the manageability/mastery aspect of caregiving consist of physical strain, such as lifting or moving the care recipient; managing their own emotional and physical stress; finding personal time or respite for self; and managing other difficult situations, such as incontinence and toileting problems. Caregivers having an enhanced sense of manageability/mastery may generally feel a sense of control, and a sense of coherence in comparison to those caregivers who do not (Antonovsky, 1979; Pearlin et al., 1990). Therefore, it is important to assess the impact of sense of manageability/mastery and the associated caregiving stressors on overall positive or negative experiences of caregivers.

Finally, the crisis or adaptability of the caregiver to the impact of stressors, coping resources, and sense of manageability/mastery has been characterized in terms of caregiver well-being (Berg-Weger, Rubio, & Tebb, 2000; Chappell & Reid, 2000; Dilworth-Anderson et al., 2002; Lyons et al., 2002; Noonan & Tennstedt, 1997; Pruchno, Burant, & Peters, 1997; Smerglia & Deimling, 1997). The definition of well-being has been commonly referred to as subjective self-appraisal of the caregiver's experience in the caregiving process as excellent, good, fair, or poor in relationship to the overall multifaceted caregiving experience (Atienza, Stephens, & Townsend, 2002; Berg-Weger et al., 2000). Well-being as an outcome implies a more positive approach to the caregiver's experiences and challenges, as opposed to the more commonly used concept of caregiver burden used more widely in the caregiving literature (Kramer, 1993, 1997; Yates, Tennstedt & Chang, 1999; Zarit, Todd, & Zarit, 1986). Having a positive sense of physical, emotional, and financial well-being promotes a more satisfying outcome by the caregiver in the caregiving experience (Kramer, 1997). This positive outcome reflects a more adaptable disposition to the multifaceted caregiving process given the stressors, coping resources, and sense of manageability/mastery as opposed to a sense of disorganization and crisis (Kramer, 1997; Lawton et al., 1989; Pearlin et al., 1990).

As a result, resilient individuals tend to view their caregiving challenges and experiences as more positive and manageable (Boss, 2002; Southwick, Vythilingam, & Charney, 2005). Moreover, it is essential to assess the important role of adaptability during the caregiving process (Atienza, Stephens, & Townsend, 2002; Berg-Weger, Rubio, & Tebb, 1999; Berg-Weger et al., 2000; Dilworth-Anderson et al., 2002). Overall, it is valuable to understand the impact of intensity of care demands, the use of formal and informal coping resources, and sense of manageability/mastery on the well-being of caregivers.

The purpose of this chapter is to understand the challenges and experiences of caregivers providing care to older, ill, or frail elders and to determine the influence of caregiving stressors coping resources, and perception of stressors on the well-being of informal caregivers. In particular, this chapter will explore the utility of the ABC-X Model of family stress theory and the foundations of family systems theory to either improve or expand our understanding of the factors that influence the well-being of informal family caregivers. In this case, the intensity of care demands in caregiving (A factors), as well as formal and informal coping resources (B factors) and perceptions or appraisals of the situation (C factors) that may lead to well-being (i.e., X-factor or adaptation or crisis) are considered.

Definition and Abbreviations of Key Terms

It is important to clarify a few terms that will be used throughout this chapter. The definitions and abbreviations are presented here:

Caregiver – A person 18 years or older providing care to a family member or friend who is 18 years or older needing helping with one or more of the activities of daily living (ADLs) or instrumental activities of daily living (IADLs) (NAC & AARP, 2004).

Caregiver stress – The degree of intense care provided by caregivers and the demand of such care which taxes the resources and potentially places the caregiver in a negative position for a decline in physical, emotional, and financial well-being (NAC & AARP, 2004).

Informal caregiver – A family member or friend who provides unpaid care provided to family members or friends (NAC & AARP, 2004).

Coping – The strategies, resources, or social support that may be external or internal that caregivers use to deal with the stresses and demands of the caregiving role (Hill, 1958; McCubbin & Patterson, 1983; NAC & AARP, 1997, 2004).

Perception of Stressor(s) – The overall meaning that family members give to particular stressor or pile-up of stressors and the family's ability to manage or respond to the crisis using the available resources available to them (Hill, 1958, McCubbin & Patterson, 1983).

Well-being – A multidimensional experience viewed as the degree to which caregivers deal with the stressors of caregiving positively or negatively and how this in turn impacts them emotionally, physically, or financially (Diener, 1984; Kramer, 1997).

Abbreviations

ABC-X Model – is the abbreviation for the theoretical stress model to denote the process by which stressors, resources, perceptions, and the associated outcomes (Hill, 1958).

Double ABC-X Model – is the abbreviation for the expanded theoretical stress model to denote the pile-up effect associated with stressors, resources, perceptions, and the associated outcomes (McCubbin & Patterson, 1983).

ADLs – is the abbreviation for activities of daily living.

IADLs – is the abbreviation for instrumental activities of daily living.

NAC & AARP – is the abbreviation for the National Alliance for Caregivers and the American Association for Retired Persons.

SPM – is the abbreviation for the Stress Process Model in Lazarus & Folkman's (1984) theory of stress, appraisal and coping of which they identified two processes: cognitive appraisal and coping as critical mediators of stressful person-environment relations.

Theoretical Frameworks for Explaining and Understanding the Caregiving Process

There are a variety of theoretical perspectives, models, and frameworks that can be used to explain or better understand the caregiving process. However, considered here will be family stress theory and family systems theory to explore a more complete understanding of stressors and associated factors of caregivers and the range of outcomes expected given different experiences and challenges of caregivers within the family context. In the past, these frameworks have provided a better understanding of how stressful situations in caregiving impact the individual caregiver and the family caregiving unit. Family stress theory has primarily been utilized to understand the stress and coping process and how families adjust based on the degree of various stressors and strains.

The concept of resiliency has been incorporated within family stress theory as a framework to better understand the contextual meanings associated with stressors within the individual and family. More importantly the resiliency framework will allow a better understanding of the adaptational and coping mechanisms that some individuals and families have that allow them to endure and "bounce back" from adverse situations or crises (Boss, 2002; Fredrickson, 2001; 2003; Tugade & Fredrickson, 2004; Walsh, 2003). Family systems theory can help explain how various stressor events can have a negative or positive impact on families. Family stress theory and family systems theory both share some common connections in the inquiry of family processes, interactions, and outcomes. Therefore, these frameworks have been integrated for use in this chapter to gain a greater understanding of the processes, impacts, influences and overall caregiver well-being outcomes.

Family Stress Theory

Reuben Hill's (1958, 1964) theory of family stress was formulated from his work with military families. Hill theorized that there are two complex variables that act to buffer the family from acute stressors and reduce the direct correlation between multiple stressors and family crisis. These were formulated into what he called his ABC-X theory of family stress. Additionally, Hill's (1949) study of families helped to better understand family as a "culturally conditioned organization reflecting the state of the culture and, at the same time, internal familial behaviors" (Boss, 2002, p. 33).

Hill's (1958) work resulted in the development of the ABC-X Model of family stress which possesses the following characteristics: A = the event as the stressor or hardship that affects the family. This event may be external or internal, B = the family's stress meeting resources, or the ability or inability of the family to organize, C = the definition or appraisal the family gives the stressor and their perception of coping resources, and X = the degree of adaptation-bond adaptation to maladaptation as a result of the stressor. The type of response the caregiver may have can be based on whether the family has in the past developed crisis-meeting resources to deal with the problem. This determines the extent to which the caregiver experiences a bondadaptive or maladaptive response. As a result of this process the family caregiver can experience a negative (burden, stressful, physiological depressive state) or a positive response (pleasure, gratifying, and satisfying state).

This model was elaborated by McCubbin and McCubbin (1989) producing the "double" ABC-X Model. The "double" ABC-X Model reflects the build-up or pile-up of stressors based on the notion that some families fail to develop techniques or crisis-meeting capabilities to deal with the stressors. Additionally, such factors ultimately produce a maladaptive or adaptive outcome. The model is also referred to as the Family Resiliency Model. Over time, as stressors build, the family's ability to utilize coping resources, along with a dismal perception that stressors are overwhelming, can further place the family in a maladaptive state (Boss, 2002).

Family stress theory by Hill (1958) sets forward acute stressors (meaning sudden onset) which when accumulated could lead to family crises, including physical, emotional, or relational crises. Examples of such family crises resulting from family stressors are episodes of domestic violence, substance abuse (relapses), illness from weakened immune systems, divorce, accidents, and children being abused or neglected. However, their impact can be muted, or buffered with protective factors that help families to survive multiple contextual stressors and continue to competently function despite chronic and acute stressors (McCubbin & Boss, 1980).

These protective factors (Hill theorized that there were basically two of them) buffer the impact of the stressors. Whereas one includes social relationships (B Factor), the other includes perceptions (C Factor) (McCubbin & Boss, 1980). Social relationships are further distinguished as being within family variables, e.g. attachment, positive family bonds, effective communication, as well as across family variables: e.g. social isolation Perceptions (C Factor) include the range in cognitions and attitudes between hope and personal effectiveness vs. despair and helplessness. These two multifaceted factors relate together with the acute stressors and ongoing social context of chronic stressors to predict family crises.

Many studies have documented the positive relationship between illness and stress. Individuals, who experience too many stressors at one time or too many changes in their daily routines and circumstances, are at increased risk within one year for having an accident, or becoming physically ill (Lyons et al., 2002). Not only individuals, but also families who experience too many stressors are at increased risk for experiencing aggravated family crises. However, not all families with multiple stresses have crises. The "B" variable refers to the complex of internal and external family resources and social support available to the family, e.g., the social connectedness within the family, as well as social connectedness outside the family. Hill theorized that social isolation would significantly increase the impact of the multiple stresses on family functioning; in contrast, positive social supports would minimize the impact.

Hill's "C" variable, the perception factor, was the second predictor of the extensiveness of the impact of stress on the family. This second complex factor referred to the shared family cognition and perceptions held about the stressors, e.g., the extent to which the family perceived the changes as a disaster or an opportunity. Some families had positive appraisals because they could make changes, increase the ability to accept their circumstances. Hill's family stress theory has been expanded by McCubbin and Patterson (1983) using the ABC-X model as its foundation and adds post-crisis variables in an effort to further describe: (a) the additional life stressors and strains which shape the course of family adaptation; (b) the critical psychological, intra-familial, and social resources families acquire and employ over time in managing crisis situations; (c) the changes in definition and meaning families develop in an effort to make sense out of their predicament; (d) the coping strategies families employ; and (e) the range of outcomes of these family efforts.

The Double ABC-X Model consists of the following components: Family Demands: Pile-up (aA Factor) which refers to the pile-up effect of stressors and strains over time that cause families to react to multiple stressor at the same time (Lavee, McCubbin, & Olson, 1987; McCubbin & Patterson, 1983). These demands or changes may emerge from a number of sources such as: (a) individual family members, (b) the family system, and or (c) the community in which the family and its members are a part. There are five broad types of stressors and strains constituting a pile-up in family systems in a crisis situation: (a) the initial stressor and its hardships, (b) normative transitions, (c) prior strains, (d) consequences of family efforts to cope, and (e) ambiguity, both intra-family and social.

The second component of the Double ABC-X model is Family Adaptive Resources (bB Factor) which refers to the resources that are a part of the family's capabilities for meeting demands and needs and include characteristics (a) of individual members, (b) of the family unit, and (c) of the community. There are two general types: existing resources and expanded family resources. Existing resources are already a part of the family's repertoire and serve to minimize the impact of the initial stressor and reduce the likelihood that the family will move to a crisis mode. The expanded family resources are those new resources individuals and families have strengthened or developed in response to the additional demands emerging out of the crisis situations or as a result of pile-up.

The third component of the Double ABC-X Model, the (cC factor) is the meaning the family gives to the total crisis situation which and includes the stressor believed to have caused the crisis, as well as the added stressors and strains, old and new resources, and estimates of what needs to be done to bring the family into balance. When families are able to successfully redefine the crisis situation and apply new meaning, they employ efforts to (a) clarify the issues, hardships, and tasks to render them more manageable and responsive to problem solving efforts; (b) decrease intensity of the emotional burdens associated with the crisis situation; and (c) encourage the family unit to carry on with its fundamental tasks promoting member social and emotional development (Lavee, McCubbin, & Olson, 1987; McCubbin & Patterson, 1983).

The coping process is critical in bridging cognitive and behavioral components for when resources, perceptions, and behavioral responses interact as families try to achieve a balance in family functioning. Further, family coping efforts may be directed at (a) eliminating and or avoiding stressors and strains; (b) managing hardships of the situation; (c) maintaining the family system's integrity and morale; (d) acquiring and developing resources to meet demands; and (e) implementing structural changes in family systems to accommodate new demands (McCubbin, 1979; McCubbin & Patterson, 1982).

The final component of the Double ABC-X Model is referred to as family adaptation balancing (xX Factor). There are three elements to be considered in family adaptation: (a) the individual family member; (b) the family system; and (c) the community of which family members and the family unit are a part. Each of these elements is characterized by both demands and capabilities. Family adaptation is therefore achieved through reciprocal relationships where the demands of one of these units are met by the capabilities of another so as to achieve a "balance" simultaneously at two primary levels of interaction. The first level referred to as *Balance: Member to family fit* is sought between individual family members and the family system such as family encouraging and supporting members' needs or participating in family shared activities. The second level is referred to as *Balance: Family to community fit* and sought between the family unit and the community of which the family is a part, such as family support or parental involvement in work and community activities and the employers' demands for extensive work times or adverse conditions (McCubbin & Patterson, 1983).

Family coherence is a critical factor as families try to achieve bondapadatation by reducing discrepancy between family resources and demands, which are never truly balanced (McCubbin & Patterson, 1983). Successful adaptation is based primarily on the family's ability to derive a sense of acceptance and understanding that they have done their best given the circumstances (Antonovsky, 1979). The feeling of confidence felt internally and externally that things will work out as reasonably as possible best describes the concept of sense of coherence for Antonovsky (1979). Families must be able to balance the two dimensions of control and trust in order to enhance their abilities. Sense of coherence is the ability to differentiate when the family should take charge or trust and believe that the situation will work out.

The concept of family adaptation is therefore used to describe a continuum of outcomes which reflect family efforts to achieve balance or "fit" at the member-to-family and the family-to community levels. The positive end of the continuum of family adaptation, called bondadaptation is characterized by a balance at both levels of functioning, which results in (a) the maintenance or strengthening of family integrity; (b) the continued promotion of both member development and family unit development; and (c) the maintenance of family dependence and its sense of control over environmental influences. Family adaptation at the negative end of the continuum is characterized by a continued imbalance at either level of family functioning or the achievement of balance at both levels but at a price in terms of (a) reduction in family integrity; (b) a curtailment of deterioration in the personal health and development of a member or the well-being of the family unit; or (c) a loss or decline in family independence and autonomy (McCubbin & Patterson, 1983).

The focus on resiliency within stress theory extends our understanding of positive and healthy family functioning to adverse or negative situations by building on the theory and research of family stress, coping, and adaptation (Boss, 2002; Hill, 1958). The concept of family resilience involves more than just managing stressful conditions and situations. It involves the capacity and potential for personal and relational transformation and growth (Boss, 2002). While resiliency is a rather new perspective it has been in the previous literature with a focus primarily on individual resilience (Walsh, 2003). Previous studies focused on children's resiliency to adverse home and family conditions (Patterson, 2002; Rutter, 1987) and on personal traits such as hardiness (Luther & Ziegler, 1991; Walsh, 1996, 2003). As the framework developed, research was expanded to include a wide range of adverse conditions, trauma, loss, and illness (Walsh, 2003).

Due to this expansion, resilience came to be viewed as a combination of multiple risk and protective factors involving the individual, the family, and the larger social forces (Walsh, 2003). Resilience, therefore, is the ability to withstand and rebound from disruptions in the life cycle (Walsh, 2003). It is a dynamic and multi-contextual process fostering positive adaption given the crisis or adversity (Luther, Cicchetti, & Becker, 2000; Patterson, 2002; Walsh, 2003).

Family stress theory and family resilience are linked through the use of the Family Adjustment and Adaptation Response Model (FAAR), which consists of four central constructs. Families engage in active processes to balance family demands with family capabilities as these interact with family meanings to arrive at a level of family adjustment or adaptation. According to Patterson (2002) family demands are comprised of (a) normative and non-normative stressors (discrete events of change); (b) ongoing family strains (unresolved, insidious tensions); and (c) daily hassles (minor disruptions of daily life). Family capabilities include (a) tangible and psychosocial resources (what the family has) and (b) coping behaviors (what the family does). An important construct in the FAAR Model is "family meaning" (Patterson, 1993; 2002).

According to Walsh (1996, 2002) the family resilience approach is grounded in family systems theory combining ecological and developmental perspectives to view the family as an open system influenced by large societal context and evolves in a multigenerational life cycle (Carter & McGoldrick, 1998). The family resilience framework developed by Walsh (1996) was a guide for use in clinical practice. While the framework has its roots in clinical settings, research in the social and family sciences has made it a useful tool for understanding variables contributing to individual resilience and well-functioning families. The key processes in family resilience fall within three domains of family functioning: 1) family belief systems, 2) organization patterns, and 3) communication processes (Walsh, 1998; 2002). Family belief systems involve making meaning of adversity, having a positive outlook, and transcendence and spirituality. Organizational patterns consist of flexibility, connectedness, and social and economic resources. Communication and problem solving processes consist of clarity, open emotional expression, and collaborative problem solving. Resiliency has been defined and conceptualized in a number of ways in the literature across many disciplines (Boss, 2002; Walsh, 1998). Nonetheless, resiliency is viewed as a way an individual or family is able to "bounce back" or respond to adversity with positive or satisfying outcomes (Fredrickson, 2001; 2003; Tugade & Frederickson, 2004). Further, the process of resiliency is such that many people may become rejuvenated or replenished as they become more experienced and begin to possess feelings of control and have a sense of mastery over an adverse event or a series of adverse situations. This process can result in greater well-being over time given different challenges in the caregiving process (Ryff, 1989; Ryff & Keyes, 1995; Southwick et al., 2005).

Family Systems Theory

The foundations of Family Systems Theory were laid by von Bertalanffy (1968). Family systems theory has three key assumptions that systems theory can unify science; that a system must be understood as a whole rather than in component parts; and that human systems are unique in their self-reflexivity. Von Bertalanffy (1975) asserted that disciplines of the natural and social sciences integrate toward one another because of certain concepts or "unifying principles" that occur in every discipline (Boss, et al, p. 328, 1993). Family systems theory considers the interconnectedness and interrelationships of all the members of the family when dealing with any one member. Systems theory involves the basic idea that objects in the world are interrelated with one another (Whitchurch & Constantine, 1993). The theory was derived from General Systems Theory (GST), which was in part a response to positivist thinking about applying the principles of natural sciences models to social science. Systems theorists argue that the system needs to be perceived at as a whole rather than as individual components, which can then be put together. General System Theory's Composition Law states that the whole is greater than the sum of all its parts. These elements are the interactions between different subsystems within the main system. These interacting components add characteristics to the whole that make it to some slight degree qualitatively different from each individual member.

This systems-oriented model enhances the linear cause and effect model of the natural sciences considering that individual elements reacting within a family is due to a variety of interacting factors rather those happening in a linear style. Systems theory then is much less concerned with the cause and effect of various systems, as opposed to how different subsystems interact to make up the whole system. Additionally, human systems are also self-reflective, which means, that unlike machines or unconscious matter, humans can look at themselves as though they were outside observers. This self-reflectivity allows human systems to establish and work toward goals, and construct their own sense of social reality, which contains shared definitions upon which to communicate with others.

Other components of systems theory are the concepts of boundaries and feedback loops. A system boundary helps to determine what is and is not part of the system. A related concept is the idea of an open versus closed system or boundary permeability. Theoretically, more open the system is, the more information will be allowed into and out of the system. Additionally, the concept of feedback loops is important to systems theory. A feedback loop is defined as a "path by which information can be traced from one point in a system, through one or more other parts of the system, and back to the point of origin" (Whitchurch & Constantine, 1993). Feedback loops are of two types: positive and negative. A positive feedback loop amplifies the deviations, whereas, a negative feedback loop has been compared to a homeostatic system, in which the feedback loop provides information that returns the system to some preset level and reduces distortions or deviations to the system.

Consistent with systems theory, Olson (1993) developed the *Circumplex Model*. The circumplex model describes families in terms of three main dimensions, family cohesion, flexibility and communication. Olson (1993) defined each of the dimensions: "family cohesion is the emotional bonding that family members have toward one another" (Olson, 1993, p. 105); "family flexibility is the amount of change in its leadership, role relationships, and relationship rules") and "family communication is measured by focusing on the family as a group with regard to their listening skills, speaking skills, self-disclosure, clarity, continuity-tracking, and respect and regard." Family cohesion has four separate levels, disengaged, separated, connected, and enmeshed. Similarly, family flexibility has four levels, chaotic, flexible, structured, and rigid. Olson (1993) makes less definitive distinctions in family communication, considering communication to be either good or poor. The model combines the flexibility and cohesion dimensions to form 16 different family system types. Olson (1993) arranged these family types from balanced to unbalanced. There are four main balanced types, which revolve around the middle ranges of each of the two dimensions including flexibly separated, flexibly connected, structurally separated and structurally connected. There are four unbalanced extreme types, which center around the extremes of the two dimensions: chaotically disengaged, chaotically enmeshed, rigidly disengaged and rigidly enmeshed. Within these unbalanced and balanced types are eight other mid-range family types.

Families that are more balanced have greater functionality and competence than unbalanced families, in particular, through more positive communication skills (Olson, 1993). Each one of these family types does not represent a convenient nomenclature for a particular family, but rather each family type describes the way the family system operates within each type. The family type is determined not by an individual member, but rather as an interactive system. In assessing family types, Olson (1993) uses a multisystem assessment, which includes looking at different subsystems within the family, such as the martial system, parent-child system, and the family. Family types then describe more of the collective additive contributions of each member of the family, rather than family system as an entire unit, something that is greater than the sum of its members. In this way, each family type can very much be thought of as separate family cultures, in which underlying group norms, role, behaviors, and expectations appear in a relatively consistent fashion. The family system would operate to reinforce the norms and expectations of the family with appropriate sanctions, if these norms or expectations are violated (Olson, 1993).

Prevalence and Phenomenon of Family Caregiving

Definitions of Caregiving

Caregiving as a unique issue has been a very important topic in the family and gerontological literature for the last three decades and as such, much research has been conducted on the various experiences and challenges associated with the caregiving role. However, some ambiguity exists in defining what caregiving is and to what extent caregiving is differentiated from other forms of assistance (Walker et al., 1995). The manner in which caregiving is defined determines the prevalence and magnitude of caregiving.

Since there is no consensus in the caregiving literature of what caregiving is or how to distinguish a caregiver; there is much debate around the topic (Montgomery & Kosloski, 1994; Walker et al., 1995). Nonetheless, most researchers agree that caregiving involves helping or providing assistance above and beyond the normal assistance generally given to family members and friends (NAC & AARP, 1997, 2004; Stone et al., 1987; Walker et al., 1995;). This type of intense care could be short or long term in relationship to the duration of care or positive or negative in terms of appraisal and perception of overall impacts on the caregiver (Beach & Schulz, 2000; Kramer, 1997; NAC & AARP, 1997; 2004; Ory, Hoffman, Yee, Tennstedt, & Schulz, 1999).

An earlier national study of the National Alliance for Caregivers (NAC) and Americans Association for Retired Persons (AARP) (1997) caregivers were defined as those persons 18 years or older providing unpaid care to someone 50 years of age or older needing assistance. The primary purpose of the study was to document the magnitude, intensity, and types of informal caregiving engaged in by caregivers across the four main racial/ethnic groups. This study estimated that there were 22.4 million or 23% of U.S. households involved in caregiving for an individual 50 years or older at some point during the previous year (NAC & AARP, 1997). In more recent national studies of the NAC & AARP (2004, 2009, 2015) caregivers were defined as persons 18 years or older providing unpaid care to family or friends 18 years or older.

Spector, Fleishman, & Pezzin (2000) documented the characteristics of long-term care users and estimated that there were 5.9 million caregivers, who were defined as family or friends providing help to a disabled elder 65 years of age or older living in the community with a need that lasted or was expected to last for 3 or more months. In contrast, another study focused on the economic value of informal caregiving, and estimated that there were 24 million caregivers. This study defined caregivers as anyone 15 years of age or older who needed or provided assistance with everyday activities based on a condition that lasted or was expected to last 3 months or longer (Arno, Levin, & Memmott, 1999).

Several other studies using the well documented National Long Term Care Survey (NLTCS) data and the companion survey, Informal Caregvier Survey (ICS) have been conducted to estimate the prevalence and magnitude of caregiving (Manton, Corder, & Stallard, 1997; Stone, Cafferata, Sangl, 1987; Wolff & Kasper, 2006). The NLTCS is a nationally representative survey of Americans aged 65 and older that was designed to study the prevalence of chronic disability (Manton et al., 1997; Manton & Gu, 2001; Wolff & Kasper, 2006).

In a recent updated national profile of caregivers, Wolff & Kasper (2006), identified caregivers as those persons who were screened from the Medicare enrollment files and considered chronically disabled and reported that they had problems with activities of daily living, i.e., ADLs, or instrumental activities of daily living, i.e., IADLs that had lasted or were expected to last at least 3 months. Among the eligible caregivers drawn from the ICS were relatives or unpaid non-relatives who provided care for one or more hours of help to NLTCS participants with ADL or IADL activities in the previous week.

The aforementioned prevalence studies and definitions provide both previous and current evidence of the variance and difficulty in defining the incidence and nature of caregiving. The issue of defining caregiving should be noted when considering findings and results from studies on caregiving (Walker et al., 1995). However, for the purposes of this review, caregiving is defined as anyone 18 years or older who provided assistance to a family member or friend who was also 18 years of age or older with at least 1 ADL or IADL (NAC & AARP, 2004, 2009).

Caregiving Support and Resources

Another concept in the caregiving literature that requires defining is the distinction between formal and informal caregiving. Walker and colleagues (1995) asserted that the caregiving literature is unclear as it relates to the relationship between family or informal caregiving and paid or formal caregiving. A first step is to define these concepts based on the previous literature and patterns of use. Formal caregiving generally refers to paid assistance for care or services and is generally associated with a professional or bureaucratic service system (Lipman & Longino, 1982; NAC & AARP, 1997; 2004). Informal caregiving refers to individuals or families who provide unpaid care to family members, friends, and neighbors. They may be considered primary or secondary caregivers, and can spend most or part of their time providing this type of care (NAC & AARP, 1997; 2004).

Primary caregivers spend the bulk of their time and resources providing care, whereas secondary caregivers are generally noted as providing assistance to the primary caregivers in the care role (NAC & AARP, 1997, 2004). It is expected that given the current demographic and health care trends, the number of primary informal family caregivers will increase with the unmet needs of many older or ill adults (Bertand, Fredman, & Saczynski, 2006; Spillman & Pezzin, 2000). Thus, the role of informal caregiving will become even more important to the family given the trend of reduced availability of family caregivers and the growing demand for long-term care needs of older and ill family members (Spillman & Pezzin, 2000).

Characteristics and Contextual Profiles of Family Caregivers

Caregiving often requires the use of many family members and their available resources in order to meet the care needs of older or ill family members. Additionally, available family members can help balance the stresses and demands of caregiving. Since the family is the preferred source of assistance for informal care (Doty, 1986, Stone et al., 1987) and is considered the long-term care backbone (Cox, 2005; Montgomery, 1999; NAC & AARP, 1997, 2004; Wolff & Kasper, 2006) for most of its family members; it is important to understand the characteristic profile of informal caregivers and those who experience the most stress, strain, and burden as a result of caring for a family member with long-term needs. Caregiver characteristics across gender, race, age, physical and mental health status, as well as a profile of the most common types of caregivers in families have been thought to influence the caregiver in the care process (Beach & Schulz, 2000; Pinquart & Sorenson, 2003; Vitaliano, Zhang, & Scanlan, 2003; Bookwala & Schulz, 2000; Center on an Aging Society, 2005; Clipp & George, 1990; Dilworth-Anderson, Williams, & Gibson, 2002; George & Gwyther, 1988;

Knight, Silverstein, McCallum, & Fox, 2000; Lawton, Rajagopal, Brody, & Kleban, 1992; NAC & AARP, 1997; 2004; Navie-Waliser, Feldmen, Gould, Levine, Kuerbis, & Donelan, 2001; Pruchno & Resch, 1989; Robinson, Moen, Dempster-McClain, 1995; Stone et al., 1987; Tennstedt, Cafferata, & Sullivan, 1992; White, Townsend, & Stephens, 2000; Yee & Schulz, 2000). While some studies report inconsistent outcomes across these contextual factors, several studies have found these aspects to be linked to caregiving (NAC & AARP, 1997, 2004, 2009, & 2015). These characteristics and contextual factors are briefly explored in relationship to the caregiving role, as well as those family members who are more likely to provide this type of care.

Gender and Caregiving

Gender has been associated with the caregiving role with women serving as the primary caregivers in most families (Yee & Schulz, 2000). Some researchers have attributed this outcome to the traditional roles of women in society as impacted by the socialization process (Gilligan, 1993; Pinquart & Sorenson, 2006; Stone, Cafferata, & Sangl, 1987). Thus, the caretaker and nurturer roles have placed women in a vulnerable position to provide long-term caregiving to children, spouses, other relatives, and friends (Gilligan, 1993). Gender and caregiving is commonly reported in the literature noting the higher levels of depression, stress, and burden among women as compared to men (NAC & AARP, 2004; Yee & Schulz, 2000). The majority of caregivers are typically women: wives, daughters, or daughters-in-law (NAC & AARP, 1997, 2004; Stone, et al., 1987). Similarly, based on a profile of caregivers from the Center on an Aging Society (2005) the majority or 64% of all primary caregivers were women. Spouses or adult children are the most common caregivers followed by other relatives, neighbors, or friends (NAC & AARP, 1997; 2004).

In a study of caregivers in the U.S., male caregivers were more likely to be Asian-American (54%) as compared to the other ethnic groups, White (38%), African American (33%), and Hispanic (41%) (NAC & AARP, 2004). More than 7 of 10 caregivers were female (73%) compared to males (27%). In the same study, Asian-American caregivers were evenly split between females (52%) and males (48%) (NAC & AARP, 2004). Gender is increasingly associated with the likelihood that women have a higher probability of becoming caregivers as compared to men across their life span (Robinson et al., 1995). While, most studies have documented the stress, distress, depression, and burden of women caregivers, several other studies have revealed no gender differences in depressive outcomes among adult caregivers (Pinquart & Sorenson, 2006; Parks & Pilisuk, 1991). Nonetheless, gender remains an important indicator and central focus on the well-being of caregiving women. In comparative study of husband's and wives' primary and secondary stressors and depressive symptoms, it was revealed that caregiving husbands experienced fewer stressors and depressive symptoms compared to caregiving wives. Multiple group analysis revealed that primary stressors were more useful in terms of explaining differences associated with the secondary stressors across both groups (Bookwala & Schulz, 2000). Therefore, it is important to expand our understanding of how gender, meanings attached to caregiving, and care situations impact the caregiving process (Berkman, 2005; Krause, 2004).

Race and Caregiving

With respect to race, research has shown mixed results relative to the experiences and challenges in the caregiving process. One issue in terms of race and caregiving is that the majority of the research has been sparse relative to the well-being of diverse racial and ethnic minority groups in the U.S. (Dilworth-Anderson et al., 2002; Knight et al., 2000). Most of the research in this area has been on large white samples with very small samples of other ethnic groups (Dilworth-Anderson et al., 2002;

Knight et al., 2000; Lawton et al., 1992; Navie-Waliser et al., 2001; White et al., 2000). As a result of this disparity in the literature, many studies have documented the effects of caregiving on self-reported emotional distress and depression among mostly white caregivers (Knight et al., 2000). However, of those studies focusing on race and caregiving, findings suggest that African American caregivers appraise caregiving as less burdensome than do White caregivers. Additionally, lowered stress appraisal has been commonly associated with lower depression outcomes (Dilworth-Anderson et al., 2002; Lawton, et al., 1992). In contrast, when comparing African American and White women in the parent care role, one study examined the potential differences in depressive symptomatology, parent-care stress and rewards, parent-care mastery, and the quality of the parent-care relationship. Results indicated that race did not have a significant effect on caregivers' depressive symptomatology, parent-care mastery, or the quality of the relationship with the parent (White et al., 2000).

In a review of the experiences and challenges among White, Black, and Hispanic informal caregivers, Black caregivers were more likely to have provided higher intense care, reported having unmet needs with care provisions and have experienced increased religiosity since becoming caregivers. However, they were less likely to report difficulty with providing care compared to White caregivers. In the same study, Hispanic caregivers were more likely than White caregivers to receive help from formal caregivers and to experience increased religiosity since becoming a caregiver, which is similar to Black caregivers (Navie-Waliser et al., 2001).

In a more recent national study of caregivers in the U.S., African American caregivers were more likely to report that caregiving was a financial burden when compared to Whites, Hispanics, and Asian caregivers (NAC & AARP, 2004, 2009). Similarly, African American caregivers requested more information on how to get financial help for the person they provide care for as compared to Asian-American caregivers. Moreover, African American caregivers and Hispanic caregivers reported spending more than eight hours a week providing care, whereas Hispanic caregivers experienced higher levels of burden in care (NAC & AARP, 2004). In the same study conducted by the NAC & AARP (2004), Asian-American caregivers reported less financial hardship due to higher incomes, however, like White caregivers, more Asian-American caregivers provided care for a family member who lived in the suburbs than did African Americans and Hispanics. Asian-American caregivers experienced less emotional stress; only 23% rate 4 or 5, on a 5-point scale where 5 was very stressful vs. 36% White, and 36% Hispanic respondents. Additionally, among Asian-Americans, 43% were more likely to say that they tried to cope with the stress of caregiving by going to the internet to seek information as compared to 33% of Whites, and 29% of African Americans. White caregivers were more likely to report higher incomes and education similar to Asian-American caregivers and were older than the other ethnic groups, with 42% reporting they earned $50,000 or more a year. Moreover, like Hispanic caregivers, White caregivers (43%) were more likely to say they had to give up vacations, hobbies, or their own social activities compared to 35% of African American caregivers. Yet, White caregivers (69%) were less likely to say caregiving was a physical strain when compared to African American caregivers (61%). White caregivers (79%) were also less likely to report that caregiving was a financial hardship compared to African Americans (66%) (NAC & AARP, 2004).

Most studies have found that African American caregivers were younger, which, in turn, increased the likelihood of increased burden and poorer subjective health (Knight et al., 2000). Additionally, African American caregivers were less likely to use institutionalized care, despite poorer health, finances, and needs for formal caregiving supportive services (Belgrave, Allen-Kelsy, Smith & Flores, 2004). Further, White Americans relied on spouses for care, whereas African Americans depended more on a diverse group of friends and relatives (Chatters, Taylor, & Jackson, 1985; Dilworth-Anderson et al., 2002). Overall, African Americans report less dissatisfaction, stress, and burden than do others in the care process (Dilworth-Anderson et al., 2000).

Age and Caregiving

Age of the caregiver has been linked to the caregiving experience in many ways. Earlier studies have documented the association between advancing age of individuals and more depression, memory loss, and anxiety in the caregiver (George & Gwyther, 1988). A more recent comparative trend report with data drawn from the 1999 National Long Term-Care Survey of caregivers and care recipients found that both caregiver and care recipients were much older in 1994 (40%) than in 1999 (34%) (Spillman & Black, 2005). Many older caregivers may experience mild psychiatric symptoms and an increased use of psychotropic medications (Clipp & George, 1990). Mental health disorders tend to increase as people age, making it more difficult for caregivers to care for themselves if they too are older. This situation can lead to increased stress and burden in the caregiving process (Zarit, Reever, & Bach-Peterson, 1980).

Another study linking age and caregiving reported that older caregivers experienced several types of problems as they cared for a family member, such as dementia caregivers who had a mean age of 74.8 years compared to those providing care for lung cancer family members (mean 68.2), and non-dementia caregivers as a control had a mean age of 70.6 years of age (Haley, LaMonde, Han, Narramore, & Schonwetter, 2001).

Recent studies continue to link age to the caregiving experience with the majority of caregivers, 65% being middle-aged (35–64) (NAC & AARP, 1997; 2004). Additionally, those caregivers functioning at the highest level of care (level 5) were more likely to be 65 years of age (30%) as compared to only 10% of those caregivers functioning at the lowest level (level 1) (NAC & AARP, 2004). However, in another study more than half or 58% of all caregivers were between the ages of 18–49 (NAC & AARP, 2004). This study found that younger caregivers cared for younger care recipients and that caregivers functioning at the highest care levels were more likely to be age 50 or older (60%) compared to caregivers functioning at a much lower care level (39%).

Mental and Physical Health Conditions and Caregiving

Probably one of the most studied areas in caregiving has been on the mental and physical health of caregivers (Gallagher-Thompson, 2006). While investigating the impacts of caregiving on the physical and mental health of caregivers, only a few studies have begun to focus on actual physical or mental health indicators or markers (Gallagher-Thompson, 2006; Vitaliano et al., 2003). This situation has been viewed as a limitation given the amount of research of self-reported mental and physical health status of the caregiver as opposed to objective reports from medical files, records, or other official health documents (Gallagher-Thompson, 2006). Nonetheless, there are many studies linking the physical and mental health of caregivers to the caregiving role across many illnesses and disease specific domains such as depression, Alzheimer's disease, Parkinson's disease, cancer, diabetes, heart disease, schizophrenia, developmental disabilities, general chronic ailments and physical frailty (Barrow & Harrison, 2005; Beach & Schulz, 2000; Center on an Aging Society, 2005; Covinsky, Newcomer, Dane, Sands, & Yaffe, 2003; Marks, Lambert, & Choi, 2002; NAC & AARP, 1997; 2004; Ory, Hoffman, Yee, Tennstedt, & Schulz, 1999; Pinquart & Sorensen, 2003; Schulz, Newson, Mittlemark, Burton, Hirsch, & Jackson, 1997; Schulz, Obrien, Bookwals, & Fleissner, 1995; Spector & Tampi, 2005; Whitlatch, Feinberg, & Sebesta, 1997; Whitlatch, Feinberg, & Stevens, 1999).

The most studied area is depression of caregivers in the care role. Depression has historically been studied as an outcome measure and as an eventual route for care recipient's institutionalization given the potential mental, physical and psychological drain on caregivers (Andel, Hyer, & Slack, 2007; Bookwala & Schulz, 2000; Tennstedt, Cafferata, & Sullivan, 1992). This type of burdensome and negative approach has dominated the caregiving literature for the last two decades and has gained wide acceptance among other researchers.

In a study investigating the pathways of psychiatric morbidity and stress of caregivers and non-caregivers found that among non-caregivers who reported severe parental disability were significantly more likely to experience depressive symptoms. Evidence of increased manifestations of depression was not found among those caring for severely disabled relatives nor was it found among those caring in the absence of severe parental needs. However, the researchers found that having a sibling was associated with increased depressive scores among non caregivers (Amirkhanyan & Wolf, 2003).

A considerable body of literature exists on dementia caregiving as well, namely, Alzheimer's disease. Research in this area suggests that dementia caregivers experience more stress, strain, burden and depressive outcomes when compared to non-caregivers (Ory et al., 1999). In a recent study examining the relationship between the mental and physical health of caregivers of persons with dementia found that problem behavior among persons living with dementia, were significant predictors of caregivers' mental and physical health (Hooker, Bowman, Coehlo, Lim, Kay, Guariglia, & Li, 2002).

A national survey study of 2,032 African American and White female informal caregivers of elderly male veterans with dementia examined the relationship between race and psychotropic drug use in informal caregivers with symptoms of depression. Also examined was the racial difference in medication use and if these use patterns related to predisposing, enabling, and need factors (Sleath, Thorpe, Landerman, Doyle, & Clipp, 2005). The authors concluded that of the caregivers with depressive symptoms, 19% used antidepressants, 23% used anti-anxiety agents, and 2% used sedatives/hypnotics. As in previous studies, African American caregivers with depressive symptoms were less likely than Whites with depressive symptoms to use antidepressants and anxiety type medications. Additionally, caregivers, who reported more social support and more doctor visits within the last 6 months, were significantly more likely than others to be taking antidepressants (Sleath et al., 2005).

A variety of mental health issues have been linked to the caregiving role. Conditions such as, schizophrenia, severe mental illness or other developmental disabilities in adult children have been found to be especially stressful across the life span of many caregivers and their families (Greenberg, Greenley, McKee, Brown, & Griffin-Francell, 1993; Heller, Caldwell, & Factor, 2007; Cook, Lefley, Pickett, & Cohler, 1994; Harvey & Burns, 2003). Greenberg and associates (1993) in their study of families of persons with schizophrenia, sought to understand more about the long-term care effects of burdens associated with dealing with mental illness and the potential health consequences on caregivers. A sample of 81 mothers of adult children with schizophrenia revealed that the subjective burden associated with the stigma and worries were related to lowered levels of physical well-being among caregivers (Greenberg et al., 1993). A recent review of later life family support for adults with developmental disabilities using a life course perspective; Heller, Caldwell, & Factor (2007) found that caregiving seemed to have a negative impact on maternal employment and family income and noted that some families are at risk for poorer physical and mental health outcomes. The researchers also found that overall, families adapted well to having a family member with disabilities.

Among caregivers whose adult children suffer from severe mental disorders Harvey & Burns (2003) examined caregivers' characteristics and experiences in 22 multiple caregiving families (primary, non-primary and lone caregivers). A comparison of these groups found lone and primary caregivers' experiences were very similar, whereas non-primary caregivers' experiences were less adverse. Nonetheless, the authors noted that greater psychological distress in the primary caregivers indicated greater psychological distress in secondary caregivers.

Another area that can affect the health status of caregivers is the stress and burden of providing care for persons with Parkinson's disease (PD) (Barry & Murphy, 1995). In a non- random convenience sample of 30 spousal caregivers of older members diagnosed with Parkinson's disease (PD), researchers found a statistically significant linear relationship between stages of (PD) and care receivers' functional ability and between care receivers' functional and social ability and caregivers' hours of caregiving. Caregivers' health was associated with diminished physical functioning of care receivers. Caregivers' ages, years of marriage, and educational levels were associated with their social, psychological, and financial well-being (Barry & Murphy, 1995). Additionally, PD caregivers spent considerably more hours on average providing care to the care recipient, mainly on managing physical and mobility problems as the disease progressed (Hobson & Meara, 1999; Slaughter, Slaughter, Nichols, Holmes, & Martens, 2001).

Similarly, there are many types of cancer that may be classified as a chronic disease which can require long-term treatment, as well as the additional time, energy and demands of informal family caregivers (Nijboer, Triemstra, Tempelaar, Mulder, Sanderman, & Geertrudis, 2000). Cancer and its progressive physical, psychological, social, and economic dimensions have been documented to have a direct and deleterious impact on caregivers and the caregiving family (Nuboer, Tempelaar, Sanderman, Mattanja, Triemstra, Spruijt, & Geertrudis, 1998). Caregiver burden and unmet needs have been associated with cancer caregiving (Nuboer et al., 1998; Siegal, Raveis, Houts, & More, 1991). A study of 483 patients with cancer and their informal caregivers was conducted. It was found that when patients reported their met and unmet needs across ADLs and IADLs, that they were more likely to report on their unmet needs as their illness progressed and resulted in limited activities and when their finances became restrained. Moreover, the likelihood of an unmet need decreasing was associated with the caregivers providing care to care recipients within that particular domain of need (Siegal, Raveis, Houts, & Mor, 1991).

Clipp and George (1991) examined the patterns of response of 30 patients with cancer dyads-spouse caregiver couples for a total of 60 patients with lung or colon cancer and their spouse caregivers to determine the reliability of spouse informants in research and clinical settings. This study concluded that caregivers can serve as proxies for cancer patients in research when objective data are needed.

Diabetes mellitus (DM) is another health area in which caregivers spend considerable time providing care to family members or friends (Langa, Vijan, Hayward, Chernew, Blaum, Kabeto, Weir, Katz, Willis, & Fendrick, 2002). DM is a common chronic disease affecting about 10 million people in the U.S. and more often the elderly (Harris, Flegal, Cowie, Eberhardt, Goldstein, Little, Weidmeyer, & Holt, 1998). A recent study of informal caregiving for DM complications among the elderly found that those with DM received an average of 6.1 hours per week of informal care, no medications received 10.5 hours, taking oral medications received 10.1 hours, and insulin received 14.1 hours of care. Additionally, other disabilities related to DM such as heart disease, stroke, and visual problems were all found to be predictors of diabetes-related informal care (Langa et al., 2002).

Heart disease issues and caregiving have also been linked in the literature (Schulz et al., 1997). Cardiovascular disease (CHD) studies involving the role of informal caregivers, found that women were at a greater risk for stress, burden, and increased heart disease issues (Lee, Colditz, Berkman, Kawachi, 2003; Schulz et al., 1997). A recent prospective study of caregiving and risk of coronary heart disease in women was conducted on 54,412 women from the Nurse's Health Study (NHS). The NHS is a cohort of female registered nurses residing in 11 U.S. states. Women aged 46–71 years of age who had not been diagnosed with coronary heart disease (CHD) stroke, or cancer baseline in

1992 and follow-up in 1996 were used in this study. As a result of the 4-year follow-up, the researchers documented 321 incidents of CHD, 231 of those were non-fatal cases of myocardial infarction and 90 resulted in CHD deaths. After researchers controlled for covariates such as age, smoking, exercise, alcohol intake, body mass index, history of hypertension, and diabetes mellitus; caregiving for ill or disabled spouses who spent more than 9 hours per week was associated with increased risk of CHD. In contrast, providing care for ill or disabled parents or others was not significantly associated with any increased risks of CHD (Lee et al., 2003).

Finally, caregiving for frail and the more chronically impaired family members has also been linked to experiences of stress, strain, and burden, as well as to the commitment and rewards of caregiving (Boaz & Muller, 1991; NAC & AARP, 1997; 2004; Piercy, 2007; Rose, Bowman, O'Toole, Abbott, Love, Thomas, & Dawson, 2007). The rapid growth of the elderly population among the very old has increased which means that these elders will need to depend on others to fulfill their basic daily activities and assist in general household responsibilities (Boaz & Muller, 1991; NAC & AARP, 1997; 2004; U. S. Census Bureau, 2000). Several recent studies have focused on family caregiving. A study examined frail elderly veterans receiving care and focused on the objective burden of the family caregivers and the extent to which the objective burden was associated with perceptions of patient-focused, family-focused care (PCFFC) and the extent to which PCFFC mediated the influence of other variables on perceptions of PCFFC (Rose et al., 2007). The authors purported that family caregivers are often in a unique position to evaluate the care of the care recipient, and found that caregivers' assessments of PCFFC were positively associated with the care recipients' instrumental activity of daily living limitations and perception on the quality of their own patient care. Greater objective burden was found to be negatively associated with caregiver assessments of PCFFC and mediated the relationship between care recipient perceptions of the quality of their own patient care and caregiver assessments of PCFFC.

Piercy (2007) conducted two qualitative studies using in depth interviews with primary and secondary intergenerational caregivers. The purpose of the study was to examine characteristics of strong commitment of family caregivers to home-based elder care from an intergenerational standpoint. The researcher interviewed 45 primary caregivers, 10 spouses, and 11 adult great-grandchildren who shared information about their relative's care, their caregiving experiences, use of paid services, and how caregiving affected their lives. Using the McCracken (1988) model, the authors found that half of the total sample consisted of strong committed caregivers. Females were noted as being the most strongly committed followed by male secondary caregivers. Caregivers not only reported deep religious and affectionate reasons and feelings regarding caregiving, but also found caregiving to be rewarding (Piercy, 2007).

Spouse and Adult Child Caregivers

As mentioned earlier in this review, the two most common types of family caregivers are spouses and adult children (NAC & AARP, 1997; 2004; Stone et al., 1987; Tennstedt, McKinlay, & Sullivan, 1989). Spouses have been referred to as the natural caregivers (Zarit, Birkel, & Beach, 1989) and generally report more stress and burden, as well as depressive symptoms due to the nature of the care situation, co-residence, competing demands, and role captivity (Deimling, Bass, Townsend, & Noekler, 1989; George & Gwyther, 1986; NAC & AARP, 1997; 2004; Strawbridge, Wallhagen, Shema, & Kaplan, 1997; Zarit, Todd, & Zarit, 1986). According to Stone and colleagues (1987) in their earlier profile of the family caregiver hierarchy included, spouses (36%) followed by adult children (39%) were the most common family caregivers. Several studies have found consistent results among family caregivers (Cantor, 1983; Tennstedt, McKinlay, & Sullivan, 1989). These studies have documented the experience and challenges of these two groups and their differences in the role as caregivers (Burton et al., 2003; Ingersoll-Dayton, & Raschick, 2004; Kramer & Lambert, 1999; Lyons et al., 2002; Townsend & Franks, 1997).

Studies consistently show differences between husband and wife caregivers with wife caregivers experiencing more stress, depression, and burden in care as compared to husbands. Other studies have documented the role and outcomes of adult child caregivers to older or ill family members (Mui, 1995). A study of caregiver strain and burden of husband and wives caring for older frail elders, revealed high prevalence of all three domains of role strain among both groups. Moreover, regression analysis indicated that caregiving role demand, role conflict, coping resources, and care recipient characteristics had differential effects on the role strain experienced by husband versus wife caregivers (Mui, 1995).

Adult child caregivers have also been studied widely within the social and gerontological literature (Dilworth-Anderson et al., 2002; Silverstein, Parrott, & Bengtson, 1995; Smerglia & Deimling, 1997; Stein et al., 1998). Specifically, adult child caregivers have been found to be the second tier of available caregivers followed by spouses (Stone et al., 1987). However, if the spouse caregiver is widowed, divorced, or separated, the next expected caregiver is usually an adult child, preferably a daughter and in some cases a daughter-in-law (Stone et al., 1987). In a study of adult daughter and son caregivers, it was found that adult daughter caregivers tended to have stronger attachments to parents than did sons (Silverstein et al., 1995).

In an another study of the role of parental obligation of parental caregiving, moderate correlations were found between scores of filial responsibility and felt obligation. Felt obligation was a better predictor of adults' reports of parental caregiving than was the gender of the adult child. The authors contend there was little evidence for intergenerational similarity in reports of felt obligation between young adults and their middle-aged parents. Overall, results demonstrated the association between felt obligation and caregiving were generally stronger between middle-aged adults and their older parents than between young adults and their middle-aged parents (Stein et al., 1998).

Stress, Strain, and Burden of Caregiving

While family caregiving has been noted as an important family value, many of the tasks, demands, and expectations associated with the needs of the care recipient can create circumstances beyond the control and available resources of many family members in the care process (Hoffman & Mitchell, 1998). The failure or inability to meet these demands and expectations may create stress, strain, and burden among many caregivers. These concepts have been used separately and collectively in the caregiving research to measure the experiences of caregivers and determine physical, emotional, and financial well-being (Hoffman & Mitchell, 1998, Sales, 2003; Teschendorf, Schwartz, Ferrans, O'Mara, Novotny, & Sloan, 2007). The meanings of each of these concepts are sometimes unclear, or in many cases, they may conceptually overlap (Chappell & Reid, 2002; George & Gwyther, 1986; Zarit et al., 1980). This results in the ambiguity of each of these terms, as well as measurement inconsistencies (Hoffman & Mitchell, 1998). Nonetheless, these concepts continue to be widely used and accepted within caregiving studies to explore and understand their impacts on the well-being of informal caregivers. This review will discuss the distinctions between stress, strain, and burden in describing the experiences, challenges, and outcomes in the care process by defining each of these concepts along with how they have been used in the literature and their impact on the intensity of care demands experienced in the caregiving process.

Stress, Strain, Burden and Intensity of Care Demands in Caregiving

Stress

Hans Seyle (1956) is credited for originating the concept of stress from his work among laboratory animals. He defined stress as nonspecifically-induced changes within a system and as the "sum of all non-specifically induced changes in a biological system" (Viner, 1999, p. 392). Since that time, stress has been widely used as an integrating phenomenon in the course of human common experiences (Viner, 1999). Other researchers have defined stress as any environmental, social, or internal demand which requires the individual to readjust his or her usual behavior patterns (Holmes & Rahe, 1967). More recently, stress has generated more definitions and has been used across many disciplines and disease-specific domains. Stress has also been defined as both a cause and a result of some phenomenon that alters equilibrium (Hunt, 2003). In contrast, Lazarus and Folkman (1984) defined stress from a "transactional perspective as a process rather than merely a response to an environmental stimulus" (p.23). Using the Lazarus & Folkman (1984) definition of stress, the focus is on the relationship among persons, his or her characteristics, and the environmental event presented.

Yet, other definitions of stress have focused on the accumulation of events and the person's abilities to cope or deal without depleting their physical, emotional, financial, and social resources (Thoits, 1995). In the literature, stress or stressors have been studied in the form of life events, chronic strains, and daily hassles (Thoits, 1995). Life events are referred to as acute changes that require major behavioral readjustments within a short period of time, such as an initial birth or a divorce. Chronic strains are referred to as persistent and recurrent demands that require readjustments over prolonged periods of time such as poverty, chronic illness, or mental problems and disabilities. Chronic strains as a stressor will be the primary focus of this chapter. Finally, daily hassles are small or mini events which require only small or minute behavioral adjustments during the course of a day, such as traffic jams or having unexpected visitors. Historically, most of the research has focused on the effects of life events and chronic strains and their effects on the physical, emotional, and financial well-being of individuals and families (Thoits, 1995).

In earlier work, stress was viewed as emerging from the convergence of the occurrence of discrete events and the presence of relatively continuous problems. Consistent with this earlier work, stress was further differentiated into primary and secondary stressors. Primary stressors refer to stress arousing demands that are directly tied to the caregiving situation such as behavior problems of the care recipient. Secondary stressors, on the other hand, refer to stressful experiences that are triggered by primary caregiving stressors, such as restrictions in carrying out one's ordinary everyday roles and activities (Pearlin, Mullan, Semple, & Skaff, 1990). Alternately, other researchers defined stress as a change or disturbance in the steady state of the family system (Boss, 1988).

In a recent study of depressive symptoms among spousal caregivers of institutionalized mates with Alzheimer's, stress and strain were conceptualized together to represent the coping and stress profiles of respondents (Kaplan & Boss, 1999). Subscales from the Coping and Stress Profile were utilized in this study. Defining stress in the caregiving experiences can often be different based on the researcher's goals and conceptualization; however, it is widely accepted that stress causes some adverse effect on the caregiver in the care experience (Olson, Stewart, & Wilson, 1992; Zarit & Zarit, 1986). Additionally, stress has been noted as having some positive outcomes as well, such as greater in meaning in life, life satisfaction, happiness, and caregiver gain (Braithwaite, 1996; Kinney & Stephens, 1989; Kramer, 1997).

Strain

In the caregiving literature, strain has been defined as both a stressor and as perceived Stress (Pearlin et al., 1990). Strain has been defined as incumbent of a particular role or status (Pearlin et al., 1990). Yet, other researchers have described strain as the effects of caregiving on the caregiver (Ory, Hoffman, Yee, Tennstedt, & Schulz, 1999). Strain has also been defined as the subjective difficulty experienced by caregivers as they perform daily tasks for the care recipient (Archbold, Stewart, Greenlick, & Harvath, 1990). Strain and burden share some commonalities, in terms of their objective and subjective dimensions. For example, both burden and strain reflect the difficulty or load experienced by the caregivers as they perform the needed tasks for the care recipient. While this strain can tax the physical, emotional, and financial resources of the caregiver, it can also restrict the caregivers' ability to do other things and in some instances, caregivers must cease other activities completely. This perceived or subjective strain and burden may worsen as the care recipient's condition worsens. Similarly, these situations may objectively show "wear and tear" on the caregiver through physical and mental health issues, as well as increased financial demands if the care recipients' resources are limited.

Burden

Burden as a concept has been heavily explored and researched as an outcome measure in the caregiving literature. While burden is generally perceived as the "load" carried by the caregiver and has a negative conceptualization; its popular use has been more recently challenged as the focus shifts to more positive approaches, such as caregiver satisfaction (Hunt, 2003; Kramer, 1997). Nonetheless, burden has been defined widely as the consequences of the activities involved with providing needed direct care to a relative, friend, or other family member that result in observable and perceived costs to the caregiver (Hunt, 2003).

Other researchers have defined burden as a state resulting from necessary caregiving tasks or restrictions that cause discomfort for the caregiver (Zarit, et al., 1980). While others have conceptualized defined burden as the negative subjective experience of the caregiver (Chwalisz, 1996). Caregiver burden has also been viewed as the "extent to which meeting caregiving demands conflicts with the basic needs of the caregiver" (Braithwaite, 1996, p.28). Burden has also been explored as an external demand or potential threat that has been appraised by the caregiver as a stressor (Lawton et al., 1989). Other researchers mark a clearer distinction by conceptualizing burden as subjective and objective. Objective burden consists of the observable, concrete, tangible cost to the caregiver resulting from the care situation (Jones, 1996; Maurin & Boyd, 1990). Alternately, an extended definition of objective burden was conceptualized as the time and effort required of one person to attend to the needs of another (Montgomery, Gonyea, & Hooyman, 1985; Sales, 2003). Subjective burden is also viewed as the positive or negative feelings that may be experienced carrying out the objective stressors mentioned above. Emotional responses to the care process can consist of distress, worrying, stigma, shame, and guilt (Maurin & Boyd, 1990; Nijober et al., 1999; Sales, 2003). These emotional appraisals of the care process can also be positive such as happiness, satisfaction, uplift, and gain during the care process (Braithwaite, 1996; Kramer, 1997; Kinney & Stephens, 1989).

There are several issues in the conceptualization and measurement of caregiver burden. Schene and colleagues (1994) suggest that the following issues are 1) multidimensional; 2) measure both objective and subjective burden; 3) composed of only negative items; 4) administered on a single occasion; 5) a composite of various dimensions, most commonly, actual care demands, added domestic task, readjustments in other role demands, and emotional reactions of caregiver; and 6) administered to only to the primary caregiver, despite recognition that all family members are impacted by the care recipient's illness or disability (Sales, 2003). Additionally, ambiguities in the conceptual meaning of subjective burden result in many measures either blending or failing to distinguish between the objective and subjective dimensions (Braithwaite, 1996; Poulshock & Deimling, 1984; Sales, 2003). Nonetheless, burden continues to be a dominant and pervasive concept in the caregiving literature. However, more emphasis must be placed on the positive aspects of caregiving as people often experience dual emotions in the care process and in different situations.

Intensity of Care Demands in Caregiving

Given the popular use of the concepts of stress, strain, and burden, these terms need to be viewed from a multidimensional standpoint because of their wide use in the literature and their over lapping meanings. Further, the term, "intensity of care demands" can serve as the "umbrella" concept that encompassed the broader facets of stress, strain, and burden and their associated characteristics. Therefore, intensity of care demands consisted of measures of the tasks or duties performed by caregivers such as activities of daily living (ADLs) and instrumental activities of daily living (IADLS) and the number of hours required to perform these tasks (NAC & AARP, 1997; 2004). The National Alliance for Caregiving and AARP (1997; 2004) created a scale referred to as "Level of Burden" or the "Level of Care Index," which is comprised of two major dimensions in the care demand concept: number of hours per week certain caregiving tasks are preformed, and the type of caregiving services provided by the caregiver. The intensity of care demands varies in terms of the amount of time spent and the kinds of care provided (NAC & AARP, 1997; 2004). Characteristically, caregivers who spent 40 hours or more per week (17%) and lived with the care recipient (44%), reported fair or poor health (29%), were 65 or older (28%), were caring for someone with Alzheimer's or dementia (24%), reported lower income (23%), and were less educated (21%) (NAC & AARP, 2004). The age of care-recipients coupled with functional status may induce intense care demands on the part of caregivers. A national caregiving survey in the U.S. found the two greatest predictors of caregivers' physical strain were the caregivers reported health and whether they felt they perceived a choice in taking on the caregiving responsibilities (NAC & AARP, 2004). Similarly, the analysis also showed that the two greatest predictors of caregivers' emotional stress was their level of burden and whether or not the caregiver had a choice to take on care responsibilities. Consequently, other factors that contributed to the caregivers' emotional stress were caregiver's self-reported health, co-residing with care recipient, and being female (NAC & AARP, 2004). Caregivers who had to modify their homes or obtain medical assistive devices such as: bathing benches, hearing aids, or other similar devices experienced a certain degree of inconvenience (NAC & AARP, 2004). Likewise, those caregivers who had to administer medications to the care recipient found themselves under enormous stress as the care situation became more intense (NAC & AARP, 1997; 2004). These intense care demands may further place the caregiver in a negative emotional and physical state (Zarit, Reever, & Bach-Peterson, 1989). As the impairment of the care recipient increases; so does the amount, intensity, and degree of stress of the caregiver. Types of assistance that include the provision of physical strength and personal hygiene are generally more taxing and burdensome for caregivers. These types of care demands are much more salient indicators of the level of burden experienced in the care context, placing older spouses at a greater disadvantage (Kramer, 1997; Pearlin et al., 1990).

Therefore, as care requirements increase and the ability to provide this type of intense care is diminished due to fewer caregivers and formal and informal resources, the quality of the relationship between the caregiver and care-recipient tends to suffer (Bookwala & Schulz, 2000). Similarly, higher care demands, intensity, and extended periods of care under these conditions often leave the caregiver with no choice but to institutionalize the care-recipient or face decreased physical, emotional, mental, and financial well-being (Colerick & George, 1986; Dilworth-Anderson et al., 2002; Draper, Poulos, Poulos, & Ehrlich, 1995; George, 1987; NAC & AARP, 2004).

Caregiver Supportive Resources

Historically, research has documented the role and impact of social or coping resources available to caregivers as they perform needed tasks for the care recipient (Thoits, 1996). The type and degree of resources available to caregivers has been linked to their ability to continue or cease the care role (George & Gwyther, 1986). Nonetheless, these resources assist caregivers to cope with the demands of caregiving. The literature has been inconsistent relative to which type of coping resources better buffer or mediates the stress of caregiving. Additionally, the number of resources needed to reduce the stressors of caregiving is even less consistent in the literature, yet they both remain important factors in the care process. Coping resources consist broadly of social and personal characteristics of which people draw upon when dealing with stressors. While it is recognized that there may be many types of resources available to caregivers as they perform their daily tasks of caregiving, formal and informal resources are the focal types for this review (NAC & AARP, 1997; 2004).

This section focuses on the utilization of formal and informal coping resources that the caregiver may utilize in the coping process. Formal coping resources may be viewed as the resources available to the caregiver that are outside of the home and are accessed externally as supportive services from the community. Whereas, informal coping resources are considered resources that are intrinsic, personal, and accessed through the caregiver's informal networks. While coping has also been linked to mastery of the care situation; the focus in this review is on the formal and informal coping resources available to caregivers in the care process (Thoits, 1996).

Formal and Informal Coping Resources

Formal Coping Resources

Social support has been conceptualized as both coping resources (Folkman & Lazarus, 1980; Vaux & Wood, 1987) and coping strategies (Pratt et al., 1985). The use of formal coping supportive resources or services in the community has included requesting information about financial assistance, obtaining formal training, using transportation services, using Meals on Wheels, enrolling care recipient in a recreation camp or Adult Day Care, taking part in support groups, or using respite care. There are many of the types of formal support services utilized by caregivers. Formal helpers and their support services generally operate within the context of a bureaucratic structure offering professional skilled services in a predictable organized fashion sometimes for a fee (Lipman & Longino, 1982; NAC & AARP, 1997; 2004). Resources of this nature may serve as coping and adaptation strategies for the caregiver in cases where professional care services are needed as higher levels of family care are required and in cases where the informal networks have either become strained or limited (Cox, 2005). In many cases the use of formal support services does not diminish the use of informal support by family members, but some functions may merely shift (Horowitz, 1985).

One study examined rural and urban differences in formal and informal resource use of Alzheimer's caregivers, various cognitive and behavioral coping strategies, and differences in social support patterns. There were significant differences in caregivers' coping patterns by race and area of residence. White caregivers attended support groups more frequently than did Blacks. Black caregivers reported more frequent utilization of cognitive strategies reframing the situation in positive terms and expressing determination to survive. Rural Blacks sought information about the disease or about services less frequently than did White or urban caregivers. Black caregivers had available, and used extensively, a broad range of informal supports. Additionally, Blacks perceived a higher spiritual authority in a very intrinsic manner in the care process (Wood & Parham, 1990).

Another study using a national sample of 597 caregivers of non-institutionalized dementia patients examined the specific coping strategies that caregivers used and how they were associated with negative and positive outcomes for the caregivers. Results from this study indicated that although caregivers used predominately "problem-focused" coping strategies, these strategies were not associated with lower caregiver burden. In contrast, "avoidant-evasive" and "regressive" coping strategies were most damaging in terms of their association with lower levels of life satisfaction and higher levels of caregiver burden (Wright, Lund, Caserta, & Pratt, 1991).

The degree to which caregivers utilize formal support systems as a coping strategy in the care process is based largely on factors of income, educational level, and care recipient involvement, need, level of care required, race/ethnicity, and other cultural expectations and experiences. Research has shown that formal care use might be temporary or episodic to offer respite for caregivers or as care recipients' needs require that they move from one care setting to another (McFall & Miller, 1992). However, for some caregivers a move to a nursing home facility or other permanent care arrangement may result in a reduction of the traditional and expected informal care responsibility (McFall & Miller, 1992). Nonetheless, the use of formal support systems as a coping resource is important to the context of caregiving in families and will become more important as many care recipients advance in age and in level of physical and cognitive impairment. The ability of caregivers to utilize both formal and informal mechanisms to cope with caregiving will be vital to their objective and subjective response to caregiving.

Informal Coping Resources

Like formal coping resources, informal or personal coping resources allow the caregiver greater adaptability in the care process considering the associated demands of caregiving. Informal coping can also be conceptualized as both coping resources and coping strategies (Folkman & Lazarus, 1980; Pratt et al., 1985; Segall & Wykle, 1988; & Vaux & Wood, 1987). In this review, this concept refers to the mechanisms that caregivers use such as, praying, talking with or seeking advice from friends or relatives, reading about caregiving, exercising or working out, going on the internet to find information, talking to a professional or spiritual counselor, or taking medication (NAC & AARP, 2004). Resources of this type serve as coping and adaptation mechanisms for the caregiver and their informal networks. Because most family members prefer the use of informal networks, it is not unusual for older or ill family members to rely on friends, family, and extended kin networks for support (NAC & AARP, 1997, 2004; Owens-Kane, 2007).

Receiving emotional support from families has been associated with decreased feelings of depression or burden (Aneshenal et al., 1995; Franks & Stephens, 1996). Among wives and daughter caregivers, research has indicated that emotional support for both groups buffered the effects of stress as a result of the care recipient's behavior (Li, Seltzer, & Greenberg, 1997). "Psychological resources are individual characteristics that increase the person's resilience or capacity to cope with stress" (Greenberg, Seltzer, & Brewer, 2006, p. w344). These resources that may enhance caregiver functioning have focused on coping strategies and an individual's sense of mastery.

Lazarus & Folkman (1984) posited two types of coping strategies: problem-focused coping and emotion-focused coping. Problem-focused coping consists of cognitive and behavioral problem-solving strategies designed to alter or manage stressful situations. In comparison, emotion-focused coping consists of cognitive and behavioral attempts to reduce or manage emotional stress that are not focused on solving the problem. The research suggested, the use of problem-focused strategies result in improved well-being (Aldwin, 1991; Seltzer, Greenberg, & Krauss, 1995). Other studies have found little support or inconsistent outcomes in this area (Patrick & Hayden, 1999; Pruchno & Kleban, 1993; Seltzer et al., 1995).

Sense of Caregiver Manageability/Mastery of the Care Situation

Caregivers can often feel overwhelmed or sense a lack of control in the care role when the demands and expectations of the care recipient tax their available resources and expertise. Their available resources coupled with the manner in which they perceive or appraise their tasks determine to some extent their sense of manageability/mastery of the situation (Lawton et al., 1991). Caregivers often express the need for more assistance or resources as they provide care or deplete their own resources. In some cases, caregivers do not have many resources to invest in the care process, especially if the caregiving role was thrust upon them unexpectedly or in an untimely manner (NAC & AARP, 1997; 2004). Caregivers who provide care and feel that they have unmet needs ultimately weaken their ability to gain a sense of control over the care situation (Foley et al., 2002). This perception or appraisal of the care situation based on unmet needs can jeopardize the caregiver, as well as the care recipient. This review focuses on understanding the general concepts of perception and appraisal and how these concepts are linked to a caregiver's sense of manageability/mastery given the unmet needs of the caregiver in the care process.

Perception and Appraisal

The Stress Process Model

Lazarus and Folkman (1984) identified two processes: cognitive appraisal and coping as critical mediators of stressful person-environment relations. The theory primarily asserts that potentially stressful situations are evaluated in terms of their significance to the personal well-being and that these evaluations guide affective, physiological, and behavioral coping outcomes. Primary appraisals at one level are evaluated as: 1) being without implications for well-being or irrelevant, 2) maintaining or enhancing well-being (positive) and 3) stressful. Stressful appraisals can be characterized further as 1) involving harm or loss, 2) threat, or potential for harm or loss, and 3) challenge, or potential for gain and growth. These stressful appraisals involve an assessment of the nature of the stressor and the individual's resources for coping with it. Once coping responses are put into motion, subsequent appraisals called secondary appraisals include the evaluation of their effectiveness. Thus, this primary and secondary appraisal process is termed dynamic and continuous.

Appraisal is dynamic and continuous and can be expected to change as the stressor is modified, such as the demands of caregiving, or the resources available to caregivers. Reappraisal is the third type of cognitive appraisal and refers to the changed appraisal based on new information from the environment and or the person. A reappraisal follows an earlier appraisal which demonstrated change over-time in the caregiving process. Additionally, there are both "person" factors and situation or environmental influences that impact appraisal. These factors or variables are properties that influence the judgment that something of importance is at stake in any encounter or caregiving situation.

The two most important "person" factors affecting cognitive appraisals are commitments and beliefs (Lazarus & Folkman, 1984). Commitments undergird the choices people tend to make and are an expression of what is important to people, whereas beliefs determine how a person evaluates what is happening or may happen in the future. There are many situational factors that have great relevance to appraisal and the potential for creating threat. These situational factors consist of novelty, predictability, ambiguity, timing, event uncertainty, and temporal factors such as imminence and duration. All of these factors could be important in determining the significance of an encounter for the person's well-being (Lazarus & Folkman, 1984).

Coping is defined as constantly changing cognitive and behavior efforts to manage specific external or internal demands that are appraised as burdensome or exceeding the resources of the person providing care. The two main functions of coping consist of 1) managing or changing the problem with the environment causing distress or 2) problem-focused coping or regulating the emotional response to the problem which is referred to as emotion-focused coping (Lazarus & Folkman, 1984). Thus, problem and emotion-focused coping influence each other throughout the caregiving situation. Finally, the importance of the appraisal and coping processes is that they affect adaptational outcomes. There are three basic kinds of outcomes: morale or life satisfaction, functioning in work and social living, and somatic health (Lazarus & Folkman, 1984).

There is additional research supporting the contextual nature of this stress process model and as such, converges on several other research areas. Coping has had multiple functions and is not limited to the regulation of distress or the management of problem causing (Parker & Endler, 1996). Others have viewed coping as influenced by appraised characteristics of the stressful context (Baum, Fleming, & Singer, 1983; Folkman, Lazarus, Dunkel-Schetter, DeLongis, & Gruen, 1986). Coping as an influence of personality disposition was advanced by the work of McCrae and Costa (1986). Finally, other researchers have viewed coping as influenced by social resources (Holahan, Moos, & Schaefer, 1996; Pierce, Sarason, & Sarason, 1996).

The notion of positive affect has recently been advanced as a much neglected yet viable view of the stress process (Folkman & Moskowitz, 2000). Positive affect is related to primary appraisal of stressful situations as challenges that signal the possibility of mastery or gain as characterized by positively toned emotions such as eagerness, excitement, and confidence. Positive affect is also related to appraisal of the resolution of a stressful encounter as favorable or successful, leading to emotions such as happiness and pride (Folkman & Lazarus, 1985). Additionally, a number of studies have examined other kinds of positive outcomes of stressful events even though the events themselves may not have had favorable resolutions (Folkman & Moskowitz, 2000). Such outcomes include the perception of benefit from the stressful encounters (Affleck, Tennen, Croog, & Levine, 1987), acquisition of new coping skills and resources (Schaefre & Coleman, 1992), perception of growth related to their stress (Holahan & Moos, 1991; Nolen-Hoeksema & Larson, 1999; Park Cohen, & Murch, 1996), and spiritual or religious transformation resulting from the stressful experiences (Aldwin, 1994; Pargament, 1997). The following arguments regarding the use of positive affect are: (a) positive affect can occur with distress during a given period; (b) positive affect in the context of stress has important adaptational significance of its own, and (c) coping processes that generate and sustain positive affect in the context of chronic meaning.

Impact of Unmet Needs

Many caregivers provide care for family members with insufficient or no assistance or support in the care process. A recent national study found that 35% of caregivers needed help finding more time for themselves and 29% reported needing assistance or information about balancing work and family responsibilities, as well as managing emotional and physical stress (NAC & AARP, 2004). Unmet needs in caregiving can consist of not having enough information or assistance in making important decisions about the care recipients' physical or mental health status as it improves or deteriorates (NAC & AARP, 2004). Additionally, having to transfer a family member from a home environment to an assisted living facility or nursing home can challenge the emotional status of caregivers. When caregivers report that they have numerous unmet needs, they may feel that they lack a sense of control or the ability to support the needs of the care recipient. Other areas of unmet needs of the caregiver can be emotional, physical, or financial. Emotional unmet needs refer to the need that the caregiver may have for finding personal time, keeping the care recipient safe, talking to health care professionals, or managing challenging behaviors of the care recipient (NAC & AARP, 2004). Physical unmet needs may consist of the caregiver's inability to lift, transfer, or manage the care recipient physically due to their own physical limitations, illness, or frailty (NAC & AARP, 1997, 2004). Financial unmet needs may consist of the caregiver's need for more information or support to enhance or augment their costs of caring for the care recipient. This support may be other family members providing paid support or care to expand the resources of the primary caregiver (NAC & AARP, 2004).

Perceptions of the Care Context

Perceptions of manageability and mastery in the provision of care are common dilemmas faced by caregivers (Gilliam & Steffen, 2006). Some researchers have recently found that objective stressors may not be directly related to negative outcomes, such as depression. Instead, recent research has found a link between caregivers' perceptions of the caregiving situation and their ability to manage the associated demands or needs of the care recipient (Gilliam & Steffen, 2006). Concepts such as mastery, self-efficacy, competence, preparedness, and quality of life have all been globally linked to how caregivers may be performing their caregiving duties (Schumacher, Stewart, Archbold, 1998). For example, caregiver mastery as defined by Lawton and colleagues (1992) is a positive view of one's ability and behavior while caring for a family member in the care process. This may also be viewed as a feeling of competence (Schumacher et al., 1998). In this case, mastery is specific to the caregiving role and behavior, but does not encompass the task itself (Lazarus & Folkman, 1984; Lawton et al., 1992). This view of mastery is closely tied to the concept of manageability/mastery in this study because it is one of the five dimensions of cognitive appraisal purported by Lazarus & Folkman (1984). The other dimensions are caregiver burden, caregiving satisfaction, and caregiving ideology. In all cases, appraisal mediates the relationship between the objective measures of stress and the overall well-being as experienced by the caregiver (Schumacher et al., 1998). Therefore, it is important to link unmet needs of the caregiver and their perceptions or appraisal of these unmet needs in relationship to their sense of ability to manage or master the care situation.

Manageability/Mastery

Because caregivers have their own beliefs along with different ways in which they perceive their caregiving efforts; attention to the appraisal of the caregiving role is important in understanding the complexities of effects caregiving has on the caregiver (Braithwaite, 2000). Caregiving appraisal is a term used to denote the way caregivers may perceive the caregiving situation. Lawton et al., (1989) used the term "caregiver appraisal" to describe all of the cognitive and affective appraisals and reappraisals of the potential stressor and the efficacy of one's coping efforts. This definition is important to understanding what care recipients are capable of doing based on the stressors associated with their physical and mental capacities and the social supportive resources available (formal or informal). Similarly, appraisals of the caregiving situations are critical factors that shape the adaptation of caregivers (Folkman & Lazarus, 1984). Given our understanding of appraisals, mastery in caregiving refers to the extent to which people see themselves as being in control of the forces that affect them (Jang, Haley, Small, & Mortimer, 2002; Pearlin et al., 1990; 2007). Manageability as a concept in this current review is an inclusive and "umbrella" concept that refers to the amount, extent, and degree to which caregivers feel they are managing or controlling the care situation. Thus, manageability consists of the caregivers' subjective feelings of whether or not all of their needs are met as they engage in the caregiving role. Therefore, manageability/mastery can be situational and dynamic. Further, the more unmet needs identified by the caregiver in the care role will serve as an indicator that the caregiver may be experiencing difficulty in manageability/mastery in the caregiving situation. On the other hand, the fewer unmet needs identified by the caregiver in the care role; the greater their manageability/mastery of the care situation.

Many studies have found sense of "control" or "mastery" as important factors influencing the physical and emotional health of persons (Krause, 1994; Pearlin, Lieberman, Menagham, & Mullan, 1981; Skaff, Pearlin, & Mullan, 1996). Thus, manageability/mastery is conceptualized as a multidimensional, broad, and inclusive concept that includes mastery and sense of coherence. Taken all together, manageability/mastery consisted of the understanding that people harbor about their ability to manage the circumstances of their lives and sense of coherence as the extent to which one regards one's life-chances as being under one's own control as opposed to being fatalistically controlled (Antonovsky, 1987; Pearlin & Schooler, 1978). These are important concepts in understanding manageability/mastery as they represent the larger concepts of definition of the situation, perceptions and appraisals as described in various stress process models (Aneshenal et al., 1995; Boss, 2002; Hill, 1949, 1958; Lazarus & Folkman, 1984; McCubbin & Boss, 1980; McCubbin & Boss, 1989; McCubbin & Patterson, 1983; Pearlin et al., 1990; 2007).

Sense of Coherence

Theory of salutogenesis focuses on the origins of health (well-being) rather than pathogenesis, which pertains to the underlying mechanisms of illness (Antonovsky, 1979; 1987). Additionally, Antonovsky's (1987) concept of sense of coherence is a global orientation that expresses the extent to which one's world is seen as comprehensible, manageable, and meaningful. Therefore, sense of coherence is important to the concept of manageability/mastery. First, sense of coherence focuses on the factors derived from a person's internal and external environments in the course of their daily lives. This is referred to as the comprehensibility aspect. Second, the resources available to meet the demands posed by these daily factors or situations are referred to as the manageability aspect. Finally, these demands are challenges worthy of investment and engagement, which is referred to as meaningfulness (Antonovsky, 1987). When all of these are taken together, these components are referred to as comprehensibility, manageability, and meaningfulness. The concept of mastery is closely tied to comprehensibility and manageability. Additionally, factors related to personal orientation, such as feelings of competence, obligation, guilt, and reciprocity can evolve from the caregiving experience (Goodman, Zarit, & Steiner, 1997). The challenges and experiences of caregiving affect the personal orientation of caregivers, thus influencing a caregiver's interpretation of the caregiving situation. As a result, a caregiver who feels competent in meeting the needs of the care recipient may not perceive caregiving as overwhelming compared to a caregiver who interprets the care situation as stressful (Goodman, Zarit, & Steiner, 1997). The aspects of competence in caregiving and commitment to the caregiver relationship are important factors in understanding manageability/mastery.

The Concept of Caregiver Well-being

An ultimate goal in most caregiving research has been to determine the extent that caregiving results in positive or negative outcomes (Kramer, 1997; Walker et al., 1995). As established earlier in this review, not all care situations result in negative experiences, but are comprised of various outcomes in this dynamic process (Lawton et al., 1991). Andrew and Withey (1976) addressed three major components of well-being: positive affect, negative affect, and life satisfaction. A major outcome of importance in the recent literature has been a focus on well-being as a more positive construct versus the traditional focus on burden or negative outcomes (Braithwaite, 2000; Kramer, 1997). This section of the review will highlight the multidimensional aspects of well-being across emotional, physical, and financial consequences in the care process. Additionally, a conceptual definition of well-being is presented.

Multidimensional Aspects of Well-being

Well-being

Well-being is a multidimensional concept and has been measured in the family, gerontological, and behavioral science literature in a variety of ways. Psychological well-being, happiness, and emotions have been studied consistently by Bradburn, 1969; Diener, Emmons, Larsen, & Griffin, 1984; 1985; Diener, Oishi, & Lucas, 2003. Additionally, researchers have taken into consideration the demands, intensity of care, and the consequences associated with caregiving (Pearlin et al., 1990; Skaff et al., 1996). Several researchers have viewed the outcomes differently, including the creation of different measures and scales (Kosberg & Cairl, 1986; Siegal et al., 1991; Stull et al., 1994; Zarit & Zarit, 1986). As a result, the concept of psychological well-being has been widely published in the field of psychology focusing on the emotional, mental, and depressive health aspects of caregiver outcomes (Hoyt, O'Donnell, & Mack, 1995; McBride, 1990; Yee & Schulz, 2000). Moreover, a variety of constructs have been used to measure well-being through various scales, indices, or subscales such as, life satisfaction, quality of life, burden, and strain. A few examples consist of the Cost of Care Index (CCI) (Kosberg & Cairl, 1986) which focused on 5 domains: personal, social, physical, emotional value, and economic. Also, the Caregiver Burden Measures (CBM) which consist of the domains of employment, financial, physical, social, and time have been used (Siegal et al., 1991). Additionally, the Caregiver Burden (CB) scale consisted of the 3 subscales of physical strain, social constraints, and financial strain (Stull et al., 1994). While all of these measures focus on the outcome of well-being, they do so in various ways, capturing multidimensional aspects of well-being.

As noted earlier, caregiver well-being has been mostly studied as a negative outcome measure focusing on depression, burden, and illness. However, since the focus of this chapter I son the more positive and satisfying effects of caregiving, attention was placed on the implicit meaning of subjective well-being. Subjective well-being refers to individuals' evaluation of their lives and includes cognitive and affective evaluations (Diener, Oishi, & Lucas, 2003). Subjective well-being includes the positive and the negative emotional outcomes experienced by caregivers which can represent a global experience and an evaluation of their lives at the moment and for longer periods of time (Diener, 1984; Diener, Larsen, & Griffin, 1985). Given negative life situations, stresses, and disadvantages; there is a tendency for most people to report feelings of global happiness (Diener & Diener, 1996). People in the lowest income categories, persons with disabilities, and even caregivers who provide intense care often report feelings of overall happiness and contentment with life (Aneshenal et al., 1995; Diener, 1984; Diener et al., 1985; Dilworth-Anderson et al., 2002; Foley et al., 2002).

Well-being as a Positive Concept

Using the conceptual measures of physical strain, emotional stress, and financial hardship as self-reported feelings by caregivers on (NAC & AARP, 2003) survey, the generic term "well-being" rather than "subjective well-being" is used in accordance with the suggestion of Diener, Suh, Lucas, and Smith (1999). Using the term well-being in this manner avoids any suggestion that there is something arbitrary or unknowable about the concepts involved (Diener et al., 1999). However, the general meaning that is attached to subjective well-being as characterized by Diener et al., (1999) referred to all of the various types of evaluations, both positive and negative, that people make of their lives. Accordingly, subjective well-being can include evaluations of life satisfaction, marital satisfaction, quality of life, joy, happiness, and sadness. Well-being is viewed here as the "umbrella" term that included the related concepts of physical strain, emotional stress, and financial hardship (NAC & AARP, 2004). All of these domains have been studied separately or together in some combination to produce the outcome of global or overall well-being in the literature (Kramer, 1997).

Positive Aspects

Most of the research on caregiving has been largely negative in its conceptualization, orientation, and outcome (Kramer, 1997; Pratt et al., 1995). A movement to focus on the more positive or holistic aspects of caregiving experiences is increasing (Kramer, 1997). Some of the more positive concepts related to caregiver experiences and challenges have been based on approaches looking at satisfaction, esteem, uplifts, gain, and finding meaning (Farran, Keane-Hagerty, Salloway, Kupferer, & Wilkin, 1997; Farran, Miller, Kaufman, Donner, & Fogg, 1999; Given, Given, Stommel, Collins, King, & Franklin, 1992; Hunt, 2003; Kinney & Stephens, 1989; Kramer, 1997).

Satisfaction in caregiving is a common term used in caregiving and is used to address aspects correlated with the benefits and potential intrinsic gratitude and growth gained from the caregiving experience (Kramer, 1997). While identifying a precise definition for satisfaction has been difficult, it has gained acceptance as a concept that seeks to measure not only positive but also negatives aspects of caregiving which supports the duality of positive and negative experiences in the care process (Hunt, 2003; Kramer, 1997).

The concept of self-esteem has gained recent importance. Specifically, self-esteem has been used to link the caregiver's experience not only as satisfying, but also an opportunity to gain confidence in the care process (Hunt, 2003). Several studies have shown that as caregivers' self-esteem increased, lower reports of depression resulted (Nijboer et al., 2000). Additionally, Hunt (2003) reviewed the concept of uplifts as purported by Kinney & Stephens (1989), which refers to daily events that stimulate joy, gladness, or satisfaction. Uplifts and hassles as experienced on a daily basis by caregivers are likely to have good things happen to them that make them feel elevated or improved, whereas, negative events may make them feel down, troubled, or threatened. When uplifts outweigh hassles, caregivers report less distress (Kinney et al., 1995).

Caregiver gain is characterized as the extent to which the caregiver role is perceived or appraised as enhancing or enriching the caregiver's life (Kramer, 1997). While caregiver gain is a form of appraisal, caregivers generally expect some type or return as a result of their caregiving experience (Hunt, 2003; Kramer 1997). Caregivers' gain is a form of adaptation, because as they adapt in their caregiving roles, they may experience enrichment or enhancement. This process has a mediating effect within the entire caregiving process (Kramer, 1997).

The concept of "finding meaning" has its orientation in qualitative research (Hunt, 2003). Six themes were identified in a qualitative study from caregivers of patients with dementia (Farran et al., 1991. The six themes led to finding meaning as a "positive psychological resource" in the caregiving process. From these outcomes, a quantitative scale called, "Finding Meaning Through Caregiving Scale" for "assessing positive factors and ways of finding meaning" in the caregiving process for families with Alzheimer's disease was created (Farran et al., 1999; Hunt, 2003).

Emotional, Physical, and Financial Aspects of Well-being

Emotional Well-being

Emotional well-being in the literature has been noted by a variety of concepts such as psychological well-being, mental well-being or health, and other subjective evaluations (Andrews & Withey, 1976; Burgener & Chiverton, 1992; Lawton et al., 1983). Like most of the concepts in the caregiving literature, emotional well-being is a multidimensional concept which involves various interpretations, measures, and constructs. As a result of these varied interpretations of the concept of emotional well-being, there are some inconsistencies in the way it is measured. For example, Lawton's (1983) conceptualization of psychological well-being consists of four aspects: 1) negative affect, which encompasses depression, anxiety, agitations, worry, pessimism, and distressing psychological symptoms; 2) happiness, which encompasses the cognitive judgment of positive affect over a long time interval; 3) positive affect, which, is an active pleasure or emotional state versus a cognitive judgment; 4) psychological well-being, which is a balance between positive and negative affect. (Burgener & Chiverton, 1992; Lawton, 1983).

In a recent national caregiver's study, emotional well-being was characterized as the emotional impact that caregiving had on the caregiver. The report noted that caregiving caused more emotional stress than physical strain (NAC & AARP, 2004). According to the report, 35% of 1,247 caregivers taking care of the care recipient rated a four on the five-point scale where five was considered very stressful emotionally. Those who rated four or five on the five-point scale and were considered at the greatest emotional risk were females (40%), between the ages of 35–64 (76%), living with the care recipient (43%), White or Hispanic (36% and 36%), and in fair or poor health themselves (47%). The need to bridge the gap between the concepts of psychological well-being in relationship to other orientations such as, research, theory, and practice, is needed to better inform the research community on the unique and overlapping nature of this aspect of well-being. In a recent study of psychological well-being in the face of serious illness, Folkman & Greer (2000) described a theoretical framework for the discussion of psychological stress during serious illness. This framework defined the variables that research had indicated some specific contribution to psychological well-being in serious illnesses. A major goal of this review is to encourage researchers and clinicians to focus on the development and maintenance of psychological well-being as it pertains to serious illness and the treatment of psychiatric symptoms. Nonetheless, emotional well-being, regardless of the terminology used focuses on the feelings expressed and experiences on the possible mental or psychological outcomes realized in the care process (Folkman & Greer, 2000; Folkman & Lazarus, 1984; Lawton et al., 1991). These emotional outcomes remain central within the caregiving research, as well as the experiences and challenges of caregivers.

Physical Well-being

Similar to emotional well-being, physical well-being has been the focus of a great deal of research in caregiving. Physical well-being is often referred to as the physiological health or actual physical impacts on the caregivers' health and physical abilities. For example, several studies have used self-reports of respondents' perceptions of their physical health. The global or general questions of "how do you rate your health?" and the choices generally presented are: excellent, very good, good, fair, or poor. The use of self-reports in determining physical well-being have been met with some concerns as they may not actually reflect the objective health condition of the respondent. Nonetheless, subjective ratings of health have been widely used and accepted in the caregiving research community. For example, in a recent national study of 1,247 caregivers, respondents were asked "How would you describe your own health?" Interestingly, 74% reported that being a care-giver had no effect on their health, whereas, 15% reported that caregiving had made their health worse. Less than 9% reported that being a caregiver made their health better (NAC & AARP, 2004). Several national studies have linked age to caregivers' perception of fair or poor physical health. For example, older caregivers are more likely to report that caregiving has made their health worse or to report that their current health is either in a fair or poor condition (NAC & AARP, 1997, 2004). The Center on an Aging Society (2005) prepared a profile based on data from the Informal Caregiver Supplement (ICS) to the 1999 National Long Term Care Survey (NLTCS) and found that 21% of male and 77% of female respondents reported that they were physically strained due to caregiving. An-other 22% reported that they felt exhausted when they went to bed at night and many stated that they could not handle all of the caregiving responsibilities. Overall, 10% of the respondents in this national study reported that taking care of the care recipient was difficult for them physically. In terms of general health, chronic conditions are common among many caregivers. Among the top chronic conditions suffered by caregivers were arthritis (46%), hypertension (39%), and heart con-ditions (14%) (Center on an Aging Society, 2005).

Financial Well-being

Providing informal care to family members is not only an emotional or physical chore but also can potentially become a financial hardship for many caregivers and caregiving families. By definition, informal caregiving implies that the duties, tasks, and roles carried out in the caregiving process are of no cost to the caregiver, however, this is not true, according to a recent study. A decade ago, it was estimated that care provided by family members and friends was estimated to be valued at $196 billion relative to what is spent on home health care, which was estimated at 32 billion and nursing home care estimated at 83 billion (Arno, Levine, & Memmott, 1999). Recent estimates sug-gest that informal caregivers of older adults by friends and family is approximately $522 billion a year (Chari, Engberg, Ray & Mehrotra, 2015). For families, this means a considerable amount of financial resources is devoted to the overall care and maintenance of the care recipient. A recent profile of caregivers' resources found that 76% of caregivers were unpaid and of those who were compensated, their sources of income was from Medicaid or another insurance (National Academy on an Aging Society, 2000). The Center on an Aging Society (2005) reported that 28% of males and 72% of females felt "very strained" financially due to providing care for the care recipient. How-ever, this same study reported that most of the primary caregivers were not low income and had more wealth on average than non-caregivers. Consistent with other national studies, lower income caregivers were more likely to experience financial burdens or hardships due to long-term care and a high dependence on family and friends to provide care (NAC & AARP, 1997, 2004, 2009). The financial hardships of caregiving are also evident in missed work, reduced hours, and early leave by the caregiver in order to meet the demands of caregiving. This is especially troublesome for women, minorities, and those who themselves are older caregivers (NAC & AARP, 1997, 2004, 2009; National Center on an Aging Society, 2005).

The financial hardship experienced by these groups is generally much higher than those with higher incomes and those who reported having completed college (NAC & AARP, 1997, 2004,

2009). As a result, African American caregivers (22%) are more likely to experience financial hardships as result of being a caregiver compared to Whites (10%), Hispanic (14%), or Asian-American (11%). In an analysis by the NAC & AARP (2004), the best predictors of a caregivers' financial hardship were level of burden and whether the caregivers felt that they had a choice in providing care to the care receipts. Other factors that contributed to financial hardships associated with caregiving were age of caregiver, health status, and whether the caregiver co-resided with the care recipient (NAC & AARP, 2004). Overall, the financial demands associated with caregiving often places the well-being of the caregiver in jeopardy, especially among women and minority groups.

Conclusion

In sum, caregiving is a broad, multidimensional, dynamic, and diverse human phenomenon that requires a great amount of personal and human support and sacrifice. Recent estimates of this type of care is exhausting when one calculates the human labor and social capital expended on this social and cultural task that families feel obligated to perform in many cases. Therefore, it is important to acknowledge that there are a number of factors that produce stress within and among caregiving families that result in different outcomes for different people. The primary focus of this chapter has been on the integrative quality of factors in the ABC-X model (Hill, 1949; McCubbin & Patterson, 1983) to focus on differences in the stressors, coping resource use, manageability/mastery, of caregivers and its utility in detecting differences in the overall well-being among caregivers. Therefore, this chapter addressed the theoretical and conceptual understanding of caregiving in general, its definition, as well as the characteristics and contextual linkages of gender, race, age, health condition, and the most common types of caregivers in our society. Nonetheless, caregivers experience a wide array of challenges and experiences in the caregiving role and as such draw upon various coping resources to either reduce or mediate the stress producing event. Additionally, caregivers are often faced with what seems like insurmountable challenges in terms of unmet needs in the care role. These unmet needs, if appraised or perceived as impossible may negatively impact experience as well as overall well-being. Likewise, unmet needs that are appraised or perceived as comprehensible or manageable may be viewed as positive thus resulting in a more favorable outcome by the caregiver. This review sought to expand our knowledge of the factors that account for the difference in well-being considering the amount of stress, level of coping resource use, and manageability/mastery among caregivers.

Taken all together, there is strong evidence of the increasing number of older, ill, and disabled family members in the U.S., and worldwide. At the same time, recent research has pointed to demographic changes that may adversely affect the availability of family members to provide this care, especially secondary caregivers, and the potential financial burden on society, formal service providers, and the health care system (Spillman & Pezzin, 2000; Wolf & Kasper, 2006). Even with improved health and reduced disability, these trends indicate that family caregivers will play an even more pivotal role in helping maintain older, ill, or disabled persons within their own homes, with relatives, or within the community in the future (Pandya & Coleman, 2000). For diverse racial and ethnic caregivers, this shift in demographics will be further exacerbated due to chronic illness, inadequate or no health coverage, an economic downturn, and fewer family caregivers to assist with this care (Spillman & Pezzin, 2000; Wolf & Kasper, 2006). This situation may increase the likelihood of more joint formal and informal support use for some, while for others, it may stimulate the use of more formal support services in order to cope.

Naturally, the challenges for caregivers will be even more important for the research community to understand and to assess the differences that exist relative to levels of stress, coping, and manageability/mastery in the caregiving experience among racial groups but also within other sub-groups, like among women. As families become more diverse, spend more hours in the work force, and live with more chronic and debilitating illnesses, the possibility of experiencing stress pile-up within the family system may adversely affect how many families will be able to cope and achieve a sense of adaptation and resilience. Attempts to explore these contextual and cultural differences can advance the caregiving agenda to new heights, and provide the necessary support and tools to caregiving families, and inform policy makers of the impact caregiving has on families and offer relief and assistance to those who find themselves in this role by choice or by circumstance.

References

Aldwin, C. M. (1991). Does age affect the stress and coping process? Implications of age differences in perceived control. *Journals of Gerontology, 46,* P174–P180.

Affleck, G., Tennen, H., Croog, S., & Levine, S. (1987). Causal attribution, perceived health benefits, and morbidity after a heart attack: An 8-year study. *Journal of Consulting and Clinical Psychology, 55,* 29–35.

Amirkhanyan, A. A., & Wolf, D. A. (2003). Caregiver stress and noncaregiver stress: Exploring the pathways of psychiatric morbidity. *The Gerontologist, 43,* 817–827.

Andel, R., Hyer, K., & Slack, A. (2007). Risk factors for nursing home placement in older adults with dementia. *Journal of Aging and Health, 19(2),* 213–228.

Andrew, P. M., & Withey, S. B. (1976). *Social indicators of well-being.* New York: Plenum Press.

Aneshensel, C. S., Pearlin, L. I., Mullan, J. T., Zarit, S. H., & Whitlatch, C. J. (1995). *Profiles in caregiving: The unexpected career.* San Diego: Academic Press.

Antonovsky, A. (1979). *Health, stress, and coping.* San Francisco: Jossey-Bass.

Antonovsky, A. (1987). *Unraveling the mystery of health.* San Francisco: Jossey-Bass.

Archbold, P., Stewart, B., Greenlick, M., & Harvath, T. (1990). Mutuality and preparedness as predictors of caregiver role strain. *Research in Nursing and Health, 13,* 3775–384.

Arno, P. S. (2002, February 24). *Economic value of informal caregiving: 2000.* Presented at the American Association for Geriatric Psychiatry, Orlando, Fla. Available: http://www.thefamilycaregiver.org/pdfs/pa2000.ppt#1.

Arno, P. S., Levine, C., & Memmott, M. M. (1999). The Economic value of informal caregiving. *Health Affairs (Millwood), 18(2),* 182–188.

Atienza, A. A, Stephens, M. A., Townsend, A. L. (2002). Dispositional optimism, role-specific stress, and the well-being of adult daughter's caregivers. *Research on Aging, 24(2),* 193–217.

Barrow, S., & Harrison, R. A. (2005). Unsung heroes who put their lives at risk? Informal caring, health, and neighbourhood attachment. *Journal of Public Health, 27(3),* 292–297.

Barry, R. A., & Murphy, J. F. (1995). Well-being of caregivers of spouses with Parkinson's Disease. *Clinical Nursing Research, 4(4),* 373–386.

Baum, A., Fleming, I., & Singer, J. E. (1983). Coping with technological disaster. *Journal of Social Issues, 39,* 117–138.

Beach, S. R., & Schulz, R. (2000). Is caregiving a risk factor for mortality? *Geriatric Times, 1,* 26–27.

Belgrave, L. L., Allen-Kelsey, G, J., Smith, K. J., and & Flores, M. C. (2004). Living with dementia: Lay definitions of Alzheimer's disease among African American caregivers and sufferers." *Symbolic Interaction 27,* 199–222.

Berg-Weger, M., Rubio, D. M. & Tebb, S. S. (2000). Living with and caring for older family members: Issues related to caregiver well-being. *Journal of Gerontological Social Work, 33(2),* 47–62.

Berkman, B. (2005). *Handbook of social work in health and aging.* Oxford: New York.

Bertalanffy, L. (1968). *General system theory: Foundations, development, applications.* New York: Braziller.

Bertalanffy, L. (1975). *Perspectives on general systems theory: Scientific-philosophical studies.* New York: Braziller.

Bertrand, R. M., Fredman L., & Saczynski, J. (2006). Are all caregivers created Equal? Stress in caregivers of adults with and without dementia. *Journal of Aging and Health, 18,* 534–51.

Bookwala, J., & Schulz, R. (2000). A comparison of primary stressors, secondary stressors, and depressive symptoms between elderly caregiving husbands and wives: The caregiver health effects study. *Psychology and Aging, 15(4),* 607–616.

Bradburn, N. (1969). *The structure of psychological well-being.* Chicago: Adeline.

Braithwaite, V. (1996). Between stressors and outcomes: Can we simplify caregiving variables? *The Gerontologist, 36,* 42–53.

Braithwaite, V. (2000). Contextual or general stress outcomes: Making choices through caregiving appraisals. *The Gerontologist, 40(6),* 706–717.

Boaz, R. F., & Muller, C. F. (1991). Why do some caregivers of disabled and frail elderly quit? *Health Care Financing Review, 13(2),* 41–48.

Boss, P. (1988). *Family stress management: A contextual approach (1st ed.).* Thousand Oaks, CA: Sage.

Boss, P. (2002). *Family stress management: A contextual approach (2nd ed.).* Thousand Oaks, CA: Sage.

Burgener, S. C., & Chiverton, P. (1992). Conceptualizing psychological well-being in cognitively impaired older persons. *Journal of Nursing Scholarship, 24(3),* 209–213.

Burton, L. C., Zdaniuk, B., Schulz, R., Jackson, S., & Hirsh, C. (2003). Transitions in spousal caregiving. *The Gerontologist, 42(2),* 230–241.

Cantor, M. H. (1983). Strain among caregivers: A study of experience in the United States. *The Gerontologist, 31,* 246–255.

Center on an Aging Society. (2005). *How do family caregivers fare? A closer look at their experiences.* (Data Profile, Number 3). Washington, DC: Georgetown University.

Chappell, N. L., Reid, R. C. (2002). Burden and well-being among caregivers: Examining the distinction. *The Gerontologist, 42(6),* 772–780.

Chari, A. V., Engberg, J., Ray, K. N., & Mehrotra, A. (2015). The opportunity costs of informal elder-care in the United States: New estimates from the American time use survey. *Health Services Research, 50(3),* 871–882.

Chatters, L. M., Taylor, R. J., & Jackson, J. S. (1985). Size and composition of the informal helper networks of elderly blacks. *Journal of Gerontology, 40,* 605–614.

Chwalisz, K. (1996). The perceived stress model of caregiver burden: Evidence from spouses of persons with brain injuries. *Rehabilitation Psychology, 41(2),* 91–113.

Clipp, E. C., & George, L. K. (1990). Psychotropic drug use among caregivers of patients with dementia. *Journal of the American Geriatric Society, 38,* 227–235.

Clip, E. C., & Heorge, L. K. (1991). Patients with cancer and their spouse caregivers: Perceptions of the illness experience. Cancer, 69(4), 1074–1079.

Cohen, J., & Cohen, P. (1983). *Applied multiple regression /correlation for the behavioral sciences* (2nd ed.). Hillsdale, NJ: Erlbaum.

Colerick, E. J., & George, L. K. (1986). Predictors of institutionalization among caregivers of Alzheimer's patients. *Journal of American Geriatrics Society, 34,* 493–498.

Cook, J. A., Lefley, H. P., Pickett, S. A., & Cohler, B. J. (1994). Age and family burden among parents of offspring with severe mental illness. *American Journal of Orthopsychiatry, 64(3),* 435–447.

Cox, C. B. (2005). *Community care for an aging society: Issues, policies, and services.* Springer Publishing Company.

Covinsky, K. E., Newcomer, R., Dane, C. K., Sands, L. P., Yaffe, L. P., & Yaffe, K. (2003). Patient and caregiver characteristics association with depression in caregivers of patients with dementia. *Journal of General Internal Medicine, 18,* 1006–1014.

Crimmins, E. M. (2001). Americans living longer, not necessarily healthier lives. *Population Today.* February/March: 1, 8.

Deimling, G. T., Bass, D. M., Townsend, A. L. & Noelker, L. S. (1989). Care-related stress: A comparison of spouse and adult-child caregivers in shared and separate households. *Journal of Aging and Health, 1,* 67–82.

Diener, E. (1984). Subjective well-being. *Psychological Bulletin, 95(3),* 542–575.

Diener, E. Larsen, R. J., & Griffin, S. (1985). The satisfaction with life scale. *Journal of Personality Assessment, 49(1),* 71–75.

Diener, E., & Diener, C. (1996). Most people are happy. *Psychological Science, 7(3),* 181–185.

Diener, E., Suh, E. M., Lucas, R. E., Smith, H. L. (1999). Subjective well-being: Three decades progress. *Psychological Bulletin, 125(2),* 276–302.

Diener, E., Oishi, S., & Lucas, R. (2003). Personality, culture, and subjective well-being: Emotional and cognitive evaluations of life. *Annual Review of Psychology, 54,* 403–425.

Dilworth-Anderson, P., Williams, S. W., & Cooper, T. (1999). The contexts of experiencing emotional distress among family caregivers to elderly African Americans. *Family Relations, 48,* 391–396.

Dilworth-Anderson, P., Williams, S. W., & Gibson, B. E. (2002). Issues of race, ethnicity, and culture in caregiving research: A 20 year review (1980–2000). *The Gerontologist, 42,* 237–272.

Donelan, K., Hill, C. A., Hoffman, C., Scoles, K., Feldman, P. H., Levine, C., & Gould, D. (2002). Challenged to care: informal caregivers in a changing health system. *Health Affairs. 21(4):* 222–31.

Doty, P. (1986). Family care of the elderly: the role of public policy. *Milbank Memorial Fund Quarterly, 64,* 34–75.

Draper, B. M., Poulos, R., Poulos, C. J., & Ehrlich, F. (1995). Risk factors for stress in elderly caregivers. *International Journal of Geriatric Psychiatry, 11,* 227–231.

Farran, C. J., Miller, B. H., Kaufman, J. E., & Davis, L. (1997). Race, finding meaning, and care distress, *Journal of Aging and Health, 9(3),* 316–333.

Farran, C. J., Miller, B. H., Kaufman, J. E., Donner, E., & Fogg, L. (1999). Finding meaning through caregiving: Development of an instrument for family caregivers of persons with Alzheimer's Disease. *Journal of Clinical Psychology, 55(9),* 1107–1125.

Foley, K. L., Tung, H. J., & Mutran, E. J. (2002). Self-gain and self-loss among African American and white caregivers. *Journals of Gerontology: Social Sciences, 57,* S14–S22.

Folkman, S. & Greer, S. (2000). Promoting psychological well-being in the face of serious illness: When theory, research, and practice inform each other. Psycho-Oncology, 9, 11–19.

Folkman, S., & Lazarus, R. S. (1980). An analysis of coping in a middle-aged community sample. *Journal of Health and Social Behavior, 21,* 219–239.

Folkman, S., Lazarus, R. S., Dunkel-Schetter, C., DeLongis, A., & Gruen, R. (1986). The dynamics of a stressful encounter: Cognitive appraisal, coping, and encounter outcomes. *Journal of Personality and Social Psychology, 50,* 992–1003.

Folkman, S. & Moskowitz, J. T. (2000). Positive affect and the other side of coping. *American Psychologist, 55,* 647–654.

Franks, M. M., & Stephens, M. A. P. (1996). Social support in the context of caregiving: Husband's provision of support to wives involved in parent care. *Journals of Gerontology Psychological Sciences and Social Sciences, 51,* 43–52.

Frederickson, B. L. (2001). The role of positive emotions in positive psychology. *American Psychologist, 56(3),* 218–226.

Frederickson, B. L. (2003). The value of positive emotions: The emerging science of positive psychology is coming to understand why it's good to feel good. *American Scientist, 91(4),* 330–336.

Gallagher-Thompson, D. (2006). Mental and physical caregiving issues: Covering the spectrum from detection to end of life. *American Journal of Geriatric Psychiatry, 14(8),* 635–641.

George, L. K. (1987). Easing caregiver burden. The role informal and formal supports. In R. A. Ward & S. S. Tobin (Eds.), *Health in aging: Sociological issues and policy direction* (pp. 133–158). New York: Springer.

George, L. K., Blazer, D. G., Winfield-Laird, I., Leaf, P. J., Fischbach, R. L. (1988). Psychiatric disorders and mental health service use in later life. In J. A. Brody & G. L. Maddox (Eds.), *Epidemiology and aging* (pp. 189–221). New York: Springer.

George, L. K., & Gwyther, L. P. (1988). Support groups for caregivers of memory-impaired elderly: Easing caregiver burden. In L. A. Bond & B. M. Wagner (Eds.), *Families in transition: Primary prevention programs that work* (pp. 309–331). Beverley Hills, CA: Sage.

George, L. L., & Gwyther, L. P. (1986). Caregiver well-being: A multidimensional examination of family care-givers of demented adults. *Gerontologist, 26 3,* 253–259.

Gilliam, C. & Steffen, A. M. (2006). The relationship between caregiving self-efficacy and depressed mood in dementia family caregivers. *The Journal of Aging and Mental Health, 10,* 79–86.

Gilligan, C. (1993). *In a different voice: Psychological theory and women's development.* Cambridge, MA: Harvard University Press.

Given, C., Given, B., Strommel, M. Collins, C., King, S., & Franklin, S. (1992). The caregiver reaction assessment (CRA) for caregivers to persons with chronic physical and mental impairments. *Research in Nursing and Health, 15,* 271–283.

Goodman, C. R., Zarit, S. H., & Steiner, V. L. (1997). Personal orientation as a predictor of caregiver strain. *Aging and Mental Health, 1(2),* 149–157.

Greenberg, J. S., Greenley, J., McKee, D., Brown, R., & Griffin-Francell, C. (1993). Mothers caring for an adult child with schizophrenia: The effects of subjective burden on maternal health. *Family Relations, 42,* 205–211.

Greenberg, J., Seltzer, M., & Brewer, E. (2006). Caregivers to older adults. In B. Berkman & S. Ambruso (Eds.), *Handbook of social work in health and aging.* Oxford University Press: New York.

Haley, W. E. (2003). The costs of family caregiving: Implications for geriatric oncology. *Critical Reviews in Oncology/Hematology, 48,* 151–158.

Haley, W. E., LaMonde, L. A. Han, B., Narramore, S., & Schonmwetter, R. (2001). Family caregiving in hospice: Effects on psychological and heal functioning among spousal caregivers of hospice patients with lung cancer or dementia. *Hospital Journal, 15,* 1–18.

Harris, M., Flegal, K., Cowie, C., Eberhardt, M., Goldstein, D., Little, R., Weidmeyer, & Holt. (1998). Prevalence of diabetes impaired fasting glucose, and impaired glucose tolerance in U.S. adults: The third national health and nutrition survey, 1988–1999. *Diabetes Care, 21,* 518–524.

Harvey, K. & Burns, T. (2003). Relatives of patients with severe mental disorders: Unique traits and experiences of primary, nonprimary, and lone caregivers. *American Journal of Orthopsychiatry, 73(3),* 324–333.

Heller, T., Caldwell, J., & Factor, A. (2007). Aging and family caregivers: Policies and practices. *Mental Retardation and Developmental Disabilities Research Reviews, 13,* 136–142.

Hill, R. (1949). *Families under stress: Adjustment to the crises of war separation and reunion.* New York: Harper and Row.

Hill, R. (1958). Generic features of families under stress. *Social Casework, 49,* 139–150.

Hill, R., & Rodgers, R. H. (1964). The developmental approach. In H. Christensen (Ed.) *Handbook of marriage and the family.* Chicago: Rand McNally.

Hobson, P., & Meara, J. R. (1999). The detection of dementia and cognitive impairment in a community population of elderly people with Parkinson's disease by use of the CAMCOG neuropsychological test. *Age and Ageing, 28(1),* 39–43.

Hoffmann, R. L. & Mitchell, A. M. (1998). Caregiver burden: historical development. *Nursing Forum, 33(4),* 5–11.

Holahan, C. J., & Moos, R. H. (1991). Life stressors, personal and social resources, and depression: A 4-year structural model. *Journal of Abnormal Psychology, 100,* 337–348.

Holahan, C. J, Moos, R. H., & Schaefer, J. A. (1996). Coping, stress, resistance, and growth: Conceptualizing adaptive functioning. In M. Zeidner & N. S. Endler (Eds.), *Handbook of coping* (pp. 24–43). New York: Wiley.

Hooker, K., Bowman, S. R., Coehlo, D. P., Lim, S. R., Kaye, J., Guarglia, R., & Li, F. (2002). Behavioral change in persons with dementia: Relationships with mental and physical health of caregivers. *Journal of Gerontology: Psychological Sciences, 57B, 5,* P453-P460.

Horowitz, A. (1985). Family caregiving to the frail elderly, In C. Eisdorfer, M. P. Lawton, & G. L. Maddox (Eds.), Annual review of gerontology and geriatrics, 3. New York: Springer.

Hoyt, D. R., O'Donnell, D., & Mack, K. Y. (1995). Psychological distress and size of place: The epidemiology of rural economic stress. *Rural Sociology, 60,* 707–720.

Hunt, C. K. (2003). Concepts in caregiver research. *Journal of Nursing Scholarship, 35(1),* 27–32.

Ingersoll-Dayton, B., & Raschick, M. (2004). The relationship between care-recipient behaviors and spousal caregiving stress. *The Gerontologist, 44(3),* 318–327.

Jang, Y., Haley, W. E., Small, B. J., & Mortimer, J. A. (2002). The role of mastery and social resources in the associations between disability and depression in later life. *The Gerontologist, 42(6),* 807–813.

Jones, S. (1996). The association between objective and subjective caregiver burden. *Archives of Psychiatric Nursing, 10(2),* 77–84.

Kaplan, L., & Boss, P. (1999). Depressive symptoms among spousal caregivers of institutionalized mates with Alzheimer's: Boundary ambiguity and mastery as predictors. *Family Process, 38,* 85–103.

Kanwar, A., Singh, M., Lennon, R., Ganta, K., McNallan, S., & Roger, V. L. (2013). Frailty and health-related quality of life among residents of long-term care facilities. *Journal of Aging and Health, 25(5),* 792–802.

Kinney, J., & Stephens, M. (1989). Hassles and uplifts of giving care to a family member with dementia. *Psychology and Aging, 4,* 402–408.

Kinney, J., Stephens, M., Franks, M., & Norris, V. (1995). Stresses and satisfaction of family caregivers to older stroke patients. *Journal of Applied Gerontology, 14(1),* 3–21.

Knight, B. G., Silverstein, M., McCallum, T. J., & Fox, L. S. (2000). A sociocultural stress and coping model for mental health outcomes among African American caregivers in southern California. *Journal of Gerontology: Psychological Sciences, 55B,* P142–P150.

Kosberg, J. I., & Cairl, R. (1986). The cost of care index: A case management tool for screening informal caregivers. *Gerontologist, 26,* 273–278.

Kramer, B. J. (1993). Expanding the conceptualization of caregiver coping: The importance of relationship-focused coping strategies. *Family Relations, 42,* 367–375.

Kramer, B. J. (1997). Gain in the caregiving experience: Where are we? What next? *The Gerontologist, 37,* 218–232.

Krause, N. (2004). Stressors arising in highly valued roles, meaning in life, and the physical health status of older adults. *Journals of Gerontology. Series B, Psychological Sciences and Social Sciences,* 59B, S287-S297.

Langa, K. M., Vijan, S., Hayward, R. A., Chernew, M. E., Blaum, C. S., Kabeto, M. U., Weir, D. R., Katz, S. J., Willis, R. J., & Fendrick, A. M. (2002). Informal caregiving for diabetes and diabetic complications among elderly Americans. *Journal of Gerontology: Social Sciences, 57B, (3),* S177–S186.

Lawton, M. P. (1983). Environment and other determinants of well-being in older people. *The Gerontologist, 23,* 349–356.

Lawton, P. M., Moss, M., Kleban, M. H., Glicksman, A., & Rovine, M. (1991). Two-factor model of caregiving appraisal and psychological well-being. *Journal of Gerontology Psychological Sciences, 46,* P181–P189.

Lawton, M. P., Rajagopal, D., Brody, E., & Kleban, M. H. (1992). The dynamics of caregiving for a demented elder among black and white families. *Journal of Gerontology: Social Sciences, 47,* S156–S164.

Lavee, Y., McCubbin, H. I., & Olson, D. H. (1987). The effects of stressful life events and transitions on family functioning and well-being. *Journal of Marriage and the Family, 49,* 857–873.

Lazarus, R. S., & Folkman, S. (1984). *Stress, appraisal, and coping.* New York: Springer.

Lee, S. L., Colditz, G. A., Berkman, L. F. & Kawachi, I. (2003). Caregiving and risk of coronary heart disease in U.S. women: A prospective study. *American Journal of Preventive Medicine, 24 (2),* 113–119.

Li, L., Seltzer, M. M., & Greenberg, J. S. (1997). Social support and depressive symptoms: Differential patterns in wife and daughter caregivers. *Journals of Gerontology: Psychological and Social Sciences, 52B,* S200–S233.

Lipman, A., & Longino, C. F. (1982). Formal and informal support: A conceptual clarification. *Journal of Applied Gerontology, 1(1),* 141–146.

Lloyd, J., Patterson, T., & Muers, J. (2014). The positive aspects of caregiving in dementia: critical review of the qualitative literature. *Dementia, 15(6),* 1534–1561.

Luthar, S. S., & Ziegler, E. (1991). Vulnerability and competence: A review of research on resilience in childhood. *American Journal of Orthopsychiatry, 61,* 6–22.

Luthar, S. S., Cicchetti, D., & Becker, B. (2000). The construct of resilience: A critical evaluation and guidelines for future work. *Child Development, 71,* 543–562.

Lyons, K. S., Zarit, S. H., Sayer, A. G. & Whitlatch, C. J. (2002). Caregiving as a dyadic process: Perspectives from caregiver a nd care receiver. *The Journals of Gerontology Series B: Psychological Sciences and Social Sciences* 57: P195–P204.

Maurin, J., & Boyd, C. (1990). Burden and mental illness on the family: A critical review. *Archives of Psychiatric Nursing, 4(2),* 99–107.

Marks, N., Lambert, J. D., & Choi, H. (2002). Transitions to caregiving, gender, and psychological well-being: A prospective U.S. national study. *Journal of Marriage and Family, 64,* 657–667.

Manton, K., Corder, L., Stallard, E. (1997). Chronic disability trends in elderly United States populations: 1982–1994. *Proceedings of the National Academy of Sciences, 94,* 2593–2598.

Manton, K., & Gu, X. (2001). Changes in prevalence of chronic disability in the United States Black and non-Black populations above 65 from 1982 to 1999. *Proceedings of the National Academy of Sciences, 98,* 6354–6359.

McBride, A. B. (1990). Mental health effects of women's multiple roles. *American Psychologist, 45,* 381–384.

McCrae, R. R., & Costa, P. T., Jr. (1986). Personality, coping, and coping effectiveness in an adult sample. *Journal of Personality, 54,* 385–405.

McCubbin, H. I. (1998). African American military families: Military families in foreign environments. In H. I. McCubbin, E. A. Thompson, A. I. Thompson, & J. A. Futrell (Eds.) *Resiliency in African American families (pp. 67–97).* Thousand Oaks, CA: Sage.

McCubbin, H. I., & Boss, P. (1980). Family stress and adaptation. *Family Relations, 29,* 454–459.

McCubbin, M. A. & McCubbin, H. I. (1989). Theoretical orientations to family stress and coping. In C. R. Figley (Ed.), *Treating stress in families (pp. 3–43).* New York: Brunner-Mazel.

McCubbin, H. I., & Patterson, J. M. (1982). Family adaptation to crisis. In H. I. McCubbin. A Cauble, & J. Patterson (Eds.), *Family stress, coping, and social support* (pp. 26–47). Springfield, IL: Charles C. Thomas Publishers.

McCubbin, H. I. & Patterson, J. M. (1983). The family stress process: The double ABC-X model of adjustment and adaptation. In M. Sussman, H. I. McCubbin, & J. M. Patterson (Eds.), Social stress and the family: Advances and developments in family stress theory and research. *Marriage and Family Review, Vol 6.* New York: Hawthorne.

McFall, S. & Miller, B. H. (1992). Caregiver burden and nursing home admission of frail elderly persons. *Journal of Applied Gerontology, 47,* S73–S79.

Montgomery, R. J. V. (1999). The family role in the context of long-term care. *Journal of Aging and Health, 11(3),* 383–416.

Montgomery, R. J. V., Gonyea, J. C., & Hooyman, N. R. (1985). Caregiving and the experience of subjective and objective burden. *Family Relations, 34,* 19–26.

Montgomery, R. J. V., Kosloski, K. (1994). A longitudinal analysis of nursing home placement for dependent elders cared for by spouses vs. adult children. *Journal of Gerontology: Social Sciences, 49,* S62–74.

Mui, A. (1995). Multidimensional predictors of caregiver strain among older persons caring for frail spouses. *Journal of Marriage and the Family, 57,* 733–740.

National Academy on an Aging Society. (2000). *Caregiving: Helping the elderly with activity limitations.* (Data Profile, Number 7). Washington, DC.

National Alliance for Caregiving and the American Association of Retired Persons. (1997). *Family caregiving in the U.S.: Findings from a National Survey*. Bethesda, MD.

National Alliance for Caregiving and AARP. (2003). Poll # 2003-CARE: *Caregivers in the U.S.* USAARP2003-CARE. Roper Center for Public Opinion Research. Storrs, CT: The Roper Center, University of Connecticut.

National Alliance for Caregiving and the American Association of Retired Persons. (2004). *Family caregiving in the U.S.: Findings from a national survey*. Bethesda, MD.

National Alliance for Caregiving and AARP. (2009). *Caregiving in the U.S.* Retrieved from http://www .caregiving.org/data/Caregiving_in_the_US_2009_full_report.pdf

National Alliance for Caregiving and AARP. (2015). *Caregiving in the U.S.* Retrieved from https://www .caregiving.org/wp-content/uploads/2015/05/2015_CaregivingintheUS_Final-Report-June-4_WEB.pdf

Navaie-Waliser, M., Feldman, P. H., Gould, D. A., Levine, C., Kuerbis, A. N., & Donelan, K. (2001). The experiences and challenges of informal caregivers: Common themes and differences among Whites, Blacks, and Hispanics. *The Gerontologist, 41,* 733–741.

Nijboer, C., Triemstra, M., Tempelaar, M. M., Sanderman, R., & Van den Bos, G. A. M. (2000). Patterns of caregiving experiences among partners of cancer patients. *The Gerontologist, 40(6),* 738–746.

Noekler, L. S., & Bass, D. N. (1989). Home care for elderly persons: Linkages between formal and informal caregivers. *Journal of Gerontology: Social Sciences, 44,* S63–S70.

Nolen-Hoeksema, S., & Larson, J. (1999). *Coping with loss*. Mahwah, NJ: Erlbaum.

Noonan, A. E. & Tennstedt, S. L. (1997). Meaning in caregiving and its contribution to caregiver well-being? *The Gerontologist, 37,* 785–794.

Nuboer, C., Tempelaar, R., Sanderman, R., Triemstra, M., Spruijt, R. J., & Van den Bos, G. A. M. (1998). Cancer and caregiving: The impact on the caregiver's health. *Psycho-Oncology, 7,* 3–13.

Olsen, D. H. (1993). Circumplex model of marital and family systems. In F. Walsh (Ed.), *Normal Family Process*. (*2nd Ed.*). New York: Guilford Press.

Olson, D. H., Stewart, K. L. and Wilson, L. R., (1992). *Coping and stress profile*. Minneapolis: Life Innovations.

Ory, M. R., Hoffman, R., Yee, J., Tennstedt, S., & Schulz, R. (1999). Prevalence and impact of caregiving: A detailed comparison between dementia and nondementia caregivers. *The Gerontologist, 39,* 177–183.

Patterson, J. M. (1993). The role of family meanings in adaptation to chronic illness and disability, In A. Turnbull, J. Patterson, S. Behr, et al. (Eds.), *Cognitive coping research and developmental disabilities* (pp. 221–238). Baltimore: Brookes.

Patterson, J. M. (2002). Integrating family resilience and family stress theory. *Journal of Marriage and Family, 64,* 349–360.

Patrick, J. H., & Hayden, J. M. (1999). Neuroticism, coping strategies, and negative well-being among caregivers. *Psychology and Aging, 14,* 273–283.

Parker, J. D. A., & Endler, N. S. (1996). Coping and defense: A historical overview. In M. Zeidner & N. S. Endler (Eds.), *Handbook of coping* (pp. 3–23). New York: Wiley.

Parks, A. H., & Pilisuk, M. (1991). Caregiver burden: Gender and psychological costs of caregiving. *American Journal of Orthopsychiatry, 61,* 501–509.

Pargament, K. I. (1997). *The psychology of religion and coping*. New York: Guilford Press. Pearlin, L. I., Menagham, E. G., Lieberman, M. A., Mullam, J. T., (1981). The stress process. *Journal of Health and Social Behavior, 22,* 337–356.

Pearlin, L. I., Mullan, J. T., Semple, S. J., & Skaff, M. M. (1990). Caregiving and the stress process: An overview of concepts and their measures. *The Gerontologist, 30,* 583–594.

Pearlin, L. I., Nguyen, K. B., Schieman, S., & Milkie, M. A. (2007). The life-course origins of mastery among people. *Journal of Health and Social Behavior, 48(6),* 164–179.

Pearlin, L. I., & Schooler, C. (1978). The structure of coping. *Journal of Health and Social Behavior, 19,* 2–21.

Pierce, G. R., Sarason, I. G., & Sarason, B. R. (1996). Coping and social support. In M. Zeidner & N. S. Endler (Eds.), *Handbook of coping* (pp. 3–23). New York: Wiley.

Piercy, K. (2007). Charactersitcs of strong commitments to intergenerational family care of older adults. *Journal of Gerontology: Social Sciences, 62B, (6),* S381–S387.

Pinquart, M., & Sorensen, S. (2003). Differences between caregivers and noncaregivers in psychological health and physical health: A meta-analysis. *Psychology and Aging, 18(2),* 250–267.

Pinquart, M. & Sorensen, S. (2006). Gender differences in caregiver stressors, social resources, and health: An updated meta-analysis. *Journal of Gerontology: Psychological Sciences, 61B, (1),* P33–P45.

Poulshock S., & Deimling, G. (1984). Families caring for elders in residence. *Journal of Gerontology, 39,* 230–39.

Pratt, C., Schmall, V., Wright, S., & Cleland, M., (1985). Burden and coping strategies of caregivers to Alzheimer's patients. *Family Relations, 34,* 27–33.

Pruchno, R. A., Burant, C. J., & Peters, N. D. (1997). Typologies of caregiving families: Family congruence and family well-being. *The Gerontologist, 37(2),* 157–167.

Pruchno, R. A., & Kleban, M. H. (1993). Mothers and fathers of adults with chronic disabilities: Caregivng appraisals and well-being. *Research on Aging, 23,* 682–713.

Pruchno, R. A., Resch, N. L. (1989). Husband and wives as caregivers: Antecedents of depression and burden. *The Gerontologist, 29,* 159–165.

Radina, M. E. (2007). Mexican America siblings caring for aging parents: Processes of caregiving selection/designation. *Journal of Comparative Family Studies, 38,* 143–168.

Reinhard, S. C., Feinberg, L. F., Choula, R., & Huser, A. (2015). Valuing the invaluable: 2015 update. AARP Public Policy Institute. Retrieved from https://www.aarp.org/content/dam/aarp/ppi/2015/valuing-the-invaluable-2015-update-new.pdf

Robinson, J., Moen, P., & Dempster-McClain, D. (1995). Women's caregiving: Changing profiles and pathways. *Journals of Gerontology: Social Sciences, 50,* S362–S373.

Rose, J. H., Bowman, K. F., O'Toole, E. E., Abbott, H. K., Love, T. E., Thomas, C., & Dawson, N. V. (2007). Caregiver objective burden and assessments of patient-centered, family focused care for frail elderly veterans. *The Gerontologist, 47(1),* 21–33.

Roth, D. L., Dilworth-Anderso, P., Huang, J., Gross, A. L., & Gitlin, L. N. (2015). Positive aspects of family caregiving for dementia: Differential item functioning by race. *Journals of Gerontology: Psychological Sciences, 70(6),* 813–819.

Rutter, M. (1987). Psychosocial resilience and protective mechanisms. *American Journal of Orthopsychiatry, 57,* 316–331.

Ryff, C. D. (1989). Happiness is everything, or is it? Explorations on the meaning of psychological well-being. *Journal of Personality and Social Psychology, 57(6),* 1069–1081.

Ryff, C. D., & Keyes, C. L. M. (1995). The structure of psychological well-being revisited. *Journal of Personality and Social Psychology, 69(4),* 719–727.

Sales, E. (2003). Family burden and quality of life. *Quality of Life Research, 12,* (Suppl. 1), 33–41.

Schaefer, S., & Coleman, E. (1992). Shifts in meaning, purpose, and values following a diagnosis of human immunodeficiency virus (HIV) infection among gay men. *Journal of Psychology and Human Sexuality, 5,* 13–129.

Schene, A., Tessler, R., & Gamache, G. (1994). Instruments measuring family or caregiver burden in severe mental illness. *Social Psychiatry and Psychiatric Epidemiology, 29,* 228–240.

Schulz, R., Newsom, J., Mittelmark, M., Burton, L., Hirsch, C., & Jackson, S. (1997). Health effects of caregiving: The caregiver health effects study: An ancillary study of the cardiovascular health study. *Annals of Behavioral Medicine, 19,* 110–116.

Schulz, R., O'Brien, A. T., Bookwals, J. & Fleissner, K. (1995). Psychiatric and physical morbidity effects of dementia caregiving: Prevalence, correlates, and causes. *The Gerontologist, 35,* 771–791.

Schumacher, K. L., Stewart, B. J., & Archbold, P. G. (1998). Conceptualization and measurement of doing family caregiving well. *Journal of Nursing Scholarship, 30, 1,* 63–69.

Segall, M., & Wykle, M. (1988). The black family's experience with dementia. *Journal of Applied Social Sciences, 13,* 170–191.

Seltzer, M. M., Greenberg, J. S., & Krauss, M. W. (1995). A comparison of coping strategies of aging mothers of adults with mental illness or mental retardation. *Psychology and Aging, 10,* 64–75.

Selye, H. (1956). *The Stress of life.* New York: McGraw-Hill.

Siegal, K., Raveis, V. H., Houts, P., & Mor, V. (1991). Caregiver burden and unmet patient care needs. *Cancer, 68,* 1131–1140.

Silverstein, M., Parrott, T. M., & Bengtson, V. L. (1995). Factors that predispose middle-aged sons and daughters to provide social support to older parents. *Journal of Marriage and the Family, 57,* 465–475.

Skaff, M. M., Pearlin, L. I., & Mullan, J. T. (1996). Transitions in the caregiving career: effects of sense of mastery. *Psychology and Aging, 11(2),* 247–257.

Slaughter, J. R., Slaughter, K. A., Nichols, K. A., Holmes, S. E., & Martens, M. P. (2001). Prevalence, clinical manifestations, etiology, and treatment of depression in Parkinson's disease. *Journal of Neuropsychiatry and Clinical Neuroscience, 13(2),* 187–196.

Sleath, B., Thorpe, J., Landerman, L., Doyle, M., & Clipp, E. (2005). African American and white caregivers of older adults with dementia: Differences in depressive symptomatology and psychotropic drug use. *Journal of the American Geriatrics Society, 53,* 397–404.

Smerglia, V. L. & Deimling, G. T. (1997). Care-related decision-making satisfaction and caregiver well-being in families caring for older members. *The Gerontologist, 37(5),* 658–665.

Southwick, S. M., Vythilingam, M., & Charney, D. S. (2005). The psychobiology of depression and resilience to stress: Implications for prevention and treatment. *Annual Review of Clinical Psychology, 1,* 255–291.

Spector, J., & Tampi, R. (2005). Caregiver depression. *Annals of Long-Term Care: Clinical Care and Aging, 13(4),* 34–40.

Spector, W. D., Fleishman, J. A., Pezzin, L. E., & Spillman, B. C. (2000). *The characteristics of long-term care users.* Paper commissioned by the Institute of Medicine Committee on Improving Quality in Long-Term Care, published by Agency for Healthcare Research and Quality, AHRQ Pub. No. 00–0049.

Spillman, B., & Black. (2005). *The size of the long-term care population in residential care: A review of estimates and methodology.* Washington, DC: U.S. DHHS, Assistant Secretary for Planning and Evaluation.

Spillman, B. C., & Pezzin, L. E. (2000). Potential and active family caregivers: Changing networks and the sandwich generation. *The Milbank Quarterly, 78(3),* 347– 374.

Stein, C. H., Wemmerus, V. A., Ward, M., Gaines, M. E., Freeberg, A. L. & Jewell, T. C. (1998). Because they're my parents: An intergenerational study of felt obligation and parental caregiving. *Journal of Marriage and the Family, 60,* 611–622.

Stone, R., Cafferata, G. L., & Sangl, J. (1987). Caregivers of the frail and elderly: A national profile. *The Gerontologist, 27,* 677–683.

Strawbridge, W. J., Wallhagen, M. I., Shema, S. J., & Kaplan, G. A. (1997). New burdens or more of the same? Comparing grandparent, spouse, and adult-child caregivers. *The Gerontologist, 37,* 505–510.

Stull, D. E., Kosloksi, K., & Kercher, K. (1994). Caregiver burden and generic well-being: opposite sides of the same coin? *Gerontologist, 34,* 88–94.

Tennstedt, S. L., Cafferata, G. L. & Sullivan, L. (1992). Depression among caregivers of impaired elders. *Journal of Aging and Health, 4,* 58–76.

Tennstedt, S. L., McKinlay, J. B., & Sullivan, L. M. (1989). Informal care for frail elders: The role of secondary caregivers. *The Gerontologist, 29,* 677–683.

Teschendorf, B., Schwartz, C., Ferrans, C. E., O'Mara, A., Novotny, P., & Sloan, J. (2007). Caregiver role stress: When families become providers. *Cancer Control, 14(2),* 183–189.

Thoits, P. A. (1995). Stress, coping, and social processes: Where are we? What next? *Journal of Health and Social Behavior,* (Extra Issue), 53–79.

Townsend, A. L., & Franks, M. M. (1997). Quality of the relationship between elderly spouse caregivers' subjective effectiveness. *Family Relations, 46,* 33–39.

Tugade, M. M., & Frederickson, B. L. (2004). Resilient individual use positive emotions to bounce back from negative experiences. *Journal of Personality and Social Psychology, 86(2),* 320–333.

U.S. Census Bureau. (2000). *Statistical Abstract of the United States, 120*th *ed*. Washington, DC: Government Printing Office. www.census.gov/stat_abstract.

Vaux, A., & Wood, J. (1987). Social support resources, behaviors, and appraisals: A path analysis. *Social Behavior and Personality: An International Journal, 15,* 107–111.

Viner, R. (1999). Putting stress in life: Hans Selye and the making of stress theory. *Social Studies of Science, 29,* 391–410.

Vitaliano, P., Zhang, J., & Scanlon, J. (2003). Is caregiving hazardous to one's physical health? A meta-analysis. *Psychological Bulletin, 129(60),* 946–972.

Walsh, F. (1996). The concept of family resilience: Crisis and challenge. *Family Process, 35,* 261–281.

Walsh, F. (1998). *Strengthening family resilience.* New York: Guilford Press.

Walsh, F. (2002). A family resilience framework: Innovative practice and applications. *Family Relations, 51,* 130–137.

Walsh, F. (2003). Family resilience: Framework for clinical practice. *Family Process, 42(1),* 1–18.

Walker, A. J., Pratt., C. C., & Eddy, L. (1995). Informal caregiving to aging family members: A critical review. *Family Relations, 44,* 402, 411.

Whitchurch, G. G., & Constantine, L. L. (1993). Systems theory. In P. G. Boss, W. J. Doherty, R. LaRossa, W. R. Schumm, & S. K. Steinmetz (Eds.), *Sourcebook of family theories and methods: A contextual approach (pp. 325–352).* New York: Plenum.

White, T. M., Townsend, A. L., & Stephens, M. A. (2000). Comparisons of African American and white women in the parent care role. *The Gerontologist, 40,* 718–728.

Whitlatch, C. J., Feinberg, L. F., & Stevens, E. J. (1999). Predictors of institutionalization for persons with Alzheimer's disease and the impact on family caregivers. *Journal of Mental Health and Aging, 5(3),* 275–288.

Wolff, J. L., & Kasper, J. D. (2006). Caregivers of frail elders: Updating a national profile. *The Gerontologist 46,* 344–356

Wood, J. B., & Parham, I. A. (1990). Coping with perceived burden: Ethnic and cultural issues in Alzheimer's family caregiving. *Journal of Applied Gerontology, 9(3),* 325–339.

Wright, S. C., Lund, D. A., Caserta, M. S., & Pratt, C. (1991). Coping and caregiver well-being: The impact of maladaptive strategies. *Journal of Gerontological Social Work, 17, (1/2),* 75–91.

Yates, M. E. Tennstedt, S., Chang, B. H. (1999). Contributors to and mediators of psychological well-being for informal caregivers. *Journal of Gerontology: Psychological Sciences, 54B,* P12–P22.

Yee, J. L. & Schulz, R. (2000). Gender differences in psychiatric morbidity among family caregivers: A review and analysis. *The Gerontologist, 40,* 147–164.

Zarit, S., Reever, K., & Bach-Peterson, J. (1980). Relatives of the impaired elderly: Correlates of feelings of burden. *The Gerontologist, 20,* 649–655.

Zarit, S. H., Todd, P. A. & Zarit, J. M. (1986). Subjective burden of husbands and wives as caregivers: A longitudinal study. *The Gerontologist, 26,* 260–266.

Zarit, S. H., Birkel, R. C., Beach, M. E. (1989). Spouses as caregivers: Stresses and interventions. In M. Z. Goldstein (Ed.), *Family involvement in the treatment of frail elderly* (pp. 23–62). Washington, DC: American Psychiatric Association.

Zarit, S. H., Stephens, M. A., Townsend, A., & Greene, R. (1998). Stress reduction for family caregivers: effects of adult day care. *Journal of Gerontology Series B: Psychological Sciences and Social Sciences, 53(5),* S267–S277.

CHAPTER 13

The Relation Between Multiple Informal Caregiving Roles and Subjective Physical and Mental Health Status Among Older Adults: Do Racial/Ethnic Differences Exist?

Giyeon Kim, PhD,[1,*] *Rebecca S. Allen, PhD,*[2,3] *Sylvia Y,. Wang, MA,*[3] *Soohyun Park, MA,*[3] *Elizabeth A. Perkins, PhD, RNLD, FAAIDD,*[4] *and Patricia Parmelee, PhD*[2,3]

Providing care for family or friends, although sometimes rewarding, is generally demanding. According to a recent report on caregiving (National Alliance for Caregiving, 2015), 43.5 million U.S. adults (18.2%) provided care for family or friends in the past year. The cost of informal care-giving in the United States was estimated to be $522 billion a year (Chari, et al., 2015). While providing care for one person is the most common type of caregiving, recent statistics show that about 18% of caregivers provided care for two or more persons (National Alliance for Caregiving, 2015). Hereafter, we call these individuals "caregivers with multiple caregiving roles" which is our main focus in the present study.

The impact of caregiving can be wide ranging. Caregiving can affect a caregiver's career, finances, relationships, physical and mental health, and general well-being. Whereas a number of previous studies reported health risks of care provision (Chang, Chiou, & Chen, 2010; Pin quart & Sörensen,

* Address correspondence to Giyeon Kim, PhD, Department of Psychology, Chung-Ang University, 84 Heukseok-ro, Dongjak-Gu, Seoul 06974, South Korea. E-mail: gkim@cau.ac.kr
[1] Department of Psychology, Chung-Ang University, Seoul, South Korea.
[2] Alabama Research Institute on Aging, The University of Alabama, Tuscaloosa.
[3] Department of Psychology, The University of Alabama, Tuscaloosa.
[4] Department of Child and Family Studies, University of South Florida, Tampa.

2003; Schulz & Beach, 1999), others reported positive influences of caregiving such as perceived benefits, better well-being, and even decreased mortality risk (Brown et al., 2009; Capistrant, 2016; Coon et al., 2004; Lee & Bronstein, 2010; Roth et al, 2013; Roth, Fredman, & Haley, 2015). More specifically, die impact of caregiving on health outcomes can be summarized as follows. First, with regard to physical health outcomes, Pinquart and Sorensen (2003) found in their meta-analytic study integrating 84 published articles that caregivers tended to have poorer physical health than noncaregivers, showing a very small effect size in population-based samples, Second, with regard to mental health, the same meta-analysis revealed that caregivers have a tendency to be more stressed and depressed compared with noncaregivers. However, the reported effect sizes were much smaller in population- based samples than in convenience samples (Pinquart & Sorensen, 2003). Third, with regard to the caregiver-mortality link, while one study showed higher mortality in caregivers (Schulz &C Beach, 1999), recent reviews based on population-based studies (Capistrant, 2016; Roth et al., 2015) reported that caregiving is associated with reduced mortality rates compared with noncaregivers.

While limited, previous research reported unique challenges faced by caregivers providing care for more than one care recipient (e.g., Bailey et al., 2010; DePasquale et al., 2016; Perkins, 2010; Scott, Hwang, & Rogers, 2006). Caregivers with multiple caregiving roles have competing caregiving demands and often experience reduced social network/support and stress resilience; this in turn may be associated with negative mental and physical health outcomes (Bailey et al., 2010; DePasquale et al., 2016; Perkins, 2010; Scott et al., 2006). In terms of mental health, Bailey and colleagues (2010) reported, using a convenience sample, that breast cancer patients with multiple caregiving roles had increased levels of depressive symptoms compared to noncaregivers and those with a single caregiving role. Regarding physical health, Chassin, Macy, Seo, Presson, and Sherman (2010) found that caring for multiple generations impaired caregivers' physical health by less engagement in health behaviors than either noncaregivers or those who cared for parents only, after controlling for demographic variables, employment status, and total number of hours for caregiving per week. Although this study used a population-based sample, it did not include older adults. Moreover, Perkins (2010) reported special challenges among what she described as "compound caregivers." This is a type of sandwich caregiver who balances competing needs of their lifelong parenting of a dependent adult with intellectual disabilities while at the same tune having additional caregiving responsibility for their own aging parents or other family members. Perkins and Haley (2010), using a convenience sample, found that "compound caregivers" reported increased desire for residential placement outside the family home for their co-residing adult child with intellectual disabilities, compared with noncompound caregivers, but found no differences in physical or mental health. These studies highlight the need for more research using population-based samples of older adults.

Despite the reported challenges of having multiple caregiving roles, what is particularly missing in the current literature is whether racial/ethnic differences exist among caregivers with multiple caregiving roles. The role of race/ ethnicity or culture in caregiver health is well documented. Numerous studies reported racial/ethnic minority caregivers' worse physical health outcomes compared with their white counterparts (Chen, Mair, Bao, & Yang, 2015; Elliott, Burgio, & DeCoster, 2010; Fredman, Daly, &, Lazur, 1995; Knight, Longmire, Dave, Kim, & David, 2007; Pinquart & Sorensen, 2005). It should be noted that racial/ethnic minorities tended to have poorer physical health status (Chen et al., 2015; Elliott et al., 2010; Knight et al., 2007) and whites are more likely to have better self-rated health regardless of caregiving status (e.g., Danilovich, Xiang, & Pinto, 2017). Findings regarding emotional and psychological health outcomes, however, are somewhat mixed. In a review article on racial/ethnic differences among dementia caregivers, jane vie and Connell (2001) reported African American caregivers' lower depression than white caregivers. Adams and colleagues (2002) found that Latino caregivers were more depressed than any other ethnic groups. In contrast, Coon and colleagues (2004) reported no significant differences in mental well-being between Latino/Hispanic and white caregivers. It is not yet clear whether racial/ethnic minority caregivers function better or worse when they have multiple informal caregiving roles. Given the paucity of research on racial/ethnic minority caregivers with multiple informal caregiving roles, we address the interplay of race/ethnicity and the type of caregiving roles among older caregivers.

Our conceptual framework is guided by the sociocultural stress and coping model (Knight & Sayegh, 2010) and the double-jeopardy theory (Dowd & Bengtson, 1978). The sociocultural stress and coping model (Knight & Sayegh, 2010) suggests that caregiving is a life stressor, which could lead to negative health outcomes. However, depending on how individuals appraise the caregiving context, caregiving experience may turn out to be positive or negative, and culture may play an important role in how caregivers interpret caregiving experience. In addition, the double-jeopardy theory (Dowd & Bengtson, 1978) views age and race/ethnicity as disadvantaged status. Therefore, older adults with racial/ethnic minority status may suffer from the double disadvantage to health due to the interactive effects of age and race/ethnicity. Taken together, we conceptualized that older adults' cultural background (i.e., race/ethnicity) plays an important part in health status, as well as in the relationship between different types of caregiving roles and how caregivers appraise their own health.

The present study is motivated by (a) the paucity of population-based research on multiple caregiving roles among racially/ethnically diverse older caregivers and (b) the complexity of the impact of having multiple caregiving roles on caregiver health among older adults. The objectives of this study were to examine (a) whether the type of caregiving role (noncaregivers vs caregivers with a single caregiving role vs caregivers with multiple caregiving roles) was associated with subjective physical and mental health status among older adults and (b) whether race/ethnicity moderated the relation between type of caregiving role and physical and mental health status, using a population-based sample. Based on previous population-based studies, we hypothesized that (a) caregivers with multiple caregiving roles would have better physical health status than noncaregivers and single-role caregivers; (b) caregivers with multiple caregiving roles would be more psychological distressed than noncaregivers and single-role caregivers; and (c) race/ethnicity would moderate the relation between the type of caregiving *roles and* subjective physical and mental health status among older adults. The present study adds to prior caregiving literature by using a population-based sample to investigate racial/ ethnic differences in multiple caregiving roles.

Methods

Sample

The sample was drawn from the 2009 California Health Interview Survey (CHIS) that was collected between September 2009 and April 2010. The CHIS is a biannual telephone survey and the largest health survey conducted in a single state. The 2009 version is one of the few CHIS surveys that included caregiving-related variables and the most recent. More detailed information about sampling design and procedures is described elsewhere (California Health Interview Survey, n.d.; Ponce et al., 2004).

For the purpose of the study focusing on racially/ethnically diverse caregivers, we selected adults aged 55+ from diverse racial/ethnic groups (non-Hispanic whites, blacks, Hispanics, and Asians; $n = 24,241$). The selected sample was then divided into three groups by different types of caregiving roles: noncaregivers ($n = 18,626$; referent), caregivers with a single caregiving role ($n = 4,023$), and care-givers with multiple caregiving roles ($n = 1,772$).

Measures

Type of Caregiving

Before asking questions about caregiving, the interviewer explained to the respondent that some people provide help to a family member or friend who has a long-term illness or disability and this may include help with things they can no longer do for themselves (California Health Interview Survey, n.d.). To identify different types of caregiving roles, we used the following 2 questions: "During the past 12 months, did you provide any such help to a family member or friend?" and "How many people have you provided care for in the past 12 months?" If necessary, "such help" was clarified to the recipient that this may include help with baths, medicines, household chores, paying bills, driving to doctor's visits or the grocery store, or just checking in to see how they are doing. When the respondent reported that they did not provide any care to a family member or friend in the past 12 months, they were categorized as "noncaregivers"; we used this group as our reference group. Among those who provided care to a family member or friend in the past 12 months, those who reported that they had provided care to one person were categorized as "caregivers with a single caregiving role" and those who reported that they had provided care to two or more persons were categorized as "caregivers with multiple caregiving roles."

Race/Ethnicity

The CHIS provides self-identified racial/ethnic categories of respondents' origins defined by the federal Office of Management and Budget and the U.S. Census Bureau. Due to small sample sizes for older caregivers from certain racial/ethnic categories (e.g., American Indian/Alaska Native), the present study selected participants who identified as one of the four major racial/ethnic groups (non-Hispanic white, black, Hispanic, or Asian).

Self-Rated Health

A single item question, "How would you rate your own health?" was used to assess self-rated health. Response categories were from 1 (*excellent*) to 5 (*poor*), with higher scores indicating poorer self-rated health.

Psychological Distress

Psychological distress was measured with the K6 (Kessler et al., 2002). Six items included in the K6 asked the respondents to report how often they felt nervous, hopeless, restless or fidgety, worthless, so depressed that nothing could cheer them up, and that everything was an effort using a five-point Likert scale ("none of the time" coded as 0 and "all of the time" coded as 4). A total score ranges from 0 to 24 and higher scores indicated greater levels of psychological distress. Internal consistency was acceptable in the present sample: $\alpha = .807$ for the overall sample; $\alpha = .805$ for non- caregivers; $\alpha = .812$ for caregivers with a single caregiving role; and $\alpha = .808$ for caregivers with multiple caregiving roles.

Covariates

Sociodemographic and other background characteristics (age [continuous], sex [male = 0; female = 1], marital status [not married = 0; married = 1], educational attainment [less than high school = 0; high school diploma = 1; some college = 2], poverty level [0–199% federal poverty level (FPL) = 0; 200% + FPL = 1], chronic diseases and disability [continuous]) were selected as covariates. Additional caregiving-related characteristics (family vs friend caregiving [friend caregiving = 0; family caregiving = 1], receiving help from family/friends [no = 0; yes = 1], duration, of caregiving [less than 3 months = 0; over 3 months = 1), living with the care recipient(s) [no = 0; yes = 1], total caregiving hours per week [continuous], and receiving paid help [no = 0; yes = 1]) were used as covariates for the sensitivity analyses.

Data Analysis

Descriptive analyses were conducted, to report background characteristics of the sample. Chi-square or analysis of variance (ANOVA.) tests were used to compare characteristics across three caregiving groups. A two-way analysis of covariance (AMCOVA) test was used to test main and interaction effects after adjusting for covariates. Adjusted estimated marginal means were compared using Bonferroni comparisons for post hoc testing. A series of sensitivity analyses were also conducted using ANCOVA to test potential effects of caregiving-related variables.

Results

Background Characteristics of the Sample

Table 13.1 presents unadjusted comparisons of background characteristics, which were significantly different across noncaregivers, caregivers with a single caregiving role, and caregivers with multiple caregiving roles. Compared to noncaregivers, caregivers with multiple caregiving roles were more likely to be younger, female, U.S.-born, have income 200 % or higher than the FPL, and have higher educational attainment and fewer chronic diseases. In comparison with caregivers with a single caregiving role, caregivers with multiple caregiving roles were more likely to be younger and female and have higher educational attainment. With regard to outcome variables, caregivers with multiple caregiving roles had significantly better self-rated health and higher psychological distress than both noncaregive.rs and caregivers with a single caregiving role.

Caregiving characteristics were compared between caregivers with a single caregiving role and caregivers with multiple caregiving roles. All characteristics were significantly different between the two groups except for receiving paid help for caregiving. Compared with caregivers with a single caregiving role, caregivers with multiple caregiving roles were less likely to be a family caregiver, provide care over 3 months and live with care recipients and more likely to receive help from family or friends. One thing to note is that caregivers with multiple caregiving roles tended to provide fewer hours of caregiving than caregivers with a single caregiving role, which is somewhat counterintuitive.

Additional analyses confirmed that there were racial/ ethnic differences in different types of caregiving. As shown in Table 13.2, in general, more whites were engaged in caregiving roles than other racial/ethnic groups, regardless of single or multiple caregiving roles. Compared with other racial/ethnic groups, more whites were engaged in a single caregiving role and more African Americans were engaged in multiple caregiving roles.

Results From ANCOVA

Table 13.3 summarizes results from a two-way ANCOVA examining the main effects of type of caregiving and race/ethnicity and the interaction of type of caregiving by race/ethnicity after adjusting for covariates. For the self-rated health outcome (left column in Table 13.3), the main effect of type

Table 13.1. *Background Characteristics of the Sample (n = 24,421)*

		Type of caregiving		
			Caregivers (*n* = 5,795)	
	Noncaregivers (*n* = 18,626)	Caregivers with a Single CGR (*n* = 4,023)	Caregivers with Multiple CGRs (*n* = 1,772)	
Characteristics	*M ± SD* or %	*M ± SD* or %	*M ± SD* or %	F or chi-square
Race/ethnicity				162.42***
Non-Hispanic white	80.1	86.8	85.7	
Black	4.1	3.5	4.7	
Hispanic	6.6	5.0	5.6	
Asian	9.2	4.7	4.0	
Age	69.54 ± 9.35	66.34 ± 8.55	64.59 ± 7.85	393.02***
Female	58.8	64.9	69.0	108.81***
Married	48.9	53.9	50.3	33.59***
Educational attainment				187.25***
Less than high school	9.1	4.8	4.7	
High school diploma	21.7	19.3	15.0	
Some college	69.2	75.9	80.3	
Poverty				73.90***
0–199% FPL	26.5	20.6	21.8	
200% + FPL	73.5	79.4	78.2	
US born	80.9	88.8	88.5	188.35***
No. of chronic diseases				46.55***
0	35.9	39.9	41.3	
1	38.8	38.1	34.4	
2+	25.3	22.0	24.3	
Disabled	45.1	41.9	43.2	15.34***
Self-rated health (1–5)	2.63 ± 1.15	2.50 ± 1.08	2.45 ± 1.07	38.29***
Psychological distress (0–24)	2.35 ±3.27	2.76 ± 3.44	2.89 ±3.40	42.07***
Caregiving characteristics[a]				
Family caregiving	—	80.6	63.7	1.89.61***
Receiving help from family/friends	—	74.7	78.4	9.55**
Caregiving over 3 months	—	76.7	70.5	24.42***
Living with care recipient(s)	—	39.1	19.5	214.57***
No. of caregiving hours per week	—	28.97 ± 47.78	19.09 ± 35.84	60.65***
Receiving paid help for caregiving	—	5.7	6.8	2.80

Notes. CGR = caregiving role(s); FPL = federal poverty level. Self-rated health was coded as 1 (*excellent*) and 5(*poor*).

[a]Chi-square and t-test for caregiving-related variables were compared between caregivers with a single caregiving role and caregivers with multiple caregiving roles.

**p < .01. ***p < .001.

Table 13.2. *Racial/Ethnic Differences in Different Types of Caregiving*

	Type of caregiving (%)			
	Noncaregivers	Single CGR	Multiple CGR	Chi-square
Total	76.3	1.6.5	7.3	
Race/ethnicity				162.42***
White	74.9	17.5	7.6	
African American.	77.3	14.2	8.5	
Latino	80.4	13.2	6.4	
Asian	86.8	9.6	3.6	

Note. CGR = caregiving role(s).

***$p < .001$.

Table 13.3. *Results from ANCOVA (n = 24,421)*

	Outcome: self-rated health				Outcome: psychological distress			
Variable	df	SS	F	Partial η^2	df	SS	F	Partial η^2
Covariates								
Age	1	103.15	123.43***	.005	1	7757.57	816.38***	.032
Female	1	19.20	29.98***	.001	1	95.30	10.03**	.000
Married	1	19.64	23.51***	.001	1	901.46	94.87***	.004
Educational attainment	1	307.77	368.28***	.015	1	104.06	10.95**	.000
Poverty	1	363.52	434.98***	.018	1	3032.47	319.13***	.013
US born.	1	27.63	33.07***	.001	1	159.25	16.76***	.001
No. of chronic diseases	1	2410.58	2884.46***	.106	1	1282.61	134.98***	.006
Disabled	1	2701.55	3232.62***	.117	1	15674.86	1649.56***	.063
Main effect								
Type of caregiving	2	13.01	7.78***	.001	2	1.17.95	6.21**	.001
Race/ethnicity	3	107.35	42.82***	.005	3	183.32	6.43***	.001
Interaction effect								
Type of caregiving × Race/ethnicity	6	11.39	2.27*	.001	6	41.06	0.72	.000
Error	24,401	20392.26			24,401	231869.02		
Total	24,421	195765.00			24,421	415130.00		

Notes. A two-way analysis of covariance (ANCOVA) was performed; *df* = degree of freedom; SS = sum of squares; Self-rated health was coded as 1 (*excellent*) to 5 (*poor*).

*$p < .05$. **$p < .01$. ***$p < .001$.

of caregiving was significant ($F_{2, 24401} = 7.78$, $p < .001$), such that caregivers with, multiple caregiving roles had better self-rated health than noncaregivers and caregivers with a single caregiving role; caregivers with a single caregiving role also had better self-rated health than noncaregivers. There was a significant main effect of race/ethnicity ($F_{3, 24401} = 42.82$, $p < .001$), indicating that older whites had the best self-rated health, whereas older Asians had the poorest self-rated health. The interaction of type of caregiving by race/ethnicity was significant ($F_{6, 24401} = 2.27, p < .05$).

For the psychological distress outcome (right column in Table 13.3), after adjusting for covariates, the main effects of both, type of caregiving ($F_{2, 24401} = 6.21, p < .01$) and race/ethnicity ($F_{3, 24401} = 6.43, p < .001$) were significant. Results indicated that caregivers with multiple caregiving roles had higher levels of psychological distress than, noncaregivers and caregivers with a single caregiving role and that caregivers with a single caregiving role had higher levels of psychological distress than noncaregivers. Older blacks had lower levels of psychological distress, whereas older Hispanics had higher levels of psychological distress. The interaction of type of caregiving by race/ethnicity was not significant for psychological distress ($F_{6, 24401} = 0.72, p < .05$).

Interpretation of the Significant Interaction Effect

Figure 13.1 displays estimated marginal means of self-rated health by type of caregiving and race/ethnicity after adjusting for covariates. In the overall sample, self-rated health, was better as older adults had more caregiving roles, indicating that caregivers with multiple caregiving roles had the best self-rated health and noncaregivers had the poorest self-rated health. Noncaregivers and caregivers with a single caregiving role also differed significantly in self-rated health. When the sample was divided by race/ethnicity, however, two different patterns were observed. For whites, Hispanics, and Asians, self-rated health was better among caregivers with multiple caregiving roles compared to the other groups. For blacks, however, self-rated health was significantly better among caregivers with a single caregiving role compared to noncaregivers and caregivers with, multiple caregiving roles whose self-rated health did not differ significantly. Detailed adjusted means and standard errors by race/ethnicity and type of caregiving are summarized in Table 13.4.

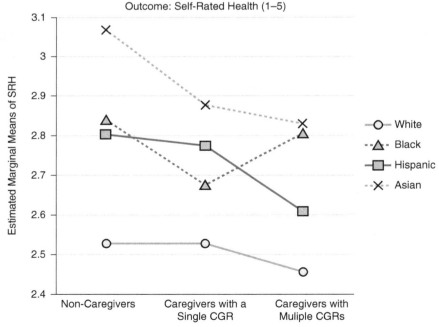

Figure 13.1. *Estimated Marginal Means of Self-Rated Health by Type of Caregiving and Race/Ethnicity*
Notes. CGR = caregiving role(s). Estimated marginal means of self-rated health (SRH) were calculated after adjusting for covariates; SRH was coded as 1 (*excellent*) and 5 (*poor*).

Table 13.4. *Adjusted Means and Standard Errors by Race/Ethnicity and Type of Caregiving (n = 24,421)*

	Self-rated health			Psychological distress		
	Noncaregivers	Caregivers with a single CGR	Caregivers with multiple CGRs	Noncaregivers	Caregivers with a single CGR	Caregivers with a multiple CGRs
	M (SE)	M (SE)	M (SE)	M (SE)	M (SE)	M (SE)
Overall						
Race/ethnicity	2.81 (.01)	2.71 (.03)	2.68 (.04)	2.27 (.05)	2.57 (.10)	2.66 (.15)
Non-Hispanic white	2.53 (.01)	2.53 (.02)	2.46 (.02)	2.40 (.03)	2.78 (.05)	2.72 (.08)
Black	2.84 (.03)	2.68 (.08)	2.81 (.10)	2.01 (.11)	2.07 (.26)	2.39 (.34)
Hispanic	2.80 (.03)	2.77 (.07)	2.61 (.09)	2.47 (.10)	3.06 (.22)	3.18 (.31)
Asian	3.07 (.03)	2.87 (.07)	2.83 (.11)	2.21 (.09)	2.39 (.23)	2.34 (.37)

Notes. CGR = caregiving role(s). Self-rated health was coded as 1 (*excellent*) to 5 (*poor*). Means were adjusted for age, sex, marital status, educational attainment, poverty, nativity status, disability status, and the number of chronic diseases.

Sensitivity Analyses

A series of sensitivity analyses was conducted to test potential influences of other confounding factors. First, to test potential differences between family and friend caregiving, we conducted a sensitivity analysis by selecting family caregivers. We compared three groups of different types of family caregiving roles: noncaregivers (n = 18,626), family caregivers with a single caregiving role (n = 3,243), and family caregivers with multiple caregiving roles (n = 1,129). Results from, the ANCOVA analysis showed the same pattern: the interaction between race/ethnicity and caregiving roles was significant only for self-rated health ($F_{6, 22978}$ = 2.20, $p < .05$) (results not shown in tables). In our subsequent post hoc analyses to interpret the significant interaction effect, we found the identical racial/ethnic patterns observed in Figure 13.1 among family caregivers. For whites, Hispanics, and Asians, caregivers with, multiple caregiving roles had better self-rated health than, noncaregivers and caregivers with a single caregiving role. For blacks, however, caregivers with a single caregiving role had significantly better self-rated health than noncaregivers and caregivers with multiple caregiving roles.

A second set of sensitivity analyses was conducted by adjusting for caregiving-related variables (family vs friend caregiving, receiving help from family/friends, duration of caregiving, living with the care recipient(s), total caregiving hours per week, and receiving paid help) in addition to covariates used in prior ANCOVA analyses. Given that caregiving-related variables were collected only for caregivers, noncaregivers were not included in this sensitivity analysis. After adjusting for all available caregiving characteristics in addition to other covariates, there was no significant main effect of caregiving type for both self- rated health and psychological distress, whereas the main effect of race/ethnicity was significant for both self-rated health and psychological distress. The interaction effects of types of caregiving and race/ethnicity were not significant. Although the caregiving role. For blacks, however, the opposite pattern was found: black caregivers with multiple caregiving roles had poorer self-rated health than those with a single caregiving role.

Discussion

We explored racial/ethnic differences in the relation between different, types of informal caregiving roles and subjective physical and mental health status using a population-based sample of older adults. Regardless of race/ ethnicity, noncaregivers reported worse self-rated health and lower psychological distress than caregivers with any type of role. As expected, we observed a significant moderating role of race/ethnicity in the relationship between caregiving roles and self-rated health. For older whites, Hispanics, and Asians, caregivers with multiple caregiving roles had better self-rated health than, noncaregivers and caregivers with a single role: caregivers with a single caregiving role had better self-rated health than noncaregivers and noncaregivers had the poorest self-rated health. Older blacks, however, showed a distinctive pattern: blacks with a single caregiving role showed better self-rated health than noncaregivers and caregivers with multiple roles whose self-rated health did not differ significantly. When the noncaregiver group was taken out and caregiving-related variables were controlled in our sensitivity analysis, the differences in mental and physical health between the two types of caregivers disappeared. Nevertheless, our major finding, using a population-based sample, on caregivers's better self-rated health in comparison with noncaregivers adds to the literature. It also suggests further research needs to identify.

Caregiving's relation to health should be highlighted, With regard to physical health, noncaregivers had worse self-rated health than caregivers with a single caregiving role and multiple caregiving roles in the overall sample and all racial/ethnic groups except for Blacks. This reflects the Healthy Caregiver Hypothesis suggested by Fredman and colleagues (Fredman, Doros, Ensrud, Hochberg, & Cauley, 2009; Fredman et al., 2010). This finding was also consistent with recent large population-based studies on the impact of informal caregiving (Brown et al., 2009; Fredman et al., 2010; Roth et al., 2013) that were reported in two recent reviews (Capistrant, 2016; Roth et al., 2015). Roth and colleagues (2015) noted that "*caregivers, as a general group, have significantly reduced mortality rates compared to their respective noncaregiving reference groups*" (p. 312), With regard to caregiving's association with mental health, noncaregivers in general had better mental health than any types of caregivers with caregivers, with multiple caregiving roles showing the worst psychological distress. This was also consistent with previous studies using large population-based data (e.g., Trivedi et al., 2014).

The role of race/ethnicity in the relation between type of caregiving role and self-rated health deserves discussion. Unlike other racial/ethnic caregivers with multiple caregiving roles reporting the best self-rated health, older blacks with multiple caregiving roles had poorer self-rated health than those with a single caregiving role. In our subsequent sensitivity analysis comparing two types of caregivers after controlling caregiving-related variables, however, the significant difference in self-rated health between the two caregiving groups disappeared, while the racial/ethnic pattern remained the same. This unexpected finding parallels results found in Hilgeman and colleagues (2009) reporting no racial/ethnic differences in paths between the latent constructs of caregiving context and objective stress, or between objective stress and role strain. Role strain may differ between multiple and single caregiving; unfortunately, it was not measured in the CHIS. In addition, the following points should be considered. First, the effect is clearly not driven by differences between family and friend caregivers, as they displayed the same pattern. Second, sensitivity analysis focusing on only caregivers after controlling caregiving-related factors uses a much smaller sample and controls for a number of factors that would reasonably be expected to affect caregiving strain. In other words, the power is grossly reduced. Third, based on information presented in Table 13.1, most of those factors are weighted against caregivers with a single caregiving role who are more likely than those with multiple caregiving roles to live with the care recipient, to have been caregiving longer, and to provide more care per week. All of these factors are known to increase caregiving strain. Given that the CHIS did not have direct measure of role strain, future research might be benefitted by examining the potential influence of role strain using appropriate data. Despite the unavailability of care recipients-related variables in the CHIS data, information on such care recipient characteristics as type of illness (e.g., dementia, cancer, disability, etc.) and severity of illness would be valuable for further detailed analyses. These plausible reasons should be examined in future research.

Despite the nonsignificant interaction effect for psychological distress, findings relating to the mental health outcome are noteworthy. The pattern observed in the overall sample was in accordance with previous research (Pinquart & Sörensen, 2003), suggesting that caregivers in general have higher levels of psychological distress compared to noncaregivers and that caregivers with multiple caregiving roles have the highest psychological distress. There were also consistent racial/ethnic patterns in the relation between the type of caregiving role and psychological distress. Regardless of caregiving roles, blacks in general had the lowest psychological distress, whereas Hispanics had the highest psychological distress. This racial/ethnic pattern was reported in previous research focusing on mental health outcomes (Kim et al., 2011).

Another notable finding was that across all three types of caregiving roles, whites consistently showed the best self-rated health, whereas Asians exhibited the poorest self-rated health. As shown in Figure 13.1, Asian caregivers in general were the most vulnerable group regardless of their caregiving roles. Asian caregivers' relatively poor global health status has been reported in previous research (e.g., Janevic & Connell, 2001; Pinquart 8c Sörensen, 2005). Kim and colleagues (2011) also reported older Asians' relatively poor self-perceptions of their own mental health. Together these data suggest that culture may play a role in self-perceptions of health regardless of caregiving roles (McMullen & Luborsky, 2006).

Findings from the present study have implications for research and practice. Given the limited research on compound caregivers, further examination on the mechanisms of caregiving burden among older caregivers with multiple caregiving roles should be prioritized. Given that caregivers with multiple caregiving roles, regardless of racial/ethnic backgrounds, may experience special challenges such as significant reduction in social network/support and stress resilience (Perkins, 2010), future research should first focus on identifying specific areas of challenges that many caregivers with multiple caregiving roles face. Also noteworthy is the potential cyclical nature of having multiple caregiving roles across one's caregiving career. Perkins and Haley (2010) reported that 37% of their sample of aging caregivers were current compound caregivers, but 66% reported they had been a compound caregiver previously, and 34% anticipated the need to become one in the near future. Clinicians should be aware that older black caregivers with multiple caregiving roles may have special challenges and need additional support from both informal and formal sources. In particular, given the heightened level of poor health status observed among older black caregivers with multiple caregiving roles, ways to address their unique instrumental needs should be considered. A problematic area noted by Perkins (2011) is the provision of respite care when there are multiple caregiving responsibilities. As described by Perkins (2011), the benefit of respite may not be optimal if the caregiver is unable to be relieved from all caregiving roles simultaneously.

Some study limitations should be noted. First, the generalizability of our findings is limited due to the geographically limited sample. Caregivers living in different states may have different resources for caregiving. Second, because the CHIS did not collect data on the relationship with die secondary or tertiary care recipient or on the care recipient's characteristics (e.g., age, health problems, presence of dementia, severity of illness), we were not able to examine the influence of these variables. Given that Penning and Wu (2015) reported differential influences of the caregiver-care recipient relationship on mental health, sandwich caregivers caring for aging parents and children may experience different levels of stress than those providing care for two or more adults. Third, given that the CHIS did not ask questions about whether the caregiver was a primary caregiver or any minimum number of hours per week: required to be considered a caregiver, the definition of caregiving used in the present study may have been limited. Fourth, we were not able to examine differences between caregivers providing care for two versus three care recipients due to small sample sizes for racial/ethnic minority groups. Future research should investigate the potential differences among caregivers with multiple caregiving roles. Fifth, as suggested by Knight and Sayegh (2010), future research should test cultural values such as familism and filial piety as potential contributors to choosing and using coping strategies that are specific to racial/ethnic groups that could explain observed differences in the relation between caregiving roles and perceptions of health status. There may be differences that manifest between people who voluntarily/involuntarily become caregivers and who subsequently voluntarily/involuntarily become multiple caregivers. Sixth, due to the cross-sectional nature of our data, the causal relation between caregiving roles and health status could not be tested. Future research should investigate the causal directionality of the relation between multiple caregiving roles and health risks using longitudinal data, and also investigate the potential cumulative effect of multiple caregiving roles across the lifespan. Seventh, despite the large sample size used in the present study, the significant interaction effects should be interpreted with caution due to extremely small effect sizes. Lastly, there may be subracial/ethnic group differences. Previous research suggests different health outcomes among different groups of Asian older adults (Kim et al., 2010). Future research should consider heterogeneity of racial/ethnic groups. Notwithstanding these limitations, one of the unique strengths of the present study was using a population-based sample to address the effect of multiple caregiving roles; in contrast, previous research on multiple caregiving roles mostly used convenience samples.

In conclusion, our findings using a population-based sample suggest that caregivers with any type of role are more psychologically distressed, but their self-rated health is better than noncaregivers. This implies that caregivers may be either self-selected to be in better health or may gain health benefits from caregiving, which deserves further investigation. Our findings also suggest that the relation between multiple caregiving roles and self-rated health may differ by race/ethnicity, with blacks differing from other racial/ethnic groups. Our sensitivity analysis controlling caregiving-related variables present only among caregivers eliminated the differences in self-rated health between the two types of caregivers. Future research should elucidate reasons for better self-rated health among racially/ethnically diverse older caregivers using a population-based sample.

Funding

Research reported in this publication is supported by the National Institute on Aging (K01AG045342, PI: G. Kim).

Acknowledgments

The content is solely the responsibility of the authors and does not necessarily represent the official views of the National Institute on Aging.

Conflict of Interest

None reported.

References

Adams, B., Aranda, M. P., Kemp, B., & Takagi, K. (2002). Ethnic and gender differences in distress among Anglo American, African American, Japanese American, and Mexican American spousal caregivers of persons with dementia, *journal of Clinical Geropsychology;* 8, 279–301.

Bailey, E. H., Pérez, M., Aft, R. L., Liu, Y., Schootman, M., & Jeffe, D. B. (2010). Impact of multiple caregiving roles on elevated depressed mood in early-stage breast cancer patients and sameage controls. *Breast Cancer Research and Treatment,* 121, 709–718. doi:1 0.1007/s10549-009-0645-1

Brown, S. L., Smith, D. M., Schulz, R., Kabeto, M. U., Ubel, P. A., Poulin, M., ... Langa, K. M. (2009). Caregiving behavior is associated with decreased mortality risk. *Psychological Science,* 20, 488–494. doi:10.1111/ j.l467-9280.2009.02323.x

California Health Interview Survey. CHIS 2009 sample design. Retrieved December 11, 2016 from http:// healthpolicy.ucla.edu/ chis/design/Documents/sample_desc_2009 .pdf

California Health Interview Survey. CHIS 2009 adult questionnaire. Retrieved June 15, 2017 from http:// healthpolicy.ucla.edu/chis/ design/Documents/CHIS2009ad ukquestion naire.pdf

Capisrrant, B. D. (2016). Caregiving for older adults and the caregivers' health: An epidemiologic view. *Current Epidemiology Reports,* 3, 72–80.

Chang, H. Y., Chiou, C. J., & Chen, N. S. (2010). Impact of mental health and caregiver burden on family caregivers' physical health. *Archives of Gerontology and Geriatrics,* 50, 267–271. doi:10.1016/ j.archger.2009.04.006

Chari, A. V., Engberg, J., Ray, K. N., & Mehrotra, A. (2015). The opportunity costs of informal elder-care in the United States: New estimates from the American Time Use Survey. *Health Services Research,* 50, 871–882. doi:10.1111/1475-6773.12238

Chassin, L., Macy, J. T., Seo, D. C., Presson, C. C., & Sherman, S. J. (2010). The association between membership in the sandwich generation and health behaviors: A longitudinal study. *Journal of Applied Developmental Psychology,* 31, 38–46. doi:10.1016/j. a ppd ev.2009.06.001

Chen, E., Mair, C. A., Bao, L., & Yang, Y. C. (2015). Race/ethnic differentials in the health consequences of caring for grandchildren for grandparents. *The Journal of Gerontology, Series B: Psychological Sciences and Social Sciences,* 70, 793–803. doi:10.1093/geronb/gbul60

Coon, D. W., Rubert, M., Solano, N., Mausbach, B., Kraemer, H., Arguelles, T., ... Gallagher-Thompson, D. (2004). Well-being, appraisal, and coping in Latina and Caucasian female dementia caregivers: Findings from the REACH study. *Aging & Mental Health,* 8, 330–345. doi: 10.1080/13607860410001709683

Danilovich, M., Xiang, X., & Pinto, D. (2017). Factors that influence self-reported health changes with caregiving. *journal of Aging and Health,* 29(8), 1444-1458. doi:10.1177/0898264316663576

DePasquale, N., Davis, K. D., Zarit, S. H., Moen, P., Hammer, L. B., & Almeida, D. M. (2016). Combining formal and informal caregiving roles: The psychosocial implications of double- and triple-duty care. *The journal of Gerontology, Series B: Psychological Sciences and Social Sciences,* 71, 201–211. doi:10.1093/ geronb/ gbul39

Dowd, J. J., & Bengtson, V. L. (1978). Aging in minority populations. An examination of the double jeopardy hypothesis. *Journal of Gerontology,* 33, 427–436.

Elliott, A. E., Burgio, L. D., & Decoster, J. (2010). Enhancing caregiver health: Findings from the resources for enhancing Alzheimer's caregiver health II intervention. *Journal of the American Geriatrics Society,* 58, 30–37. doi:l0.1111/j.1532-5415.2009.02631.x

Fredman, L., Cauley, J. A., Hochberg, M., Ensrud, K. E., & Doros, G.; Study of Osteoporotic Fractures. (2010), Mortality associated with caregiving, general stress, and caregiving-related stress in elderly women: Results of caregiver-study of osteoporotic fractures. *Journal of the American Geriatrics Society,* 58, 937–943. doi:10.1111/j.1532-5415.2010.02808.x

Fredman, L., Daly, M. P., & Lazur, A. M. (1995). Burden among white and black caregivers to elderly adults. *The Journal of Gerontology, Series B: Psychological Sciences and Social Sciences,* 50, S110–S118.

Fredman, L., Doros, G., Ensrud, K. E., Hochberg, M. C., & Cauley, J. A. (2009). Caregiving intensity and change in physical functioning over a 2-year period: Results of the caregiver-study of osteoporotic fractures. *American Journal of Epidemiology, 170*, 203–210. doi:10.1093/aje/kwp 102

Hilgeman, M. M., Durkin, D. W., Sun, E., DeCoster, J., Alien, R. S., Gallagher-Thompson, D., & Burgio, L. D. (2009). Testing a theoretical model of the stress process in Alzheimer's caregivers with race as a moderator. *The Gerontologist, 49*, 248–261. doi:10.1093/geront/gnp 015

Janevic, M. R., & Connell, C. M. (2001). Racial, ethnic, and cultural differences in the dementia caregiving experience: Recent findings. *The Gerontologist, 41*, 334–347.

Kessler, R. C., Andrews, G., Colpe, L. J., Hiripi, E., Mroczek, D. K., Normand, S. L.,... & Zaslavsky, A. M. (2002). Short screening scales to monitor population prevalences and trends in nonspecific psychological distress. *Psychological Medicine, 32*(6), 959–976.

Kim, G., Chiriboga, D. A., Jang, Y., Lee, S., Huang, C. H., & Parmelee, P. (2010). Health status of older Asian Americans in California. *Journal of the American Geriatrics Society, 58*, 2003–2008. doi:10.1111/j.l532–5415.2010.03034.x

Kim, G., DeCoster, J., Chiriboga, D. A., Jang, Y., Allen, R. S., & Parmelee, P. (2011). Associations between self-rated mental health and psychiatric disorders among older adults: Do racial/ ethnic differences exist? *The American Journal of Geriatric Psychiatry, 19*, 416–422. doi:10.1097/JGP.0b013e3181f61ede

Knight, B. G., Longmire, C. V., Dave, J., Kim, J. H., & David, S. (2007). Mental health and physical health of family caregivers for persons with dementia: A comparison of African American and white caregivers. *Aging & Mental Health, 11*, 538–546. doi:10.1080/13607860601086561

Knight, B. G., & Sayegh, P. (2010). Cultural values and caregiving: The updated sociocultural stress and coping model. *The Journal of Gerontology, Series B: Psychological Sciences and Social Sciences, 65*, 5–13. doi:10.1093/geronb/gbp096

Lee, Y., & Bronstein, L. R. (2010). When do Korean-American dementia caregivers find meaning in caregiving?: The role of culture and differences between spouse and child caregivers. *Journal of Ethnic & Cultural Diversity in Social Work, 19*, 73–86.

McMullen, C. K., & Luborsky, M. R, (2006). Self-rated health appraisal as cultural and identity process: African American elders' health and evaluative rationales. *The Gerontologist, 46*, 431–438.

National Alliance for Caregiving. (2015). *Caregiving in the US.* Berhesda, MD: The National Alliance for Caregiving and AARP.

Penning, M. J., & Wu, Z. (2016). Caregiver stress and mental health: Impact of caregiving relationship and gender. *The Gerontologist, 56*, 1102–1113. doi:10.1093/geront/gnv038

Perkins, E.A. (2010). The compound caregivers: A case study of multiple caregiving roles. *Clinical Gerontologist, 33*, 248–254.

Perkins, E. A. (2011). *Compound caregivers: Overlooked and overburdened [White paper],* Tampa, FL: University of South Florida, Florida Center for Inclusive Communities. Retrieved from http://flfcic.fmhi.usf.edu/docs/FCIC_CompoundCaregivers_070811. pdf

Perkins, E. A., & Haley, W. E. (2010). Compound caregiving: When lifelong caregivers undertake additional caregiving roles. *Rehabilitation Psychology, 55*, 409–417. doi:10.1037/ a0021521

Pinquart, M., & Sörensen, S. (2003). Differences between caregivers and noncaregivers in psychological health and physical health: A meta-analysis. *Psychology and Aging, 18*, 250–267.

Pinquart, M., & Sörensen, S. (2005). Ethnic differences in stressors, resources, and psychological outcomes of family caregiving: A meta-analysis. *The Gerontologist, 45*, 90–106.

Ponce, N. A., Lavarreda, S. A., Yen, W., Brown, E. R., DiSogra, C., & Satter, D. E. (2004). The California Health Interview Survey 2001: Translation of a major survey for California's multiethnic population. *Public Health Reports (Washington, DC: 1974), 119*, 388–395. doi:10.1016/j.phc2004.05.002

Roth, D. L., Fredman, L., & Haley, W. E. (2015). Informal caregiving and its impact on health: A reappraisal from population-based studies. *The Gerontologist, 55*, 309–319. doi:10.1093/geront/gnu177

Roth, D. L., Haley, W. E., Hovarer, M., Perkins, M., Wadley, V. G., & Judd, S. (2013). Family caregiving and all-cause mortality: Findings from a population-based propensity-matched analysis. *American Journal of Epidemiology,* 178, 1571–1578. doi:10.1Q93/aje/kwt225

Scott, L. D., Hwang, W. T., & Rogers, A. E. (2006). The impact of multiple care giving roles on fatigue, stress, and work performance among hospital staff nurses. *Journal of Nursing Administration,* 36, 86–95.

Schulz, R., & Beach, S. R. (1999). Caregiving as a risk factor for mortality: The Caregiver Health Effects Study. *JAMA,* 282, 2215–2219.

Trivedi, R., Beaver, K., Bouldin, E. D., Eugenio, E., Zeliadt, S. B., Nelson, K., … Pietre, J. D. (2014). Characteristics and wellbeing of informal caregivers: Results from a nationally-representative US survey. *Chronic Illness,* 10, 167–179. doi:10.11.77/1742395313506947

CHAPTER 14

Ten Surprising Facts about Stressful Life Events and Disease Risk

Sheldon Cohen,[1] *Michael L. M. Murphy,*[1] *and Aric A. Prather*[2]

Introduction

Definitions of stress vary in their foci from objective threatening characteristics of the environment—stressful life events—to individuals' (subjective) appraisals of the threat that an environment poses for them—psychological stress—to the activation of physiological systems that support the behaviors (e.g., fight and flight) needed to respond to that threat (Cohen et al. 2016). These varying definitions have been viewed as representing different stages in a model where stressful life events that an individual appraises as threatening trigger behavioral and physiological responses with possible downstream implications for disease (Cohen et al. 2016).

In this review, we focus on major stressful life events (also called stressors). Our interest in objectively defined events is partly attributable to a substantial literature associating events with risk for, and exacerbation of, a range of diseases including depression, coronary heart disease (CHD), HIV/AIDS, asthma, autoimmune diseases, respiratory infections, and mortality (for a review, see Cohen et al. 2007), but it is also attributable to our recognition that, from a public health perspective, reducing environmental stressors may be easier and more cost effective than treating individuals' psychological or physiological responses.

We focus on events that are threats to one's social status, self-esteem, identity, or physical wellbeing, such as divorce, the death of a loved one, the loss of a job, being arrested, retirement, or being diagnosed with a serious illness. Much of what we know about stressful life events is derived from research, using major stressful life event checklists (Monroe 2008). These scales assess the number of major events that a person reports experiencing in a defined time span, usually a year, based on the assumption that events are cumulative. That is, each event adds to the total stress burden. In contrast to the assumptions of this approach, there is also substantial evidence for an increased risk for disease among those who have experienced a single event. Most convincing in this regard are studies that identify major threatening events using a structured interview called the Life Events and Difficulties Schedule (LEDS) (Brown & Harris 1989). In this method, the threat of an event is assessed using information garnered from the interview, and the event is rated by comparison to records (a dictionary) of ratings of similar events experienced by others previously interviewed using the LEDS. Individual events that meet a common criterion for threat (the average person would be severely threatened) are thought to be substitutable in their risk for disease, but experiencing multiple events does not increase that risk.

After over 70 years of research on the association between stressful life events and health, it is generally accepted that we have a good understanding of the role of stressors in disease risk. In this review, we highlight that knowledge but also emphasize misunderstandings and weaknesses in this literature with the hope of triggering further theoretical and empirical development. We organize this review in a somewhat provocative manner, with each section focusing on an important issue in the literature where we feel that there has been some misunderstanding of the evidence and its implications.

The Ten Facts

Fact 1: There Is Little Agreement on the Characteristics that Define a Stressful Event

There is a consensus among researchers that severe circumstances such as death of a spouse, sexual assault, or learning of a diagnosis of imminent death are examples of major stressful life events—events that we expect will result in psychological and physiological stress responses for the average person. Less clear is what the necessary criteria are for an event to be classified as stressful. In this section, we present four alternative theoretical perspectives on what constitutes a stressful event.

Adaptation. The first approach views the stressfulness of an event as the amount of adaptation or change it requires of an average individual (Holmes & Rahe 1967). This implies that stressful events are cumulative, with each additional event adding to the overall burden of change. It also implies that positive events (e.g., marriage, vacations) can also be stressful events if they require substantial adaptation.

Threat or harm. The second approach defines stressful events as those that are consensually seen as harmful or threatening (e.g., Brown & Harris 1989, Cohen et al. 2016). Imminence of harm, intensity, duration, and the extent to which an event is objectively uncontrollable are all factors that contribute to the potential magnitude of consensual threat (Lazarus & Folkman 1984, Rabkin & Struening 1976). As mentioned above, although the magnitude of the threat represented by different life events is often thought to be cumulative (e.g., as assumed by stressful life event checklists), there is also evidence that the maximum risk for disease occurs when a single event meets a high criterion for threat (Wethington et al. 1995), with additional events not adding to the total risk.

Demands exceed resources. The third approach arises out of the job stress literature. The underlying assumption is that a demanding situation results in psychological distress and strain when decision latitude and control over characteristics of the situation are insufficient (e.g., Karasek et al. 1981). Although this assumption is borrowed from approaches to psychological stress where psychological demands and control are each subjectively appraised by the individual (Karasek et al. 1981, Lazarus & Folkman 1984), it has also been employed as an objective assessment of job strain through the application of consensual (e.g., the average response of workers with a specific job) or expert (supervisors') ratings of demands and control (Frese & Zapf 1988, Karasek & Theorell 1990).

Interruption of goals. Finally, the fourth approach defines stressful events as interruptions of major goals (Carver & Scheier 1999), including goals to maintain one's physical integrity and one's psychological well-being (Kemeny 2003, Lazarus & Folkman 1984). This approach is primarily rooted in evidence that interference with personal goals is associated with emotional distress, but it has not been widely studied in die prediction of illness outcomes (Carver & Scheier 1999, Wrosch et al. 2007). Goal interruption is also central to Brown & Harris's (1989) position that threat is primarily rooted in disruption of roles or plans in the context of a person's life goals. Our own view that events are threats to one's social status, self-esteem, identity, and physical well-being may also be folded in to the goal interruption theory, with each of these representing a core goal that is consensually viewed as important.

Which approach is correct? There is obvious overlap among these approaches. For example, the interruption of goals may occur when demands exceed decision latitude, and goal interruption probably generates both threat and a need to adapt. The adaptation approach has received the most direct testing of its assumptions, with only mixed results. For example, summing of judges' weights of how much change each event on a life event checklist requires is no more predictive of health outcomes than just counting the number of events, and positive events (e.g., marriage, vacation) that require adaptation are unlike negative ones in that they do not contribute to the predictability of life event checklists (Turner & Wheaton 1995).

Overall, the threat or harm approach is the most commonly accepted perspective. There is considerably less evidence addressing the validity of the demands versus control and decision latitude and goal interruption approaches. Moreover, one could argue that these two approaches are merely subsets of the threat approach. The simplicity of the adaptation approach remains attractive (Turner & Wheaton 1995), even though some key hypotheses derived from this perspective have not held up. It is a challenge for future researchers to more clearly distinguish among the sensitivities of these alternative approaches and to delineate any important differences in their predictions for the types of environmental events with the potential to influence our health and well-being.

Fact 2: Stressful Events Can Impact Most Diseases

There are a variety of mechanisms through which the experience of stressful events may influence the onset of clinically defined disease, preclinical or clinical disease progression, or both (Miller et al. 2009). The pathways linking stressful event exposure to disease that have been extensively studied include alterations in affective regulation (e.g., elevated levels of anxiety, fear, depression), health behaviors (e.g., poor nutrition, not exercising, overconsumption of alcohol, smoking cigarettes, poor sleep), and neurohormonal systems (e.g., changes in the output or tissue effects of hormones such as cortisol, testosterone, and estrogen), as well as direct innervation of tissues by the autonomic nervous system (e.g., heightened sympathetic nervous system activity resulting in increased release of norepinephrine). Modification of any of these pathways could potentially result in deleterious changes to major organs (e.g., brain, heart, liver) and bodily systems (e.g., immune, endocrine, and cardiovascular systems) (McEwen 2012). Thus, in theory, exposure to stressful events may impact any disease with an etiology involving affect regulation, health behaviors, hormones, or the autonomic nervous system. This formulation suggests that many diseases or disease processes with multifaceted etiologies may theoretically be subject to modulation by stressor exposure. While it is outside the scope of this article to provide an extensive review of research linking stressful events to all diseases, in this section, we consider evidence for the relationships between stressor exposure and a selection of common illnesses responsible for a large proportion of morbidities, disabilities, and deaths worldwide: depression, cardiovascular disease (CVD), infectious diseases, and cancer (see also Cohen et al. 2007).

Depression. Major stressful life events p respectively predict the premorhid symptoms of depression, anxiety, and fear that are risks for depression (Gotlib & Joormann 2010, Hammer) 2016, Turner et al. 1995). They also predict both the clinical onset and subsequent reoccurrences of major depressive disorder (Hammen 2005, Monroe et al. 2009). Individuals who develop depression are estimated to be between 2.5 and 9.4 times as likely to have experienced a major stressful life event prior to the first onset of depression, making recent stressor exposure one of the strongest proximal risk factors for depression in community samples (Kendler et al. 2000, Monroe et al. 2009, Slavich & Irwin 2014). Furthermore, among individuals who are depressed, stressful life events are associated with higher symptom severity, longer duration of illness, and increased likelihood of relapse (Monroe et al, 2009).

Cardiovascular diseases. Numerous mechanistic studies have documented that exposure to stressful life experiences is associated with the development of premorbid processes and states well recognized as risk factors for clinical CVD onset and progression (Steptoe & Kivimaki 2013). These factors include increased central adiposity, dysregulation of lipid and glucose levels, heightened exposure to inflammation, and elevated resting blood pressure. In line with these mechanistic studies, prospective studies have repeatedly documented that chronic stressful experiences are associated with increased risk for the development of clinical CVD (Dimsdale 2008). Moreover, experiencing chronic stressors predicts both faster progression of CVD and increased mortality from CVD (Steptoe & Kivimaki 2012). Even acute stressors can trigger adverse cardiac events, such as myocardial ischemia, cardiac arrhythmias, cardiomyopathy, and myocardial infarction, among patients with preexisting heart disease (Steptoe & Kivimaki 2013).

Infectious diseases. Infectious diseases are caused by pathogens such as viruses and bacteria. However, experiencing stressful life events, especially chronic enduring events, can increase an individual's risk of developing illness in response to exposure to an infectious agent (for a review, see Pedersen et al. 2010). Some of the most compelling evidence for the role of stressful events in increasing individuals' risk for developing illness following exposure to a pathogen comes from a series of viral challenge studies conducted by Cohen and colleagues (for an overview, see Cohen 2016). In these studies, healthy adults were experimentally exposed to a virus that causes the common cold and then quarantined and followed for 5–6 days to determine who developed a clinical illness, as manifested by infection (shedding virus) and objective signs of disease (mucus production, and congestion). Within this paradigm, exposure to recent and chronic stressful life events has repeatedly been shown to increase an individual's risk of developing clinical illness following inoculation with die challenge virus. While a cold is not generally a serious illness, these findings demonstrate that host resistance to infectious agents can be reduced by stressful events. In the case of a far more serious infectious disease, naturalistic studies of HIV/AIDS conducted since the advent of highly active antiretroviral therapy have found that stressful life events, especially exposure to traumatic experiences, are associated with poorer disease outcomes, including increased viral load, higher risk of developing an opportunistic secondary infection, and increased AIDS-related mortality (Leserman 2008).

Cancer. Findings regarding whether stressful life events increase cancer risk or progression are much more equivocal than findings for the other conditions discussed above. Mechanistic laboratory studies have demonstrated a role of stressful experiences in modulating physiological processes related to cancer development (for reviews, see Antoni et al. 2006, Fagundes er al. 2017).

Conversely, prospective studies of the association between stressful events and cancer onset and progression have not consistently found evidence for stressor exposure as a risk factor (for a review, see Cohen et al. 2007). However, this lack of consistent findings may be due to difficulties in conducting methodologically rigorous, well-powered cancer studies. Consistent with this notion, using meta-analytic techniques, Chida et al. (2008) found that, among studies that they coded as being high in quality, stressful life events were associated with poorer survival among samples of patients with cancer, as well as with higher mortality rates due to cancer in population samples. That being said, cancer is a heterogeneous disease, and the findings reviewed by Chida et al. were limited to only a relatively narrow set of possible cancer sites. Furthermore, the reported pooled effect sizes were modest, and the authors found evidence for significant publication bias. As such, the true nature of the association between stressor exposure and cancer remains much less clear than for the other diseases discussed above.

Theory versus data.   While exposure to stressful events could theoretically impact any disease that is modulated by associated behaviors or physiology, the evidence concerning stressful events and cancer highlights a divide between what theory suggests and what data show. Health behaviors, hormones, and central nervous system activity are all known to modulate various cancers (Anderson et al. 1994, Antoni et al. 2006, Lutgendorf & Andersen 2015. Sklar & Anisman 1981). However, the strongest conclusion derived from decades of research on stressors and cancer is that stressful events may be associated with decreased cancer survival but are probably not associated with disease incidence (Chida et al. 2008). From a public health perspective, the evidence that exposure to stressful events is associated with cancer survival is interesting and important. However, it is conceptually unclear why the incidence of a disease influenced by the same pathways that are activated by exposure to stressors would not show more empirical associations with stressful experiences (but see Sklar & Anisman 1981). It is possible that this issue may simply reflect eventually surmountable methodological limitations related to studying cancer in humans (Cohen et al. 2007). Nonetheless, one area that may benefit from further development is a better accounting of what disease processes may be less subject to modulation by stressor exposure and why this might be the case.

Fact 3: Most People Exposed to Stressful Events (Even Traumatic Events) Do Not Get Sick

Despite compelling evidence that stressful events have the capacity to impair health, on the whole, most people who experience stressful events do not get sick. This is true both in the case of normative stressful events (i.e., events that happen to most of us sometime in our lifetime, such as a job loss or the loss of an important relationship) and for less common traumatic events (e.g., direct exposure to violence or abuse).

This phenomenon has been highlighted in work exposing otherwise healthy participants to a common cold virus (Cohen et al. 1998). Stressful events were assessed in a sample of 276 participants using the LEDS semistructured interview discussed above (Brown & Harris 1989). Participants were then inoculated with rhinovirus, quarantined, and tracked for the development of a biologically verified cold. As predicted, those reporting an enduring (1 month or more) stressful life event had an increased likelihood of developing a cold compared to those who did not report a stressful life event. Only 72 of 201 participants (35.8%) without a stressful event developed a cold compared to 37 of 75 participants (49.3%) who reported a stressful event. What is often neglected when interpreting these data is that 38 of the 75 participants who reported a stressful life event (50.7%) did not develop a clinical cold.

While exposures to stressful and even traumatic events may not always result in physical illness, one would think that the occurrence of negative mental health outcomes, such as depression, would be commonplace. Interestingly, this does not appear to be the case. Although stressful life events are consistently found to be related to increased risk for depression, depression is not inevitable. Indeed, Bonanno et al. (2011) have demonstrated across various traumatic events that the majority of exposed individuals are resilient to later psychopathology. For example, in response to a loss of a spouse in later life, 13.2% of adults in the sample experienced the onset of depression following the loss, which is in stark contrast to the 68.2% who showed little to no evidence of depression over a 6-year follow-up period (Maccallum et al. 2015). The remaining percentage of the sample was made up of individuals who were depressed prior to the loss and remained depressed across the sampling frame (7.4%) and those who showed high levels of depression prior to the loss of their spouse that improved following the loss (11.2%). While the percentage of individuals who fall into these different groups vary by stressor exposure (e.g., combat exposure, medical illness, loss of a child) and by psychopathology outcome (e.g., depression, post-traumatic stress disorder), a large segment of those exposed to stressors (35–65%) do not suffer significant mental health problems as a consequence (Bonanno et al. 2011).

Why are some people resilient to stressful events? Accumulating data suggest that several individual difference measures play protective roles. In this regard, reports of greater perceived control, greater self-efficacy, and lesser negative affectivity and rumination have all been associated with psychological resilience in the face of stressful life events (reviewed in Adler & Matthews 1994, Bonanno et al. 2011). Access to social resources has also been shown to promote resilience under stressful circumstances (Cohen 2004). These resources include emotional, instrumental, and informational support. The influence of social support in buffering the negative effects of stressful events goes beyond mental health. For example, a prospective study of over 700 men followed over 7 years found that the presence of stressful events predicted increased risk of mortality only among participants reporting low emotional support. Those with high levels of emotional support were protected (Rosengren et al. 1993).

Fact 4: Stressful Events Do Not Fall Randomly from the Sky

With some limited exceptions (e.g., natural disasters, accidental deaths of friends or family members), stressful event exposures do not occur at random but instead are influenced by both individual differences in environmental circumstances and psychological characteristics. An example of a salient environmental circumstance at play here is the socioeconomic status (SES) of one's neighborhood. Compared to high-SES neighborhoods, low-SES environments are marked by more frequent and severe stressor exposures, such as overcrowding and the observation and experience of violence (Evans & Kim 2010). Individual SES can similarly influence exposure to stressful events. For example, those with lower SES are more likely to experience a divorce, death of a child, and violent assault than those with higher SES (Adler et al. 1994, Lantz et al. 2005).

Personality factors may also be hidden causes of stressor exposure. For example, divorce is more common in those whose personality is characterized by greater neuroticism or lesser conscientiousness and agreeableness (Roberts et al. 2007). In addition, some cognitive styles, such as a tendency to attribute negative events to stable, global, and internal causes, can lead individuals to experience more stressful life events. Examined primarily in the context of depression (Hammen 2006), individuals characterized by negative attributional style have been found to generate more interpersonal conflicts, leading to a greater likelihood of experiencing stressful life events, such as the loss of a close relationship (Liu & Alloy 2010). Notably, negative attachment, styles, such as anxious attachment, and maladaptive coping strategies, such as avoidant coping, have also been linked to a tendency to experience more future major stressful life events (Barker 2007, Hankin et al. 2005).

Interestingly, individual stressful events themselves may trigger sequences of other events (Cohen et al. 1982, Monroe 1982). Like dominos, when one event occurs, this sets into motion a cascade of subsequent stressors that can result in a clustering of stressor exposures. An example of this could be the loss of a job. An event like this can reverberate through an individual's life, leading to exposure to multiple additional stressors, including residential relocation and increased strain in one's relationships, possibly leading to marital divorce. Divorce could lead to the loss of income, health insurance, and contacts with friends. Moreover, a single stressor can have transgenerational effects. For example, parental job loss can create stressors for children, including a need to change schools (due to relocation of their home), loss of close contacts, and possible parental separation.

Fact 5: Stressful Events May Not Cause Disease in Healthy People

As noted above, there is consistent evidence that exposure to stressful life events predicts increases in risk for disease, particularly in the case of chronic medical conditions such as CVD, asthma, and depression (Monroe et al. 2009, Steptoe & Kivimaki 2013, Wright et al. 1998). However, it is important to emphasize that stressful event exposure may not be the proximate cause of disease. That is, stressful events may not trigger the initial pathogenesis of disease in otherwise healthy people. Rather, events may influence risk for disease by either suppressing the body's ability to fight invading pathogens or exacerbating the progression of ongoing premorbid processes, resulting in the eventual onset of clinically defined disease.

We view the evidence for associations between stressful events and the onset of chronic diseases as equivocal because of the difficulty of identifying when these diseases begin. That is, in many cases, baseline (prior to the onset of the stressful event) measures of disease do not convincingly rule out the possibility of unidentified signs of illness. In turn, studies of the incidence of such diseases may actually be studies of the role of stressful events in the progression of disease, or, in some cases, may reflect preexisting disease resulting in stressor exposure. For example, coronary artery disease (CAD) is marked by the accumulation of plaques in the coronary arteries that, over time, lead to blockage and reduction in blood flow. When it is severe, a reduction in blood flow can result in cardiovascular events such as a heart attack. Although CAD was once thought to be a disease that emerged in midlife, recent research suggests that the premorbid pathogenesis of CAD can begin during the first 2 decades of life (Thurston & Matthews 2009). Thus, what appears to be stressor-triggered disease onset in mid-life and older adults may actually be stressor-triggered progression of previously unidentified disease. Identifying premorbid markers of cancer at baseline involves a similar challenge, with early and premorbid disease often being difficult or impossible to detect (Cohen et al. 2007).

Exposure to stressful events can, however, exacerbate early or premorbid disease states by tipping the balance of an already vulnerable system. For example, heart attacks are a marker of the progression of CAD and occur in persons with underlying atherosclerosis. A study of the 1981 earthquake in Athens, Greece found an increased rate of fatal heart attacks on the days immediately following the earthquake compared to the days that preceded it (Trichopoulos et al. 1983). Similarly, activity from implantable cardioverter defibrillators (devices used on heart disease patients to detect and correct heart rhythm issues) was significantly higher in the 30 days following the September 11 World Trade Center attacks than in the 30 days before (Steinberg et al. 2004). Importantly, these examples suggest that stressful events may contribute to morbidity by triggering cardiovascular events in individuals already burdened by CVD. This association also plays a role in asthma exacerbation. For example, Sandberg et al. (2000) demonstrated that, in children with chronic asthma, the occurrence of severe stressful events, such as the death of a family member or parental divorce, prospectively predicted an asthma exacerbation between 2 and 4 weeks after the event.

The assertion that stressful events may not be the proximal cause of the onset of chronic diseases derives from historical limitations in measuring premorbid and early stage disease in epidemiological studies. It is not a criticism of the wealth of evidence that stressful events can perturb key biological processes that potentially play a role in disease pathogenesis (e.g., inflammatory processes, metabolic dysregulation). In other words, we are not denying the possibility that progressive biological wear and tear that occurs with chronic or cumulative stressful life events may result in increased disease risk (Juster et al. 2010, McEwen 1998). Rather, we are suggesting that the evidence that stressful life events play a causal role in the onset of chronic diseases in otherwise healthy individuals (i.e., without existing disease) is not well supported empirically.

Fact 6: Certain Types of Stressful Events Are Particularly Potent

Not all domains of stressful life events are equally impactful when it comes to shaping an individual's health. Experiences that threaten an individual's sense of competence or status within domains that make up the individual's core identity appear to be the most costly (Cohen et al. 2016; see also Crocker & Park 2004). Events of this nature generally fell into three broad categories, although there is overlap among categories. These categories are interpersonal problems, loss of social status, and employment difficulties (in particular, un- or underemployment).

Events involving interpersonal problems can be broadly construed as threatening or harmful events that are centered around interactions or relationships with other people. Examples of interpersonal events include ongoing conflict with a spouse, friend, or coworker; a close friend moving away; and the death of a loved one. Stressful events involving other people occur less frequently than positive experiences with others; however, when negative events do occur, they tend to have a more dramatic impact on well-being and health than do positive interpersonal experiences (Rook 1998). Indeed, evidence has accumulated linking stressful interpersonal events to a variety of negative health outcomes, including heightened risk of depression, upper respiratory infection, hypertension, heart disease, physical disability, and premature mortality (Cohen et al. 1998, Kendler et al. 2003, Rook 2014, Sneed & Cohen 2014).

Interpersonal stressful life events may be problematic for health; however, it is also the case that not all events within this domain are equally potent. Mounting evidence suggests that interpersonal events that specifically threaten an individual's social status (i.e., that are high in social-evaluative threat) may be particularly noxious (Dickerson & Kemeny 2004). Examples of such events include being broken up with by a romantic partner and being intentionally excluded from social activities by one's peers. Studies have shown links between stressful events marked by loss of social status and adverse health outcomes. For example, in a large epidemiological survey, Kendler et al. (2003) found that interpersonal loss was associated with increased risk for developing depression. However, the extent to which depression risk increased depended on the nature of the loss. Individuals who had experienced the death of a loved one were at similarly elevated risk for depression as individuals who broke off the relationship with their romantic partner, whereas individuals who had been broken up with by a romantic partner showed the greatest depression risk. Relatedly, in a multiwave study of youth diagnosed with asthma, Murphy et al. (2015) found that, at study waves when individuals reported having recently experienced social rejection, they showed decreased anti-inflammatory gene signaling and increased asthma symptoms compared to study waves when no rejection had occurred. Importantly, no such associations were found for other types of stressful life events (i.e., interpersonal events without rejection and noninterpersonal events) with similar severity ratings. Results from these studies also converge with research in nonhuman primates that documents threats to social status as a particularly pathogenic type of stressful event (e.g., Cohen et al. 1997, Manuck et al. 1995, Shively & Clarkson 1994).

Employment difficulties, especially becoming unemployed or being underemployed, have adverse implications for role identity, social status, and financial security and are also associated with deleterious health outcomes. For example, in a study that directly compared how various different types of major stressful life events influence disease risk, Cohen et al. (1998) found that un- or underemployment life events lasting at least 1 month, as measured using the LEDS, were die strongest predictors of developing illness among participants experimentally exposed to a cold-causing virus (interpersonal events were the next-strongest predictors of illness). More broadly, epidemiological studies have found that becoming unemployed or underemployed increases risk for depression, CVD, and premature mortality (e.g., Dooley et al. 2000, Gallo et al. 2004, Morris et al. 1994).

Fact 7: Chronic Stressful Events Are Worse than Acute Ones, Except When They Are Not

It is generally thought that stressful life events that last a long time are more harmful than acute ones. This is because, as exposure persists, there are increased probabilities of the stressor being present at points of vulnerability in the disease process; of long-term or permanent changes in the emotional, physiological, and behavioral responses that have downstream influences on disease (Cohen et al. 2007); and of increased wear and tear on the body (e.g., allostatic load) (McEwen 2004).

However, there are dimensions of chronic events, other than duration per se, that can be important for understanding the health risks that these events pose. Chronic events include both persistent chronic stressors, such as permanent disabilities, parental discord, or chronic job stress, which persist continuously for a long time, and chronic intermittent stressors, such as conflict-filled visits to in-laws or sexual difficulties, which may occur once a day, once a week, or once a month (Cohen et al. 1982). Another type of chronic exposure involves stressor sequences, or series of events that occur over an extended period of time as the result of an initiating event such as job loss, divorce, or bereavement (Cohen et al. 1982, Monroe 1982).

When do chronic events matter? We propose that chronic events should be associated with a greater risk of facilitating disease processes than should acute events. This belief is in contrast to the adaptation hypothesis—that one adapts to stressors over time, and thus shows fewer effects with increased duration of exposure. The adaptation hypothesis is based primarily on laboratory studies where physiological responses to stressful experiences habituate rather quickly (e.g., Glass & Singer 1972), as well as on work looking at long-term adaptation to physical disability (Schulz & Decker 1985). What are the characteristics of chronic events that result in increased risk versus attenuation over time? One possibility is that continued effects of exposure to prolonged stressful experiences are more likely to occur when events are severely threatening, and habituation or adaptation is more likely to occur when they are less so. Another possibility is that the type of periodicity of the event matters, with random intermittent events inhibiting habituation and continuous or predictable intermittent events promoting adaptation (Glass & Singer 1972). A final possibility is that the underlying biological process is key. Many stressor-elicited changes, for example in immune function (Anderson et al. 1994) and sympathetic activation (Kaplan et al. 1987, Skantze et al. 1998), may persist with the chronicity of a natural stressor; yet others, such as cortisol concentrations (Ockenfels et al. 1995), may habituate over time.

When do acute events matter? As alluded to above, although it plays less of a role in disease onset, exposure to acute (time-limited) stressful life events, such as taking an important exam, awaiting surgery, or being held up at gunpoint, are thought to play a significant role in exacerbating preexisting disease. For example, among individuals with CAD (atherosclerosis), exposure to acute life stressors is associated with a number of deleterious cardiovascular outcomes such as reduced oxygen delivery to the heart, which, when extreme, results in the death of heart tissue—a heart attack or myocardial infarction (Rozanski et al. 1999). Similarly, among those with asthma (underlying inflammation of the airways), acute events can trigger asthma attacks (Wright et al. 1998).

Others (Baum et al. 1993) have emphasized that traumatic events like rape or physical assault may last a short time but still have long-term effects on risk for disease. They suggest that the impact of a stressful event should be determined not only by the duration of the event, but also by the durations of the ensuing appraisal process, the affective response to the event, and the stress-related physical effects.

Fact 8: Multiple Events May Be More Potent than Individual Ones, or They May Not

Above, we mention that both definitions of stressful life events that focus on adaptation and those that focus on threat suggest the possibility that the risk associated with, stressful life events is cumulative. Unexpectedly, research with stressful life event checklists that merely count the number of events that occurred during the previous year results in as good predictions of health outcomes as summing change or threat weights assigned to the events by judges (Turner & Wheaton 1995). Thus, it is true that the more events occur, the greater is the risk, but at the same time, the data do not provide direct evidence that this effect is due to the amount of change or threat that is accumulating.

In contrast, as noted above, research using the LEDS interview suggests that experiencing a single event that meets a moderate or severe threat criterion is sufficient to put people at risk, but that experiencing multiple events does not further increase that risk (Brown & Harris 1989, Wethington et al. 1995). A possible explanation for the LEDS interview's finding that single events predict health outcomes is that the life event checklists may not be doing a good job of defining the content of events. For example, is a divorce that leads to residential relocation and loss of income one event or three? Similarly, are conflicts at work, being underpaid at work, and being overloaded at work separate events, or do they all represent a single bad work environment? The LEDS takes into account the context in which events occur, probably resulting in single events, as assessed by the LEDS, representing multiple events on a life events checklist. Some recent life events checklists have had success with aggregating events into domains (e.g., financial events, legal events, career events, relationships, safety in the home, and medical issues) and counting the number of domains in which someone is experiencing stressors, rather than die number of events across domains (Lee et al. 2017, Shalowitz. et al. 1998). Creating domains may better represent the experience of correlated events.

A related question is whether chronic background stressors, e.g., marital discord or a bad work environment, make one more or less responsive to the occurrence of acute events. The hypothesis that exposure to chronic events results in sensitization has been supported by studies of the impact of acute stressors when there is a background of chronic stress on the symptoms and signs of disease in asthmatic children (e.g., Marin et. al. 2009; Sandberg et al. 2000, 2004) and on depression among caregivers for the chronically ill (Kiecolt-Glaser et al. 1988); however, this hypothesis has received only mixed support in studies of biomarker responses to acute laboratory stressors in those suffering chronic background stress (Gump et al. 1999). The variability in results could be attributed to multiple differences between studies, for example, differences in definitions of what constitutes a chronic event, whether the chronic event has been resolved or not, the relationship between the domain of the chronic stressful event and the domain of the acute stressor, and the acute stressor study outcome (most outcomes studied in the laboratory are cardiovascular).

Overall, it is impossible at this point to know whether increases in the number of events increases risk for disease. This is because there is no overall agreement as to what constitutes an event. It is not clear whether an event needs to meet a threshold of threat or adaptation, whether events that cluster together (e.g., divorce and moving) should be considered a single experience or multiple ones, or whether event domains are a better way of defining the stress experiences than the occurrence of single events. Studies providing better comparisons of these possibilities would help in providing a clearer answer to this question.

Fact 9: Stressful Events Vary in Frequency and Potency as a Function of Where an Individual Is in the Life Course

There is substantial variability in individuals' day-to-day lives. However, structured around this variability are predictable life events that make up the typical life course. These events are common in the population, routinely happen during a particular life stage, and are consistent with sociocultural norms (Schulz & Rau 1985). Examples of such events include finishing school, getting married, and having a child during the earlier adult years and retirement from the workforce and the death of a spouse during the later adult years. Individuals have expectations about when such events are supposed to happen, and violations of these expectations can have deleterious consequences for health and well-being. To illustrate, consider the death of a spouse. Losing a loved one can represent a stressful event regardless of age (Bonanno & Kaltman 1999). Yet as painful as the death of a spouse might be, such an event is more normative among older adults relative to the same loss experienced earlier in the life course. As a result, losing a spouse should be more strongly associated with negative outcomes when it occurs earlier in life than when it occurs in later decades. Consistent with this formulation, meta-analytic evidence shows that the age at which individuals lose a spouse moderates mortality risk, with the association between stress and mortality being stronger among younger individuals than among older individuals (Shor et al. 2012). Violations of expectations of when normative events should happen also include situations where expected events do not occur; for example, not graduating high school, not getting married, or not being promoted at expected times have the potential to exert similar pathogenic effects as stressful life events that do occur (Schulz & Rau 1985).

In addition to expectations around when particular types of stressful events should or should not happen over the life course, there is evidence that there are sensitive periods of life when stressful events may exact a more pronounced and long-lasting toll on health. Childhood appears to be a particularly important sensitive period, with numerous studies linking adverse childhood experiences to increased risk of developing chronic illnesses later in life, as well as increased mortality risk (e.g., Anda et al. 2009, Norman et al. 2012, Wegman & Stetler 2009). Adverse childhood experiences are generally conceptualized as stressful early life events comprising both ongoing difficulties (e.g., parental abuse or neglect) and acute time-limited exposures with long-term threat implications (e.g., witnessing a violent crime or being sexually assaulted). Experiencing adversity during childhood may set an individual on a trajectory to being exposed to more stressors over the life course, and such excess exposure may subsequently increase disease risk (Pearlin et al. 2005). Furthermore, adverse childhood experiences are also thought to increase risk for negative health outcomes later in life by generating enduring changes in both biological processes and behavioral proclivities (Repetti et al. 2002, Taylor 2010). In some cases, such changes may confer shorter-term adaptive advantages to individuals in the context of the adverse childhood environment. However, these shorter-term advantages may come at a cost with regards to later-life disease risk (Cohen et al. 1986, Danese & McEwen 2012, Miller et al. 2011).

Fact 10: Different Types of Stressful Events Influence Women and Men

Underlying physiological differences between the biological sexes, along with differential evolutionary pressures, play a role in shaping men's and women's physiological and behavioral responses to stressful experiences (Bale & Epperson 2015, Taylor et al. 2000). However, the extent to which men and women differ in the types of stressful events that they are exposed to is thought to be driven more by differences in socialized gender roles than by underlying physiology. As reviewed by Dedovic et al. (2009), in Western cultures, men are historically more likely than women to be encouraged from an early age to develop self-focused agentic goals (e.g., getting a good job). Conversely, women are more likely than men to be encouraged to develop socially interdependent communal goals (e.g., taking care of a family). These differently cultivated goal motivations ultimately shape the sorts of experiences that young men and women seek as they develop into adolescents and adults. As a result, the types of stressful events that men and women experience should theoretically vary as a function of gender socialization.

Consistent with the idea that socialized gender roles predispose men and women to different stressful events, researchers have argued that men are more likely to be exposed to achievement-related stressful experiences such as unemployment, while women are more likely to be exposed to interpersonal stressful experiences such as caregiving (for a review, see Helgeson 2011). Moreover, whereas men tend to only report stressful events that occur directly to them, women are more likely to also report exposure to stressful events that occur to close others (Kessler & McLeod 1984, Turner et al. 1995). However, while this theoretical orientation predicting differential patterning of stressful life experiences as a function of gender continues to permeate the literature, it may not be consistent with available data. In particular, a meta-analysis of 119 studies published between 1960 and 1996 found that women consistently reported greater exposure to stressful events than men across domains, including in both interpersonal and work domains (Davis et al. 1999). It is possible that changing sociocultural norms regarding women in the workplace have closed the gap in work-related stressor exposure, as women place more importance on employment and financial success now than they did in the past (e.g., McLeod et al. 2016).

There are fewer studies addressing the extent to which gender differences in exposure to stressful life events are associated with differential vulnerability to illnesses. The clearest evidence for differential vulnerability comes from studies examining sex disparities in depression risk (Hammen 2005). While depression risk is similar between males and females during childhood, starting during adolescence, females' risk for depression increases relative to males, a pattern that remains consistent well into adulthood (Cyranowski et al. 2000). This finding is thought to be due at least in part to women developing more sensitivity to what is happening within their social networks and thus being exposed to more interpersonal stressful life events than men (Helgeson 2011, Kessler & McLeod 1984). Importantly, exposure to interpersonal events tends to be more strongly associated with depression onset for women than for men (Hammen 2005). Interestingly, women's heightened vulnerability to depression following stressful events may also help explain why, compared to men, women tend to experience worse clinical outcomes due to morbidities modulated by depression, such as CVD and metabolic diseases (for reviews, see Low et al. 2010; Möller-Leimkühler 2008, 2010; Murphy & Loria 2017).

Reflections and Conclusions

What We Know About Stressful Life Events and Disease Risk

What we can be sure of is that stressful life events predict increases in severity and progression of multiple diseases, including depression, cardiovascular diseases, HIV/AIDS, asthma, and autoimmune diseases. Although there is also evidence for stressful events predicting disease onset, challenges in obtaining sensitive assessments of premorbid states at baseline (for example, in cancer and heart disease) make interpretation of much of these data as evidence for onset less compelling.

In general, stressful life events are thought to influence disease risk through their effects on affect, behavior, and physiology. These effects include affective dysregulation such as increases in anxiety, fear, and depression. Additionally, behavioral changes occurring as adaptations or coping responses to stressors, such as increased smoking, decreased exercise and sleep, poorer diets, and poorer adherence to medical regimens, provide important pathways through which stressors can influence disease risk. Two endocrine response systems, the hypothalamic-pituitary-adrenocortical (HPA) axis and the sympathetic-adrenal-medullary (SAM) system, are particularly reactive to psychological stress and are also thought to play a major role in linking stressor exposure to disease. Prolonged or repeated activation of the HPA axis and SAM system can interfere with their control of other physiological systems (e.g., cardiovascular, metabolic, immune), resulting in increased risk for physical and psychiatric disorders (Cohen et al. 1995b, McEwen 1998).

Chronic stressor exposure is considered to be the most toxic form of stressor exposure because chronic events are the most likely to result in long-term or permanent changes in the emotional, physiological, and behavioral responses that influence susceptibility to and course of disease. These exposures include those to stressful events that persist over an extended duration (e.g., caring for a spouse with dementia) and to brief focal events that continue to be experienced as overwhelming long after they have ended (e.g., experiencing a sexual assault). Even so, acute stressors seem to play a special role in triggering disease events among those with underlying pathology (whether premorbid or morbid), such as asthma and heart attacks.

One of the most provocative aspects of the evidence linking stressful events to disease is the broad range of diseases that are presumed to be affected. As discussed above, the range of effects may be attributable to the feet that many behavioral and physiological responses to stressors are risk factors for a wide range of diseases. The more of these responses to stressful events are associated with risk for a specific disease, the greater is the chance that stressful events will increase the risk for the onset and progression of that disease. For example, risk factors for CVD include many of the behavioral effects of stressors (poor diet, smoking, inadequate physical activity). In addition, stressor effects on CVD (Kaplan et al. 1987, Skantze et al. 1998) and HIV (Capitanio et al. 1998, Cole et al, 2003) are mediated by physiological effects of stressors (e.g., sympathetic activation, glucocorticoid regulation, and inflammation).

It is unlikely that all diseases are modulated by stressful life event exposure. Rare conditions, such as those that are genetic and of high penetrance, leave little room for stressful life events to play a role in disease onset. For example, Tay-Sachs disease is an autosomal recessive disorder expressed in in fancy that results in destruction of neurons in both the spinal cord and brain. This disease is folly penetrant, meaning that, if an individual carries two copies of the mutation in the *HEXA* gene, then they will be affected. Other inherited disorders, such as Huntington's disease, show high penetrance but are not fully penetrant, leaving room for environmental exposures, behavioral processes, and interactions among these factors to influence disease onset. Note that, upon disease onset, it is unlikely that any disease is immune to the impact of stressor exposure if pathways elicited by the stressor are implicated in the pathogenesis or symptom course of the disease.

What We Do Not Know About Stressful Life Events and Disease Risk

There are still a number of key issues in understanding how stressful events might alter disease pathogenesis where the data are still insufficient to provide clear answers. These include the lack of a clear conceptual definition of what constitutes a stress till event. Alternative approaches (adaptation, threat, goal interruption, demand versus control) overlap in their predictions, providing little leverage for empirically establishing the unique nature of major stressful events. The lack of understanding of the primary nature of stressful events also obscures the reasons for certain events (e.g., interpersonal, economic) being more potent.

Two other important questions for which we lack consistent evidence are whether the stress load accumulates with each additional stressor and whether previous or ongoing chronic stressors moderate responses to current ones. The nature of the cumulative effects of stressors is key to obtaining sensitive assessments of the effects of stressful evens on disease and for planning environmental (stressor-reduction) interventions to reduce the impact of events on our health.

Evidence that single events may be sufficient to trigger risk for disease has raised two important questions. First, are some types of events more potent than others? We address this question above (in the section titled Fact 6: Certain Types of Stressful Events Are Particularly Potent) using the existing evidence, but it is important to emphasize die relative lack of studies comparing the impact of different stressors on the same outcomes (for some exceptions, see Cohen et al. 1998, Kendler et al. 2003, Murphy et al. 2015). Second, are specific types of events linked to specific diseases? This question derives from scattered evidence of stressors that are potent predictors of specific diseases [e.g., social loss for depression (Kendler et al. 2003), work stress for CHD (Kivimäki et al. 2006)] and of specific stress biomarkers [e.g., threats to social status leading to cortisol responses (Denson et al. 2009, Dickerson & Kemeny 2004)]. While it is provocative, there are no direct tests of the stressor-disease specificity hypothesis. A proper examination of this theory would require studies that not only conduct broad assessments of different types of stressful life events, but also measure multiple unique diseases to draw comparisons. Such studies may not be feasible due to the high costs of properly assessing multiple disease outcomes and the need for large numbers of participants to obtain sufficient numbers of persons developing (incidence) or initially having each disease so as to measure progression. Comparisons of limited numbers of diseases proposed to have different predictors (e.g., cancer and heart disease) are more efficient and may be a good initial approach to this issue.

Another area of weakness is the lack of understanding of the types of stressful events that are most salient at different points in development. For example, although traumatic events are the type of events studied most often in children, the relative lack of focus on more normative events leaves us with an incomplete understanding of how different events influence the current and later health of young people. Overall, the relative lack of comparisons of the impact of the same events (or equivalents) across the life course further muddies our understanding of event salience as we age.

It is noteworthy that the newest generation of instruments designed to assess major stressful life events has the potential to provide some of the fine-grained information required to address many of the issues raised in this review (for a review, see Anderson et al. 2010; see also Epel et al. 2018). For example, the Life Events Assessment Profile (LEAP) (Anderson et al. 2010) is a computer-assisted, interviewer-administered measure designed to mimic the LEDS. Like the LEDS, the LEAP assesses events occurring within the past 6–12 months, uses probing questions to better define events, assesses exposure duration, and assigns objective levels of contextual threat based on LEDS dictionaries. Another instrument, the Stress and Adversity Inventory (STRAIN)

(Slavich & Shields 2018), is a participant-completed computer assessment of lifetime cumulative exposure to stressors. The STRAIN assesses a range of event domains and timing of events (e.g., early life, distant, recent) and uses probing follow-up questions. Both the LEAP and the STRAIN are less expensive and time consuming than the LEDS and other interview techniques and are thus more amenable to use in large-scale studies.

The fundamental question of whether stressful events cause disease can only be rigorously evaluated by experimental studies. Ethical considerations prohibit conducting experimental studies in humans of the effects of enduring stressful events on the pathogenesis of serious disease. A major limitation of the correlational studies is insufficient evidence of (and control for) selection in who gets exposed to events, resulting in the possibility that selection factors such as environments, personalities, or genetics are the real causal agents. The concern is that the social and psychological characteristics that shape what types of stressful events people are exposed to may be directly responsible for modulating disease risk. Because it is not possible to randomly assign people to stressful life events, being able to infer that exposure to stressful events causally modulates disease will require the inclusion of covariates representing obvious individual and environmental confounders, as well as controls for stressor dependency—the extent to which individuals are responsible for generating the stressful events that they report.

Even with these methodological limitations, there is evidence from natural experiments that capitalize on real-life stressors occurring outside of a person's control, such as natural disasters, economic downsizing, or bereavement (Cohen et al. 2007). There have also been attempts to reduce progression and recurrence of disease using experimental studies of psychosocial interventions. However, clinical trials in this area tend to be small, methodologically weak, and not specifically focused on determining whether stress reduction accounts for intervention-induced reduction in disease risk. Moreover, trials that do assess stress reduction as a mediator generally focus on the reduction of nonspecific perceptions of stress and negative affect instead of on the elimination or reduction of the stressful event itself. In contrast, evidence from prospective cohort studies and natural experiments is informative. These studies typically control for a set of accepted potentially confounding demographic and environmental factors such as age, sex, race or ethnicity, and SES. It is also informative that the results of these studies are consistent with those of laboratory experiments showing that stress modifies disease-relevant biological processes in humans and with those of animal studies that investigate stressors as causative factors in disease onset and progression (Cohen et al. 2007).

Despite many years of investigation, our understanding of resilience to stressful life events is incomplete and even seemingly contradictory (e.g., Brody et al. 2013). Resilience generally refers to the ability of an individual to maintain healthy psychological and physical functioning in the face of exposure to adverse experiences (Bonanno 2004). This definition suggests that when a healthy individual is exposed to a stressful event but does not get sick and continues to be able to function relatively normally, this person has shown resilience. What is less clear is whether there are certain types of stressful events for which people tend to show greater resilience than for others. It seems likely that factors that increase stressor severity, such as imminence of harm, uncontrollability, and unpredictability, also decrease an event's potential to be met with resilience. Additionally, it may be possible that stressful events that are more commonly experienced are easier to adapt to due to shared cultural experiences that provide individuals with expectations for how to manage events. Conversely, less common events (e.g., combat exposure) or experiences that carry significant sociocultural stigma (e.g., rape) might be less likely to elicit resilience. As efforts to test interventions to promote resilience continue to be carried out, careful characterizations of stress exposures, including the complexities discussed in this review, will be critical to understanding the heterogeneity in physical and mental health outcomes associated with stressful life events.

Disclosure Statement

The authors are not aware of any affiliations, memberships, funding, or financial holdings that might be perceived as affecting the objectivity of this review.

Acknowledgments

This work was supported by grants from the National Center for Complementary and Integrative Health (AT006694) and the National Institute on Aging (R24AG048024).

Literature Cited

Adler N, Matthews K. 1994. Health psychology: Why do some people get sick and some stay well? *Annu. Rev. Psychol.* 45: 229–59.

Adler NE, Boyce T, Chesney MA, Cohen S, Folkman S, et al. 1994. Socioeconomic status and health: the challenge of the gradient. *Am. Psychol.* 49: 15–24.

Anda RF, Dong MX, Brown DW, Felitti VJ, Giles WH, et al. 2009. The relationship of adverse childhood experiences to a history of premature death of family members. *BMC Public Health* 9:106.

Anderson B, Wethington E, Kamarck TW. 2010. Interview assessment of stressor exposure. In *The Handbook of Stress Science: Biology, Psychology, and Health*, ed. RJ Contrada, A Baum, pp. 565–82. Berlin: Springer.

Anderson BL, Kiecolt-Glaser JK, Glaser R. 1994. A biobehavioral model of cancer stress and disease course. *Am. Psychol.* 49: 389–404.

Antoni MH, Lutgendorf SK, Cole SW, Dhabhar FS, Sephton SE, et al. 2006. The influence of bio-behavioural factors on tumour biology: pathways and mechanisms. *Nat. Rev. Cancer* 6: 240–48.

Bale TL, Epperson CN. 2015. Sex differences and stress across the lifespan. *Nat. Neurosci.* 18: 1413–20.

Barker DB. 2007. Antecedents of stressful experiences: depressive symptoms, self-esteem, gender, and coping. *Int. F. Stress Manag.* 14: 333–49.

Baum A, Cohen L, Hall M. 1993. Control and intrusive memories as possible determinants of chronic stress. *Psychosom. Med.* 55: 274–86.

Bonanno GA. 2004. Loss, trauma, and human resilience: Have we underestimated the human capacity to thrive after extremely aversive events? *Am. Psychol.* 59: 20–28.

Bonanno GA, Kaltman S. 1999. Toward an integrative perspective on bereavement *Psychol. Bull.* 125: 760–76.

Bonanno GA, Westphal M, Mancini AD. 2011. Resilience to loss and potential trauma. *Annu. Rev. Clin. Psychol.* 7: 511–35.

Brody GH, Yu T, Chen E, Miller GE, Kogan SM, Beach SRH. 2013. Is resilience only skin deep? Rural African Americans' socioeconomic status-related risk and competence in preadolescence and psychological adjustment and allostatic load at age 19. *Psychol. Sci.* 24: 1285–93.

Brown GW, Harris TO. 1989. *Life Events and Illness*. New York: Guilford Press.

Capitanio JP, Mendoza SP, Lerche NW, Mason WA. 1998. Social stress results in altered glucocorticoid regulation and shorter survival in simian acquired immune deficiency syndrome. *PNAS* 95: 4714–19.

Carver CS, Scheier MF. 1999. Stress, coping, and self-regulatory processes. In *Handbook of Personality,* ed. LA Pervin, OP John, pp. 553–75. New York: Guilford Press.

Chida Y, Hamer M, Wardle J, Steptoe A. 2008. Do stress-related psychosocial factors contribute to cancer incidence and survival? *Nat. Clin. Pract. Oncol.* 5: 466–75.

Cohen F, Horowitz. MJ, Lazarus RS, Moos RH, Robins LN, et al. 1982. Panel report on psychosocial assets and modifiers of stress. In *Stress and Human Health: Analysis and Implication of Research*, ed. GR Elliott, C Eisdorfer, pp. 147–88. Berlin: Springer.

Cohen S. 2004. Social relationships and health. *Am. Psychol.* 59: 676–84.

Cohen S. 2016. Psychological stress, immunity, and physical disease. In *Scientists Making a Difference: The Greatest Living Behavioral and Brain Scientists Talk About Their Most Important Contributions,* ed. R Sternberg, F Fiske, D Foss, pp. 419–23. Cambridge, UK: Cambridge Univ. Press.

Cohen S, Evans GW, Stokols D, Krantz D. 1986. *Behavior, Health, and Environment Stress.* New York; Plenum Press.

Cohen S, Frank E, Doyle WJ, Skoner DP, Rabin BS, Gwaltney JM. 1998. Types of stressors that increase susceptibility to the common cold in healthy adults. *Health Psychol.* 17: 214–23.

Cohen S, Gianaros PJ, Manuck SB. 2016. A stage model of stress and disease. *Perspect. Psychol. Sci.* 11: 456–63.

Cohen S, Janicki-Deverts D, Miller GE. 2007. Psychological stress and disease. *F. Am. Med. Assoc.* 298: 1685–87.

Cohen S, Kessler RC, Gordon LU. 1995a. *Measuring Stress: A Guide for Health and Social Scientists.* Oxford, UK: Oxford Univ. Press.

Cohen S, Kessler RC, Gordon LU. 1995b. Strategies for measuring stress in studies of psychiatric and physical disorders. In Cohen et al. 1995a, pp. 3–26.

Cohen S, Line S, Manuck SB, Rabin BS, Heise ER, Kaplan JR. 1997. Chronic social stress, social status, and susceptibility to upper respiratory infections in nonhuman primates. *Psychosom. Med.* 59: 213–21.

Cole SW, Kemeny ME, Fahey JL, Zack JA, Naliboff BD. 2003. Psychological risk factors for HIV pathogenesis: mediation by the autonomic nervous system. *Biol. Psychiatry* 54: 1444–56.

Crocker J, Park LE. 2004. The costly pursuit of self-esteem. *Psychol. Bull.* 130: 392–414.

Cyranowski JM, Frank E, Young E, Shear K. 2000. Adolescent onset of the gender difference in lifetime rates of major depression. *Arch. Gen. Psychiatry* 57: 21–27.

Danese A, McEwen BS. 2012. Adverse childhood experiences, allostasis, allostatic load, and age-related disease. *Physiol. Behav,* 106: 29–39.

Davis MC, Matthews KA, Twamley EW. 1999. Is life more difficult on Mars or Venus? A meta-analytic review of sex differences in major and minor life events. *Ann. Behav. Med.* 21: 83–97.

Dedovic K, Wadiwalla M, Engert V, Pruessner JC. 2009. The role of sex and gender socialization in stress reactivity. *Dev. Psychol.* 45: 45–55.

Denson TF, Spanovic M, Miller N. 2009. Cognitive appraisals and emotions predict cortisol and immune responses: a meta-analysis of acute laboratory social stressors and emotion inductions. *Psychol. Bull.* 135: 823–53.

Dickerson SS, Kemeny ME. 2004. Acute stressors and cortisol responses: a theoretical integration and synthesis of laboratory research. *Psychol. Bull.* 130: 355–91.

Dimsdale JE. 2008. Psychological stress and cardiovascular disease. *F. Am. Coll. Cardiol.* 51: 1237–46.

Dooley D, Prause J, Ham-Rowbottom KA. 2000. Underemployment and depression: longitudinal relationships. *F. Health Soc. Behav.* 41: 421–36.

Epel ES, Crosswell AD, Mayer SE, Prather AA, Slavich GM, et al. 2018. More than a feeling: a unified view of stress measurement for population science. *Front. Neutroendocrinol.* 49: 146–69.

Evans GW, Kim P. 2010. Multiple risk exposure as a potential explanatory mechanism for the socioeconomic status-health gradient. In *The Biology of Disadvantage: Socioeconomic Status and Health*, ed. NE Adler, J Stewart, pp. 174–89. Hoboken, NJ: Wiley.

Fagundes CP, Murdock KW, Chirinos DA, Green PA. 2017. Biobehavioral pathways to cancer incidence, progression, and quality of life. *Curr. Dir. Psychol. Sci.* 26: 548–53.

Frese M, Zapf D. 1988. Methodological issues in the study of work stress: objective versus subjective measurement of work stress and the question of longitudinal studies. In *Causes, Coping and Consequences of Stress at Work*, ed. CL Cooper, R Payne, pp. 375–411. Hoboken, NJ: Wiley.

Gallo WT, Bradley EH, Falba TA, Dubin JA, Cramer LD, et al. 2004. Involuntary job loss as a risk factor for subsequent myocardial infarction and stroke: findings from the Health and Retirement Survey. *Am. F. Ind. Med.* 45: 408–16.

Glass DC, Singer JE. 1972. *Urban Stress.* Cambridge, M A: Academic.

Gotlib IH, Joormann J. 2010. Cognition and depression: current status and future directions. *Annu. Rev. Clin. Psychol.* 6: 285–312.

Gump BB, Matthews KA, Raikkonen K. 1999. Modeling relationships among socioeconomic status, hostility, cardiovascular reactivity, and left ventricular mass in African American and White children. *Health Psychol.* 18: 140–50.

Hammen C. 2005. Stress and depression. *Annu. Rev. Clin. Psychol.* 1: 293–319.

Hammers C. 2006. Stress generation in depression: reflections on origins, research, and future directions. *F. Clin. Psychol.* 62: 1065–82.

Hammen C. 2016. Depression and stressful environments: identifying gaps in conceptualization and measurement. *Anxiety Stress Coping* 29: 335–51.

Hankin BL, Kassel JD, Zbela JRZ. 2005. Adult attachment dimensions and specificity of emotional distress symptoms: prospective investigations of cognitive risk and interpersonal stress generation as mediating mechanisms. *Personal. Soc. Psychol. Bull.* 31: 136–51.

Helgeson VS. 2011. Gender, stress, and coping. In *The Oxford Handbook of Stress, Health, and Coping*, ed. S Folkman, pp. 63–85. Oxford, UK: Oxford Univ. Press.

Holmes TH, Rahe RH. 1967. The social readjustment rating scale. *F. Psychosom. Res.* 11: 213–18.

Juster RP, McEwen BS, Lupien SJ. 2010. Allostatic load bin markers of chronic stress and impact on health and cognition. *Neurosci. Biobehav. Rev.* 35: 2–16.

Kaplan JR, Manuck SB, Adams MR, Weingand KW, Clarkson TB. 1987. Inhibition of coronary atherosclerosis by propranolol in behaviorally predisposed monkeys fed an atherogenic diet. *Circulation* 76: 1364–72.

Karasek R, Baker D, Marxer F, Ahlbom A, Theorell T. 1981. Job decision latitude, job demands, and cardiovascular disease: a prospective study of Swedish men. *Am. F. Public Health* 71: 694–705.

Karasek R, Theorell T. 1990. *Healthy Work: Stress, Productivity, and the Reconstruction of Working Life.* New York: Basic Books.

Kemeny ME. 2003. The psychobiology of stress. *Curr. Dir. Psychol. Sci.* 12: 124–29.

Kendler KS, Hettema JM, Butera F, Gardner CO, Prescott CA. 2003. Life event dimensions of loss, humiliation, entrapment, and danger in the prediction of onsets of major depression and generalized anxiety. *Arch. Gen. Psychiatry* 60: 789–96.

Kendler KS, Thornton LM, Gardner CO. 2000. Stressful life events and previous episodes in the etiology of major depression in women: an evaluation of the "kindling" hypothesis, *Am. F. Psychiatry* 157: 1243–51.

Kessler RC, McLeod JD. 1984. Sex differences in vulnerability to undesirable life events. *Am. Sociol. Rev.* 49: 620–31.

Kiecolt-Glaser JK, Dyer CS, Shuttleworth EC. 1988. Upsetting social interactions and distress among Alzheimer's disease family care-givers: a replication and extension. *Am. F. Community Psychol.* 16: 825–37.

Kivimäki M, Virtanen M., Elovainio M, Kouvonen A, Väänänen A, Valuers J. 2006. Work stress in the etiology of coronary heart disease: a meta-analysis. *Scand. F. Work Environ. Health* 32: 431–42.

Lantz PM, House JS, Mero RP, Williams DR. 2005. Stress, life events, and socioeconomic disparities in health: results from the Americans' changing lives study. *F. Health Soc. Behav.* 46: 274–88.

Lazaras RS, Folkman S. 1984. *Stress, Appraisal, and Coping.* Berlin: Springer.

Lee AG, Chiu Y-HM, Rosa MJ, Cohen S, Couli BA, et al. 2017. Association of prenatal and early childhood stress with reduced lung function in 7-year-olds. *Ann. Allergy Asthma Immunol.* 119: 153–59.

Leserman J. 2008. Role of depression, stress, and trauma in HIV disease progression. *Psychosom. Med.* 70: 539–45.

Liu RT, Alloy LB. 2010. Stress generation in depression: a systematic review of the empirical literature and reconunendations for future study. *Clin. Psychol. Rev.* 30: 582–93.

Low CA, Thurston RC, Matthews KA. 2010. Psychosocial factors in the development of heart disease in women: current research and future directions. *Psychosom. Med.* 72: 842–54.

Lutgendorf SK, Andersen BL. 2015. Biobehavioral approaches to cancer progression and survival. *Am. Psychol.* 70: 186–97.

Maccallum F, Galatzer-Levy IR, Bonanno GA. 2015. Trajectories of depression following spousal and child bereavement: a comparison of the heterogeneity in outcomes. *F. Psychiatr. Res.* 69: 72–79.

Manuck SB, Marsland AL, Kaplan JR, Williams JK. 1995. The pathogenicity of behavior and its neuroendocrine mediation: an example from coronary artery disease. *Psychosom. Med.* 57: 275–83.

Marin TJ, Chen E, Munch JA, Miller GE. 2009. Double-exposure to acute stress and chronic family stress is associated with immune changes in children with asthma. *Psychosom. Med.* 71: 378–84.

McEwen BS. 1998. Protective and damaging effects of stress mediators. *N. Engl. F. Med.* 338: 171–79.

McEwen BS. 2004. Protection and damage from acute and chronic stress: allostasis and allostatic overload and relevance to the pathophysiology of psychiatric disorders. *Ann. N. Y. Acad. Sci.* 1032: 1–7.

McEwen BS. 2012. Brain on stress: how the social environment gets under the skin. *PNAS* 109: 17130–85.

McLeod GFH, Horwood LJ, Fergusson DM, Boden JM. 2016. Life-stress and reactivity by gender in a longitudinal birth cohort at 30 and 35 years. *Soc. Psychiatry Psychiatr. Epidemiol.* 51: 1385–94.

Miller GE, Chen E, Cole SW. 2009. Health psychology: developing biologically plausible models linking the social world and physical health. *Annu. Rev. Psychol.* 60: 501–24.

Miller GE, Chen E, Parker KJ. 2011. Psychological stress in childhood and susceptibility to the chronic diseases of aging: moving toward a model of behaviors and biological mechanisms. *Psychol Bull.* 137: 959–97.

Möller-Leimkühler AM. 2008. Women with coronary artery disease and depression: a neglected risk group. *World F. Biol. Psychiatry* 9: 92–101.

Möller-Leimkühler AM. 2010. Higher comorbidity of depression and cardiovascular disease in women: a biopsychosocial perspective. *World F. Biol. Psychiatry* 11: 922–33.

Monroe SM. 1982. Life events assessment: current practices, emerging trends. *Clin. Psychol. Rev.* 2: 435–53.

Monroe SM. 2008. Modern approaches to conceptualizing and measuring human life stress. *Annu. Rev. Clin. Psychol.* 4: 33–52.

Monroe SM, Slavich GM, Georgiades K. 2009. The social environment and life stress in depression. In *Handbook of Depression,* ed. IH Gotlib, CL Hammen, pp. 340–60. New York: Guilford Press.

Morris JK, Cook DG, Shaper AG. 1994. Loss of employment and mortality. *Br. Med. F.* 308: 1135–39.

Murphy MLM, Slavich GM, Chen E, Miller GE. 2015. Targeted rejection predicts decreased anti-inflammatory gene expression and increased symptom severity in youth with asthma. *Psychol. Sci.* 26: 111–21.

Murphy MO, Loria AS. 2017. Sex-specific effects of stress on metabolic and cardiovascular disease: Are women at a higher risk? *Am. F. Physiol. Regul. Integr. Comp. Physiol.* 313: Rl–9.

Norman RE, Byambaa M, De R, Butchart A, Scott J, Vos T. 2012. The long-term health consequences of child physical abuse, emotional abuse, and neglect: a systematic review and meta-analysis. *PLOS Med.* 9:e1001349.

Ockenfels MC, Porter L, Smyth J, Kirschbaum C, Hellhammer DH, Stone AA. 1995. Effect of chronic stress associated with unemployment on salivary cortisol: overall cortisol levels, diurnal rhythm, and acute stress reactivity. *Psychosom. Med.* 57: 460–67.

Pearlin LI, Schieman S, Fazio EM, Meersman SC. 2005. Stress, health, and the life course: some conceptual perspectives. *F. Health Soc. Behav.* 46: 205–19.

Pedersen A, Zachariae R, Bovbjerg DH. 2010. Influence of psychological stress on upper respiratory infection: a meta-analysis of prospective studies. *Psychosom. Med.* 72: 823–32.

Rabkin JG, Struening EL Jr. 1976. Life events, stress, and illness. *Science* 194: 1013–20.

Repetti RL, Taylor SE, Seeman TE. 2002. Risky families: family social environments and the mental and physical health of offspring. *Psychol. Bull.* 128: 330–66.

Roberts BW, Kuncel NR, Shiner R, Caspi A, Goldberg LR. 2007. The power of personality: the comparative validity of personality traits, socioeconomic status, and cognitive ability for predicting important life outcomes. *Perspect. Psychol. Sci.* 2: 313–45.

Rook KS. 1998. Investigating the positive and negative sides of personal relationships: through a glass darkly? In *The Dark Side of Close Relationships,* ed. BH Spitzberg, WR Cupach, pp. 369–93. Mahwah, NJ: Lawrence Erlbaum.

Rook KS. 2014. The health effects of negative social exchanges in later life. *Generations* 38: 15–23.

Rosengren A, Orth-Gomer K, Wedel H, Wilhelmsen L. 1993. Stressful life events, social support, and mortality in men born in 1933. *Br. Med. F.* 307: 1102–5.

Rozanski A, Blumenthal JA, Kaplan J. 1999. Impact of psychological factors on the pathogenesis of cardiovascular disease and implications for therapy. *Circulation* 99: 2192–217.

Sandberg S, Järvenpää S, Pentrinen A, Paton JY, McCann DC. 2004. Asthma exacerbations in children immediately following stressful life events: a Cox's hierarchical regression. *Thorax* 59: 1046–51.

Sandberg S, Paton JY, Ahola S, McCann DC, McGuinness D, et al. 2000. The role of acute and chronic stress
in asthma attacks in children. *Lancet* 356: 982–87.

Schulz R, Decker S. 1985. Long-term adjustment to physical disability: the role of social support, perceived
control, and self-blame. *F. Personal. Soc. Psychol.* 48: 1162–72.

Schulz R, Rau MT. 1985. Social support through the life course. In *Social Support and Health*, ed. S Cohen, SL
Syme, pp. 129–49. Cambridge, MA: Academic.

Shalowitz MU, Berry CA, Rasinski KA, Dannhausen-Brun CA. 1998. A new measure of contemporary life
stress: development, validation, and reliability of the CRISES. *Health Sen. Res.* 33: 1381–402.

Shively CA, Clarkson TB. 1994. Social-status and coronary-artery atherosclerosis in female monkeys. *Arte-
rioscler. Thromb.* 14: 721–26.

Shor E, Roelfs DJ, Currefi M, Clemow L, Burg MM, Schwartz JE. 2012. Widowhood and mortality: a
meta-analysis and meta-regression. *Demography* 49: 575–606.

Skantze HB, Kaplan J, Pettersson K, Manuck S, Blomqvist N, et al. 1998. Psychosocial stress causes endothe-
lial injury in cynomolgus monkeys via β1-adrenoceptor activation. *Atherosclerosis* 136: 153–61.

Sklar LS, Anisman H. 1981. Stress and cancer. *Psychol. Ball.* 89: 369–406.

Slavich GM, Irwin MR. 2014. From stress to inflammation and major depressive disorder: a social signal
transduction theory of depression. *Psychol, Bull.* 140: 774–815.

Slavich GM, Shields GS. 2018. Assessing lifetime stress exposure using die Stress and Adversity Inventory
for Adults (Adult STRAIN): an overview and initial validation. *Psychosom. Med.* 80: 17–27.

Sneed RS, Cohen S. 2014. Negative social interactions and incident hypertension among older adults. *Health
Psychol.* 33: 554–65.

Steinberg JS, Arshad A, Kowalski M, Kukar A, Surna V, et al. 2004. Increased incidence of life-threatening
ventricular arrhythmias in implantable defibrillator patients after the world trade center attack. *F. Am.
Coll. Cardiol.* 44: 1261–64.

Steptoe A, Kivimaki M. 2012. Stress and cardiovascular disease. *Nat. Rev. Cardiol* 9: 360–70.

Steptoe A, Kivimaki M. 2013. Stress and cardiovascular disease: an update on current knowledge. *Annu. Rev.
Public Health* 34: 337–54.

Taylor SE. 2010. Mechanisms linking early life stress to adult health outcomes. *PNAS* 107: 8507–12.

Taylor SE, Klein LC, Lewis BP, Gruenewald TL, Gurung RAR, Updegraff JA. 2000. Biobehavioral responses to
stress in females: tend-and-befriend, not fight-or-flight, *Psychol. Rev.* 107: 411–29.

Thurston RC, Matthews KA. 2009. Racial and socioeconomic disparities in arterial stiffness and intima media thickness among adolescents. *Soc. Set. Med.* 68: 807–13.

Trichopoulos D, Katsouyanni K, Zavitsanos X, Tzonou A, Dallavorgia P. 1983. Psychological stress and fatal
heart-attack: the Athens 1981 earthquake natural experiment. *Lancet* 1: 441–44.

Turner RJ, Wheaton B. 1995. Checklist measurement of stressful life events. In Cohen et al. 1995a, pp. 29–58.

Turner RJ, Wheaton B, Lloyd DA. 1995. The epidemiology of social stress. *Am. Sociol. Rev.* 60: 104–25.

Wegman HL, Sterler C. 2009. A meta-analytic review of the effects of childhood abuse on medical outcomes
in adulthood. *Psychosom. Med.* 71: 805–12.

Wethington E, Brown GW, Kessler RC. 1995. Interview measurement of stressful life events. In Cohen et al.
1995a, pp. 59–79.

Wright RJ, Rodriguez M, Cohen S. 1998. Review of psychosocial stress and asthma: an integrated biopsychosocial approach. *Thorax* 53: 1066–74.

Wrosch C, Bauer I, Miller GE, Lupien S. 2007. Regret intensity, diurnal cortisol secretion, and physical health
in older individuals: evidence for directional effects and protective factors. *Psychol. Aging* 22: 319–30.

Index

9 781524 931957